LABOR RELATIONS AND PUBLIC POLICY SERIES

REPORT NO. 8

NLRB REGULATION OF ELECTION CONDUCT

A Study of the National Labor Relations Board's Policies and Standards for Setting Aside Representation Elections Based on Postelection Objections

by

ROBERT E. WILLIAMS
PETER A. JANUS
and
KENNETH C. HUHN

INDUSTRIAL RESEARCH UNIT
The Wharton School, Vance Hall/CS
University of Pennsylvania
Philadelphia, Pennsylvania 19174
U.S.A.

Foreword

In 1968, the Industrial Research Unit inaugurated its Labor Relations and Public Policy monographs as a means of examining issues and stimulating discussions in the complex and controversial areas of collective bargaining and the regulation of labor management disputes. The first four studies in the series dealt with aspects of the National Labor Relations Board and its administration. The fifth report contained papers read at the fiftieth anniversary conference of the Industrial Research Unit, at which many aspects of labor relations and public policy were discussed. The sixth monograph—*Welfare and Strikes*—was the first empirical analysis of the impact of government payments to strikers on the American collective bargaining system and on the settlements of disputes under that system. The seventh in the series, *Opening the Skilled Construction Trades to Blacks*, was the initial attempt to determine by detailed field analysis, what actually occurs when the federal government insists that the skilled construction trades make a serious effort to increase the number and percentage of Negroes in their work force.

This, the eighth in our series, marks a return to the general subject matter of the first four monographs, National Labor Relations Board policy. The NLRB has been given broad powers under Section 9 of the National Labor Relations Act to establish rules, regulations and procedures for the conduct of union representation elections. Pursuant to this authority the Board has, over the years, established a myriad of rules governing virtually every phase of the election process—how, when and where the participating union and the employer may campaign for the employees' votes; what they may say and do in the process; how the election itself should be conducted; and what safeguards must be provided against interference with the employees' freedom of choice.

These rules, which currently govern the conduct of more than 10,000 NLRB-supervised elections annually, are not codified or published in any single source so that election participants can readily determine their rights and duties. Instead, they must be gleaned from countless decisions, published and unpublished, by the NLRB and the directors of its 31 regions throughout the country, sustaining or overruling postelection objections. Such objections are filed in well over 1,000 cases a year by parties claiming that their elections were conducted unfairly or that some improper conduct by another party or a third person may have caused or contributed to their defeat. The Board's case-by-case rulings on these objections become the precedents by which the validity of subsequent elections is determined and the only source of guidance for future election participants.

This study represents an effort to discover and set forth in a comprehensive fashion the rules, principles and policies the Board actually applies in determining whether to certify the results of an election as valid or set it aside and order a rerun. It is hoped that by compiling the results of Board decisions on all major categories of election interference in a single source, this study will aid participants in NLRB elections to determine how to govern their own campaign conduct properly and to judge whether the election process in their case was conducted fairly. It is also hoped that by comparing the Board's rulings on a wide variety of election objections, examining and evaluating the principles the Board has applied and tracing their evolution, this book may be useful in some measure in bringing about a simpler, more consistent and more coherent set of rules for election conduct which will make the representation election process more efficient and effective.

The authors of this study, all members of the bar, have worked on the project for more than a year. Robert E. Williams received his J.D. at the University of Illinois College of Law and is a member of the Illinois and District of Columbia Bars. He served on the National Labor Relations Board staff for five years, concluding his work there as supervisory attorney in the appellate court branch. He is now practicing law in Washington, D.C. Peter A. Janus, a member of the Connecticut Bar, received his J.D. from the Boston University School of Law, served as an officer in the Adjutant General Corps, U.S. Army, and will be awarded the Master of Business Administration degree from the Wharton Graduate Division in May 1974. Kenneth C. Huhn received his J.D. from Rutgers-Camden Law School and is a member of the Pennsylvania Bar. Both Messrs. Janus and Huhn are serving as Legal Research Associates with the Industrial Research Unit. At this time the authors would like to express their appreciation to their wives, Susan, Lucinda and Joan, for the assistance and support which they generously provided during this lengthy and demanding period.

Initial financing of this study was provided by the ALCOA Foundation. An additional grant for this purpose was received from the Olin Corporation Charitable Trust, and two unrestricted grants from the General Electric Foundation and one from the Uniroyal Foundation were utilized in support also. Unrestricted contributions provided by the fifty companies composing the Research Advisory Group of the Industrial Research Unit made up the balance of the research and publication costs. The authors, of course, take full responsibility for the opinions expressed and conclusions reached.

The authors and the Industrial Research Unit take pleasure in thanking Mrs. Veronica M. Kent, Mrs. Toby Bridendall, Mrs. Linda Ritch, and Miss Mary Booker who typed the manuscript; Mrs. Ann C. Emerson who edited the manuscript; Mrs. Margaret E. Doyle, Office Manager of the Industrial Research Unit who handled the administrative details, and Kenneth C. McGuiness, Esq., who commented on sections of the manuscript.

HERBERT R. NORTHRUP, *Director*
Industrial Research Unit
The Wharton School
University of Pennsylvania

Philadelphia
January 1974

TABLE OF CONTENTS

PAGE

PART ONE

Introduction

CHAPTER I

The Nature Of The Issue

Our national labor policy is founded upon the dual principles of freedom of choice and majority rule. Section 7 of the National Labor Relations Act [1] gives employees the right to organize and "to bargain collectively through representatives of their own choosing," or to refrain from doing so if they prefer. However, Section 9(a) of the Act makes it clear that it is the majority's choice which controls providing that:

> Representatives designated or selected for the purposes of collective bargaining by the majority of the employees in a unit appropriate for such purposes, shall be the exclusive representatives of all the employees in such unit for the purposes of collective bargaining. . . .

This provision makes the decision of the majority of the employees regarding union representation binding not only on any nonconsenting minority within the unit, but also on the employer. Together with Section 8(a)(5) of the Act,[2] it imposes a duty on the employer to recognize and bargain with the labor organization chosen by the majority and forbids him to deal with employees individually or through any other representative.[3]

In view of the status and legal obligations thus attached to the majority's designation of a bargaining representative, it is vitally important that the process through which the majority makes its selection be fair, effective, and reliable. Various methods of determining the majority's choice have been recog-

---

[1] 49 Stat. 449 (1935), as amended, 29 U.S.C. §§ 151 et seq. (1970).

[2] Id. at § 158(a)(5). This section makes it an unfair labor practice for an employer "to refuse to bargain collectively with the representatives of his employees, subject to the provisions of Section 9(a)."

[3] See Brooks v. NLRB, 348 U.S. 96, 35 L.R.R.M. 2158 (1954); J.I. Case Co. v. NLRB, 321 U.S. 332, 14 L.R.R.M. 501 (1944).

nized,[4] but the "preferred route,"[5] and the one specifically provided for by Congress in the statute, is through secret ballot elections conducted by the National Labor Relations Board. The Board's authority to conduct representation elections derives from Section 9(c)(1) of the National Labor Relations Act, which provides:

> Whenever a petition shall have been filed, in accordance with such regulations as may be prescribed by the Board—
>
> (A) by an employee or group of employees or any individual or labor organization acting in their behalf alleging that a substantial number of employees (i) wish to be represented for collective bargaining and that their employer declines to recognize their representative as the representative defined in Section 9(a), or (ii) assert that the individual or labor organization which has been certified or is being currently recognized by their employer as the bargaining representative, is no longer a representative as defined in Section 9(a); or
>
> (B) by an employer alleging that one or more individuals or labor organizations have presented to him a claim to be recognized as the representative as defined in Section 9(a);
>
> the Board shall investigate such petition and if it has reasonable cause to believe that a question of representation affecting commerce exists shall provide for an appropriate hearing upon due notice. . . . If the Board finds upon the record of such hearing that such a question of representation exists, it shall direct an election by secret ballot and shall certify the results thereof.

The Act thus spells out to some extent the conditions and circumstances under which elections should be held, but the details of the election process itself are left almost entirely unspecified. The only requirement in the statute is that the election be "by secret ballot." Accordingly, the Act has been interpreted as granting the NLRB "a wide degree of discretion" in establishing various rules and procedures for conducting elections and determining whether or not the results are valid.[6]

---

[4] *See* NLRB v. Gissel Packing Co., 395 U.S. 575, 71 L.R.R.M. 2481 (1969). One frequently used method for establishing majority preference is through a showing of union authorization cards signed by a majority of the employees. For an analysis of the legal and practical defects of this method, see McFARLAND & BISHOP, UNION AUTHORIZATION CARDS AND THE NLRB (1969).

[5] 395 U.S. at 596, 71 L.R.R.M. at 2488-89.

[6] NLRB v. A.J. Tower Co., 329 U.S. 324, 330-331, 19 L.R.R.M. 2128, 2131 (1946); NLRB v. Waterman S.S. Co., 309 U.S. 206, 226, 5 L.R.R.M. 682, 692 (1940).

Pursuant to this broad grant of authority, the NLRB has, over the years, developed a myriad of rules, regulations, and policies governing the conduct of representation elections. One portion of this body of rules and decisions relates to what may be broadly identified as *pre-election* matters. These include such issues as whether a genuine question concerning representation exists, whether the election petition is timely, and whether the bargaining unit sought is an appropriate one. A second body of election rulings and decisions relates to *postelection* matters: challenges to eligibility of particular voters and objections charging that misconduct by one of the parties or irregularities in the process tainted the results and that the election should therefore be set aside.

It is with the latter type of postelection questions that this study deals—*i.e.* objections to the conduct of representation elections or to conduct allegedly affecting the results thereof. By hearing and deciding such objections, the Board endeavors to maintain the fairness and reliability of the election process against interference or improper influence from any source. As we shall see, the decisions of the Board in such cases are generally the only available guidelines by which the union, the company, and the employees involved can determine what they may and may not do during the campaign period and on the day of the election itself. Such decisions also provide, in many instances, the only source of guidance to the Board agent on the scene as to how to handle irregularities arising during the course of the election.

As a guide to election conduct, however, the Board's decisions on objections have certain shortcomings. It must be remembered that such decisions define only an outer limit, not an ideal or recommended standard of behavior. Moreover, the automatic sanction for conduct found to support a postelection objection is invalidation of the entire election, or even to a bargaining order. Because postelection objections thus lead to extreme remedies, and because the economic stakes in union representation elections are often potentially very high, objection cases are likely to be contested by the unions and companies involved. For these reasons, it is extremely important for the Board's rules and policies regarding election conduct to be clear, consistent, and sound. Unfortunately, as we shall see, the Board has not always achieved these standards.

DEVELOPMENT OF POLICY

With few exceptions, the Board's election policies have been developed through decisions of the Board and its regional directors on a case-by-case basis, rather than through formal rulemaking proceedings, as provided for under the Administrative Procedure Act.[7] Consequently, the Board's election-case rulings have often tended to be narrow and limited to particular fact situations, and few comprehensive statements of election policy have emerged.[8] There has also been a prevalent tendency, as the personnel on the Board have changed or political pressures on Board members shifted, for the Board's election rules and policies to shift correspondingly. The result has been the development of a vast body of decisional law regarding election standards and requirements, frequently marked by conflicts of basic policy and reversals of precedent.

IMPACT OF CASE LOAD

The impact of inconsistencies in the Board's election rulings is magnified by several factors over which the Board itself has little or no control. One is the sheer volume of elections which the Board is called upon to manage. Supervision of elections and resolution of issues related to the election process are among the Board's most important functions and consume steadily increasing amounts of the agency's time and resources. In the early period immediately following the passage of the Wagner Act in 1935, the Board conducted fewer than twelve hundred elections annually.[9] Now the Board receives nearly fifteen thousand election petitions a year and conducts almost

---

[7] 60 Stat. 273 (1946), *as amended*, 5 U.S.C. § 1001, *et seq.* (1970). *See generally* Peck, *A Critique of the National Labor Relations Board's Performance in Policy Formulation: Adjudication and Rule Making*, 117 U. PA. L. REV. 254 (1968); Vernstein, *The NLRB's Adjudication-Rule Making Dilemma Under the Administrative Procedure Act*, 79 YALE L. J. 371 (1970).

[8] *See* Samoff, *Coping with the NLRB's Growing Caseload*, 22 LAB. L. J. 739, 746 (1971).

[9] 1-5 NLRB ANN. REP. (1936-40). For the years 1936 through 1940, the official statistics of the frequency of NLRB representation elections are as follows: (1) 31 (1936); (2) 265 (1937); (3) 1,152 (1938); (4) 746 (1939); and (5) 1,192 (1940).

ten thousand elections.[10] Inevitably, faced with this enormous
expansion in its election caseload, the Board has been unable to
give each individual case protracted attention. As a result,
deficiencies in reasoning and inconsistencies in policy occasionally
escape scrutiny and are perpetuated rather than corrected.

In order to keep pace with its burgeoning representation caseload, the Board, in 1961, exercised its authority under Section
3(b) of the Act to delegate its powers in election cases to its
regional directors.[11] Since then, the details of the election
process and the initial resolution of election issues have been
handled primarily by staff personnel in the Board's 43 regional
and field offices, under the supervision of the regional directors
and with limited review by the Board itself.[12] Although this
delegation has enabled the Board to cope with more cases, it
has tended to accentuate the lack of uniformity and consistency
in the Board's election policies. For those policies are now being
implemented in the first instance by a number of separate ad-
ministrators, each with his own interpretation of prior decisions
and his own view of how elections should be conducted, rather
than by a single tribunal. In addition, decisions by the regional
directors often remain unpublished even though they may become final and binding decisions; thus, making it all the more
difficult for private parties and the Board's own staff to know
and understand what the rules actually are and how they are
applied.

COURT REVIEW

These problems are heightened by the limited availability of
review of election case determinations. According to the Board's
rules and regulations, when a regional director disposes of
a party's postelection objections, the right of any party disagreeing with his determination to obtain review by the Board

---

[10] *See* 37 NLRB ANN. REP. 19-20 (1972).

[11] NLRB STATEMENTS OF PROCEDURES, § 101.21 (a) (Series 8, *as amended,*
1959). The grant of authority to the Board to delegate such powers was
included in the Landrum-Griffin amendments to the Act in 1959, but was
not exercised until the Kennedy appointees took office in 1961. *See* McGUINESS,
THE NEW FRONTIER NLRB 97-98 (Washington: Labor Policy Ass'n, 1963).

[12] For a fuller discussion of the Board's election procedures and the requirements for obtaining Board review, *see* MORRIS, THE DEVELOPING LABOR LAW
182-199 (1971). *See also* McGUINESS, HOW TO TAKE A CASE BEFORE THE
NLRB 105-24 (3d ed. 1967).

in Washington depends upon the type of order or agreement under which the election was conducted,[13] as well as upon the type of postelection decision or report which the director decides to issue. Depending on these variables, the aggrieved party may have access only to a limited type of Board review, or his right to obtain review at all may be limited by a discretionary procedure under which the Board will consider the case only if it decides that "compelling reasons exist." [14]

Review by a court of the regional director's or Board's determinations in an election case may be even more elusive. If the result of the election proceedings at the regional or Board level is to deny the petitioning union certification as the bargaining representative, there is generally no way in which judicial review may be obtained.[15] If the result is to certify the union, review by a federal court of appeals may be obtained, but only through a lengthy, circuitous route known as a "technical" Section 8(a)(5) violation. Thus, since a certification under Section 9 of the Act is not regarded as a "final order" of the agency subject to judicial review under Section 10,[16] an employer disagreeing with the Board's action can obtain court review only by ignoring the certification, refusing to bargain with the union upon request, and waiting to be found guilty by the Board of an unfair labor practice for his action. He may then seek judicial review of the Board's resulting order in the unfair labor practice case, and can raise before the

---

[13] *See* NLRB RULES AND REGULATIONS, § 102.69(c) (Series 8, *as amended,* 1959). Elections may be conducted pursuant to (1) a direction of election issued by the regional director or the Board following a pre-election hearing; (2) a stipulated consent election agreement under which the parties waive a pre-election hearing but preserve their rights to Board review of postelection determinations by the regional director; or (3) a "pure" consent agreement, under which the regional director is given final authority to resolve all issues that may arise, subject to Board review only if his action is arbitrary or capricious. *See generally* McGuiness, How To Take a Case Before the NLRB 105-24 (3d ed. 1967).

[14] NLRB RULES AND REGULATIONS, §§ 102.67(c), 69(c).

[15] Only in "extraordinary circumstances" does a federal court have jurisdiction to review NLRB action in refusing to certify the results of an election conducted under Section 9 of the Act. Leedom v. Kyne, 358 U.S. 184, 43 L.R.R.M. 2222 (1958). *Cf.* Boire v. Greyhound Corp., 376 U.S. 473, 55 L.R.R.M. 2694 (1964).

[16] AFL v. NLRB, 308 U.S. 401, 5 L.R.R.M. 670 (1940).

court his defense that the underlying certification was defective.[17] Even then, however, the scope of the judicial review that can be obtained is limited. As noted above, the Act has been interpreted as giving the Board wide discretion in establishing election policies, and the courts frequently defer to this discretion, citing the familiar proposition of administrative law that a court should not interfere with agency action in an area in which the agency has greater "expertise." [18]

FREE SPEECH ISSUE

Contributing to the uncertainty of the Board's election policies over the years has been their fluctuating interrelationship with the unfair labor practice provisions of the Act and Section 8(c)—the so-called "free speech" provision of the Taft-Hartley amendments. Despite the clear indications that Section 8(c) was added in order to curtail the early Wagner Act Board's restrictive regulation of employer efforts to campaign against union representation, we shall see that the amendment indirectly led instead to closer Board regulation of both employers' and unions' campaign activities. Thus, we will trace the curious evolution of the Board's "laboratory conditions" doctrine, which originated shortly after the passage of the Taft-Hartley Act, as part of a rationale for not applying Section 8(c) to election cases.[19] Under this doctrine, the Board sets aside elections whenever it concludes that acceptable "laboratory" standards have not been maintained, whether or not the conduct complained of constitutes an unfair labor practice.[20]

---

[17] As the circuit court of appeals observed in NLRB v. Genesco, Inc., 406 F.2d 393, 394, 70 L.R.R.M. 2252, 2253 (5th Cir. 1969). "Unfortunately, this time-consuming round-about proceeding is the only method for challenging the Board's certification of a union because board decisions in representation proceedings are usually not reviewable by the courts of appeal. . . . We attach no opprobrium to the employer's refusal to bargain where, as here, it is the only means of inveighing the Board's findings in an underlying representation hearing."

[18] Judicial review is particularly narrow in the case of consent elections. There, the courts will generally reverse a Board determination only if it exceeds "reasonable bounds." NLRB v. Laney & Duke Storage Warehouse Co., 369 F.2d 859, 864, 63 L.R.R.M. 2552, 2554 (5th Cir. 1966).

[19] The doctrine originated in the Board's decision in General Shoe Corp., 77 N.L.R.B. 124, 21 L.R.R.M. 1337 (1948). For a fuller discussion see Chapter II, *infra*.

[20] Since its decision in Dal-Tex Optical Co., 137 N.L.R.B. 1782, 50 L.R.R.M. 1489 (1962), the Board has maintained that conduct which constitutes an

Although the Board has vacillated concerning the applicability of Section 8(c) to election proceedings,[21] it has continued to apply the "laboratory conditions" standard, with varying degrees of strictness, ever since 1948. The effect has been that neither unions nor employers may exercise as much freedom today in campaigning for employees' votes as they could during the Wagner Act period before Congress acted to guarantee their rights of "free speech."

As we shall find, the Board's methodology in applying the "laboratory conditions" standard has added to the difficulty of discerning clear, consistent rules and policies in its election-case decisions. Too often the Board's decisions are based upon untested opinions or assumptions, by the particular Board members deciding the case, as to the probable effect of the conduct in question upon the ability of the employees in the voting unit to make a free choice. In this exercise, the Board has consistently relied solely upon its own presumed "expertise" in labor relations. It has never sought to corroborate its assumptions through reference to any empirical studies or psychological analyses of the impact of campaign conduct on employees' voting behavior. The result is a set of highly subjective standards whose continuity is dependent upon the appointment of successive Board members with similar views.

PURPOSE OF STUDY

As this discussion indicates, the process through which the Board's election policies are developed is not structurally conducive to the creation of a clear-cut, consistent set of rules for election conduct. The system of case-by-case, quasi-judicial decision making by a Board subject to short-term political appointments and a widely-dispersed staff of regional officers invites inconsistency both in the development of the governing policies and in their application. The review procedures pro-

---

unfair labor practice is, *a fortiori*, conduct which warrants setting aside an election. Other conduct, not specifically unlawful under the Act, may also be found to destroy the requisite "laboratory conditions" and invalidate an election.

[21] *Compare* National Furniture Co., 119 N.L.R.B. 1, 40 L.R.R.M. 1442 (1957); *with* Dal-Tex Optical Co., 137 N.L.R.B. 1782, 50 L.R.R.M. 1489 (1962); *and* Media Mailers, Inc., 191 N.L.R.B. No. 50, 77 L.R.R.M. 1393 (1971) (Chairman Miller, dissenting).

vided by the Act do not afford an adequate means of correcting errors or inconsistencies when they do occur. Moreover, the "laboratory conditions" doctrine, the standard adopted by the Board to regulate campaign conduct, is of such an ambiquous nature that it has been subjected to a multitude of interpretations, none of which have outlasted their author's Board tenure. Consequently, no clear codification of the standards of conduct for a valid election is available, although definitive standards are badly needed both by the parties and by employees who participate in the election process and by the Board personnel initially responsible for conducting elections and resolving election issues as they arise.

In an effort to meet this need, this study undertakes to determine and, to the extent possible, reduce to a coherent set of rules the principles which the Board has enunciated which cause it or its regional directors to set aside elections as a result of the conduct of participating employers, unions, or employees or members of the Board's own staff. Where relevant, we shall trace the evolution of the principles enunciated by the Board to determine how and to what extent the Board's policies have fluctuated over the years. We shall also attempt to assess the consistency with which the Board has applied its enunciated principles within a current time span to fact situations and parties deserving similar treatment. Finally, we shall examine the principles developed by the Board in an effort to evaluate their reasonableness and determine whether they should be retained, modified, or abandoned.

Although, as noted, the election process involves other important, often complex issues—*e.g.*, whether the petition is timely and not barred, whether the unit sought is appropriate, whether individual voters whose ballots have been challenged should be considered eligible to vote—we do not deal with those subjects here.[22] Rather, this study is confined to the grounds and criteria upon which the Board sustains postelection objections—*i.e.* the kinds of conduct prior to and during the election which, if objected to, will cause the Board to set the election aside.

Broadly speaking, elections may be invalidated for either of two reasons: (1) the employer or union involved (or persons

---

[22] For a thorough study of Board rulings regarding appropriate bargaining units, see ABODEELY, THE NLRB AND THE APPROPRIATE BARGAINING UNIT (Labor Relations and Public Policly Series, Rep. No. 3, 1971).

acting on their behalf) may be found to have interferred with the voters' freedom of choice by making statements or engaging in conduct deemed likely to coerce, mislead or otherwise improperly influence the voters; or (2) the election procedures themselves may be found to have been defective because of outside interference, improper conduct by the presiding Board agent, or some deficiency in the handling of the mechanics of the process. We shall review the cases dealing with the many kinds of conduct and varieties of issues arising within each of these broad, general categories.

Although we confine our consideration primarily to the substantive policies and principles the Board applies in ruling on objections, certain procedural requirements should be borne in mind in evaluating the Board's overall approach to election objections. One is the rule that the objecting party, not the Board or its agents, must sustain the burden of searching out and producing specific evidence supporting his objections before the Board need act on them.[23] This requirement may derive in part from administrative necessities, but it reveals something of the true nature of the objection process. Although the Board often justifies its election rulings in terms of its obligation to provide "laboratory conditions" for the voters,[24] this obligation apparently applies only if one of the parties actually complains and carries the initial burden of making his own investigation. The machinery provided by the Board is thus primarily geared, not toward detecting and preventing any conduct which might interfere with the voters' freedom of choice, but only toward resolving those infractions actually charged by one of the parties and supported by an affirmative showing of evidence.

Another procedural rule applicable to all of the categories of election objections considered herein is the rule which establishes a cutoff date for the "pre-election period." Only conduct occurring between the cutoff date and the election will be considered as grounds to set the election aside. For a number of years, the recognized cutoff date was either the execution date

---

[23] NLRB v. Mattison Machine Works, 365 U.S. 123, 124, 47 L.R.R.M. 2437 (1961) (per curiam); NLRB v. Tennessee Packers, Inc., 379 F.2d 172, 178, 65 L.R.R.M. 2619, 2622 (6th Cir.), cert. denied, 389 U.S. 958, 66 L.R.R.M. 2507 (1967); NLRB v. National Survey Service, Inc., 361 F.2d 199, 207, 61 L.R.R.M. 2712, 2716 (7th Cir. 1966); NLRB v. Zelrich Co., 344 F.2d 1011, 1015, 59 L.R.R.M. 2225, 2228 (5th Cir. 1965).

[24] General Shoe Corp., 77 N.L.R.B. 124, 21 L.R.R.M. 1337 (1948).

of a consent election agreement, or, where no such agreement was present, the date of issuance of the Board's order directing the election.[25] In 1961, however, after delegating its decisional authority in election cases to its regional directors, the Board determined that an earlier date was needed in light of the anticipated decrease in the agency's handling time for such cases. Therefore, the Board announced that the date of filing of the petition would henceforth serve as the cutoff date.[26] Accordingly, under the current rule, only conduct occurring between the filing of the petition and the election will be considered objectionable. The same rule is applied even in uncontested elections, where the parties consent after the petition is filed to proceed to an election.[27]

The following three parts of this study deal with the major categories of speech and conduct by employers or unions during the applicable pre-election period which may be found by the Board to constitute interference with the voters' freedom of choice. Of principal concern in this area are campaign speeches and propaganda. Board decisions impose limits upon when, where, and how election parties may communicate their campaign messages and what they may say. Part Two explores the restrictions upon the substance of campaign statements with specific attention to the rules regarding misrepresentations; promises, predictions, and expressions of opinion; and appeals to racial prejudice. Part Three examines other forms of campaign speech and conduct which may be found to interfere with the voters' freedom of choice: offers and inducements; reprisals for nonallegiance; threats; questioning, polling, and surveillance; favoritism or assistance by the employer to a competing union; and third party interference. The Board's regulation of the time, place, and manner of campaign communications is then examined in Part Four. The fifth part of this study concerns the limits and safeguards the Board has established against interference with the fairness or effectiveness of the election process itself, whether through misconduct or noncooperation by one of the parties, or through some deficiency in the mechanics of the election or misconduct by the Board agent in charge.

---

[25] *See* F.W. Woolworth Co., 109 N.L.R.B. 1446, 34 L.R.R.M. 1584 (1954); Great Atlantic & Pacific Tea Co., 101 N.L.R.B. 1118, 31 L.R.R.M. 1189 (1952).

[26] Ideal Electric & Mfg. Co., 134 N.L.R.B. 1275, 49 L.R.R.M. 1316 (1961).

[27] Goodyear Tire & Rubber Co., 138 N.L.R.B. 453, 51 L.R.R.M. 1070 (1962).

PART TWO

*Regulation of the Substance of
Campaign Statements*

CHAPTER II

Misrepresentations

The National Labor Relations Board policies in regard to misrepresentation in campaign statements have varied from non-involvement to detailed regulation. The evolvement of Board policies from one position to the other is examined here beginning with the early Wagner Act position that employers had no interest in a representation dispute.

THE EVOLUTION OF BOARD POLICY

In its early decisions under the Wagner Act, the Board took the position that the Act obliged employers to maintain complete neutrality regarding their employees' decisions for or against union representation. Therefore, the Board applied a strict rule that any pre-election antiunion speech by an employer would constitute an unfair labor practice and a ground for setting the election aside.[1] The importance of providing for exposure of managements' views was discounted, under this early approach, on the theory that the employer had no legitimate interest in whether his employees selected a union. To the early Wagner Act Board, this decision was the exclusive concern of the employees and the petitioning union.

THE EARLY POLICY OF NONINVOLVEMENT
WITH CAMPAIGN PROPAGANDA ISSUES

Accordingly, the Board had little occasion to consider the truth or falsity of employers' campaign statements; virtually all management remarks relating to an election were deemed objectionable, even if they were true. With respect to union campaign statements, although the Board followed a diametrically opposite approach, it also avoided any extensive inquiry into

---

[1] *E.g.*, Rockford Mitten & Hosiery Co., 16 N.L.R.B. 501, 5 L.R.R.M. 244 (1939); Virginia Ferry Corp., 8 N.L.R.B. 730, 2 L.R.R.M. 525 (1938); Nebel Knitting Co., Inc., 6 N.L.R.B. 284, 2 L.R.R.M. 151 (1938). *See* 1 NLRB ANN. REP. 73 (1936).

issues of substantive truth or falsity. The early Board policy, as expressed in *Maywood Hosiery Mills, Inc.*,[2] emphasized the avoidance of agency involvement with questions of the substance of union campaign propaganda:

> Absent violence, we have never undertaken to police union organization or union campaigns, to weigh the truth or falsehood of official union utterances, or to curb the enthusiastic efforts of employee adherents to the union cause in winning others to their conviction.[3]

Under this rule, election results were certified despite union campaign misrepresentation which the Board described as "reprehensible"[4] and "highly offensive and unethical,"[5] so long as the Board concluded that the employees did not vote under actual coercion or duress.[6] The Board's reasoning was that "employees undoubtedly recognize [campaign] propaganda for what it is, and discount it."[7]

Under this early approach, it was only in certain extreme circumstances that the Board would hold a union's campaign representations so improper as to render elections invalid. In *Sears Roebuck & Co.*[8] the Board set aside an election where one of two competing unions had implied in its campaign propaganda that it was favored by the Board and circulated a leaflet purporting to contain an endorsement of the union by the Board's regional director.[9] Again, in *Continental Oil Co.*[10]

---

[2] 64 N.L.R.B. 146, 150, 17 L.R.R.M. 90 (1945).

[3] *Id.* at 150, 17 L.R.R.M. at 90-91. *See also* General Plywood Corp., 83 N.L.R.B. 197, 199 (1949).

[4] Curtiss-Wright Corp., 43 N.L.R.B. 795, 797 n.2, 11 L.R.R.M. 1, 2 (1942) (election sustained despite false claim by one of two competing unions that it was not bound by wartime agreement renouncing overtime pay, whereas its rival was).

[5] Corn Products Refining Co., 58 N.L.R.B. 1441, 1442, 15 L.R.R.M. 104, 105 (1944) (election sustained despite false claim by one of two competing unions that it had NLRB approval, whereas its rival was not recognized by the Board as a legitimate labor organization).

[6] 43 N.L.R.B. at 797, 11 L.R.R.M. at 2.

[7] 58 N.L.R.B. at 1442, 15 L.R.R.M. at 105.

[8] 47 N.L.R.B. 291, 11 L.R.R.M. 247 (1943).

[9] The Board distinguished the *Sears Roebuck* case in *Corn Products Refining Co.*, indicating that the *Sears* decision applied only to propaganda which appeared to have emanated from the agency itself. 58 N.L.R.B. at 1442 n.5, 15 L.R.R.M. at 105.

[10] 58 N.L.R.B. 169, 15 L.R.R.M. 30 (1944).

the Board invalidated an election because the incumbent union had posted a prematurely released notice indicating approval of a wage increase by the War Labor Board immediately before the scheduled election, and a notification from the wartime agency that the notice had been released in error was not posted until too late for it to be seen by most employees before they voted.

The Board's real objective in these cases appears to have been to prevent the parties from utilizing propaganda tactics that would tend to reflect adversely on the processes of the government.[11] But the Board explained its holding in *Continental Oil* in broad language which laid the groundwork for future holdings providing for more extensive inquiry into the substance of union campaign representations: "Elements, regardless of their source or of their truth or falsity, which, in the experienced judgment of the Board, make impossible an impartial test, are grounds for the invalidation of an election." [12]

The Development of the "Laboratory Conditions" Standard

With the passage of Section 8(c) of the Act in 1947, it became clear that the Board could no longer adhere to the strict rule that any employer expressions of opinion relative to a pending representation election would be grounds for valid objection.

In view of 8(c), employers had to be allowed some freedom in campaigning against union representation. Yet, the Board plainly did not relish the prospect of granting employers the same broad leeway in pre-election propaganda that it had extended to unions in its decisions prior to Section 8(c). Instead, some new formula had to be devised which would permit closer agency supervision of the substance of employer campaign communications, and still allow for certification of election results when the Board felt that the employees' choice had not suffered undue interference.

The Board's resolution of this problem appeared in its *General Shoe* decision.[13] Here the Board announced that Section 8(c) is specifically applicable only to unfair labor practice cases. In

---

[11] *Id.* at 172-74, 15 L.R.R.M. at 31-32 (Member Reilly, concurring).

[12] *Id.* at 172 n.2, 15 L.R.R.M. at 31.

[13] General Shoe Corp., 77 N.L.R.B. 124, 21 L.R.R.M. 1337 (1948).

the election context, the Board stated, the question is not whether the speech or conduct complained of constituted an unfair labor practice as such, but whether it "created an atmosphere calculated to prevent a free and untrammeled choice by the employees." The Board went on to declare that its duty in election cases is to provide:

> a laboratory in which an experiment may be conducted, under conditions as nearly ideal as possible, to determine the uninhibited desires of the employees. It is our duty to establish those conditions; it is also our duty to determine whether they have been fulfilled. When . . . the standard drops too low . . . the requisite laboratory conditions are not present and the experiment must be conducted over again.

Although the Board made some efforts to reconcile this newly announced "laboratory conditions" standard with its previous liberal treatment of campaign propaganda excesses by unions,[14] the *General Shoe* opinion left little room for doubt that the Board had adopted a basic change of policy in response to the addition of Section 8(c). Rather than to allow employers the same free rein in matters of campaign speech that unions had previously enjoyed, the Board had opted in favor of applying a stricter standard against pre-election communications by all parties.

The actual effectuation of this policy of stricter regulation was gradual. In 1951 the Board slightly modified its familiar declaration that "absent threats" it would not inquire into the truth or falsity of union campaign statements, by adding, after "threats," the words "or other gross misconduct."[15] There followed several cases in which campaigning parties employed deliberate deceptions in an effort to discredit rival parties.[16]

---

[14] The Board cited the *Continental Oil* case, notes 10-12, *supra*, to illustrate that it had set aside elections based on union conduct in certain "glaring" instances in the past. Although the Board admitted that it had used this power "sparingly," it said this was in part because "we cannot police the details surrounding every election. . . ." 77 N.L.R.B. at 126, 21 L.R.R.M. at 1340.

[15] West-Gate Sun Harbor Co., 93 N.L.R.B. 830, 27 L.R.R.M. 1474 (1951). *See also* Kearney & Trecker Corp., 96 N.L.R.B. 1214, 29 L.R.R.M. 1014 (1951).

[16] United Aircraft Corp., 103 N.L.R.B. 102, 31 L.R.R.M. 1437 (1953) (one of two competing unions sent a letter over the signature of the other union's president, apologizing for conduct attributed to the latter union's organizers and implicitly praising the former union). Timken-Detroit Axle Co., 98 N.L.R.B. 790, 29 L.R.R.M. 1401 (1952) (employer sent employees a letter opposing the union over the signature of one of their fellow employees, without identifying management as the real source of the letter).

The Board concluded that such tactics would make it impossible for the employees to recognize the propaganda "for what it is" and would render them "helpless to exercise good sense in appraising it."[17] As a result, by 1953 a new qualification had been appended to the Board's statement of its prevailing policy. It now read:

> Absent threats or other elements of intimidation we will not undertake to censor or police union campaigns or consider the truth or falsity of official union utterances, *unless the ability of the employees to evaluate such utterances has been so impaired by* the use of forged campaign material or other campaign trickery *that the uncoerced desires of the employees cannot be determined in an election.*[18]

Thus, the Board had begun to place greater emphasis on the ability of the employees to evaluate campaign claims rationally, and less reliance on its general policy of noninvolvement with issues of propaganda. Once the Board had recognized that the deceptive *manner* in which a representation was made could prevent its proper evaluation by the employees, it was but a short step to the proposition that some claims, because of their very *substance*, were beyond the voters' powers of rational evaluation. In *The Gummed Products Co.*[19] the union issued campaign handbills which misstated the wage rates it had negotiated with a nearby competitor of the employer, and it reiterated these misstatements on the eve of the election, after the employer had denied their accuracy. The Board, without expressly overruling any precedents, set the election aside.

The rationale of the Board indicated an increased willingness to look into the substance of campaign claims to determine how serious a departure from the truth had occurred:

> The Board *normally* will not censor or police preelection propaganda by parties to elections, absent threats or acts of violence. *However*, . . . the Board has imposed some limits on campaign tactics. Exaggerations, inaccuracies, partial truths, name-calling, and falsehoods, while not condoned, may be excused as legitimate propaganda, *provided they are not so misleading as to prevent the exercise of a choice by employees* in the election of their bargaining representative. The ultimate consideration is whether the chal-

---

[17] 103 N.L.R.B. at 105 & n.9, 31 L.R.R.M. at 1438.

[18] Merck & Co., Inc., 104 N.L.R.B. 891, 892, 32 L.R.R.M. 1160, 1161 (1953) (emphasis added).

[19] 112 N.L.R.B. 1092, 36 L.R.R.M. 1156 (1955).

lenged propaganda has lowered the standards of campaigning to the point where it may be said that the uninhibited desires of the employees cannot be determined in an election.[20]

The Board emphasized that the falsified wage rates in *Gummed Products* related to a matter with which the employees were "vitally concerned"; that the union's claims were likely to be relied upon by the employees because it was "in an authoritative position to know" what rates it had negotiated with another employer; and that the false claims were "repeated on the very eve of the election" and, therefore, were "entitled to greater than ordinary weight."[21] Under these circumstances, the Board held, the standards of the campaign had been lowered to a point where the election results could not be relied upon to represent the free choice of the employees, and a new election was necessary.

With the *Gummed Products* decision, it became apparent that, despite the Board's continued disclaimers of any intent to serve as a general campaign censor, it would now closely examine the substance of election propaganda in an effort to prevent employees from being substantially misled and would subject last-minute claims relating to key election issues, such as wages, to particular scrutiny. This purpose was reaffirmed in a subsequent series of cases in which the Board appeared steadily to be tightening its rein on misleading propaganda claims. In *The Calidyne Co.*[22] the Board held that a party's failure to tell the *whole truth* in election literature was just as objectionable as an outright falsification, since technically true statements could be made misleading by the omission of relevant facts.[23] In *Kawneer Co.*[24] the Board gave an indication that, notwithstanding language in its prior opinions limiting the *Gummed Products* rule to *deliberate* misrepresentations, it would also

---

[20] *Id.* at 1093-94, 36 L.R.R.M. at 1156-57 (emphasis added).

[21] *Id.* at 1094, 36 L.R.R.M. at 1157.

[22] 117 N.L.R.B. 1026, 39 L.R.R.M. 1364 (1957).

[23] *Id.* at 1028, 39 L.R.R.M. at 1365. In *Calidyne*, the union distributed a flyer purporting to show wage rates it had negotiated with another employer, but did not indicate that the rates it quoted were the maximum rates provided for, and that some employees in the job classifications listed might actually be receiving as much as thirty cents an hour less. *Id.* at 1027-28, 39 L.R.R.M. at 1364-65. *Cf.* Horder's Inc., 114 N.L.R.B. 751, 753, 37 L.R.R.M. 1049 (1955).

[24] 119 N.L.R.B. 1460, 41 L.R.R.M. 1333 (1958).

apply the rule to misstatements resulting from a party's error or misunderstanding. The controlling factor, in the Board's view, was that "the effect on the Employer's employees of such a misrepresentation would be no different from that of a deliberate misstatement." [25] And in *Cleveland Trencher Co.*[26] the Board held that it would not tolerate misstatements about vital campaign subjects (in this case, certain claims relating to fringe benefits) even though they involved only a few specific items in an extensive, and otherwise accurate, list of similar claims.[27]

The Courts' Application of the "Laboratory Conditions" Test

The Board's zeal to impose greater control upon the substance of election statements did not match that of the courts.[28] For the courts tended to take the Board's "laboratory conditions" standard seriously, and undertook to ensure that it would be applied as strictly against campaign abuses by unions as against those by management. In the *Celanese* case, for example, the Court of Appeals for the Seventh Circuit concluded that the Board had erred in overruling an objection based on a union's campaign letter claiming credit for "Celanese fringes, as well as other plant conditions." [29] In reality, the court pointed out, only *some* of the employees' fringe benefits had been won through collective bargaining, and since the court felt that union's letter could reasonably be interpreted to refer to *all* such benefits, it held that the letter did not meet the standards of "veracity demanded in respect to material statements made immediately

---

[25] *Id.* at 1461 n.4, 41 L.R.R.M. at 1434. *Cf.* Otis Elevator Co., 114 N.L.R.B. 1490, 37 L.R.R.M. 1198 (1955). This issue was not definitively resolved, however, until 1962, when the Board, in Hollywood Ceramics Co., Inc., 140 N.L.R.B. 221, 224 n.8, 51 L.R.R.M. 1600, 1602 (1962), specifically overruled decisions indicating that a misrepresentation would not be held objectionable unless it was deliberate.

[26] 130 N.L.R.B. 600, 47 L.R.R.M. 1371 (1961).

[27] The Board also rejected the regional director's conclusion that the claims were not objectionable because they were too ambiguous to be misleading. *Id.* at 602, 47 L.R.R.M. at 1371.

[28] Indeed, the Board's initial decision in the *Gummed Products* case to scrutinize substantive misrepresentations in campaign propaganda appears to have been influenced by prodding from the courts. *See, e.g.,* NLRB v. Trinity Steel Co., 214 F.2d 120, 34 L.R.R.M. 2377 (5th Cir. 1954).

[29] Celanese Corp. v. NLRB, 279 F.2d 204, 46 L.R.R.M. 2445 (7th Cir. 1960).

prior to a representation election."[30] Although the Supreme
Court subsequently remanded the case for reconsideration in
light of an intervening decision holding that "trivial irregularities" will not support election objections where there has
been "no prejudice to the fairness of the election,"[31] the Seventh
Circuit adhered to its position that the union's statement was
a material misrepresentation which prevented a fair vote.[32]

Similarly, in the Houston Chronicle case[33] the Fifth Circuit
overturned a Board holding that a pre-election union letter
containing statements that were "not completely accurate; speculative; exaggerated; half-truths; [and] misrepresentations" did
not afford grounds for setting the election aside. The regional
director, in rejecting the employer's objection to the letter, had
emphasized that the wage claims made by the union simply
rested on certain unstated hypotheses; that the bargaining unit
consisted of editorial employees who were trained in critically
evaluating such data; and that, in any event, the employer had
specifically taken advantage of the opportunity to reply to the
union's claims before the election. The court, however, quoted
the Board's own language respecting the need for "laboratory
conditions" in representation elections, and held that here the
standards had dropped too low.[34] In response to the Board's
argument that a certain amount of "prattle" ought to be tolerated
in election campaigns, the courts rejoined, "purportedly authoritative and truthful assertions concerning wages and pen-
sions . . . are not mere prattle; they are the stuff of life for
unions and members, the selfsame subjects concerning which
men organize and elect their representatives to bargain."[35]

The courts' decision in cases such as Celanese and Houston
Chronicle clearly reflected a judicial determination to see to it
that the Board's self-proclaimed "laboratory conditions" stand-

---

[30] Id. at 206, 46 L.R.R.M. at 2447.

[31] NLRB v. Mattison Machine Works, 365 U.S. 123, 47 L.R.R.M. 2437
(1961).

[32] Celanese Corp. v. NLRB, 291 F.2d 224, 48 L.R.R.M. 2406 (7th Cir.),
cert. denied, 368 U.S. 925, 49 L.R.R.M. 2173 (1961). See also Allis-Chalmers
Mfg. Co. v. NLRB, 261 F.2d 613, 43 L.R.R.M. 2246 (7th Cir. 1958).

[33] NLRB v. Houston Chronicle Publishing Co., 300 F.2d 273, 49 L.R.R.M.
2782 (5th Cir. 1962).

[34] Id. at 278, 49 L.R.R.M. at 2786.

[35] Id. at 280, 49 L.R.R.M. at 2787.

ard would be enforced as strictly against labor as against management. In this regard it is noteworthy that the Board itself had made attempts, early in the Eisenhower period, to back away somewhat from its "laboratory conditions" language. It issued opinions stating that elections "do not occur in a laboratory" and that "elections should be judged realistically and practically, and should not be judged against theoretically ideal, but nevertheless artificial, standards." [36] The Board's contemporaneous decisions [37] suggest, however, that this language should be read not as an attempt to return to a policy of noninvolvement in campaign propaganda issues, such as the policy pursued prior to *General Shoe*, but more as an attempt by the Board to stake out a broad area of discretion for itself in election cases. The "laboratory conditions" standard was to be retained as a theoretical goal, but the Board wished to preserve greater flexibility for itself to decide in each case whether the conditions came close enough to this "ideal." Such a flexible standard, of course, always carries with it possibilities for abuse of discretion, particularly in an area as politically charged as that of labor-management relations. Court decisions such as those discussed above simply illustrate judicial reaction in instances where it appeared to the courts that the Board was abusing this flexible standard to favor unions over management.

THE CURRENT TESTS FOR MISREPRESENTATIONS

Against the backdrop of adverse judicial decisions such as those discussed above, the Board undertook late in 1962 to restate and, to some extent, to codify its policies regarding election misrepresentations.[38] What is essentially involved in such cases, the Board pointed out, is a process of balancing "the right of the employees to an untrammeled choice, and the right of the parties to wage a free and vigorous campaign with all the normal legitimate tools of electioneering." [39] After listing

---

[36] The Liberal Market, Inc., 108 N.L.R.B. 1481, 1482, 34 L.R.R.M. 1270, 1271 (1954). *See also* Morganton Full Fashioned Hosiery, 107 N.L.R.B. 1534, 1538, 33 L.R.R.M. 1421, 1423 (1954).

[37] *See* text accompanying notes 17-25, *supra*.

[38] Hollywood Ceramics Co., Inc., 140 N.L.R.B. 221, 51 L.R.R.M. 1600 (1962).

[39] *Id.* at 224, 51 L.R.R.M. at 1601.

various reasons why the results of an election should not be lightly set aside on the basis of electioneering overstatements, the Board, in *Hollywood Ceramics,* enunciated the following formula:

> We believe that an election should be set aside only where there has been a misrepresentation or other similar campaign trickery, which involves a substantial departure from the truth, at a time which prevents the other party or parties from making an effective reply, so that the misrepresentation, whether deliberate or not, may reasonably be expected to have a significant impact on the election. However, the mere fact that a message is inartistically or vaguely worded and subject to different interpretations will not suffice to establish such misrepresentation as would lead us to set the election aside. Such ambiguities, like extravagant promises, derogatory statements about the other party, and minor distortions of some facts, frequently occur in communication between persons. But even where a misrepresentation is shown to have been substantial, the Board may still refuse to set aside the election if it finds upon consideration of all the circumstances that the statement would not be likely to have had a real impact on the election. For example, the misrepresentation might have occurred in connection with an unimportant matter so that it could only have had a *de minimis* effect. Or, it could have been so extreme as to put the employees on notice of its lack of truth under the particular circumstances so that they could not reasonably have relied on the assertion. Or, the Board may find that the employees possessed independent knowledge with which to evaluate the statements.[40]

The Board continues to refer to *Hollywood Ceramics* as the definitive statement of its policies regarding campaign misrepresentations.[41] From the discussion in the *Hollywood Ceramics* decision and subsequent cases, the following factors can be isolated as the Board's officially proclaimed tests for deciding whether or not to set aside an election on the basis of misrepresentations:

1) *Substantiality*—Was the misrepresentation enough of a departure from the truth to be likely to have influenced the voters' choice?

---

[40] *Id.,* 51 L.R.R.M. at 1601-1602.

[41] *See* 37 NLRB ANN. REP. 155 (1972). *See also* Modine Mfg. Co., 203 N.L.R.B. No. 77, 83 L.R.R.M. 1133 (1973). In the latter case, the Board adverted to certain factors which, it said, "make it in some degree tempting to abandon the approach taken in *Hollywood Ceramics,* but this we are not prepared to do." Member Penello concurred, stating that the *Hollywood Ceramics* rule should be changed in a future case, and Member Kennedy concurred only in the result, but refused, without explanation, to adopt his colleague's discussion of *Hollywood Ceramics.*

2) *Materiality*—Was the subject matter of the misrepresentation closely enough related to election issues to influence the voters?

3) *Timing*—Did the opposing party have an adequate opportunity to reply to the misrepresentation prior to the election?

4) *Source*—Did the misrepresentation come from a party in a position to have special knowledge of the subject matter, so that voters would be likely to rely on, or unable to check, its accuracy?

5) *Voters' independent knowledge*—Did the misrepresentation relate to a matter about which the voters lacked independent knowledge, thus precluding a finding that they were able to evaluate the claim for themselves?

If each of these questions is answered in the affirmative, the election will be set aside. It is usually said that unless *all* of the *Hollywood Ceramics* tests are met, the election will be considered valid, notwithstanding the presence of misrepresentation.[42] As we shall see, however, this has not always proved true in practice. Moreover, since the tests themselves entail a number of subjective determinations, their application has been far less predictable and consistent than a reading of the *Hollywood Ceramics* opinion itself would suggest.[43] In the discussion which follows, we shall seek to define each of the foregoing

---

[42] *E.g.*, NLRB v. Cactus Drilling Corp., 455 F.2d 871, 79 L.R.R.M. 2551 (5th Cir. 1972); NLRB v. O.S. Walker Co., Inc., 469 F.2d 813, 81 L.R.R.M. 2726 (1st Cir. 1972). The courts, however, do not always enumerate the same factors when they purport to list the *Hollywood Ceramics* tests. The Fifth Circuit, for example listed three of the above five factors in Pepperell Mfg. Co. v. NLRB, 403 F.2d 520, 523, 69 L.R.R.M. 2679, 2681 (5th Cir. 1968), and a different group of three in S.H. Kress Co. v. NLRB, 430 F.2d 1234, 1239, 75 L.R.R.M. 2064, 2068 (5th Cir. 1970). Omitted from both lists was the "substantiality" requirement, yet that factor is clearly included in the *Hollywood Ceramics* criteria and has been recognized by the courts as a prerequisite to setting aside elections in other cases. *See, e.g.*, Southwestern Portland Cement Co. v. NLRB, 407 F.2d 131, 134, 70 L.R.R.M. 2536, 2538 (5th Cir.), *cert. denied*, 396 U.S. 820, 72 L.R.R.M. 2431 (1969). Other courts have enumerated four of the five tests. Bausch & Lomb, Inc. v. NLRB, 451 F.2d 873, 78 L.R.R.M. 2648 (2d Cir. 1971); NLRB v. Trancoa Chemical Corp., 303 F.2d 456, 460, 50 L.R.R.M. 2407, 2408 (1st Cir. 1962).

[43] "[I]n large measure, each case must turn on its particular facts." Aerovox Corp. of Myrtle Beach v. NLRB, 409 F.2d 1004, 1008, 70 L.R.R.M. 3391, 3393 (4th Cir. 1969). Hence, the courts have emphasized the need to apply the above criteria with an awareness of the entire pattern of circumstances attending the election. *E.g.*, Foremost Dairies of the South v. NLRB, 416 F.2d 392, 400, 71 L.R.R.M. 2663, 2668 (5th Cir. 1969).

factors through reference to Board and court opinions and explore the problems encountered in its application.

APPLICATION OF THE CURRENT TESTS

The Board tried to make it clear in *Hollywood Ceramics* that its intention was not to eliminate every misstatement made during election campaigns, but only to prevent "*gross* misrepresentation about some material issue in the election." [44] Accordingly, it would limit its attention to statements which involved a "substantial departure from the truth." Lesser propaganda offenses, such as "ambiguities, . . . extravagant promises, derogatory statements about the other party, and *minor distortions of some facts* . . ." would be disregarded.[45] Clearly, then, the Board's intent was only to regulate the use of *major* distortions of the facts in campaign propaganda, and not to intervene if the propaganda claims, even though false, were relatively close to the truth.

Substantiality

The Board thus envisioned a much less exacting standard of truth—and implicitly a much less rigorous adherence to the "laboratory conditions" standard—than the Seventh Circuit had required in *Allis-Chalmers Mfg. Co. v. NLRB*.[46] In that case, overturning a Board decision which held that certain union propaganda was permissible because it was "virtually accurate," the court had declared:

> If the truth is diluted, it is no longer truth. A glass of water is no longer pure if a one-ninth part thereof is contaminated, nor is it "virtually pure." There cannot be "virtually" the truth any more than there can be "virtually" a virgin.[47]

---

[44] 140 N.L.R.B. at 223, 51 L.R.R.M. at 1601 (emphasis added).

[45] *Id.* at 224, 51 L.R.R.M. at 1601-1602. *See also* Florida Mining & Materials Corp., d/b/a McCormick Concrete Co., 198 N.L.R.B. No. 81, 80 L.R.R.M. 1848, *enforced*, 481 F.2d 65, 83 L.R.R.M. 2793 (5th Cir. 1973), wherein the Board declined to impose an "affirmative disclosure" requirement under which an election would be invalidated whenever it could be shown that one of the parties had concealed relevant information from the electorate.

[46] 261 F.2d 613, 43 L.R.R.M. 2246 (7th Cir. 1958).

[47] *Id.* at 616, 43 L.R.R.M. at 2248.

One can easily predict the effect on the volume of rerun elections if so rigorous a standard of purity for campaign speech were widely accepted. The contrast between this stringent approach and the Board's more flexible view is apparent in the Board's declaration in *Hollywood Ceramics* that "complete honesty" is not always attainable in an election campaign, "nor [is it] expected by the employee." [48]

As a practical matter, a test allowing some leeway for insubstantial departures from the truth is a necessity. The election machinery of the Act simply could not function if a new election had to be ordered every time any election party made a campaign statement which was untrue. But the alternative of a standard which requires the Board to differentiate among the degrees of falsehood involved in each case has proved difficult to administer. Not the least of the problems inherent in such an approach is that, under a standard so subjective and so flexible, the individual predelictions of the Board members or regional director deciding the issue may often become controlling.

Several decisions illustrate the kinds of difficulties encountered in the Board's application of the substantiality test. In *Cross Baking Co.*[49] the Board overruled an objection based on a union's distribution of propaganda claiming that a competitor's employees had obtained a seventy-five cents-an-hour increase under a union contract, when in fact the increase had amounted to about sixty cents and was spread over a three-year period. In the Board's view, this was not a sufficient departure from the truth to warrant invalidation of the election. The Court of Appeals for the First Circuit reversed the decision finding that the union's misrepresentation was substantial and deliberate.[50] The court stated, "Eleventh hour misrepresentations, manifestly deliberately untrue, have obviously been carefully timed to obtain the utmost benefit of the untruth, and presumably have

---

[48] 140 N.L.R.B. at 223, 51 L.R.R.M. at 1601. In so stating, the Board cited its decision in the *Celanese* case, without making any reference to the subsequent adverse rulings of the Seventh Circuit in that case. It is noteworthy that the Seventh Circuit has since become one of the more lenient circuits in regard to insubstantial departures from the truth in campaign propaganda. *See, e.g.*, NLRB v. Red Bird Foods, Inc., 399 F.2d 600, 68 L.R.R.M. 2943 (7th Cir. 1968).

[49] 186 N.L.R.B. 199, 75 L.R.R.M. 1359 (1970).

[50] Cross Baking Co. v. NLRB, 453 F.2d 1346, 78 L.R.R.M. 3059 (1st Cir. 1971).

been phrased to go just far enough to meet what the misrepresenting party believes to be necessary."[51] The court pointed out that where an *employer* had made misrepresentations of a less substantial nature than the *union's* misrepresentations in the case before it, the Board had held that the election was tainted.[52]

The Board recently incurred the ire of another court of appeals through its application of the substantiality test in the *Walled Lake Door* case.[53] There, although the union actually had been certified at only two of the company's four other plants, the union distributed a campaign leaflet urging the employees to "join hands with employees of the 4 Walled Lake plants who are represented by unions." The Board dismissed the discrepancy as not sufficiently substantial to invalidate the election, but the Fifth Circuit saw it differently. It ordered the election set aside and branded as a "crepuscular euphemism" the Board's attempt to characterize the union's misrepresentation as a mere "arithmetical inaccuracy."

In cases involving employers' campaign statements, the Board has not always allowed as much room for departure from the liberal truth. For example, in *The Trane Co.*,[54] the employer deducted five dollars from the employees' paychecks and enclosed it in a separate envelope which he distributed to the employees on the morning of the election as an attachment to their regular pay envelopes containing the balance of their usual pay. Accompanying the envelope with the five dollars was the written statement: "This is the estimated amount the union would want you to take out of your paycheck every month and hand over to them." The Board found that this was a substantial misrepresentation by the employer, since the actual

---

[51] *Id.* at 1350, 78 L.R.R.M. at 3061. *But cf.* Kalvar Corp., 204 N.L.R.B. No. 132, 83 L.R.R.M. 1385 (1973) (union's "eleventh hour" misrepresentations concerning hospitalization insurance negotiated with another employer held not sufficient to invalidate election).

[52] The court cited Bausch & Lomb, Inc. v. NLRB, 451 F.2d 1222, 78 L.R.R.M. 2648 (2d Cir. 1971), upholding a Board decision which set aside an election because the employer had told the voters that the union, at another location, had given up the employees' right to receive a Christmas bonus without explaining that the union had obtained other benefits in exchange for this concession.

[53] Walled Lake Door Co. v. NLRB, 472 F.2d 1010, 82 L.R.R.M. 2499 (5th Cir. 1972).

[54] 137 N.L.R.B. 1506, 50 L.R.R.M. 1434 (1962).

dues charged by the union were only four dollars a month. The difference to the employees, of course, would be twelve dollars a year—considerably less than a difference of one cent-an-hour in their wages. Yet no case has been found where the Board has required a union's claims concerning wages to be accurate to the exact cent.[55] Moreover, as the dissenting Board members pointed out in *Trane,* the employer did not claim its representation regarding the union's dues was exactly accurate, but only that it was an "estimated amount."[56]

In *Haynes Stellite Co.*[57] the Board went even further in insisting that the employer adhere to the literal truth. There the Board found an unfair labor practice and set aside an election based upon the employer's reading at pre-election meetings of the following statement:

> Customers arc buying products on the basis of prices, delivery and dependability. The facts are that in some cases we are the sole source of supply at present for some of our customers. We have been told that we would not continue to be the sole source of supply if we became unionized, due to the ever present possibility of a work stoppage due to strikers or walkouts.

The truth was that *one* customer had informed the company that it would seek other sources of supply if the company became unionized. But the Board read the employer's statement as implying that "some of [its] customers" had said they would take such action, and held that, in loosely equating "some" with

---

[55] *Compare* Gooch Packing Co., Inc., 200 N.L.R.B. No. 151, 82 L.R.R.M. 1171 (1972) (union agent's overstatement of her wage rate at a unionized plant by eight and one-half cents-an-hour held not sufficient to sustain objection), *with* Follet Corp., 164 N.L.R.B. 378, 65 L.R.R.M. 1102 (1967), *enforced,* 397 F.2d 91, 68 L.R.R.M. 2474 (7th Cir. 1968) (same; union's overstatement of unionized competitor's wage rate by seven cents per hour).

[56] 137 N.L.R.B. at 1512, 50 L.R.R.M. at 1437. *Cf.* The Singer Co., Friden Div., 199 N.L.R.B. No. 162, 82 L.R.R.M. 1019 (1972), where the Board held it was permissible for an employer to post seventy one-dollar bills in ten columns of seven bills each under the legend, "one-years minimum union dues looks like this," together with a display of groceries under the legend, "it can buy this." The seventy-dollar figure was accurate, and the Board held that "however graphic and dramatic," the employer's display did not transgress legitimate campaign tactics. *See also* Peachtree City Warehouse, Inc., 158 N.L.R.B. 1031, 1041, 62 L.R.R.M. 1169 (1966).

[57] 136 N.L.R.B. 95, 49 L.R.R.M. 1711 (1962).

"one," the employer "had materially misrepresented the facts." [58] Obviously some consideration of the substantiality factor is essential if the Board is to evaluate fairly the probable impact of campaign misrepresentations on the electorate. But as the foregoing cases illustrate, the Board's application of the test has been so uneven as to virtually preclude election parties from predicting in any case whether a given factual inaccuracy will be considered substantial enough to disturb the election results. This, of course, leads to increased litigation in an area where the benefits of delay already provide more than ample encouragement to litigate.

Although it might not be feasible for the Board to enunciate a more precise standard than it has in the past for determining how great a departure from strict truth it will tolerate in campaign communications, the Board could reduce the uncertainty in this area in the future by renouncing decisions such as *Trane* and *Haynes Stellite*, and adhering more faithfully to its early policy of considering only gross and deliberate campaign trickery as grounds for invalidation, without regard to which party commits such misconduct. A trend in this direction appears to be gaining support in opinions of Chairman Miller decrying what he sees as the Board's "belabored examination of minutiae . . . [resulting from] too purist a view of what parties may be permitted to say in election campaigns." [59]

Recently, in *Modine Mfg. Co.*,[60] the Board gave a strong indication that it is moving in the direction Chairman Miller has suggested:

> We do not wish to have unrealistic standards, or insist upon such improbable purity of word and deed that we will obstruct our administrative task of conducting elections in a high number of cases that any hard-fought campaign will almost inevitably result in our elections being invalidated.[61]

---

[58] *Id.* at 97, 49 L.R.R.M. at 1712. The court of appeals subsequently denied enforcement of the Board's finding that the same management statements constituted coercion violative of Section 8(a)(1), *sub nom.*, Union Carbide Corp. v. NLRB, 310 F.2d 844, 52 L.R.R.M. 2001 (6th Cir. 1962). However, since the election-case rulings in *Haynes Stellite* did not result in issuance of a bargaining order, those specific rulings were never reviewed by the court of appeals.

[59] Bill's Institutional Commissary Corp., 200 N.L.R.B. No. 151, 82 L.R.R.M. 1171 (1972); Allis-Chalmers Mfg. Co., 194 N.L.R.B. No. 150, 79 L.R.R.M. 1148 (1972); National Mobil Homes, 186 N.L.R.B. 891, 75 L.R.R.M. 1477 (1970).

[60] 203 N.L.R.B. No. 77, 83 L.R.R.M. 1133 (1973).

[61] *Id.*, 83 L.R.R.M. at 1136.

However, the Board specifically stated that it is not presently prepared to abandon the *Hollywood Ceramics* approach.[62] It appears, rather, that the Board majority will strive to take advantage of the flexibility inherent in the *Hollywood Ceramics* tests to reduce its involvement in matters of election propaganda without specifically enunciating any new tests. It will remain to be seen whether, in doing so, the Board will be able to reach more intelligible and uniform results than it has under its past application of the current tests, and whether it will be able to satisfy the courts that it is applying its new standards fairly.

Materiality

Even a gross and deliberate misrepresentation affords no reason to set aside an election unless it is so related to the issues at stake in the election that it can fairly be presumed to have had an impact on the voters' choice. Claims relating to certain key issues, such as wages and benefits, obviously meet this test. To repeat the Fifth Circuit's often quoted language, "assertions concerning wages . . . are the stuff of life for unions and members, the selfsame subjects concerning which men organize and elect their representatives to bargain." [63] For this reason, the courts have repeatedly held that the Board should apply a more exacting standard when evaluating the probable impact of union propaganda concerning wages and benefits received under union contracts at other locations.[64] Despite such adverse decisions, however, the Board still frequently fails to apply a rigorous enough standard in regard to union wage propaganda to satisfy the courts.[65]

In addition to claims relating to wages and working conditions, other campaign statements which would appear presumptively

---

[62] *But cf.* 203 N.L.R.B. No. 17, 83 L.R.R.M. 1138 (1973) (Members Penello and Kennedy, concurring). *See also* note 41, *supra.*

[63] NLRB v. Houston Chronicle Publishing Co., 300 F.2d 273, 49 L.R.R.M. 2782 (5th Cir. 1962).

[64] *E.g.*, Cross Baking Co. v. NLRB, 453 F.2d 1346, 78 L.R.R.M. 3059 (1st Cir. 1971); NLRB v. Bill's Institutional Commissary Corp., 418 F.2d 405, 72 L.R.R.M. 2782 (5th Cir. 1969); Gallenkamp Stores Co. v. NLRB, 402 F.2d 525, 69 L.R.R.M. 2024 (9th Cir. 1968); Collins & Aikman Corp. v. NLRB, 383 F.2d 277, 68 L.R.R.M. 2320 (4th Cir. 1968); NLRB v. Houston Chronicle Publishing Co., 300 F.2d 273, 49 L.R.R.M. 2782 (5th Cir. 1962).

[65] *See, e.g.*, NLRB v. Millard Metal Service Center, Inc., 472 F.2d 647, 82 L.R.R.M. 2345 (1st Cir. 1973); Gulton Industries, Inc. v. NLRB, 469 F.2d 1371, 81 L.R.R.M. 2885 (5th Cir. 1972).

to meet the test of materiality include claims by either party relating to the union's dues and membership requirements,[66] its policies regarding fines and assessments,[67] and its policies regarding strikes and the necessity for strike votes.[68] Each of these subjects bears directly upon the nature of the relationship the employees will be entering into if they choose to be represented by a union. Accordingly, each is material to the central decision facing the voters—whether the potential benefits of union representation are worth the costs in dues and surrender of individual freedom.

The Board, however, has tended to deemphasize the materiality of union claims regarding their policies and performance, as compared with similar claims by employers. For example, in *Graphic Arts Finishing Co.*,[69] the Board rejected objections based upon a union's gross exaggeration of the amount it had recently paid in strike benefits to the employees of a neighboring firm. The union had distributed an election-eve circular containing the claim that because of generous union strike fund payments to its members and their families during that strike, "NOT ONE PERSON LOST A THING." There could be no doubt about the substantiality of this misrepresentation since, in fact, the striking employees had sustained about $600 thousand in uncompensated wage losses. Nevertheless, the Board's regional director ruled that the union's misstatements were not likely to have a significant impact on the electorate. The Court of Appeals for the Fourth Circuit, in reversing the Board's decision, pointed out why claims about strike benefits are particularly likely to influence employees in deciding whether or not to choose a union:

> If the employees believed this statement, . . . any doubts they entertained about joining the union for fear of being involved in a costly strike would be substantially removed, if not totally removed. It is common knowledge that strikes play a major role in labor relations and that they constitute the most potent weapon in the employees arsenal.[70]

---

[66] The Trane Co., 137 N.L.R.B. 1506, 50 L.R.R.M. 1434 (1962).

[67] *Compare* Chemi-Trol Chemical Co., 190 N.L.R.B. No. 56, 77 L.R.R.M. 1120 (1971); *with* Allis-Chalmers Mfg. Co., 194 N.L.R.B. No. 150, 79 L.R.R.M. 1148 (1972).

[68] *See* Bailey Meter Co., 198 N.L.R.B. No. 162, 81 L.R.R.M. 1087 (1972).

[69] Case No. 5-RC-4826, 59 L.R.R.M. 1644 (1965).

[70] Graphic Arts Finishing Co. v. NLRB, 380 F.2d 893, 65 L.R.R.M. 3038 (4th Cir. 1967).

Thus, despite the Board's contrary view, it would appear that, if materiality is to be considered at all, misrepresentations regarding the amount a union can or will pay in strike benefits to its members clearly should be considered relevant to the central issues at stake in any representation election.

The materiality of some types of campaign claims may depend on the context in which they occur. In several 1972 cases, for example, the Board was called upon to decide whether union statements concerning the potential effect of "Phase II" wage controls on bargaining were likely to have had an improper impact on the employees' decision whether to elect the union.[71] In view of the then-current status of wage controls and the uncertainty as to their duration, the employees might reasonably have concluded that selection of a bargaining representative at that time would be of little benefit to them in securing higher wages. Against this background, any union claims relating to ways it could use to "get around" the controls [72] would clearly have been material to their decision.

Several recent cases illustrate the kind of difficulties that may be encountered in borderline situations in attempting to determine whether certain types of campaign representations meet the materiality test. In one case [73] the union falsely represented to employees that it had filed unfair labor practice charges with the NLRB on behalf of two employees who had been discharged during the union campaign. The employer argued that this misrepresentation was likely to influence votes, since it would tend to convince the employees that the presence of the union afforded them greater protection against unfair labor practices than they would otherwise have had, when in fact the union had done nothing. The Board disagreed, holding that the union's statement, although false, was not material because even without the union the employees could have filed a charge on their own behalf, and the union's participation or nonparticipation would not affect the vindication of their rights.

The problem with the Board's analysis is that it fails to consider the matter from the employees' point of view. The

---

[71] Thiem Industries, Inc., 195 N.L.R.B. No. 200, 79 L.R.R.M. 1614 (1972); Barfield Cleaning Co., Case No. 7-RC-10818, 79 L.R.R.M. 1200 (1972).

[72] 79 L.R.R.M. at 1201.

[73] Indiana Rock Wool Div., Susquehanna Corp., 201 N.L.R.B. No. 19, 82 L.R.R.M. 1155 (1973).

grounds and procedures for filing unfair labor practice charges may well have been unfamiliar to the employees, and the belief that the union had actively piloted their cause through the agency process could logically have induced them to retain the union to aid them in such matters by electing it as their bargaining representatives. Hence, although one may well agree with the Board's holding on the ground that it has no business setting aside elections on the basis of statements such as this, the Board's rationale that the misrepresentation was not *material* is highly questionable.

Another recent case, *Westlock Division*,[74] involved a union's false campaign charges that the employer had assigned an employee to a hazardous new machine and then callously discharged him when he sustained an injury. In truth, the employee had not been hurt on the job, and the employer had made attempts to find him another position before discharging him. The employer's objection to the union's propaganda was rejected by the Board's regional office on the ground that the misrepresentation was not material, but was merely "typical campaign rhetoric describing the Employer as insensitive to the needs of the employees. . . ." The region's approach was consistent with a line of Board cases holding that campaign rhetoric attacking the character of the other party, no matter how unjustified, will not be considered to invalidate the election.[75]

In this instance, however, the Board overturned the region's determination and sustained the objection.[76] Apparently the Board felt that the union's story was so unjustified and its potential emotional impact on the voters was so great that the election should be set aside, even if the misrepresentation was not *rationally* related to any legitimate campaign issues.[77]

---

[74] Westlock Div., Tool Research & Eng. Corp., 199 N.L.R.B. No. 25, 81 L.R.R.M. 1278 (1972).

[75] *See* Georgia Pacific Corp., 199 N.L.R.B. No. 43, 81 L.R.R.M. 1214 (1972) (employer's charge that union was undemocratic and corrupt did not void election even though "short of complete honesty"); Calcor Corp., 106 N.L.R.B. 539, 32 L.R.R.M. 1498 (1953) (election upheld despite "virtually libelous" handbills distributed by union).

[76] 199 N.L.R.B. No. 25, 81 L.R.R.M. at 1279.

[77] The Board, after highlighting the emotional pitch of the union's communications, did make an attempt to tie the representation question into the issue of job security, but the link is obviously rather remote. *Id.*, 81 L.R.R.M. at 1278-79.

A comparable problem was presented in the earlier *Tyler Pipe* case,[78] but there the Board reached the opposite result. The employer objected to union propaganda charging that the company's officers and stockholders were getting wealthy through callous exploitation of the wage earners. The Board found that the union had used falsified figures which grossly exaggerated the company's profits. Although the union's tactic was, as the Board put it, "reprehensible," its claims were essentially irrelevant to genuine campaign issues. The employees' basic economic interest depended not on whether the company's officers and stockholders were getting wealthy, but on what the union could actually get for the workers if elected. It was not disputed that the company had been profitable, even though not as profitable as the union had claimed. As the Board's trial examiner observed, "the very nature of these representations are (sic) such that they are likely to be taken with a grain of salt by the employees, for it is obvious that no one can determine with precision the extent to which the work of employees contributes to the worth of the employer." [79]

The Court of Appeals for the Fifth Circuit found this result unacceptable. The court did not address the question of whether the disputed propaganda was *material* to issues genuinely at stake in the election, but emphasized that it was deliberately falsified and emotionally pitched and, therefore, had a probable impact on the employees' choice. This in itself was enough to invalidate the election in the court's view.[80]

What the court may have had in mind, although it did not expressly say so, is that inflammatory campaign propaganda can have a powerful impact on the voters' choice even if it is not really material to genuine issues at stake in the election. The issues are only one part of the overall reality of an election. It is also, in a sense, a referendum on the employer's popularity

---

[78] Tyler Pipe Industries, Inc., 161 N.L.R.B. 784, 63 L.R.R.M. 1359 (1966), *remanded*, 406 F.2d 1272, 70 L.R.R.M. 2739 (5th Cir. 1969), *reaffirmed*, 180 N.L.R.B. 880, 76 L.R.R.M. 1830 (1970), *enforcement denied*, 447 F.2d 1136, 77 L.R.R.M. 2416 (5th Cir. 1971).

[79] 180 N.L.R.B. at 889, 76 L.R.R.M. at 1830-31.

[80] *See also* Schneider Mills, Inc. v. NLRB, 390 F.2d 375, 67 L.R.R.M. 2413 (4th Cir. 1968), wherein the court reversed a Board decision which had refused to invalidate an election because of union statements comparing the employer's president to Hitler and falsely charging him with having said he would like to see employees tied and incinerated.

and sometimes even a medium of protest. Experienced organizers know this and can use exaggerated *ad hominem* attacks to as great an advantage as misrepresentations about such matters as wages. The court obviously felt such tactics should have no place in a government sponsored and supervised election.[81]

Yet the question the court ignored is whether it is truly desirable or practical for the Board to intervene routinely to "protect" the employees from such emotional appeals. The Board is on shaky ground in any circumstances when it attempts to predict what statements will interfere with the voters' opportunity to make a rational choice.[82] But at least the Board has limited its intervention, for the most part, by applying a presumption that the voters will generally act as rational beings and disregard matters that are irrelevant. For the Board to go further and purport to determine when and how the voters' choice may be affected by irrational and emotional appeals that are essentially irrelevant to genuine campaign issues would be for it to assume a role it is totally incompetent to perform.

The view represented by the Board's holding in *Tyler Pipe* has obvious administrative advantages; it would keep the agency from becoming embroiled in the unpleasant and fruitless task of sorting the truth from among derogatory campaign exchanges and speed the resolution of representation questions. It has a practical appeal in that it would place the voters on basically the same independent footing in regard to inflammatory appeals in Board elections as they are accustomed to in normal civil elections. Also, it would be supportive of the free speech concept embodied in Section 8(c) of the Act. Unfortunately, the Board has never made either the existence of its policy of noninterference in such circumstances or the reasons favoring that policy sufficiently clear in its own opinions to provide a firm basis for acceptance of its view by the courts of appeals.

---

[81] *See also* NLRB v. Southern Paper Box Co., 473 F.2d 208, 82 L.R.R.M. 2482 (8th Cir. 1973), where the court refused enforcement of a Board order based on a certification, saying, "We are simply unwilling to accept . . . that such an *ad hominem* accusation [that the employer's president had used bonus money due the employees to finance a trip to Europe] . . . was . . . permissible campaign propaganda which the employees could be expected to evaluate for themselves." *Id.* at 211, 82 L.R.R.M. at 2485.

[82] *See* Getman & Goldberg, *The Myth of NLRB Expertise*, 39 U. CHI. L. REV. 681 (1972); Samoff, *NLRB Elections: Uncertainty and Certainty*, 117 U. PA. L. REV. 228 (1968); Bok, *The Regulation of Campaign Tactics in Representation Elections Under the N.L.R.A.*, 78 HARV. L. REV. 38 (1964).

The Board's decision overturning its regional director in the recent *Westlock Division* case,[83] suggests that the Board may now be wavering from the resolve it showed in *Tyler Pipe* and modifying its views as to the materiality of campaign appeals which raise emotional or personal issues not genuinely relevant to the selection or rejection of a bargaining representative. Perhaps the decision can be explained as an attempt by the Board to redress in some measure the comparatively permissive treatment of certain other types of union misrepresentations in some of its previous decisions.[84] But the better way to correct such imbalance, if that is truly the Board's objective, is not for the Board now to increase its regulation of what is essentially irrelevant propaganda when it is used by unions, but rather to decrease its role in policing the content of *both* employers' and unions' campaign statements, and to limit agency involvement with issues of the campaign propaganda of either party to a level commensurate with that applied to unions in the early period of the Act, prior to the addition of Section 8(c).

Timing

In *Hollywood Ceramics* the Board said that it would treat as objectionable only those misrepresentations which are made "at a time which precludes the other party or parties from making an effective reply. . . ." [85] Thus, if the opposing party knows of the misrepresentation far enough in advance of the election so that he can communicate the truth to the voters, whether or not he actually does so, he will be barred from objecting on that ground.

This requirement reflects the Board's basic belief that if the opposing party responds with the truth, the employees can generally be relied on to recognize it as such, and any adverse impact the misrepresentation might otherwise have had will thereby effectively be neutralized. The presumption may be un-

---

[83] *See* text accompanying notes 74-77, *supra*.

[84] It is particularly significant that Chairman Miller participated in the *Westlock* decision, since it would seem to represent a step away from the view he has expressed in other cases, to the effect that the Board should avoid playing too protective a role where campaign propaganda is concerned. *See* cases cited at note 59, *supra*.

[85] 140 N.L.R.B. at 224, 51 L.R.R.M. at 1601.

warranted in many individual cases, but it is in accord with the Board's basic policy of leaving the voters to their own rational defenses in regard to matters of campaign propaganda, except in those glaring instances where the circumstances and the nature of the propaganda itself make rational evaluation impossible.

There are also administrative considerations underlying the timing requirement. The Board seeks to structure its election policies so as to ensure that the parties themselves will use their own best efforts during the pre-election period to neutralize or eliminate any objectionable conditions and thus minimize the incidence of rerun elections. Accordingly, if a party knows a misrepresentation has been made and has it within his power to neutralize its impact by a timely reply, the Board holds that he must do so or he will be precluded from objecting thereafter that the misrepresentation interfered with the election results. This restriction eliminates the tactical advantage a party might otherwise gain from allowing a misrepresentation to go unanswered and then using it afterward as a basis for overturning the election if the results are unsatisfactory to him. It is for these reasons that the Board's policy is phrased in terms of whether an actual reply was made.

In one view, this approach places excessive emphasis on the lack of diligence of the company or union which failed to reply when it could have, and ignores the fact that, nevertheless, because no reply was made, the employees' freedom of choice may have been impaired. As the Fifth Circuit has stated:

> It seems, in passing, that the Board relies too heavily on the Company's *Opportunity* to rebut the Union's misstatements. Rebuttal is significant; *opportunity* to rebut, taken alone, is a different matter. It must be remembered that the stated purpose of these proceedings is to determine the uninhibited desires of the *employees*. Too often, the battle raging between the company and the union obscures the very subject of the focus of our attention. The fact that the company or the union fails to exercise an opportunity to rebut the lies of the other is of little moment in attempting to determine the effect of those falsehoods on the employees.[86]

---

[86] NLRB v. Cactus Drilling Corp., 455 F.2d 871, 79 L.R.R.M. 2551 (5th Cir. 1972); Tyler Pipe & Foundry v. NLRB, 406 F.2d 1272, 70 L.R.R.M. 2739 (5th Cir. 1969). For a view very much in accord with the language quoted above, but in a slightly different context, see the Board's opinion in Sterling Faucet Co., 203 N.L.R.B. No. 144, 83 L.R.R.M. 1530 (1973) (Chairman Miller, dissenting).

The Board, however, has taken the position that as the agency primarily responsible for effectuating the election mechanisms of the Act, it must choose the policy which will do the most to promote the principle of free choice in all elections. Although it might arguably protect the freedom of choice of the particular employees in each individual case to order rerun elections whenever unrebutted misrepresentations are shown, this would do little to encourage parties to take affirmative action during the pre-election period to prevent voters from being misled. The latter objective can be promoted only by imposing a strict doctrine of waiver against any party who could have acted prior to the election to neutralize an opponent's campaign misstatements, but failed to do so. The Board has resolved the balance in favor of the latter policy, reasoning that it best serves the interests of "all majorities" despite its necessary infringement on the rights of "particular majorities." [87] This determination clearly seems to represent a proper exercise of the Board's administrative discretion.[88]

Deciding whether a misrepresentation occurred far enough in advance of the election to afford an adequate opportunity for reply sometimes poses difficult questions of fact for the Board. Ordinarily the process begins by measuring the elapsed time between the moment when the opposing party became aware of the misrepresentation and the opening of the polls. It must then be determined whether, with reasonable diligence, the objecting party could have composed an effective answer and communicated it to the voters within that available time period. A week will almost certainly be considered adequate time to reply if, in fact, any reply is possible.[89] Three or four days will generally be enough.[90] Two days may even be enough, de-

---

[87] *See* 455 F.2d at 876, 79 L.R.R.M. at 2554.

[88] NLRB v. A.J. Tower Co., 329 U.S. 324, 331, 19 L.R.R.M. 2128, 2131 (1946), where the Supreme Court said: "The principle of majority rule, however, does not foreclose practical adjustments designed to protect the election machinery from the everpresent dangers of abuse and fraud."

[89] *E.g.*, Lipman Motors, Inc. v. NLRB, 451 F.2d 823, 78 L.R.R.M. 2808 (2d Cir. 1971).

[90] *E.g.*, Hardy Herpolsheimer Div., Allied Stores, Inc., 173 N.L.R.B. 1109, 70 L.R.R.M. 1121 (1968); Ralston Purina Co., 147 N.L.R.B. 506, 56 L.R.R.M. 1243 (1964).

pending on the circumstances.[91] However, when the misrepresentation occurs on the "eve of the election"—that is, within the final 24 hours—it will generally be considered too late to allow time for an effective reply.[92]

As the time available for reply decreases, the Board pays closer attention to such factors as the size of the voting unit and any special problems of communicating with the employees in the time available.[93] The Board may look to the manner and promptness with which the objecting party has replied to other statements during the course of the campaign as an indication of how much time he would have needed to reply to the challenged statement.[94] Finally, if the Board finds that the general subject matter which the alleged misrepresentation concerned was raised and discussed earlier in the campaign, it may conclude that the objecting party could have formulated an effective reply in a shorter time than would otherwise have been needed, since the employees would already be generally familiar with the issue.[95]

The subject matter of a misrepresentation may have an important bearing on how much time an opponent will reasonably need to formulate an effective reply. Although the Board has never placed much emphasis on the point, several courts of appeals have stressed that adequate time to reply "must mean adequate time to make an *effective* reply." [96] As the First Circuit pointed out in *Cross Baking Co.*, where one party makes elaborate assertions of fact purportedly supported by docu-

---

[91] *Compare* S.H. Lynch & Co. v. NLRB, 406 F.2d 766, 70 L.R.R.M. 2217 (5th Cir. 1968); *and* General Electric Co., 162 N.L.R.B. 912, 64 L.R.R.M. 1104, *enforced*, 383 F.2d 152, 66 L.R.R.M. 2262 (4th Cir. 1967); *with* Gulton Industries, Inc. v. NLRB, 469 F.2d 1371, 81 L.R.R.M. 2885 (5th Cir. 1972); *and* Zarn Inc., 170 N.L.R.B. 1135, 67 L.R.R.M. 1549 (1968).

[92] *E.g.*, Gallenkamp Stores Co. v. NLRB, 402 F.2d 525, 69 L.R.R.M. 2024 (9th Cir. 1968); Collins & Aikman Co. v. NLRB, 383 F.2d 277, 68 L.R.R.M. 2320 (4th Cir. 1968).

[93] 147 N.L.R.B. at 509, 56 L.R.R.M. at 1244.

[94] *See, e.g.*, General Electric Co., 162 N.L.R.B. 912, 918, 64 L.R.R.M. 1104 (1967).

[95] *Id.* at 913 n.3, 64 L.R.R.M. at 1104.

[96] Cross Baking Co. v. NLRB, 453 F.2d 1346, 1350, 78 L.R.R.M. 3059, 3061 (1st Cir. 1971) (emphasis added); *accord*, NLRB v. Cactus Drilling Corp., 455 F.2d 871, 79 L.R.R.M. 2551 (5th Cir. 1972); NLRB v. Houston Chronicle Publishing Co., 300 F.2d 273, 49 L.R.R.M. 2782 (5th Cir. 1962).

mentary evidence of materials within its special knowledge, the other party's "last minute bare denial cannot be an effective reply." [97] In such circumstances, the courts have insisted that the objecting parties be given sufficient time to make whatever investigation and assemble whatever data are reasonably necessary to enable them to frame an effective reply. Where the facts have shown that time for that kind of investigation was lacking, the courts have rejected the Board's application of the time-for-reply test to overrule objections. [98]

Difficult questions may arise in determining what sort of reply would have been "effective." In the *Cactus Drilling* case, the Board's regional director concluded that the employer had an adequate opportunity to reply effectively to a union campaign letter which came to its counsel's attention at least four days before the election. [99] The union's letter claimed that other unnamed drilling companies in the area had said that they would be forced to "roll back" wage increases previously granted unless Cactus, a leader in the area, granted similar raises. The possibility of such rollbacks was of interest to the unit employees since, in the highly transitory drilling business, many of them worked intermittently for other area companies. The union's letter urged that this was a reason for voting in its favor, speculating that if it won the election it could obtain a raise at Cactus and thereby prevent the allegedly threatened rollbacks at other locations. [100]

Cactus contended that it had no opportunity to reply effectively to this propaganda, because the union's letter did not identify the "other contractors" who had allegedly suggested the possibility of rollbacks. Hence, the company protested, there was no way, short of contacting every drilling contractor in the Permian Basin, for it to determine whether the union's claim was true and formulate a response, and this could not be done within the available four days.

---

[97] 453 F.2d at 1350, 78 L.R.R.M. at 3061.

[98] *See* cases cited at note 96, *supra; see also* NLRB v. Millard Metal Service Center, Inc., 472 F.2d 647, 82 L.R.R.M. 2345 (1st Cir. 1973).

[99] 455 F.2d at 875, 79 L.R.R.M. at 2554.

[100] Serious questions arise as to whether this statement was a misrepresentation at all and, if so, whether it met the "substantiality" test, discussed *supra*. The Board overruled the objection in part on those grounds, but the court of appeals was clearly of the opinion that the statement was a material misrepresentation.

The Board was not persuaded that an exhaustive canvas of other drillers was truly necessary for an effective reply. It argued before the court of appeals that the company should simply have telephoned the union agent who composed the letter and asked him which other contractors had made the alleged "rollback" statements. If the union had identified them, the company could have checked with those contractors and, if the union's claim proved untrue, framed an appropriate reply. On the other hand, if the union had refused to identify its sources, the company could have reported that fact to the employees and challenged the union to defend its claim.

Under this theory, a simple statement from the company that it did not know of any contractors who were contemplating wage rollbacks and that the union had refused to identify any such contractors, should have been sufficient to equip the employees to evaluate the union's letter for themselves. In either case, the company would have had adequate time to respond within four days. The company's failure to take even this minimal step in the interest of avoiding a rerun election, the Board argued, justified the conclusion that the company was not truly interested in protecting the employee's free choice, but only in delaying its bargaining obligation.

The court's refusal to enforce the Board's order clearly indicates a rejection of that inference and of the Board's premise that an answer merely pointing out the union's refusal to identify the sources of its information would have been "effective" to neutralize the impact of its campaign letter.

An earlier decision by the Fifth Circuit provides an interesting contrast with its ruling in *Cactus Drilling* insofar as it relates to the obligation of a party to take affirmative steps to verify pre-election claims made by his opponent in order to prevent the employees from being misled. In *NLRB v. Trinity Steel Co.*[101] a union agent learned prior to an election that company representatives had told employees that the company had applied to some unidentified government agency for permission to grant a wage increase to its employees. The union agent contacted the local Wage Stabilization Board Office and was told that no such application had been filed. Relying on this information, he told the employees that the company representatives' claim was false. In fact, the company had filed

---

[101] 214 F.2d 120, 34 L.R.R.M. 2377 (5th Cir. 1954).

for approval of an increase with the Wage and Hour and Public Contracts Division of the U.S. Department of Labor, which the union agent had failed to contact. Accordingly, the information conveyed by the union agent, while given in good faith, was misleading because his investigation had not been complete enough.

The Board had overruled company objections based on these events, but the Fifth Circuit reversed the Board and declared the election invalid. Significantly, the court criticized the union agent for never contacting the company prior to the election in an effort "to reconcile the discrepancy between what the company officials had told the employees about the matter in question and what he . . . had ascertained from his own inquiry."

It seems quite reasonable to hold, as the court did, that the union agent in *Trinity Steel* should have telephoned the company officials and asked what agency, if any, they had applied to for permission to raise wages, before representing to the employees that the company had not made any such application.[102] But, by the same token, it seems equally reasonable to suggest that the employer in *Cactus Drilling* should have telephoned the union agent and asked which drilling contractors, if any, had warned of possible wage rollbacks before protesting to the Board that there was no way he could have rebutted the union's claims. All that is suggested in either instance is that the parties in question should have been required to exert certain obvious, minimal efforts in advance of the election to ensure that the employees would not be misled, and thus, to eliminate the need for a rerun election.

Such a requirement would be in accord with the basic objective of improving the efficiency and reliability of the Act's election machinery in general, and, as discussed above,[103] would thereby accrue to the benefit of "all majorities." As this analysis demonstrates, the Board's recent application of the time-to-reply test appears to be generally consistent with that basic policy, whereas the more limited application of the test envisioned by the courts in such cases as *Cactus Drilling* would tend to undermine these general objectives in favor of greater

---

[102] Whether the union agent's misstatement in *Trinity Steel* was actually substantial or material enough to justify setting the election aside is a separate issue.

[103] *See* text accompanying notes 87-88, *supra*.

concern for the possibility of occasional impairment of the rights of "particular majorities" in individual cases. It is submitted here that the Board's approach is better calculated to effectuate the overall goals of the Act's election provisions.

Source

The source of a misrepresentation may have an important bearing on its effect on the election, since voters may be more likely to rely—or less able to check—on the accuracy of a statement if it comes from a party in a position to have special knowledge of what the Board has called "the true facts." [104]

The *Gummed Products* case,[105] one of the leading cases in the development of the Board's current set of tests for misrepresentations, illustrates the customary application of the source test. There, the Board considered objections to union handbills asking employees to compare their wages with the rates allegedly received by employees at three similar companies within the same general labor market. The rates listed by the union as being paid by one of these competitors were six to 57 cents-an-hour higher than the rates actually in effect at that company. When the employer responded pointing out this error to the employees, the union retaliated with an election-eve distribution falsely claiming that it had negotiated a new contract with the competitor which did in fact contain the rates it had originally quoted. In evaluating the effect of the unions' statements, the Board emphasized that "as one of the parties to [the] alleged new contract at the [competitor's] plant, the [union] was in an *authoritative position to know* whether a new contract had been signed and whether it contained higher wage rates. . . ." [106] Therefore, applying the source test, the Board voided the election.

The significance of the source factor has been variously explained. In early cases, the Board indicated that it would overturn an election because of misrepresentations, only if the subject related to "matters peculiarly within the knowledge" of the party making the statement.[107] The use of the word "peculiarly"

---

[104] Hook Drugs, Inc., 119 N.L.R.B. 1502, 1505, 41 L.R.R.M. 1351, 1352 (1958).

[105] The Gummed Products Co., 112 N.L.R.B. 1092, 36 L.R.R.M. 1156 (1955).

[106] *Id.* at 1094, 36 L.R.R.M. at 1157 (emphasis added).

[107] *E.g.,* Craft Mfg. Co., 122 N.L.R.B. 341, 343, 43 L.R.R.M. 1116, 1117 (1958).

suggested a strict requirement that the speaker be the *only* one with knowledge of or access to the facts. Thus, the Board would not set aside an election if the voters could have found out the truth, either by investigating on their own or by checking with some third party. This approach was in line with the Board's general policy at that time of placing primary responsibility on the employees themselves to evaluate election campaign statements, and intervening to void the election only in the most extreme situations.[108]

Under this construction, application of the source test would limit election invalidation to cases in which a party made misrepresentations about some subject within his exclusive knowledge. For example, a union's statement about plans to decrease its dues or fees, an employer's claims about impending changes in the structure of his business, or either party's accounts of relevant dealings with some remote third person not readily accessible to the other election participants, all could be grounds for voiding an election, because there would be no way even a skeptical voter could check on the validity of such statements.

In *Hollywood Ceramics*, however, the Board merely said that the source of a misrepresentation is "one factor which the Board will consider" in evaluating "the probable impact of a party's statement on the election." [109] This suggests a deemphasis of the factor, implying it would be used more as a makeweight than as a necessary prerequisite to overturning an election. This change of emphasis indicated a basic shift in the Board's focus away from a consideration of whether it was *possible* for the employees to evaluate the matter for themselves, and toward a determination of whether it was *probable* that the misrepresentation had an actual impact on votes. *Hollywood Ceramics* also states that the reason for considering the source factor is that the voters "may be expected to attach greater significance" to assertions coming from a party with "intimate" knowledge of the subject matter.[110] This language seems to indicate that the important consideration is the employees' probable reliance on the false statements, rather than the nonexistence of any other source with whom the employees could have checked the accuracy of the party's claim to avoid being misled.

---

[108] *See* discussion at pp. 17-19, *supra*.

[109] 140 N.L.R.B. at 224 n.10, 51 L.R.R.M. at 1602.

[110] *Id.*, 51 L.R.R.M. at 1602. For a recent application of the same rationale, see TRW Credit Data, 205 N.L.R.B. No. 143, 84 L.R.R.M. 1077 (1973).

Comparing *Hollywood Ceramics* with earlier Board decisions, one can see the contrast between the early policy of minimal intervention in questions of campaign propaganda, with safeguards only against the most blatant violations of fair play, and the later, more protectionist approach, whereby the Board actively involves itself in trying both to identify the types of statements and to determine how these statements most likely influence voters. But the Board has never totally abandoned its earlier approach, with its emphasis on the voters' own powers of evaluation. Instead, the Board has again sought to preserve maximum flexibility for itself, at the expense of a clearly-defined standard which election parties can use to determine their rights without litigation. Thus, the Board's decisions have intermittently reflected, in varying degrees, the influence of both the *Hollywood Ceramics* approach and the earlier rationale, with the controlling emphasis in each particular case seemingly depending on the result the Board desired to reach.

The Board's recent decision in *Modine Mfg. Co.*[111] perpetuates this ambivalence. The decision averts to various factors which can only be viewed as weighing in favor of greater emphasis on voters' self-reliance. Among these are: "the fact that the voters in most of our elections have benefited, along with the bulk of our citizenry, by improvements in our educational processes;" and "the fact that our elections have now become almost commonplace in the industrial world so that the degree of employee sophistication in these matters has doubtless risen substantially during the years of the Act's existence." Nevertheless, the Board concludes that it will not "leave all our voters in all our elections and in all circumstances to sort out, with no protection from us, from among a barrage of flagrant deceptive misrepresentations." The Board fails to acknowledge, of course, that for approximately the first twelve years of its existence it saw nothing wrong with leaving voters to evaluate misrepresentations by *unions*, however flagrant, with virtually no "protection" from the Board.

This sort of ambivalence in the Board's decisions has produced difficulties for the Board in the courts of appeals in regard to the application of the source factor. For example, in the *A.G. Pollard* case,[112] the Board upheld an election despite objections

[111] 203 N.L.R.B. No. 77, 83 L.R.R.M. 1133 (1973).

[112] NLRB v. A.G. Pollard Co., 393 F.2d 239, 67 L.R.R.M. 2997 (1st Cir. 1968).

based on a union organizer's election-eve statements to the effect that the union's loss in an election at the company's Boston office several years earlier had resulted in the discharge of a number of employees. The organizer who made this claim had worked at the Boston office at the time of the earlier election. The Board's regional director, purporting to apply *Hollywood Ceramics* principles, found that the organizer had no "special knowledge" of the incident he referred to, and that the employees were therefore capable of evaluating his remarks. This result was, in fact, more in the tradition of earlier Board cases than of *Hollywood Ceramics*.

On review, the court of appeals concluded that the regional director's holding was inconsistent with *Hollywood Ceramics*. For if the ultimate question is whether the misrepresentation had a probable impact on the election, "the test cannot be whether the speaker in fact had special knowledge, but must be whether the listeners would believe he had." [113] Since the speaker in question had worked at the Boston office, the court said, "it is difficult to think who could be thought to know better than he the Boston situation, or be thought by the . . . employees more reliable." [114] Hence, the court concluded that the Board's finding that employees could have critically evaluated the organizer's misrepresentation showed "either an erroneous appraisal of basic human nature that no amount of expertise can justify, or an impossible standard of what is a sufficiently trustworthy representation." [115]

If the determinative question is whether it was probable that the employees would have relied on the organizer's false statements, then it is impossible to determine whether the Board or the court was correct in *A.G. Pollard*. The answer must depend, as the court indicated, on an "appraisal of basic human nature." But, with due deference to the court, this is a matter upon which reasonable opinions could differ, and it is highly doubtful whether either it or the Board is qualified by "expertise" or otherwise to make that kind of appraisal.[116] Yet this is the test *Hollywood Ceramics* appears to dictate.

---

[113] *Id.* at 242, 67 L.R.R.M. at 2999. The Board itself later applied this view in Cranbar Corp., 173 N.L.R.B. 1287, 69 L.R.R.M. 1581 (1968).

[114] 393 F.2d at 242, 67 L.R.R.M. at 3000.

[115] *Id.*, 67 L.R.R.M. at 3000.

[116] For an extensive treatment of the question of Board "expertise" by the commentators, see the articles cited at note 82, *supra*.

On the other hand, if specific consideration is given to the factor underlying earlier Board opinions—whether the circumstances were such that the employee reasonably *could have* evaluated the statements in question—then the result reached by the Board in *A.G. Pollard* is readily defensible. The Boston organizer was well known as a strong advocate of the union's viewpoint, and a reasonably wary voter could easily have recognized the possibility that there might be another side to the story he told. Moreover, the circumstances were not such as to make it impossible for cautious voters to have checked further before relying on the organizer's assertions. The record showed he had no "special" knowledge of the earlier Boston events. Thus, there were undoubtedly others within the company who also had knowledge of those events, and any truly concerned voter could have obtained a different point of view, by making a telephone call if necessary.

To follow the latter approach would be to hold, in effect, that the Board should not intervene to protect voters from their own gullibility. Rather, Board intervention would be limited to instances where, because of unique circumstances—such as the use of intentional deception or trickery—even an ordinarily skeptical voter would have had no reason to suspect that a given campaign statement was untrue and no way to check on it if he did have suspicions. This approach would accord with the Board's earlier view of the scope of its responsibilities under the election provisions of the Act. It would put the Board in the role, not of paternalistically protecting employees from any misstatement they might rely on, but merely of overseeing the election process to ensure that no breach of fundamental fairness occurred.

Such limited intervention would encourage voters to apply the same critical powers in representation elections they are expected to apply in other types of elections if they wish to make a reasoned choice. At the same time, it would encourage the parties to engage in the sort of "uninhibited, robust and wide open" debate which both the first amendment and Section 8(c) of the Act contemplate and which the Supreme Court has recognized is essential to the effective functioning of the election process.[117] In order to achieve these beneficial results, however, the Board must clearly redefine its policy. It cannot maintain

---

[117] Linn v. United Plant Guards, Local 114, 383 U.S. 53, 61 L.R.R.M. 2345 (1966).

parallel rationales and preserve its option of selecting reasoning to fit the desired result on a case-by-case basis.

Voters' Independent Knowledge

Closely related to the source factor discussed above is the question of the voters' own knowledge—*i.e.* whether they have sufficient independent knowledge of the subject matter of the misrepresentation to enable them to evaluate statements about it without reference to other sources of information. The most frequent application of this test occurs when the misrepresentation in question concerns the voters' own working conditions. For example, in *Uniroyal, Inc.*[118] the union seeking certification distributed a handbill claiming that the truckdrivers in the petitioned-for bargaining unit drove 500 miles a day and received similar pay as union members who drove only 350 miles a day. Actually, the 500-mile figure was a substantial exaggeration. The voting unit employees' true daily average was approximately 365 miles, not materially different from that of the employees in the other unit. Hence, the thrust of the union's handbill—that the voters were being treated unfairly as compared to employees at another location—was false. The Board, however, found no basis to invalidate the election. The employees had (or certainly should have had) independent knowledge of their own daily mileages and could readily determine that their own average was not significantly greater than the asserted average of the drivers in the other unit. Accordingly, even though a substantial and presumably material misrepresentation had been made, there was no need for the Board to intervene to protect the voters from being misled.

Where a misrepresentation concerns not the employees' own working conditions, but other conditions within the plant, community or industry with which the voters are likely to be familiar, the same result should follow. But it is more difficult to predict how the Board will actually rule in such cases. *Allis-Chalmers Mfg. Co.,*[119] one of the early cases to analyze this factor, dealt with union misstatements concerning the wage rates of unionized workers in another unit within the same plant where the voting unit employees worked. The Board refused to set the election aside, noting that the necessary information to evaluate the union's claims "was close at hand, if not in the

---

[118] 169 N.L.R.B. 918, 67 L.R.R.M. 1301 (1968).

[119] 117 N.L.R.B. 744, 747-48, 39 L.R.R.M. 1317, 1318 (1957).

immediate possession of the employees in the unit. . . ." [120] Indeed, it seems safe to assume that employees would know the wage rates received by employees in other units within the same plant, and if they did not, it should have been easy for them to find out. The test, the Board declared, is whether "the circumstances were such that knowledge of the true facts (sic) was readily available to the publisher of the utterance but *not readily available to the employees* or the other party or parties." [121]

But if the decisive factor is whether information needed to evaluate the propaganda was "readily available" to the employees, the Board may be faced with difficult questions requiring a thorough examination of the facts of the particular case. Since the Board seeks to avoid basing its decision in election cases on subjective evidence of the voters' state of mind, it may be forced to draw a number of inferences as to what the employees in the unit probably knew or could have found out. In this regard, the Board often gives significant weight to evidence showing that the subject matter of the misrepresentation had been raised earlier in the campaign, either by one of the parties or through contemporaneous news reports. If the particular subject has previously been elevated to the status of an important issue in the campaign, the Board is more likely to conclude that the employees were in a position to evaluate statements about it than if the subject was injected as a new issue at the last minute. The Board's decision in *Millard Metal Services Center, Inc.*[122] provides a good illustration. There the Board's regional director overruled objections based on a union's allegedly misleading wage claims, stating that "previous campaign references to wages . . . [by both parties] were sufficiently explicit to give the electorate a fair opportunity to appraise the wage issue and to vote their preference concerning representation." [123]

The Board's decision in the *Dorado Beach Hotel*[124] case suggests a slightly different approach to the question of the voter's

[120] *Id.* at 748, 39 L.R.R.M. at 1319.

[121] *Id.*, 39 L.R.R.M. at 1318 (emphasis added).

[122] 80 L.R.R.M. 1221 (1971).

[123] *Id.*

[124] 144 N.L.R.B. 712, 54 L.R.R.M. 1121 (1963).

independent knowledge. There the Board overruled an objection charging that a Puerto Rico local of the Hotel Employees' Union had interfered with an election by misrepresenting the terms of an agreement between its international president and Teamsters' president, James Hoffa, under which a former organizer for a Teamsters' local which had been rejected by the employees in an earlier election was to become a trustee for the Hotel Employees local. There was no question that the union had engaged in a deliberate fraud. However, the Board stated:

> It is clear that the subject matter of the alleged misrepresentation was the very thing concerning which charges and countercharges were made [during the campaign]. . . . It was also under extensive investigation by the Puerto Rico Senate and all of these events and contentions were well publicized throughout the area. Accordingly, we do not believe that the total impact of the campaign upon employees was such as to impair unduly their freedom of choice, but, rather, we find that this is the type of propaganda which the Board leaves to the good sense of the voters to evaluate.[125]

The Board reached this result in *Dorado Beach* without specifically overturning the finding of its trial examiner that the employees were in no position "to learn the truth when all they saw was a flood of vituperative propaganda." [126] Hence, the import of the Board's ruling seems to be that, even if knowledge of the "true facts" was *not* "readily available" to the employees, the election should not be set aside where the circumstances were such as to put the voters on notice that the union's claims *might* not be true. Thus, the Board seems to be saying, in effect, that it will not intervene to protect employees from uncritical reliance on campaign propaganda when the circumstances themselves should have made the employees skeptical.

A similar approach seems to underlie the result recently reached by the Board in *Essex Wire Corp.*,[127] a case in which *both* parties made false statements about the same subject. The union distributed a pre-election handbill containing wage misrepresentations, and the employer responded on the morning of the election with its own handbill which also contained wage misrepresentations. The union lost the election and objected

---

125 *Id.* at 714-15, 54 L.R.R.M. at 1122.

126 *Id.* at 727.

127 188 N.L.R.B. No. 59, 77 L.R.R.M. 1016 (1971).

that the employer's last-minute handbill had polluted the election atmosphere. Rejecting the union's contention, the Board observed:

> Both [handbills] involved regrettable inaccuracies. But where, as here, each party had an opportunity to present its own [inaccurate] argument, we are unwilling to conclude that the employees were so unable to evaluate the issue presented that on the basis of the mutual inaccuracies the election should be set aside.[128]

Obviously, an exchange of "mutual inaccuracies" is not likely to lead the employees any closer to an understanding of the "true facts." The most that can be said is that such an exchange is not likely to mislead voters either. For, in the face of inconsistent and conflicting claims from both sides, a reasonable voter would not base his decision upon what either party said on that subject, but rather would make a choice based upon his own knowledge.

The Court of Appeals for the First Circuit has repeatedly rejected Board decisions which it felt required too much from the employees in the way of independent investigation and evaluation of campaign claims. As the court recently put it:

> We are not favorably disposed toward a rule which permits a party to circulate misleading campaign propaganda and then escape harmless on the ground that the deceived employees had an opportunity to investigate and discover the truth.[129]

This judicial view reflects an understandable reaction to the Board's wavering approach in cases of this sort,[130] but the court's comment should be limited to cases in which the facts and circumstances surrounding the misrepresentation contain nothing that should have suggested to the employees that the statement in question might not be wholly accurate.

The test, in other words, should not focus on whether it was *probable* that the employees would have relied on the false communication, but rather on whether it would have been *reasonable* for them to do so under the circumstances. Under such an approach, the Board would not have to speculate as to whether it was likely that the employees relied uncritically on

---

[128] *Id.*, 77 L.R.R.M. at 1019 n.3.

[129] NLRB v. Millard Metal Service Center, Inc., 472 F.2d 647, 651, 82 L.R.R.M. 2345, 2348 (1st Cir. 1973). *See also* Cross Baking Co. v. NLRB, 453 F.2d 1346, 78 L.R.R.M. 3059 (1st Cir. 1971).

[130] *See* discussion at pp. 46-54, *supra.*

alleged misrepresentations. If the circumstances *should* have raised a question in the voters' minds as to the accuracy of the statements, then the election would not be set aside. Such an approach would serve the interests of fundamental fairness as well as effective administration. Fairness does not require that employees be given a second chance to vote if the only interference with their first choice was attributable to their own unreasonable reliance on false propaganda, under circumstances which should have suggested caution. Nor does it promote the policies of the Act to reward the losing party with a second election if it has engaged in the same sort of campaign deceptions that it charges its successful opponent with using. It is suggested that adoption of a test specifically articulating a requirement of reasonableness on the part of the employees would aid the Board in clarifying a point which it has sporadically emphasized, and which it seems anxious to make at present—*i.e.* that the Board should not be regarded as a general campaign censor charged with prohibiting every departure from the truth. The current Board members—or at least some of them—now seem to recognize that they are not well qualified to serve in such a role and that the Board's past efforts in this direction have done little to enhance the reliability of the election process. That process can be made a more reliable mechanism for determining the employees' free choice only by placing maximum responsibility upon the employees themselves to evaluate and investigate campaign propaganda in a reasonable, cautious, and deliberate manner.

CONCLUDING REMARKS

As we have seen, under the original Wagner Act the Board avoided any extensive involvement with issues concerning the truth or falsity of election campaign statements by either employers or unions. In the case of employers, virtually all comments concerning pending elections were prohibited, whether true or false. As for unions' statements, the Board limited its intervention to cases in which a deliberate deception was employed which reflected adversely on the fairness or impartiality of the government itself.

In 1947, pursuant to the Taft-Hartley amendment, Congress added Section 8(c) with the objective of extending full freedom of speech to employers and giving them the same right to express their views in regard to unionization as unions had enjoyed under the Wagner Act. The Board's reaction, however, declared that this right was not specifically applicable to election cases, and developed a new policy toward campaign speech under which it would invalidate the results of an election if it found that either party had made statements which might mislead the voters. This new policy was rationalized in the *General Shoe* case on the theory that the Board has a duty to provide "laboratory conditions" for elections and to conduct the "experiment" over again whenever there is a possibility that some party's statement may have tainted the result.[131] The Board attempted to disguise its departure from precedent in *General Shoe* by citing various pre-8(c) cases and disclaiming any role as a campaign censor, but a comparison of those cases with the Board's subsequent decisions leaves no room for doubt that the Board, faced with a Congressional mandate to apply the same standards to speech by both parties, had opted to vastly increase its involvement with all issues of election propaganda rather than allow employers the same free rein in campaign speech previously accorded to the unions.

To retain the degree of control over employers' campaign speech that it desired, the Board has paid a high price in rerun elections, representation case litigation, and the invalidation of many elections on the basis of union statements which, at least under its Wagner Act standards, the Board would have been content to tolerate. There is no doubt that the Board has felt uncomfortable at times with its self-imposed "laboratory conditions" standard.[132] Experience has shown the Board that strict adherence to that standard would require it to invalidate many elections it would prefer to sustain. Accordingly, as we have seen, the Board has backed away from its "laboratory" metaphor at times and has tried in a variety of ways to impart greater flexibility to its rules regarding misrepresentations. The result has been the development of a number of tests, each of which turn on a variety of subjective considerations whose weight and application may vary from case to case.

The foregoing review of cases applying the *Hollywood Ceramics* tests demonstrates the problems inherent in the Board's

---

[131] General Shoe Corp., 77 N.L.R.B. 124, 21 L.R.R.M. 1337 (1948).

[132] *See, e.g.,* Modine Mfg. Co., 203 N.L.R.B. No. 17, 83 L.R.R.M. 1133 (1973); The Liberal Market, Inc., 108 N.L.R.B. 1482, 34 L.R.R.M. 1270 (1954).

attempt to apply such flexible standards. Determinations regarding the *substantiality* and *materiality* of particular misrepresentations are necessarily highly subjective. It would be difficult for any tribunal —let alone an agency with frequent
politically-related personnel shifts and widely dispersed decision-
making authority in election cases—to reach uniform and consistent results in the application of such standards. The *timing*
test represents a logical and necessary attempt to limit agency
involvement to cases of "last-minute" abuses, but even it may
raise vexatious issues of fact regarding what is required for
an "effective" opportunity for reply. With respect to the *source*
and *independent knowledge* factors, the Board's decisions reflect a fundamental ambivalence as to how much emphasis
should be placed upon the voters' own abilities to recognize
campaign propaganda for what it is and either disregard it or
take independent steps to verify it before voting in reliance
thereon. In some cases, the Board appears to have regarded
the employees as exceptionally naive and in need of extensive
protection from the agency. In others, the Board has seemed
willing to impose a high degree of responsibility on the voters
themselves to protect themselves from being misled by campaign
claims.

Although the Board has struggled to maintain maximum flexibility for itself in deciding whether to sustain or overturn an
election on the basis of misrepresentation, it has repeatedly met
resistance from the courts of appeals. For, as pointed out earlier,
the courts have tended to take the Board's "laboratory conditions" standard seriously and have tried to ensure that the
standard will be applied as faithfully against labor as against
management. Although the courts have generally refrained from
openly accusing the Board of bias, their opinions have, not in-
frequently, reflected a belief that the Board was abusing its
discretion in its treatment of campaign misrepresentations to
favor unions over employers. Accordingly, the courts have felt
compelled to admonish the Board in such terms as these:

> The right of free speech guaranteed by Section 8(c) of the Act
> applies to employers and labor unions alike. There is no basis for
> adopting a narrow and restrictive rule for one party and a liberal
> one for the other.[133]

---

[133] Automation Div., Bendix Corp. v. NLRB, 400 F.2d 141, 69 L.R.R.M.
2157 (6th Cir. 1968). For other expressions of the same sentiment, *see,*
e.g., Boaz Spinning v. NLRB, 439 F.2d 876, 76 L.R.R.M. 2956 (6th Cir.

As another court observed, in holding that the Board has applied its standards improperly in favor of a union seeking certification: "While we recognize the considerable discretion with which the Board has been entrusted, it is proper to observe that with discretion goes responsibility." [134]

It is significant that judicial disagreement with the Board's treatment of election misrepresentations has almost always resulted in the court's ordering the Board to apply a more rigorous, rather than a more lenient, standard. This might appear incongruous at first blush. As an abstract matter, one might assume that the courts, faced with the suspicion that the Board was using its control over election propaganda unfairly, would order less use of that control against employers rather than more control against unions. This would seem the surest way to reduce the impact of the agency's abuse of discretion and to reduce the work of the courts in such cases. But because of the indirect procedural route to obtaining court review of representation case determinations, the contrary has been true. For the fact is that the courts seldom have an opportunity to rule that the Board has applied too strict a standard. If the Board rules against the party charged with making misrepresentations, it sets the election aside and, barring exceptional circumstances, that decision never goes to a court for review.[135] Instead, it is normally only the decisions in which

---

1971) ("Nor is the right of free speech to be unequally applied as between employers and labor unions."); NLRB v. Lord Baltimore Press, Inc., 370 F.2d 307, 401-402, 64 L.R.R.M. 2055, 2059 (9th Cir. 1968) ("It should hardly need saying that [the *Hollywood Ceramics* standard] no less applies to material misrepresentation by a union than by an employer."); and *see generally*, Cross Baking Co. v. NLRB, 453 F.2d 1346, 49 L.R.R.M. 2782 (1st Cir. 1971); Foremost Dairies of the South v. NLRB, 416 F.2d 392, 399-400, 71 L.R.R.M. 2663, 2666 (5th Cir. 1969); Gallenkamp Stores Co. v. NLRB, 402 F.2d 525, 69 L.R.R.M. 2024 (9th Cir. 1968); Sonoco Products Co. v. NLRB, 399 F.2d 835, 843, 69 L.R.R.M. 2037, 2040 (9th Cir. 1968).

[134] NLRB v. Bonnie Enterprises, Inc., 341 F.2d 712, 714, 58 L.R.R.M. 2395, 2397 (4th Cir. 1965).

[135] An exception would be where the Board sets aside a first election which the union lost based on employer misrepresentations, directs a new election, certifies the union as the winner of the second election, and then orders the employer to bargain. In a subsequent Section 8(a)(5) proceeding, the employer could raise the defense that the first election was valid despite his alleged misrepresentations and thus obtain review of the Board's invalidation of the first election. *See, e.g.,* Boaz Spinning v. NLRB, 439 F.2d 876, 76 L.R.R.M. 2956 (6th Cir. 1971); Automation Div., Bendix Corp. v. NLRB, 400 F.2d 141, 69 L.R.R.M. 2157 (6th Cir. 1968).

the Board sets aside election objections, certifies the union as winner, and orders bargaining that are reviewed by the courts. Under the circumstances, courts seeking to correct what they may view as agency favoritism toward unions have little choice but to insist that the Board stick closer to its "laboratory conditions" ideal when considering alleged union propaganda abuses.

It becomes apparent, then, that the Board has gotten itself into a sort of trap. For a myriad of practical and policy reasons, it would be desirable from the Board's point of view for it to reduce its role in policing campaign propaganda. Reason, scholarly analysis, and empirical evidence all support a shift in this direction,[136] and the Board itself seems to recognize this.[137] The problem is that, having taken a strict position on misrepresentations in the past in order to maintain the control it then desired over employer speech, the Board is now blocked by the courts from retreating gracefully to a policy of reduced control. Because the courts' opportunities to review Board election rulings have been largely restricted to cases in which the Board has ruled leniently in favor of unions, and because the courts have long suspected that any loosening of the Board's standards in such cases was undertaken selectively to favor the unions, the courts have tended to act as a ratchet, allowing tighter Board control but preventing any slippage toward a looser approach.

As a result, although the Board may now wish it could take advantage of the flexibility of its *Hollywood Ceramics* tests to reduce the extent of its control over election speech without expressly overruling any precedents or promulgating new tests, it has so far been unsuccessful in doing so. Instead, its efforts in this direction have only produced frequent conflicts with the courts as to what standard should be applied. The result is a state of uncertain law which does much to undermine the effectiveness of the election process.

The question which remains is: what must the Board do to free itself from this predicament and accomplish a much-needed policy shift? One answer, of course, would be for the Board to overrule *Hollywood Ceramics* and announce new tests for misrepresentations. If the Board did so with a clear ex-

---

[136] *See* the authorities cited at note 82, *supra*.

[137] *See* Modine Mfg. Co., 203 N.L.R.B. No. 77, 83 L.R.R.M. 1133 (1973).

pression of purpose to administer the new standard fairly, there is no reason to expect resistance from the courts. But the majority of the Board members apparently are not yet ready to take this step. As indicated in *Modine Mfg. Co.*,[138] they would prefer to retain the *Hollywood Ceramics* tests, at least for the present, but to modify the application of those tests to place greater responsibility on the employees and less on the government. In obvious anticipation of resistance from the courts, the Board's majority have tried to make it clear through their language in *Modine* that they are not merely relaxing their standards for the benefit of the union in the case at hand, but declaring a general shift to a less restrictive policy for all election parties. To the same end, the Board emphasizes various administrative considerations favoring the application of a more lenient standard, including "the prudent husbandry of the funds appropriated to us for administering this Act." And the Board interjects a consideration which it obviously hopes will help to reconcile its new approach with its earlier, more restrictive decisions purportedly applying the same tests—*i.e.* because of better education and greater experience with Board elections, "the degree of employee sophistication in these matters has doubtless risen substantially during the years of this Act's existence. . . ."[139]

Even if the Board is able to accomplish a shift in policy in the manner contemplated by *Modine* without resistance from the courts, there is still likely to be a continued high volume of litigation over charges of campaign misrepresentations. For the Board will still be applying—albeit more sparingly—a policy whereby the validity of elections will turn upon a series of vague tests, each of which involves a number of highly subjective considerations varying with the facts of each case. As long as the Board continues to probe into the truth or falsity of campaign statements and measure their effect on election results by these uncertain standards, parties unsuccessful in the balloting will object routinely to their opponents' campaign statements, and the Board will be forced to engage in a painstaking analysis of everything that was said in the campaign, with the certification of the election results delayed in the interim.

---

[138] *Id.*, 83 L.R.R.M. at 1134-36.

[139] *Id.*, 83 L.R.R.M. at 1136.

It is suggested here that a better approach would be for the Board to overrule *Hollywood Ceramics,* repudiate its "laboratory conditions" notion, and announce a new policy according campaign statements by all parties, treatment which is similar to that given to union campaign statements prior to the Taft-Hartley amendments. That is, the Board should declare that it will not review the truth or falsity of the parties' statements, and that it is up to the voters to protect themselves against distorted, misleading, or inflammatory propaganda. Agency intervention should be explicitly limited to instances of violence, coercion or intentional deception rising to the level of actual fraud.

CHAPTER III

Campaign Promises, Predictions, and Expressions of Opinion

The NLRB's inquiry into the substance of campaign state-ments does not end with the question of their truth or falsity. Many statements made during the election period are not susceptible to evaluation on that basis. In a typical campaign, the union's propaganda will be filled with references to benefits and improvements in wages and working conditions assertedly obtainable through unionization, while the company's statements will emphasize possible deleterious effects of such a course upon the employees and the business upon which the employees' job security depends. In short, much of the campaign propaganda by both sides will consist, not of assertions of fact, but of speculation, prophecy, and expressions of opinion.

In other contexts, statements of this nature by parties com-peting for votes are recognized as the most fundamental sort of free expression protected by the first amendment. Not so, however, in the realm of NLRB elections. Instead, as we shall see, the limitations imposed by the Board on statements of this sort are in many respects more stringent than those applied to outright misrepresentations of fact. As we have noted, this is despite the fact that Congress added Section 8(c) to the Act in 1947 to guarantee both unions and management the right to express their views, arguments, and opinions without inter-ference from the Board. This guarantee has been held applicable only to unfair labor practice cases,[1] and in election cases, closer Board scrutiny of the parties' statements is undertaken on grounds of the asserted need to provide "laboratory conditions." [2]

---

[1] See General Shoe Corp., 77 N.L.R.B. 124, 21 L.R.R.M. 1337 (1948); Dal-Tex Optical Co., 137 N.L.R.B. 1782, 50 L.R.R.M. 1489 (1962). But see the dissenting opinion of Chairman Miller in Media Mailers, Inc., 191 N.L.R.B. No. 50, 77 L.R.R.M. 1393 (1971).

[2] 77 N.L.R.B. at 127, 21 L.R.R.M. at 1341. For a general criticism of this approach to the question of campaign speech, see Bok, The Regulation of

STATEMENTS REGARDING POSSIBLE
CONSEQUENCES OF UNIONIZATION

Almost all cases in which the Board has set aside elections based upon campaign promises or predictions involve statements by employers. Union promises are routinely condoned by the Board as mere "puffing," [3] and union predictions of adverse economic consequences, if the union is rejected, are deemed mere "accusations" against the employer. The Board has rationalized this disparate treatment on the ground that unions generally lack the power to effectuate their campaign promises and predictions through their own volition. Hence, their assertions are treated as permissible speculation or expressions of opinion. Management campaign statements, on the other hand, often relate to matters over which the company has decisional authority. Accordingly, the argument runs, the employees are apt to view management's campaign predictions as either promises of reward or threats of reprisal contingent upon how they vote.[4]

Because of this reasoning, employers are required to be extremely cautious in making any predictions about potential changes in the business or in the working conditions as a result of unionization. The Supreme Court summarized the narrow scope of expression open to employers in *NLRB v. Gissel Packing Co.*:[5]

> [T]he prediction must be *carefully phrased* on the basis of *objective fact* to convey an employer's belief as to *demonstrably probable* consequences *beyond his control.* . . . If there is *any implication* that an employer may or may not take action solely on his own initiative for reasons unrelated to economic necessities and known only to him, the statement is no longer a reasonable prediction based on available facts but a threat of retaliation based on misrepresentation and coercion, and as such without the protection of the First Amendment.

Campaign Tactics in Representation Elections under the National Labor Relations Act, 78 HARV. L. REV. 38 (1964). *See also* MCGUINESS, THE NEW FRONTIER N.L.R.B. 28-48 (1963).

[3] *See, e.g.*, Producers' Cooperative Ass'n, 191 N.L.R.B. No. 78, 71 L.R.R.M. 1581 (1971); Southern Foods, Inc., 174 N.L.R.B. 154, 70 L.R.R.M. 1108 (1969); Otis Elevator Co., 114 N.L.R.B. 1490, 1493, 37 L.R.R.M. 1198, 1199 (1955).

[4] *See, e.g.*, Oak Mfg. Co., 141 N.L.R.B. 1323, 1325, 52 L.R.R.M. 1502, 1503 (1963).

[5] 395 U.S. 575, 618, 71 L.R.R.M. 2481, 2497 (1969) (emphasis added).

One problem with this reasoning is that, if an employer may predict only what he can reasonably prove, much realistic and noncoercive discussion based upon the employer's acquired business judgment may be lost to the employees, regardless of how valuable it might be to them in making a rational choice in the election. For, obviously, it is much easier to make accurate economic predictions than to prove that they are accurate. The benefits to the electorate of "uninhibited, robust and wide open debate" [6] become illusory when management's freedom to express its opinions and judgments is thus limited.

Another problem with the test approved in *Gissel*, limiting the employer's commentary to matters "beyond his control," is that it is applied without regard to the relative economic strengths of the parties. If the employer technically has the authority to make the ultimate decision whether or not a particular business change will be made, the matter is treated as being wholly within his volition. But such a notion of management control is often largely fictional. We may consider, for example, the situation of a small independent businessman whose employees are being organized by a powerful international union. If elected, the union may well be able to dictate terms of employment or changes in the business to which the employer must agree if he is to continue to operate. In such circumstances, the employer's paper decisional authority would be meaningless in terms of the impact of his predictions on the workers. Since the union would have the economic power to force the employer to "decide" upon working conditions in accordance with its wishes, his forecasts would take on the character of speculation.

To concede that the foregoing example is extreme is not to say that such situations do not exist. [7] In any event, the example illustrates a point that applies to a wide range of labor-management relationships—*i.e.* that in the context of labor relations, few decisions about changes in the business or in employees' working conditions are entirely volitional with the employer. Most such decisions result from an interplay of economic forces in which the unions as well as the employers have significant input. And where the employees are represented by a strong international union, management prerogatives may be severely

---

[6] Linn v. United Plant Guards, Local 114, 382 U.S. 912, 61 L.R.R.M. 2345 (1966).

[7] *See generally*, COURT, THE PROBLEMS OF UNION POWER 86-101 (1961); JOHNSON & KOTZ, THE UNIONS 124-50 (1972).

curtailed. To apply a broad presumption that employers alone have the power to make changes in operations and working conditions, without any recognition of these contrary economic realities, is either naive or discriminatory.

The Board has never given much weight to these practical limitations upon an employer's power to implement changes. *Media Mailers, Inc.*[8] illustrates the point well. The employer told a group of employees, including some women, during an election campaign that if the union got in, they would no longer be permitted to work on inserting machines because the union's standard contract did not cover such machines. He also stated that their job opportunities would be better if they stayed out of the union because there were more nonunion than union shops in the area, and that he would have to call the union to get surplus employees and the union would not refer women. No contention was made that these statements were false,[9] but the Board majority found that they invalidated the election because they "clearly threatened that if the union won the election it would be detrimental to the future employment opportunities of the employees."

Only Chairman Miller, who dissented in *Media Mailers*, recognized that the employer was not saying he would take any action on his own part to the employees' detriment. He was only stating his understanding of how the union's established policies would affect them. As such, his remarks merely amounted to a tacit acknowledgement that if the union was elected, he would undoubtedly have to bring his operation into line with other union shops in the area. To treat this as a threat of reprisal by the employer is to ignore the widespread power of unions to compel adherence to standard, area-wide contracts which allow small employers little or no freedom to operate their businesses in a nonconforming manner.

What the employer sought to convey to his employees in *Media Mailers* was a realistic picture of how their interests could be adversely affected by choosing the union.[10] This is,

---

[8] 191 N.L.R.B. No. 50, 77 L.R.R.M. 1393 (1971).

[9] The union pointed out that its constitution provided for women members, and that it had no policy against women, but it admitted it had no women members. Accordingly, the employer's comment that the union did not refer women could hardly be deemed a substantial misrepresentation.

[10] However, the Board did accept this in Appleton Discount, Inc., 205 N.L.R.B. No. 58, 83 L.R.R.M. 1674 (1973). During a pre-election question

of course, the central issue facing employees in every representation election, and unless both parties are free to inform the employees of the potential implications of the decision facing them, the employees may not be in a position to make the rational, informed decision the election process contemplates. Bribery and threats of reprisal, of course, have no proper place in a campaign. But the fact is that there often are potential adverse consequences to employees if they choose a union. Increased labor costs and decreased flexibility, for instance, may prompt management to consider relocation or closure of the plant for valid business reasons, particularly if the operation is marginal.[11] If the employees are unaware of the economic considerations facing management and hear only the union's promises of better pay, increased benefits, and job security, they will scarcely be in a position to make a valid assessment of how their own best interests will be served.

The problem facing the Board, then, in regulating the election process, is to develop rules which will eliminate coercive threats and promises of benefit without foreclosing either party from communicating views, opinions, and economic judgments calculated to educate the voters concerning all possible consequences of unionization, both favorable and adverse. In the following pages, we shall analyze a number of Board decisions in an effort to determine how the Board has approached this task and how well it has succeeded. Since certain common economic themes tend to recur in cases dealing with employers' campaign predictions, we will separate the cases for purposes of discussion into several rough categories based on the subject matter of the prediction.

Plant Closure or Relocation

Unionization accompanied by increased benefits, job classification requiremens, or reduced productivity as the result of

---

and answer period in reply to questions concerning job security for part-time employees, the employer stated his opinion that the union preferred full-time employees. The Board dismissed the union's complaint that this constituted a threat to discharge part-time employees if they chose the union. The employer's statement was held to be an expression of his opinion concerning union policy.

[11] For a detailed discussion of the economic factors the employer may consider in a decision to relocate, see Swift, *Plant Relocation: Catching Up With the Runaway Shop*, 14 B.C. IND. & COM. L. REV. 1135 (1973).

strikes may well push the marginally profitable employer into a situation where he must shut down or relocate. "To many businesses in precarious stages of growth or of marginal profitability, the possibility of plant relocation or closure is the most significant ramification of unionization." [12] There is, of course, nothing unlawful in an employer's taking such steps so long as his preponderant motive is economic.[13] The possibility of relocation or closure can be of substantial concern to the employee not only in terms of continued job security, but also with respect to his choice of bargaining agent in a representation election. Thus, the issue may be extremely relevant to the campaign. In contrast with other possible consequences of unionization, this one affects the entire work force rather than selected individuals or specific groups.[14] Conceivably a statement by an employer suggesting a plant shutdown if the union wins the election could be a strong weapon of opposition by the employer. The Board has considered objections to the outcome of an election alleging that statements of this nature constituted improper threats.

In the early cases of the 1950's the Board placed a great deal of emphasis upon the effect of statements on the self-organization rights of the employees and upon the presence of threats. It was not strict in the definition of these rights.[15] *Chicopee Mfg. Corp.*[16] indicated that the predictions that unionization might force the employer to move the plant did not interfere with the election when the employer did not overtly suggest that he would "use [his] economic power to make its prophecy come true." [17] The exact employer statement at issue was that "if the union won, they would be forced to move the plant." Another employer's statement to the effect that meet-

---

[12] Swift, "NLRB Overkill: Predictions of Plant Relocation and Closure and Employer Free Speech," mimeographed preliminary research paper (Philadelphia: Industrial Research Unit, The Wharton School, University of Pennsylvania, 1973).

[13] *See generally* MORRIS, THE DEVELOPING LABOR LAW 122 (1971).

[14] For a more detailed study of such employer statements see article cited at note 11, *supra*.

[15] *See generally* DAYKIN, SINICOP & WHITEHILL, FREE SPEECH RIGHTS (1967).

[16] 107 N.L.R.B. 106, 33 L.R.R.M. 1064 (1953).

[17] *Id.* at 107, 33 L.R.R.M. at 1064.

ing the demands of the union would force a plant shutdown was similarly upheld in *National Furniture.*[18]

The *Lux Clock Mfg.* case,[19] in particular, reflects the wide degree of latitude afforded employer speech during this period. When asked if the plant would shut down if the union won, the employer said, "Unfortunately, if I made the proper answer to that I think—no, I'm sorry, I cannot make any comments on that particular question—it's against the law." [20] The Board relied on the overall content of the employer's election statements during the campaign in finding there was no election interference.

In *Nash-Finch Co.*[21] the Board approved a speech where the employer recounted the experience of past branches of the company which had closed after unionization. The discontinued profitability of their operations was given as the reason. Two factors likely were significant in this decision. "Profitability" had been a significant campaign issue in this election, and the employer specifically had disclaimed any intention to shut down the plant, regardless of the outcome of the election.

A later decision in 1959 apparently rejected the *Chicopee Mfg.* and *National Furniture* attitudes regarding employer speech and predictions. In *Benjamin Electric Mfg. Co.*[22] the central theme of the employer's campaign was that it "needed the I.B.E.W. label on its products to sell them and that therefore unless [it] won the election, the Employer would be forced to move its plant to another locality." [23] This was found to be a threat of reprisal for employee selection of the independent union. The Board no doubt was influenced by the resemblance of the statement to an ultimatum for the union's victory, but it ignored the purely economic nature of this campaign issue.

A different Board in the 1960's took a stricter approach with respect to the acceptable limits of employer campaign predictions. In *Somiso, Inc.,*[24] the employer primarily had discussed

---

[18] National Furniture Mfg. Co., Inc., 106 N.L.R.B. 1300, 33 L.R.R.M. 1004 (1953).

[19] 113 N.L.R.B. 1194, 36 L.R.R.M. 1432 (1955).

[20] *Id.* at 1198, 36 L.R.R.M. at 1433.

[21] 117 N.L.R.B. 808, 39 L.R.R.M. 1329 (1957).

[22] 122 N.L.R.B. 1517, 43 L.R.R.M. 1332 (1959).

[23] *Id.* at 1517, 43 L.R.R.M. at 1332.

[24] 133 N.L.R.B. 1310, 49 L.R.R.M. 1030 (1961).

the likelihood of strikes if the union won and maintained its demands. He also stated that "whether we go out of business or not I am not saying right now. Use your own judgment. Most of you, as I have said, have been here a long time, and you know what we can withstand." [25] The Board found that the employer was threatening to go out of business if it had to deal with the union. The above statement appears less threatening than the employer's comment which was approved in *Lux Clock*. Significantly, a dissenting opinion in *Somiso* maintained that this was merely a prediction of consequences which would result from union demands not from the employer's action.

Since the early 1960's the Board has often based findings of "veiled" or "implied" threats upon strained interpretations of statements framed as predictions.[26] In *Lake Catherine Footwear, Inc.*[27] the election was set aside because the employer indicated the plant would shut down if faced with a strike or continued union demands. Apparently, the fatal error was in not being more specific about the impact of the union's insistence on economic issues upon continued operations. The Board implied a threat by the *Maremont Corp.*[28] from the presence of a poster on a company bulletin board depicting a building with boards across the windows and the door with the word "closed" written on the boarded door. The poster had not specifically showed the plant in question, however, previous posters with different messages plainly had depicted the plant.[29]

In a very recent decision, *State Supply Warehouse Co.*,[30] the Board held that the appearance of a "FOR SALE" sign [31] on the day of the election constituted election interference, and it set aside a tied election (6 to 6). The Board based its decision upon the existence of plant rumors dealing with alleged re-

---

[25] *Id.* at 1311, 49 L.R.R.M. at 1030.

[26] Bok, *The Regulation of Campaign Tactics in Representation Elections under the National Labor Relations Act*, 78 HARV. L. REV. 38 (1964).

[27] 133 N.L.R.B. 443, 48 L.R.R.M. 1683 (1961).

[28] Case No. 10-RC-6415, 65 L.R.R.M. 1135 (1966).

[29] Grede Foundries, Inc., 205 N.L.R.B. No. 12, 83 L.R.R.M. 1661 (1973), there was no implied threat from a poster depicting a locked plant gate with the legend "Vote No, Avoid This."

[30] 206 N.L.R.B. No. 36, 84 L.R.R.M. 1233 (1973).

[31] The sign did not specifically identify the company warehouse being sold. It merely said, "FOR SALE, BY OWNER. Call 583-5708, Tulsa."

marks by the company president that a union victory would
bring about a plant shutdown and the presence of the sign
near the polling area for an extended period of time. The
Board did not indicate whether it viewed the sign as a campaign
ploy or otherwise. The regional director had dismissed the
union's objection in this case, because he found that the employer had posted a notice requesting the employees to disregard any threatening rumors in the plant. He also felt the
employer had offered a legitimate explanation for the presence
of the sign:

> During the investigation of the objections, [the employer] explained
> that he had brought the sign to the Tulsa warehouse intending to
> take it to [another warehouse] the following day, but, as the sign
> was freshly painted and not thinking of the ramifications involved,
> he placed it in the shipping department to dry.[32]

Subsequently the sign was used for the stated purpose. The
Board responded to this point by saying:

> Accepting the Employer's alleged business justification concerning
> the purpose and use of the sign, we nevertheless conclude that in
> the circumstances here the mere presence of the sign near the polls
> during the election was likely to have affected the election results.[33]

In cases involving allegedly threatening campaign statements
and posters, or "FOR SALE" signs as here, the Board must
evaluate the overall tenor of the campaign, and it must be
careful in applying literal interpretations to specific statements or in extending others beyond their intended meaning.
In *Tunica Mfg. Co., Inc.*[34] the Board held that a speech by
the employer indicating that the company was the sole source
of benefits and it could continue to provide benefits only so
long as economic conditions permitted did not constitute election
interference. This was so even though the speech made repeated references to plant closings and included the statement
that "you stand to lose if the Union gets in and to gain if you
keep it out."
In the same case, however, a company cartoon showing
hands above the surface of the water grasping for a life pre-
server with the caption "Don't run the risk" was deemed to

---

[32] 206 N.L.R.B. No. 36, 84 L.R.R.M. at 1233.

[33] *Id.*, 84 L.R.R.M. at 1234.

[34] 182 N.L.R.B. 729, 76 L.R.R.M. 1535 (1970).

be an implied threat. The Board's trial examiner stated that although the "exact meaning of the cartoon was not clear" it was "difficult to conjure up an innocuous meaning" to it. The possibility that the "risk" referred to might stem from economic conditions, rather than company reprisals, was not considered. The Board also found threats implied in the employer's leaflet asking employees rhetorically where they had been employed before, what their earnings had been, and whether they could get their old jobs back. The trial examiner stated that, since the leaflet itself did not expressly relate these questions to economic conditions, the only possible implication of the leaflet was "that selection of the Union would inevitably cause employees to lose their jobs." The lesson of *Tunica* seems to be that it is all right to make references to plant closings and loss of employment, but only so long as some explanation tying these eventualities to economic conditions is included *in the same document*. The fact that other campaign communications clearly indicated that any decision to close would turn on economic considerations was not considered sufficient to impart an "innocuous meaning" to the company's cartoon and leaflet.

The 1969 *Gissel* decision, as mentioned earlier, specifically held that an employer's conveying the possibility of a plant closure must be based on objective evidence of such a likelihood, and it must not be dependent upon the employer's volition. It has been suggested that the requirement of proof of closure "approaches a *per se* rule forbidding any communication of prediction on this subject." [35] The *McLaughlin Co.*[36] decision found an implied threat to shut down from two letters in which the employer referred to plant closings elsewhere in the course of the union's bargaining history. Not only did the Board apparently reject the *Nash-Finch* case, but also it seemingly ignored the employer's specific indications that his reference to the previous history should not be construed to suggest that a union's victory here would mean a shutdown. He had said, "we will sit down at the bargaining table and try to arrive at a contract." [37]

Chairman Miller supplied a vigorous dissent in *McLaughlin*, not only attacking the Board's specific findings, but also sug-

---

[35] Swift, at note 11, *supra*.

[36] 187 N.L.R.B. 897, 76 L.R.R.M. 1317 (1971).

[37] *Id.* at 898, 76 L.R.R.M. at 1317.

gesting dissatisfaction with the Board's use of implied threats to set aside elections. The dissent in *McLaughlin* may kindle a hope that a more flexible Board approach to such employer statements is emerging. The *Birdsall Construction Co.*[38] would seem to indicate this. The employer's statement with respect to continued plant operations was:

> I predict that if [the union] wins this election, and if we have to operate under [a union contract] which adds considerably to our cost, then we are certainly, as businessmen, going to have to consider very strongly the necessity of moving our operations so as to reduce our cost.[39]

The Board held that under the *Gissel* standard, no employer threat of retaliation or coercion had occurred, but merely an objective statement of the financial problem which it would face. Importantly, too, there was the suggestion in the campaign that the employees could continue their employment at the new location.

If these opinions spark optimism that the Board may be moving toward a fuller recognition of the employer's right of free speech in election campaigns, that spirit is substantially squelched by a reading of the Board's subsequent decision in *The Singer Co., Friden Div.*[40] There the trial examiner, whose election case rulings were adopted by the Board, purported to apply the *Gissel* standards to a series of company statements issued in response to a union campaign which the examiner himself characterized as "vigorous and militant." The decision warrants special consideration, because it illustrates how a union can engage in a free-wheeling campaign of lavish promises and broadside attacks, but management will be faulted if it attempts to turn some of the union's own pet issues to its advantage.

The employer in *Singer* had recently opened a new plant in Albuquerque, New Mexico, and frankly informed the employees that one of its chief reasons for locating there was to take advantage of lower labor and operating costs which would enable it to better compete against foreign and domestic manufacturers. One of the principal themes of the union's organiz-

---

[38] 198 N.L.R.B. No. 20, 80 L.R.R.M. 1580 (1972).

[39] *Id.*, 80 L.R.R.M. at 1581.

[40] 199 N.L.R.B. No. 162, 82 L.R.R.M. 1019 (1972).

ing campaign at the Albuquerque plant was that it had recently obtained higher wages and benefits for employees at the company's San Leandro, California, plant and that it could obtain similar increases at Albuquerque. The company countered that the higher rates at San Leandro had actually made that plant uncompetitive in certain respects, and that, in fact, one thousand San Leandro employees had lost their jobs when work was transferred to other plants, including Albuquerque, which could operate more competitively. The company also attributed job losses at other unionized plants to loss of competitive status as a result of unionization.

No contention was made that the company's statements were inaccurate, but the trial examiner said that "the truth or accuracy of the statements is not the sole determining factor in deciding whether they exceeded the permissible limits of free speech." [41] Here, the examiner concluded, the thrust of the company's remarks was to suggest that job losses would "inevitably" result from unionization, and this was held to constitute both election interference and unlawful coercion under Section 8 (a) (1).

It should be pointed out that the employer never said jobs would "inevitably" be lost if the union won the election. This was the trial examiner's interpretation of the overall thrust of the company's campaign. The company did say, in fact, that wages and job security would be dependent on economic conditions, and not on the selection of the union. But the examiner felt that these reassurances were insufficient in view of the company's frequent campaign references to strikes and plant closures.

Those references, however, were part and parcel of the company's economic argument. They were simply used to illustrate what the company contended would be the likely economic consequences if the union's extravagant promises were realized. If the result appeared as "inevitable" in the company's propaganda, it was because it was portrayed as an *economic* inevitability. Again, it is important to bear in mind that there was no finding that this economic judgment was inaccurate. To hold, under these circumstances, that the company's statements did not meet the "demonstrably probable" requirements of *Gissel* seems a particularly harsh application of that test.

---

[41] Slip Opinion (Trial Examiner's Decision), p. 36.

The Board's holding becomes even more difficult to accept when it is realized that it was the union, not the employer, which initiated the issue of plant closure in the *Singer* case. Apparently, recognizing that an organizing drive would provoke fears among the employees of loss of competitive status and subsequent loss of jobs, the union had sought to allay those fears through repeated assertions that the company had signed a twenty-year lease on its Albuquerque plant and, therefore, could not close. The trial examiner acknowledged that the company's references to plant relocation or closure were framed as responses to the union's claim, but he nevertheless held that they were improper. In a like vein, the examiner faulted the company for making references to "the inevitability of strikes" even though he conceded that the company's statements on that subject were merely in answer to the union's claim that the company "could not take a strike."

The perspective in which the trial examiner viewed this exchange of campaign statements can readily be seen in the following language from his opinion:

> Whether, as claimed by the company, the Union itself raised the "straw man" of plant closure only to knock it down, the fact remains that, despite widespread rumors of the possibility of plant closure, the company remained silent, and did nothing to reassure or allay the apprehension of the employees in this regard. On the contrary, the company permitted the employees to harbor the belief, if, indeed, it did not foster or encourage it, regardless of whether it has any intention of actually closing the plant, that the selection of the Union could lead to that result.[42]

The question which arises is why an employer should be required to "reassure" employees or "allay their apprehensions" about eventualities which very well might actually—and lawfully—materialize if they vote for the union. The trial examiner seems to tacitly concede that the selection of the union, accompanied by the possibility of wage increases which would make the plant uncompetitive with foreign producers or strikes which could result in loss of business, might well have led the company to decide to close or relocate for lawful business reasons. Would the employees be better off not knowing this? The examiner further acknowledges that the union was falsely advising the employees, in effect, that the company could not resist its wage demands because it could neither close its

---

[42] *Id.* at 38.

plant nor take a strike. Should the employer have let this false impression stand uncorrected?

The facts of the *Singer* case, as found by the trial examiner, indicate that the company had valid grounds for representing that its Albuquerque plant was particularly vulnerable to any increases in labor costs. Under the circumstances, for the company merely to have reassured employees or allayed their fears of a possible plant closure would have been a disservice to them and would not have promoted a rational choice in the election. It may well be, as the examiner stated, that the company's frequent campaign references to the possibility of strikes culminating in plant closure had a "chilling effect upon the self-organizational aspirations of the employees," but where such a chilling effect stems from legitimate economic probabilities, rather than any implication of antiunion retaliation, it should afford no ground for voiding the results of the election.

Loss of Business, Job Security, and Benefits

The employer's campaign theme may stress less drastic effects of unionization than a plant shutdown. It is actually more common to find that the campaign centers upon job security, wages, and benefits. The union will promise improvements in these areas and the employer may counter with arguments that the union cannot create jobs, it cannot ensure job security, and it does not provide the wages and benefits. The Board's opinions acknowledge the right of the employer to express his opposition to the unions and to attack the credibility of its campaign promises, but the limits of that right are not so clearly established. The difficulty in the application of the Board's policy to regulate such statements increases as the intensity of the campaign rises.

In an early case an employer's statement that there would be a loss of overtime and a worsening of general conditions if the union won was held to be interference.[43] The employer's mistake probably was in not specifying the reason for the predicted loss. Similar conditions were present in *Shovel Supply Co.*[44] where the employer emphasized the possibility of a return to the forty-hour week and loss of the Christmas bonus under

---

[43] Hercules Motors Corp., 73 N.L.R.B. 650, 20 L.R.R.M. 1026 (1947).

[44] 121 N.L.R.B. 1485, 43 L.R.R.M. 1014 (1958).

the union. A slight change in the employer's language in *Cleveland Plastics, Inc.*[45] affected the outcome. The employer in a letter wrote "[w]e do know that any increase in the hourly rate would probably mean a reduction in the overtime work that you have been getting."[46] The Board held this to be mere prediction of the consequences of unionization. The Board also approved of a statement indicating collective bargaining with the union would mean a reduced contribution to the employees profit sharing plan.[47] The reason given was that bargaining would involve legal costs which would reduce profits. On the other hand, the Board's acceptance of the basis for an employer's campaign statement is not always predictable. In *Lafayette National Bank*,[48] for example, the bank indicated that joining the union would make it "difficult if not impossible" for the employees to obtain jobs with other financial institutions in that area, since the union had no contracts with them. The Board said this was a threat of economic reprisal.

The argument that economic factors may cause an unfavorable impact as the result of unionization does not always guarantee Board approval. The employer often may argue that because of the particular nature of its market or competitive conditions it may face a loss of customers or reduction in business. In *Aeronca Mfg. Corp.*[49] the employer supplied aircraft parts to Boeing. Its principal campaign issue was that should the union be elected, a loss of orders would result when strikes curtailed production because Boeing could not afford to wait and would go elsewhere. The Board felt that the constant reference to a withdrawal of orders created a fear of loss of jobs even though the employer's competitive status was unquestioned. The Board indicated it may have been influenced by the intensive electioneering and villification of the union conducted by the employer. However, upon similar facts and campaign issues another employer's argument that strikes would mean a loss of business and a resultant loss of jobs was upheld.[50]

---

45 85 N.L.R.B. 513, 24 L.R.R.M. 1433 (1949).

46 *Id.* at 514, 24 L.R.R.M. at 1433.

47 Rospatch Corp., 193 N.L.R.B. 772, 78 L.R.R.M. 1360 (1971).

48 77 N.L.R.B. 1210, 22 L.R.R.M. 1136 (1948).

49 118 N.L.R.B. 461, 40 L.R.R.M. 1196 (1957).

50 Freeman Mfg. Co., 148 N.L.R.B. 577, 57 L.R.R.M. 1047 (1964).

Apparently the intensity of the campaign was the same since the dissent in the latter case felt the issue of the employer's competitive market position was "relentlessly" argued before the employees with the result that "coercion replace[d] fact and fear dominate[d] reason." [51] It is unfortunate that the vigor of the campaign should be a determinative factor in assessing the impact of economic arguments.

One employer argued that, in the event of a strike, the Air Force would take over the function, as it had done elsewhere in the past.[52] The Board held this to be a threat, while the dissent urged that this was merely a statement of the likely consequences of unionization outside of the employer's control. The case probably may be explained on the basis that the employer's language implied the likelihood of a strike.

The *Formex Co.*[53] case lends support to this analysis. Here the employer indicated that because of its market and competitive conditions unionization *could* create the possibility of a loss of patronage. Furthermore, if a strike were to occur and the company was unable to supply its customers, they *might* seek a substitute. The Board held there was no interference. The distinction between these words suggesting the conditional nature of events and the others creating the implication of the likelihood of them lacks meaningful support, but apparently the Board was convinced that this subtle difference warranted a different result.

The Board has often found implied threats in the content of an employer's statements. *Moksnes Mfg. Co.*[54] is a case where one employer referred to another company, which when faced with unionization cancelled a contract thereby causing layoffs. The contract offered no profit, but it would have kept the work force employed. On the basis of this story with no further suggested similarity between the two employers, the Board found an implied threat of economic reprisal.

The Board in *Mohawk Bedding Co.*[55] ordered a second election as the result of the employer's antiunion campaign which re-

---

[51] *Id.* at 582, 57 L.R.R.M. at 1049.

[52] Serv-Air, Inc., 183 N.L.R.B. No. 32, 74 L.R.R.M. 1284 (1970).

[53] 160 N.L.R.B. 835, 63 L.R.R.M. 1043 (1966).

[54] 106 N.L.R.B. 1230, 32 L.R.R.M. 1651 (1963).

[55] 204 N.L.R.B. No. 1, 83 L.R.R.M. 1317 (1973).

ferred to the experience of the earlier company which had faced unionization. He mentioned the other company went out of business and the employees lost their jobs. The employer also referred to the high rate of unemployment in the locality, suggesting that many of the unemployed had formerly worked in unionized shops. The Board applied the *Gissel* standard for evaluating predictions; thus, it noted that the employer had not provided any cost comparisons which would have suggested the necessity to shut down in the event of unionization. The Board automatically assumed that the employer was making a prediction and that his sole purpose was to threaten a shutdown at his own plant. However, it is quite reasonable to consider that the employer was relating a factual account and was presenting valid data about the employment situation. It then becomes apparent that the employer had satisfied the *Gissel* standards. In his dissenting opinion, Chairman Miller agreed with the hearing officer's determination that there was insufficient basis to set aside the election.

Another employer referred to union contracts in other plants which offered generally lower wages than he paid and suggested that the worst that could happen would be that wages would go down to the union level. The Board said this created an implied fear of reprisal.[56] In *General Electric Wiring Devices, Inc.*[57] the employer referred to the closing of another plant and cited inflated union demands and a loss of business as reasons. The Board found the closing to be a retaliatory act and, therefore, reference to it constituted an implied threat of retaliation in the present case. The implication that the closing was retaliatory arose from a statement by a supervisor of the closed plant, "I believe that if a union had not interfered at Micro I would still be there."[58] However, the *Louis-Allis* decision,[59] reached near the time of *General Electric Wiring*, expressed the opposite viewpoint based on almost identical facts. In essence the Board said the employer had not asserted or inferred that the other unionized plants had closed for retaliatory reasons. The difference in wording between the em-

---

[56] Oak Mfg. Co., 141 N.L.R.B. 1323, 52 L.R.R.M. 1502 (1963).

[57] 182 N.L.R.B. 876, 74 L.R.R.M. 1224 (1970).

[58] *Id.*, at 877, 74 L.R.R.M. at 1225.

[59] The Louis-Allis Co., 182 N.L.R.B. 433, 74 L.R.R.M. 424 (1970).

ployer's speech in *General Electric Wiring* and the employer's letter in *Louis-Allis* does not reconcile these conflicting decisions. *Allied/Egry Business Systems, Inc.*[60] presents an interesting Board approach to a vigorous campaign characterized by extensive partisan electioneering by both parties in the campaign. The employer indicated it would not yield to pressure by the union where such pressures were unreasonable. In response to objections to the election results by the union, the Board stated:

> The Union nowhere showed that any of the Employer's statements were untrue, grossly exaggerated, materially misrepresentative, or indeed anything but permissible puffing and expression of partisan opinion. The Union had time to answer and answered in an equally vigorous, exaggerated, and partisan manner. This is the give and take of campaigning.[61]

The *Allied/Egry* case is significant from the viewpoint of suggesting that greater flexibility be given to the content and nature of campaign statements, and of indicating that the ability of the union to respond to employer statements should be a factor in determining election interference.[62] The Board has not yet accepted in general practice the doctrine suggested by *Allied/Egry*.

Strikes

The strike is, without question, the union's greatest economic weapon at the bargaining table. In most cases it is used when collective bargaining negotiations have broken down. The ultimate decision to strike is usually made either by union officials or by an employee strike vote. It is reasonable to assert, therefore, that strikes are, at least, as directly subject to the control of the union as shutdowns, job security, wages, and benefits are subject to the control of the employer. The ability of the employer to coerce employees during an election by means of statements concerning the possibility of strikes must, therefore, be considered in a different light than other alleged employer

---

[60] 169 N.L.R.B. 514, 67 L.R.R.M. 1195 (1968).

[61] *Id.* at 515, 67 L.R.R.M. at 1196.

[62] Member Brown, dissenting in this case, suggested that union attempts to counteract vigorous employer campaigning would be ineffective because of the employer's superior economic power. 169 N.L.R.B. at 516, 67 L.R.R.M. at 1196.

threats. Just as a powerful union can force its terms upon an employer, a determined employer can force a strike by bad faith bargaining or the refusal to bargain. The employer *can only create* the *threat* of a strike by means of anticipatory refusals to bargain during the election campaign period.

A rather clear statement of Board policy with respect to employer strike forecasts was made in *Boaz Spinning Co., Inc.*:[63]

> In arguing against unionism, an employer is free to discuss rationally the potency of strikes as a weapon. . . . It is, however, a different matter when the employer leads the employees to believe that they *must* strike in order to get concessions. . . . When an employer frames the issue of whether or not the employees should vote for a union purely in terms of what a strike might accomplish, he demonstrates an attitude of predetermination that bargaining itself will accomplish nothing. . . . Policy considerations dictate that employees should not be led to believe, before voting, that their choice is simply between no union or striking.[64]

Aside from those cases, where during the campaign the employer explicitly challenges his employees to a strike if they unionize, the Board cannot deny the employer the right to use the possibility of strikes as a campaign issue. While the strike is the most potent of union bargaining weapons, it is also the most costly one to both the union and the employees. Strikes can occur whenever collective bargaining fails to produce an agreement. Economic strikers can be permanently replaced by the employer. These are all facts which the employer may choose to emphasize as his campaign issues. Yet, the Board would deny the employer this right:

> [T]he more the employer persists in referring to strikes and what they entail—replacement, violence, unemployment, walking picket lines, unpaid bills—the more the employee is likely to believe that the employer has already determined to adopt an intransigent bargaining stance which will force employees to strike in order to gain any benefits.[65]

In addition, a strike may well be an inevitability of unionization where the two parties have indicated wide disagreement in their respective proposals. Yet, any argument by the employer conjuring the "vision" that a strike is inevitable is deemed to carry

---

[63] 177 N.L.R.B. 788, 71 L.R.R.M. 1506 (1969).

[64] *Id.* at 789, 71 L.R.R.M. at 1508.

[65] Thomas Products Co., 167 N.L.R.B. 732, 733, 66 L.R.R.M. 1147, 1148 (1967).

an "obvious potential for interference." [66] Thus, the employer cannot emphasize the impact of the substantial disagreement he may show with the union.

The Board generally will set aside an election when it feels the inevitability of a strike was conveyed by the employer. In *Utica-Herbrand Tool Division of Kelsey-Hayes Co.*[67] the employer stated that "the only way this union can get any concessions from the company is by a strike." [68] The employer also warned of replacement of strikes, loss of jobs, and possible bitterness and violence. The election was set aside because of the creation of an atmosphere of reprisal. Perhaps the Board failed to consider that the employer was not obligated to grant concessions at the bargaining table. The other points mentioned by the company were only the by-products of strike activity, many independent of employer conduct.

The Board said that another employer threatened the employees with the inevitability of a strike because it did not affirmatively suggest that selection of the union "need not result in a strike . . . but could result in a collective bargaining agreement." [69] No such duty to express both sides of the picture was imposed on the union. It had promised the employees a favorable contract and had not emphasized that unionization could result in a strike. The employer had merely indicated in its campaign statements that if the union made economic demands beyond the company's ability, the sole course for the union would be to strike. A closer reading of the campaign statements suggests that the employer was saying a strike would result if it was determined that "the company refused to fulfill the promises of the union." [70] The Board, in effect, faulted the employer for focusing its campaign upon the negative aspects of unionization, of which he felt the employees should be aware.

---

[66] Campbell Chain, Division of Unitec, 180 N.L.R.B. 51, 52, 72 L.R.R.M. 1587, 1589 (1969).

[67] 145 N.L.R.B. 1717, 55 L.R.R.M. 1223 (1964).

[68] *Id.* at 1718, 55 L.R.R.M. at 1224.

[69] Ideal Baking Co. of Tennessee, Inc., 143 N.L.R.B. 546, 552, 53 L.R.R.M. 1270, 1272 (1973).

[70] *Id.* at 548, 53 L.R.R.M. at 1270.

A comparison of two cases, decided within a short period of time of each other, illustrates further the difficulty of applying the Board's standard to employer statements about the inevitability of a strike. The Board approved of the employer's campaign, in *Coors Porcelain Co.*,[71] which included references to prior strike trouble and suffering, permanent replacement of some strikers, and several strikes in the area. The Board said the statements were factual, relevant, and were not accompanied by the employer's unwillingness to allow the union a "legitimate role in representing the employees." On the other hand, identical facts involving similar campaigning by the employer were found to constitute interference in *Everest and Jennings, Inc.*[72] Apparently the Board felt the employer did express an "unwillingness" and it based its decision on his general antiunion animus and certain references to union supporters as "malcontents." The employer's only alternative would have been express neutrality.

The judiciary has indicated a reluctance to accept the Board's conception of a threat of inevitability of a strike. The Court of Appeals for the Tenth Circuit reversed a Board finding and stated that the campaign should be "uninhibited, robust, and wide open." [73] It would find nothing wrong with an employer's campaign theme emphasizing that "a strike is the union's chief economic weapon and [there are] immediate economic detriments inherent in a strike. *Emphasis and repetition of a valid argument is fair campaigning. . . .*" [74] The court seems to be reminding the Board of its own pronouncements in *Allied/Egry.*

Hard Bargaining

Section 8(d) of the NLRA imposes upon both parties the statutory obligation "to bargain collectively . . . in good faith." Considerable litigation has been raised in the attempt to clarify the meaning of good faith. Certain basic principles are

---

71 158 N.L.R.B. 1108, 62 L.R.R.M. 1158 (1966).

72 158 N.L.R.B. 1150, 62 L.R.R.M. 1192 (1966), *enforced*, 384 F.2d 999, 67 L.R.R.M. 2032 (9th Cir. 1967).

73 NLRB v. Sanitary Laundry, Inc., 441 F.2d 1368, 1370, 77 L.R.R.M. 2359, 2361 (10th Cir. 1971).

74 *Id.* at 1371, 77 L.R.R.M. at 2361 (emphasis added).

unquestioned however. The Act does not compel the parties to *reach* an agreement,[75] it only attempts to regulate the process of trying to reach agreement. The Act does not force either party to make concessions.[76] The parties are not required to continue bargaining if they have reached an "impasse." While recognizing that these are only generalizations, it is important to stress their relevance to the election campaign. In response to union promises of increased benefits and improved conditions, the employer's only recourse may be to inform the employees that campaign promises are not automatically incorporated into a union contract and that negotiated benefits may increase, decrease or remain the same.

A common campaign theme used by the employer is to indicate that it will bargain "from scratch." Such an attitude is permissible in both the economic and legal sense.[77] The Board has said:

> [i]n considering the impact on employee free choice of "bargaining from scratch" statements . . . [it] has distinguished circumstances in which such remarks could reasonably be read in context as a threat to discontinue existing benefits from instances in which such remarks are merely descriptive of the employer's bargaining strategy, designed to let employees know that unionization does not mean automatic increases in benefits.[78]

In principle, this approach is entirely proper. But the factual determination thereby required—whether a remark can "reasonably be read as a threat to discontinue existing benefits"—is exceedingly difficult to make. In some cases, the Board has upheld statements by the employer indicating that because of his economic situation the level of benefits are subject to negotiation and the union is not necessarily a guarantee of benefit increases.[79] It has also approved statements which indicated that

---

[75] NLRB v. Highland Park Mfg., 110 F.2d 632, 6 L.R.R.M. 786 (4th Cir. 1940).

[76] NLRB v. Reed & Prince Mfg. Co., 205 F.2d 131, 32 L.R.R.M. 2225 (1st Cir.), *cert. denied*, 346 U.S. 887, 33 L.R.R.M. 2133 (1953).

[77] Host International, Inc., 195 N.L.R.B. No. 66, 79 L.R.R.M. 1322 (1972).

[78] *Id.*, 79 L.R.R.M. at 1323.

[79] Trent Tube Co., Subsidiary of Crucible Steel Co., 147 N.L.R.B. 538, 56 L.R.R.M. 1251 (1964). *See also* Terry Coach Mfg. Inc., 103 N.L.R.B. 754, 31 L.R.R.M. 1575 (1953).

bargaining in fact could produce less than the current benefits.[80] On the other hand, in *Rein Co.*[81] an employer's statements that he was neither required to negotiate present benefits into a union contract nor did he believe that the law prohibited him from telling his employees before an election that benefits given in the past could be discontinued were found to be a threat to discontinue the existing benefits. The reasoning was that both statements had been included in the same speech. In addition, the employer had misinterpreted the case law—at his peril. The dissent accused the majority of failing to read the speech in its entirety. The employer's reference to the "law of the land" was merely being used in support of its intent to "bargain from scratch." In another case where an employer combined "bargaining from scratch" predictions with statements that a strike might be necessary, accompanied by job losses, the Board said, "the sum total of the Employer's separate communications to its employees constituted a clear message that it was futile . . . to select [the union]."[82] The dissent argued that each separate act of conduct was not interference.

A restrictive viewpoint to employer statements was taken in the *Thomas Products* case:[83]

> When the employer additionally warns that he will never grant to the union benefits that he would not grant without a union, and, indeed, that he stands ready to demand a reduction in employee benefits in exchange for security measures which the union might request, the employees can well believe that the employer has decided in advance to refuse to accord to the union in bargaining the good faith and open mind the law requires.[84]

Perhaps the most realistic policy was stated by the Court of Appeals for the Sixth Circuit in a decision upholding an employer's campaign statements.[85] There was a heated campaign

---

[80] The Guiberson Corp., 121 N.L.R.B. 260, 43 L.R.R.M. 1322 (1958). *See also* Appleton Discount, Inc., at note 10, *supra*, where the employer said a new employee pension plan to go into effect would be a subject of bargaining if the union won the election.

[81] 111 N.L.R.B. 537, 35 L.R.R.M. 1517 (1955).

[82] General Industries Electronics Co., 146 N.L.R.B. 1139, 1141, 56 L.R.R.M. 1015 (1964). *See also* Georgia-Pacific Corp., 181 N.L.R.B. 377, 73 L.R.R.M. 1365 (1970).

[83] 167 N.L.R.B. 732, 66 L.R.R.M. 1147 (1967).

[84] *Id.* at 733, 66 L.R.R.M. at 1148.

[85] Automation Div., Bendix Corp. v. NLRB, 400 F.2d 141, 69 L.R.R.M. 2157 (6th Cir. 1968).

and the employer stated that collective bargaining is a "two-way street," that "wages and benefit programs would be altered *upward or downward, created or eliminated,*" and that bargaining would begin from the *"zero point* item by item!" [86] The court indicated that the Board should take into account the timing of the statements, the opportunity of the union to respond, and the nature of its responses:

> The statements made by both should be considered by the Board after which a reasoned determination could be made as to whether either interfered with the employee's freedom of choice.[87]

A recent dissent by Chairman Miller suggests that there may be developing sentiment among the current Board members for a view that would allow employers greater latitude in announcing a hard bargaining stance in such circumstances.[88]

Legal Position

The basis for the general principle permitting the employer to declare a "hard bargaining" approach during the campaign period was that this merely constituted a statement of the employer's legal position—*i.e.* the intent to bargain in good faith. Other statements by employers are also protected when they represent an assertion of a legally endorsed position or fact. Although this policy has been long-established, the Board's application of it has changed as the Board has altered its response to other statements or conditions coincident with the statement of legal position.

Initially, the Board displayed a reluctance to permit such statements automatically. In *Metropolitan Life Insurance* [89] an employer's letter recited the belief that the Board had erred in allowing a union to participate in a representation election. It stated that "if the [union] should be certified as bargaining representative, it is our intention to contest through the courts the issue of its failure to comply with the law." [90] The Board held this to be a threat impressing upon the employees the

---

[86] *Id.* at 143-144, 69 L.R.R.M. at 2158.

[87] *Id.* at 146, 69 L.R.R.M. at 2160.

[88] Monroe Mfg. Co., 200 N.L.R.B. No. 11, 82 L.R.R.M. 1042 (1972) (Chairman Miller, dissenting).

[89] 90 N.L.R.B. 935, 26 L.R.R.M. 1294 (1950).

[90] *Id.* at 937, 26 L.R.R.M. at 1295.

futility of voting for the union. The dissent said it was a proper declaration of a bona fide intention of testing the Board's decision in the courts. In the *Capital Transit* case [91] the employer disagreed with the Board's determination of nonsupervisory status for a group of employees and announced its intent to treat them as supervisors until the court ruled on the decision. The Board said a ruling by the court would only occur when the employer had engaged in an unfair labor practice, and his statement, therefore, was a threat to disregard the eligible voters' protected rights. The Board applied the procedural requirement of "finality" for judicial review into an unintended context.

One employer declared that because he felt the union was Communist dominated, he would only bargain with the union if required and vowed, therefore, to employ all legal means available to avoid doing so. The Board's strict interpretation of this statement found it to be an "anticipatory refusal to bargain" since there was no "legal" means to avoid an existing duty to bargain. [92]

Following a change of Board personnel under the Eisenhower administration, the *Metropolitan Life* decision was specifically overruled by *National Furniture Mfg. Co., Inc.* [93] The employer expressed disagreement with the Board's unit determination and indicated it would not recognize the union until it had appealed the decision. The Board said an expression of legal position does not warrant setting aside an election. By implication *Capital Transit* was also overruled because here the refusal to recognize the unit (pending an appeal of the unit determination) constitute an unfair labor practice.

Several subsequent decisions reflected the approach taken in *National Furniture*. An employer's statement, which suggested that striking workers during an economic strike could be permanently replaced, was protected as an expression of legal position. [94] The announced decision by a company to appeal a Board ruling

---

[91] 100 N.L.R.B. 1173, 30 L.R.R.M. 1416 (1952).

[92] Legion Utensils Co., 103 N.L.R.B. 875, 31 L.R.R.M. 1586 (1953).

[93] 106 N.L.R.B. 1300, 33 L.R.R.M. 1004 (1953).

[94] F.W. Woolworth Co., 111 N.L.R.B. 766, 35 L.R.R.M. 1561 (1955).

accompanied by the statement that the appeal would delay collective bargaining for about two years was also upheld.[95]

In 1963, the *Dal-Tex* case reversed precedents set by earlier Board rulings regarding expressions of legal positions. It was the start of a period of rigid evaluation of the employer's statements. *National Furniture* was specifically overruled. Statements of legal position now would be evaluated in the context of the employer-employee economic relationship and with "due consideration" of other statements suggesting hostility to the union.

Shortly after the *Dal-Tex* decision the Board applied this new policy in the *Lord Baltimore Press*[96] case. The employer disagreed with a bargaining unit determination and announced he would appeal the decision. The campaign language suggested that the appeal would be a time-consuming process, and that the employer would not recognize and bargain with "an inappropriate unit." The Board said the statements constituted a "threat to use the delaying processes of the law to the fullest extent possible. . . ."[97] The employer, in effect, was being denied the rightful assertion of his legal position because procedural delays in the NLRA appeals process transformed his statements into threatening delay tactics.

Statements by employers which assert simple facts evident under the provisions or procedures of the NLRA are usually accepted. An employer's statement that a vote in favor of severance from the bargaining unit would restrict flexible interchange between jobs was merely a representation of fact.[98] Comments that unionization would restrict individual grievance resolution between the employee and employer has been protected as a prediction of the impact of Section 9(a) of the NLRA.[99] However, the Board in *General Electric Wiring Devices*[100] said that such a statement was a threat, since the

---

[95] Aeronca Mfg. Corp., 121 N.L.R.B. 777, 42 L.R.R.M. 1435 (1958).

[96] 142 N.L.R.B. 328, 53 L.R.R.M. 1019 (1963).

[97] *Id.* at 329, 53 L.R.R.M. at 1020.

[98] Weil-McLain Co., 130 N.L.R.B. 19, 47 L.R.R.M. 1232 (1961).

[99] Bostitch Division of Textron, Inc., 176 N.L.R.B. 377, 71 L.R.R.M. 1241 (1969).

[100] At note 57, *supra.*

selection of a union does not preclude individuals from going to the employer with their problems unless precluded by the collective bargaining agreement. There is no doubt that there was an implied understanding of this fact in the other cases which entertained such an issue.

Form and Context of Statements

As noted above, the Board's task has been to distinguish between predictions of the impact of unionization and *threats* by an employer of actions he would take in the event a union was selected as the bargaining agent. Generally, the former is permissible conduct while the latter constitutes election interference, if not an unfair labor practice. As the foregoing review of cases demonstrates, the distinction has not been simple.

The Board has indicated that statements "couched" in the form of carefully phrased opinions may have as much coercive potential as threats.[101] The "emphatic" manner in which one employer concluded his remarks was held to make his speech a threat rather than a prediction.[102] The Board has also indicated:

> [it] may set aside an election because of speeches which are not coercive, conduct which does not constitute unfair labor practices, or coercive remarks even if made to relatively few employees, or even if they are veiled, hinted or merely implied. . . .[103]

In addition, "statements which on their face contain improper threats" are not permissible "because external circumstances, to which no reference is made in the statements themselves, would give those statements a different meaning." [104] In effect, the employees are not required to "look behind" the meaning of such words.

The Board, however, is quick to look behind employer statements which are noncoercive on their face. The Board has often stated that it will interpret an employer's statements by looking at the entirety of the employer's words and actions.[105] It would be wrong to evaluate the impact of such statements

---

[101] Shovel Supply Co., 121 N.L.R.B. 1485, 43 L.R.R.M. 1014 (1958).

[102] New England Upholstery Co., Inc., 121 N.L.R.B. 234, 42 L.R.R.M. 1234 (1958).

[103] Aeronca Mfg. Corp., 118 N.L.R.B. 461, 466-67, 40 L.R.R.M. 1196, 1198 (1957).

[104] Telechron, Inc., 93 N.L.R.B. 474, 475, 27 L.R.R.M. 1412 (1951).

[105] Lux Clock Mfg. Co., Inc., 113 N.L.R.B. 1194, 36 L.R.R.M. 1432 (1955).

by means of selected passages.[106] But what is the exact relationship between the "whole" and the "sum of its parts?" One opinion by a Board member was that "the whole consists only of its parts, and therefore a consideration of the whole speech necessarily requires an examination of its *specific* parts." [107] In other words, every part of the speech would not have to contain unlawful statements in order to find that the speech as a whole was coercive. Other cases have shown the tendency of the Board to focus on selected portions of an employer's campaign material and to fail to consider the entire context of the same material. Thus, the whole often has become greater than the sum of its parts.[108] Such an approach has been especially evident where the campaign has been vigorous. But it is necessary to remember:

> So long as there is no requirement that an employer maintain an attitude of neutrality during a union election campaign, there can be no legitimate reason why there should be any fetters upon the intensity of his electioneering activities.[109]

The Board has often condemned antiunion propaganda, however, on the principal ground that it was presented in an overly vivid or dramatic form. It is chiefly for this reason that the Board has repeatedly set aside elections because of the employers' showing of the motion picture *And Women Must Weep*. The film has been characterized by one court as "an exposé of what happens to union members when dominated by ruthless and unthinking union officials." [110] The Board has had some difficulty in deciding whether to label it a "misrepresentation" or a "threat," [111] but it has been convinced, in any event, that it is beyond the ambit of protected campaign speech. The Board's

---

[106] Storkline Corp., 142 N.L.R.B. 875, 53 L.R.R.M. 1160 (1963) (dissenting opinion).

[107] 113 N.L.R.B. at 1202, 36 L.R.R.M. at 1435.

[108] Ideal Baking Co. of Tennessee, Inc., 143 N.L.R.B. 546, 53 L.R.R.M. 1270 (1963).

[109] Aeronca Mfg. Corp., 118 N.L.R.B. 461, 486, 40 L.R.R.M. 1196 (1957).

[110] Luxuray of N.Y., Div. of Beaunit Corp. v. NLRB, 447 F.2d 112, 77 L.R.R.M. 2820 (2d Cir. 1971).

[111] *Compare* Plochman & Harrison—Cherry Lane Foods, Inc., 140 N.L.R.B. 130, 51 L.R.R.M. 1558 (1962); *with* Southwire Co., 159 N.L.R.B. 394, 62 L.R.R.M. 1280 (1966).

objection is that the movie "paint[s] a fearful picture" through a medium "more powerful . . . than the printed or spoken word in arounsing emotions and influencing attitudes." [112] The courts of appeal have consistently rejected the Board's view.[113] The Second Circuit recently acknowledged that the film is a "one-sided brief against unionism, devoid of rational content perhaps," but pointed out that a prounion film *Anatomy of a Lie*, designed to refute *And Women Must Weep* was available and could have been used. Under the circumstances, the court could see no reason for concluding that the company's use of the movie invalidated the election. One comment in the court's opinion deserves particular attention:

> It is primarily the responsibility of the employees, and not of the Board, to evaluate the merit of competing propaganda. "Congress did not intend the Board to act as a censor of the reasonableness of statements by either party to a labor controversy. . . ." [114]

Perhaps the Board has retreated from its evaluation of *And Women Must Weep*. In *Hawesville Rolling Mill, Nat'l Aluminum Div. of Nat'l Steel Corp.*,[115] the Board recently held that showing the film, without other illegal or objectionable conduct accompanying it, was an insufficient basis for setting aside an election. This decision did not alter *Plochman & Harrison* [116] because that decision involved other objectionable employer conduct in addition to the showing of the film.

Despite the emphasis the Board has sometimes placed on the form of campaign communications, it stated in the *Dal-Tex* case that election interference could be found "regardless of the form in which the statement was made." [117] More important

---

[112] 140 N.L.R.B. at 132, 51 L.R.R.M. at 1559.

[113] Luxuray of N.Y., Div. of Beaunit Corp. v. NLRB, 447 F.2d 112, 77 L.R.R.M. 2820 (2d Cir. 1971); Kellwood Co. v. NLRB, 434 F.2d 1069, 75 L.R.R.M. 2814 (8th Cir. 1970); Southwire Co. v. NLRB, 383 F.2d 235, 65 L.R.R.M. 3042 (5th Cir. 1967).

[114] Luxuray of N.Y., Div. of Beaunit Corp. v. NLRB, 447 F.2d at 117, 77 L.R.R.M. at 2824; *accord*, NLRB v. Golub Corp., 388 F.2d 921, 66 L.R.R.M. 2769 (2d Cir. 1967).

[115] 204 N.L.R.B. No. 42, 83 L.R.R.M. 1305 (1973).

[116] At note 111, *supra*.

[117] Dal-Tex Optical Co., Inc., 137 N.L.R.B. 1782, 1787, 50 L.R.R.M. 1489, 1492 (1962).

than the form of the communication, the *Dal-Tex* opinion states, are "the economic realities of the employer-employee relationship" in which the statement must be evaluated. But as we have seen before, the Board's analyses of "economic realities" for these purposes have often tended to be somewhat one-sided. The Board has restricted its analysis to weighing the employees' asserted economic pressures that could make it difficult or impossible for the company to retaliate against employees.[118]

The Supreme Court's decision in *Gissel* reinforced this unilateral view of "economic realities." The Court stated that the "economic dependence of the employees on their employers, and the necessary tendency of them because of that relationship, to pick up intended implications" of the employer's statements is an important consideration in the determination of threats. There is questionable merit in perpetuating the notion of the inherent insecurity faced by employees in their relationship with the employer. There is also a distinct irony in the readiness of the Board and the courts to attribute to employees such keen powers of perception in picking out subtle "implications" in management statements when, in related contexts, these same tribunals have persistently refused to credit employees with even an average ability to evaluate campaign propaganda for themselves and avoid being misled by this very propaganda.

CONCLUDING REMARKS

We have had occasion to mention several instances in which Chairman Miller, in dissent, took a more limited view of the proper scope of Board intervention in the area of campaign predictions and expression of opinion than his colleagues on the Board.[119] In part, his views have been based upon a more realistic assessment of the economic considerations facing management in a union campaign, and of the legitimacy of management's communication of those considerations to employees.[120] In part, too, they have been based upon administrative considerations which weigh against the desirability of lengthy "postmortum examinations" of the propaganda exchanged in

---

[118] *See* discussion at pp. 46-47, *supra*.

[119] *See* cases cited at notes 8, 34, *supra*.

[120] *See, e.g.*, Blaser Tool & Mold Co., 196 N.L.R.B. No. 45, 80 L.R.R.M. 1014 (1972).

every contested election campaign.[121]   And finally, Chairman Miller's opinions in such cases have reflected greater sensitivity than the Board has shown for a number of years to the concept of free speech embodied in Section 8(c) of the Act.[122]

If the Miller view gains majority acceptance at the Board, it could do much to promote the fairness and efficiency of the election process and could also help to foster the free exchange of opinions and ideas necessary to make that process effective. A Board opinion, issued just prior to Miller's appointment, indicates a framework within which the Board could apply such an approach:

> Although attempting to establish ideal conditions insofar as possible, we acknowledge that actual facts must be considered in light of realistic standards of human conduct and that elections must be appraised realistically and practically, and should not be judged against theoretically ideal, but nevertheless artificial standards. . . . [W]e are not unmindful of the fact that the 'laboratory' for election purposes is usually an industrial plant where vigorous campaigning and discussion normally take place, and where isolated deviations from the above mentioned standard will sometimes arise, not withstanding the best directed effort to prevent their occurrence.[123]

Not surprisingly, these words appeared in a Board decision overruling an employer's objections to the campaign statements of a union seeking certification. If the same basic principles could be borne in mind in judging objections to employers' promises and predictions, the Board might well advance to a much more realistic overall approach to the regulation of campaign speech.

---

[121] Essex Wire Corp., 188 N.L.R.B. No. 59, 77 L.R.R.M. 1016 (1971) (dissenting opinion).

[122] *See, e.g.*, Miller's dissenting opinion in Spartus Corp., 195 N.L.R.B. No. 17, 79 L.R.R.M. 1351 (1971).

[123] Owens-Corning Fiberglas Corp., 179 N.L.R.B. 219, 223, 72 L.R.R.M. 1289, 1293 (1969).

CHAPTER IV

Appeals To Racial Prejudice

Speech or conduct during the election campaign period, which appeals to racial prejudice or injects race as an issue regardless of the manner of presentation, carries the high potential of evoking emotional responses by the voters to the issue of union representation. In determining whether such speech or conduct by an employer or union constitutes election interference, the Board faces certain policy considerations: should the employees, like voters in political elections, be free to vote on emotional grounds? To what extent can the Board accurately determine the probable impact of emotional appeals on the voters' choice? When are racial appeals relevant to the campaign? Above all, the Board must remember that it has not been empowered to take an active role in combatting racial discrimination. Its powers to prohibit discriminatory practices are specifically limited by the Act to those relating to union membership or protected concerted activity.

APPEALS TO RACIAL PREJUDICE AS AN
UNFAIR LABOR PRACTICE

The early Board cases which considered appeals to racial prejudice made during union organization attempts were primarily unfair labor practice proceedings arising under Section 8(a)(1) of the Act. The typical case involved employer statements to white employees which emphasized that, if the union won the election, Negroes would be introduced into the plant.

The Board indicated that although it did not consider racial prejudice to be an acceptable issue in a campaign, it would not police or censor all such appeals. It was necessary to show that the racial appeals constituted interference, restraint, and coercion within the meaning of the NLRA. The Board interpreted this general standard in such a manner that only racial appeals which suggested economic punishment or threatened job security constituted objectionable conduct. Statements which emphasized the other "social" consequences of integration of the work force were tolerated. Consequently, it was not an unfair labor practice to suggest that employees would work side-by-side with Negroes,[1] or that they would share the same rest room facilities.[2] However, an employer threat to replace white workers with Negroes, if the union won, was an unfair labor practice.[3]

This distinction between social threats and economic ones did not always lead to predictable or consistent results. In *Empire Mfg. Corp.*,[4] an employer's statement that, if the union won, he "would hire Negroes who would work together with the whites" was held to be a threat to job security and an 8(a)(1) violation. This case seems indistinguishable from earlier accepted employer remarks. More recent Board decisions also illustrate the problem of applying this distinction. An employer's statement that there would be "enforced association" between whites and Negroes and a sharing of rest rooms and drinking fountains was held to be a Section 8(a)(1) violation, since it could be interpreted as a threat by the employer to change working conditions by instituting the "enforced association."[5] In another case,[6] the employer claimed that if the union should win the election, the union would replace Negroes with whites and there was nothing management could do to prevent the replacements. The Board said the first statement was permissible because it was truthful and relevant, but the other comprised a threat which predicted that the employer would yield to the demands of the union. It was deemed objectionable to impress upon the employees that the employer would yield to the demands of the union and relinquish its right to hire, discharge, or replace employees.

In most of the early cases, the Board evaluated racial appeals as unfair labor practices almost exclusively by the impact such statements were thought to have upon the employees' economic

---

[1] Happ Bros. Co., Inc., 90 N.L.R.B. 1513, 26 L.R.R.M. 1356 (1950).

[2] American Thread Co., 84 N.L.R.B. 593, 24 L.R.R.M. 1334 (1949).

[3] Bibb Mfg. Co., 82 N.L.R.B. 338, 23 L.R.R.M. 1557 (1949).

[4] 120 N.L.R.B. 1300, 42 L.R.R.M. 1153 (1958).

[5] Atkins Saw Division, Borg Warner Corp., 148 N.L.R.B.. 949, 57 L.R.R.M. 1097 (1964).

[6] Boyce Mfg. Corp., 141 N.L.R.B. 756, 52 L.R.R.M. 1393 (1963).

interests. No real attempt was made to consider racial prejudice as an emotionally inflammatory issue affecting the individual. In the *Bibb Mfg.* case,[7] however, the threat of job loss was accompanied by remarks suggesting that working side-by-side would promote interracial marriages, and that the union wanted to break down the color barrier. The Board merely called the entire series of racial appeals "clear and patent" violations of 8(a)(1) while remaining silent on their inflammatory nature.

Under this early approach, the Board was dealing with only a part of the problem of racial appeals during the election period —threats or promises with racial overtones—and remaining silent about the impact of deliberate, inflammatory appeals.

APPEALS TO RACIAL PREJUDICE AS ELECTION INTERFERENCE

The standard which had been developed in the unfair labor practice cases was initially applied in substance to cases where an objection to the outcome of a representation election was raised as a result of racial appeals made during the campaign period.[8] The early rule or test for determining if such appeals constituted election interference was formulated in *Sharnay Hosiery Mills.*[9] There, the Board held that there was no basis for setting aside the election, if there was no misrepresentation, fraud, violence, or coercion and the statements were temperate and factually correct. The Board apparently recognized that inflammatory appeals as such could constitute election interference. In *Sharnay*, the Board upheld an election where the employer sent a lengthy letter to his employees which discussed the union's prointegration stand on the racial issue. In the Board's view, the letter was temperate in nature and relevant to the campaign since the employees were entitled to know more about the union.

In the period following the *Sharnay* decision, the Board generally was reluctant to set aside elections in the absence of threats or coercion arising from racial appeals made during the campaign period. Without difficulty, the Board made it clear that the mere mention of a religious or racial issue was not

---

[7] At note 3, *supra*.

[8] Westinghouse Electric Corp., 118 N.L.R.B. 364, 40 L.R.R.M. 1191 (1957).

[9] 120 N.L.R.B. 750, 42 L.R.R.M. 1036 (1958).

grounds for setting aside an election.[10] In *Mead-Atlanta Paper Co.*,[11] the Board held that there was no interference and no threat or coercion because the employer made no specific charges and no reference to the union when he stated that in a number of unionized plants in the area there was a lower ratio of Negroes to whites than in his plant. These statements, however, were made at conference meetings where the employees attending were either all white or Negro. *Mead-Atlanta* suggested an appropriate standard which should be considered by the Board in cases where racial appeals have been made. This standard evaluates whether or not the appeals have distorted the issues of the election from the question of unionism to one of racial prejudice. Such a test effectively encompasses the issues of relevancy, truthfulness, and temperateness into a test which probes the essence of election interference. The Board has never fully pursued this approach in later cases.

A rather interesting decision was reached in *Chock Full O'Nuts* [12] when the Board, relying on *Sharnay*, held that there was no election interference when a Negro vice-president of the firm stated to his Negro employees that he "was the reason for this union," that "some of the employees didn't want to be represented by me because of my race," and that the "white employees were jealous of my position with the company." The Board said that it did not condone the conduct of the executive in raising the racial issue, but it did not find sufficient grounds to set aside the election. The Board apparently gave no weight to the fact that such statements had been made repeatedly over a period of several months.

In *Heintz Division, Kelsey Hayes Co.*[13] the Board appeared to dispense with the requirement of a finding of threats or coercion as a prerequisite to finding election interference. The Board set aside an election where the intervenor union hired eight non-employees (5 Negro and 3 white) to pass out leaflets bearing the name of the other union. The Board construed this conduct as an implicit misrepresentation of the other union's position on racial matters, and held that this constituted a basis for setting

---

[10] Paula Shoe Co., Inc., 121 N.L.R.B. 673, 42 L.R.R.M. 1419 (1958).

[11] 120 N.L.R.B. 832, 42 L.R.R.M. 1053 (1958).

[12] 120 N.L.R.B. 1296, 42 L.R.R.M. 1152 (1958).

[13] 126 N.L.R.B. 151, 45 L.R.R.M. 1290 (1960).

aside the election. It was called "pernicious" deception, highly capable of "misleading and misdirecting the interests and desires of voters in many ways." [14] The mere presence of the Negroes passing out leaflets was apparently sufficient to constitute an objectionable appeal to racial prejudice.

The effect upon the election of predictions related to racial issues was an interesting question raised in the *Westinghouse Electric Corp.*[15] case. Normally, in representation election cases, the Board has found that statements seeking to forecast what will occur as a result of union demands and practices are permissible predictions. It was suggested in *Westinghouse* (although not ruled upon) in a concurring opinion by Member Leedom that it was doubtful whether predictions involving "an advantage or disadvantage to an employee growing out of racial prejudice" [16] should be allowed (absent any threat or coercion). However, this question has never been resolved.[17]

SEWELL RULE

Sewell Manufacturing Co.[18] was the first case where deliberate and sustained appeals to racial prejudice rather than threats or promises with racial overtones—by the employer—were considered as grounds for election invalidation. The Board enunciated a distinction between rational (reasoned) and emotional (inflammatory) racial statements made to the employees. It stated:

> So long, therefore, as a party limits itself to *truthfully* setting forth another party's position on matters of racial interest and does not deliberately seek to overstress and exacerbate racial feelings by irrelevant, inflammatory appeals, we shall not set aside an election on this ground.[19]

When an objection is raised, the burden of proof rests with the party making the statements to show that they are truthful and

---

[14] *Id.* at 153, 45 L.R.R.M. at 1290.

[15] 119 N.L.R.B. 117, 41 L.R.R.M. 1005 (1957).

[16] *Id.* at 118, 41 L.R.R.M. at 1006.

[17] In Boyce Mfg. Corp., at note 6, *supra,* a prediction was held to be interference on the ground it constituted a threat.

[18] 138 N.L.R.B. 66, 50 L.R.R.M. 1532 (1962).

[19] *Id.* at 71-72, 50 L.R.R.M. at 1535.

germane to the election issues. While *Sewell* was considered to be the new leading case on racial campaign appeals, it does not represent a significant departure from earlier cases. The element of temperateness given controlling importance in *Sewell* had been included in the earlier *Sharnay* rule, although the Board's opinion gave it less emphasis.

In the *Allen-Morrison* case,[20] decided the same day, the Board applied the *Sewell* rule to statements made by an employer which outlined in detail the union's position favoring integration. The letter discussed segregation and integration and how it was an individual choice rather than one to be forced upon the individual by a union which favored integration, and which used union dues to eliminate segregation. The Board characterized the employer's campaign as temperate in tone. It said that it was germane to the election because the employees had the right to make the choice between integration and segregation.

A comparison between the rational racial statements in *Allen-Morrison* and the inflammatory propaganda in *Sewell*[21] is quite easy, but the general application of such a distinction is more difficult. Under what conditions can appeals to racial prejudice conclusively be determined to be emotion-free? One writer has stated:

> However valid the common sense distinction between a rational appeal and an emotional appeal, between a "calm orderly, restrained presentation" and a "complex fusion of excitement, resentment, vague enthusiasm, strangely aroused fears and hopes," it cannot be applied to issues where, owing to the nature of the issue itself, the predictable response of any appeal is primarily emotional. . . . While such attitudes may also be founded upon sustained value preferences, the fundamental difficulty in applying a common sense distinction between emotional and rational appeals in this area is that no criteria have been derived for ascertaining the nature and form of propaganda which activates emotional rather than rational processes on emotionally charged issues.[22]

---

[20] Allen-Morrison Sign Co., 138 N.L.R.B. 73, 50 L.R.R.M. 1535 (1962).

[21] The employer had sent to the employees: (a) a picture of a Negro dancing with a white woman with the caption indicating the union endorsed this conduct; (b) a reproduction of a newspaper photo showing a white man dancing with a Negro lady, the caption indicated this was the union leader; (c) a letter indicating the union supported the NAACP and CORE; and (d) a racist newspaper *Militant Truth* which alleged that integration was supported by communists. This campaigning occurred in two small Georgia towns.

[22] Note, *Employee Choice and Some Problems of Race and Remedies in Representation Campaigns*, 72 YALE L. J. 1243, 1251 (1963).

The difficulty of this distinction is illustrated in cases decided subsequent to *Sewell* and *Allen-Morrison.*

THE SEWELL RULE AND THE CIVIL RIGHTS CASES

Appeals to racial prejudice in representation election campaigns assumed a new dimension following *Sewell* during the civil rights movement of the 1960's. Not only did the Board receive more cases involving racially-oriented campaigns than in the past, but also objections began to be raised by employers alleging interference as the result of prointegrationist campaign conduct by unions.

The union campaigns were directed at Negro employees and they stressed the issue of social and economic inequality. In the *Archer Laundry Co.* case,[23] the Board held that campaign propaganda which appeals to racial self-consciousness is permissible when the purpose is not to inflame racial hatred or engender conflict between black and white, but to encourage concerted action by the Negroes. The Board approved of the following campaign materials issued by the union: (1) a leaflet entitled, *Freedom is Everyone's Fight,* which included a picture of a dog, a policeman with a club, five horses, and a caricature of "the boss" as a fat, bald-headed man with money; (2) a leaflet indicating a labor-hater is also anti-Negro; (3) a leaflet indicating an antiunion Negro is also an "Uncle Tom." A serious question may be raised as to the correctness of the Board's conclusion that the above literature did not deliberately invoke the hatred of the Negro for the white. The Board claimed it advised the Negroes that because they were black, they were discriminated against in the economic sphere and thus they were urged to join the union, not as an act against the white race, but to gain equality.

A later case, *Baltimore Luggage Co.*,[24] approved union campaign appeals to Negro employees on the ground they were appeals to economic and social self-betterment. During the campaign, however, several references were made to the violent deaths of two civil rights workers and the sniper slaying of Medgar Evers. A letter and two speeches on behalf of the union

---

[23] 150 N.L.R.B. 1427, 58 L.R.R.M. 1212 (1965). *See also* Aristocrat Linen Supply Co., Inc., 150 N.L.R.B. 1488, 58 L.R.R.M. 1216 (1965).

[24] 162 N.L.R.B. 1230, 64 L.R.R.M. 1145, *enforced,* 387 F.2d 744, 67 L.R.R.M. 2209 (4th Cir. 1967).

emphasized that the civil rights and labor movements were parallel. The Board said that "campaign material of this type is directed at undoing disadvantages historically imposed . . . upon Negroes because of their race, through an appeal to collective action of the disadvantaged." [25] It was held to be relevant for the employees to know of the union's attitude to Negroes and its advantages for them. Upon the petition for enforcement of this order to the court of appeals, the order was approved but the dissenting judge argued the campaign was both inflammatory and not germane to the issues of the election. This appeal "had the effect of bringing the election into an improper perspective, namely that the election was an integral part of the civil rights struggle of the American Negro."

Later, in the *Hobco* case,[26] the Board upheld an election on the same grounds as *Baltimore Luggage*. Again, there had been references to the killing of Medgar Evers, and the Board rejected the assertion that this was inflammatory, since it was less graphic than the leaflets in *Archer Laundry*.

NLRB v. Schapiro & Whitehouse, Inc.[27] denied enforcement of a Board order by taking a stricter approach to permissible union campaign propaganda and, in particular, to the determination of the relevancy of the racial appeals to the campaign. The union urged the employees (almost all were Negro) to consider and act upon race as a factor; it alleged that the company had held the employees down over the years. The court made the important statement that equality of race in privilege or economic opportunity had not been an issue of the campaign, *that a majority of the employees were Negroes did not make it so*. It rejected the Board's automatic acceptance of the parallelism of the civil rights and labor movements. "For the union to call upon racial pride or prejudice in the contest could 'have no purpose except to inflame the racial feelings of the voters in the election.' "[28] The court also determined that the campaign was highly inflammatory because several references to the Cambridge race riot had been made in leaflets distributed during the cam-

---

[25] *Id.* at 1233, 64 L.R.R.M. at 1145.

[26] Hobco Mfg. Co., 164 N.L.R.B. 862, 65 L.R.R.M. 1173 (1967).

[27] 356 F.2d 675, 61 L.R.R.M. 2289 (4th Cir. 1966), *denying enforcement to* 148 N.L.R.B. 958, 57 L.R.R.M. 1094 (1964).

[28] *Id.* at 679, 61 L.R.R.M. at 2293.

paign. In *Hobco Mfg.*, however, the Board indicated that *Archer Laundry* and similar cases were still controlling in spite of *Schapiro & Whitehouse*.

The civil rights cases, in general, evidence the Board's willingness to accept racial self-consciousness and economic and social self-betterment as valid campaign issues. Moreover, although the Board continues to refer to *Sewell* as its leading case, it has in fact departed significantly from *Sewell* in its current willingness to overlook the inflammatory nature of many union appeals. The courts, on the other hand, look to *Sewell* as the definitive statement of Board policy on racial propaganda and are understandably reluctant to ignore the potential impact of campaign statements about race which, in the language of *Sewell* are obviously "emotional" as much as "rational" appeals.

CONCLUDING REMARKS

What emerges from an analysis of these cases is a conflict between the standard the Board actually follows in judging appeals to racial discrimination and the standard it describes when it discusses the principles it purports to follow. In actual practice, the Board frequently treats inflammatory racial statements, especially those aimed at inspiring blacks to collective action, in much the same manner as it does *ad hominem* attacks on the character or personality of an opposing party. As discussed earlier in the context of misrepresentations,[29] the Board prefers to leave the voters to their own rational defenses in evaluating such propaganda, even if it is inflammatory in nature. In the misrepresentations context, the Board reaches that result by classifying the inflammatory statements as nonmaterial. However, in the racial context, particularly with employer appeals, the Board follows a different and not entirely consistent route. It broadly defines the *Sewell* concept of "reasoned" appeals so as to bar much racial propaganda which is clearly emotionally pitched and which, under the more straightforward approach of the misrepresentation cases, would unquestionably be classified as "inflammatory."

In establishing a satisfactory policy for determining which conduct constitutes election interference through racial appeals, the Board perhaps should reconsider its own suggestion in the *Mead-Atlanta Paper* case of the test of "distortion" of the elec-

---

[29] *See* pp. 36-39, *supra.*

tion issues. This would more effectively incorporate threats of an economic nature and the most extreme inflammatory appeals, while making it clearer that not every emotional appeal on racial grounds will be enough to invalidate the election. It would also deemphasize the current *Sewell* distinction between "reasoned" and "emotional" appeals.

The Board's current approach does not necessarily lead to the wrong results. It is probably desirable for the agency to ignore most racially-pitched propaganda because of the impossibility of determining when the voters are actually influenced by such appeals. But the conflict between the language of the *Sewell* opinion, which the Board continues to cite, and the results actually reached during the civil rights movement, creates considerable uncertainy over the Board's policy. In this context, it is difficult for the Board's regional office staffs, who have the initial responsibility for applying Board election policies, or the courts, who must occasionally review the application of such policy, to reach results consistent with the Board's real objective.

Although the civil rights movement has taken on different dimensions and future cases involving appeals to human rights will inevitably differ, a reconsideration of the issues discussed in *Sewell*, followed by a clear statement of the Board's present policy is in order.

PART THREE

Regulation of Other Campaign Conduct

CHAPTER V

Offers And Inducements

The Board seeks to prevent employers and unions from using economic incentives as campaign tools to restrain or bribe employees in their selection of a bargaining representative. Accordingly, the Board has imposed limits on the promising or granting of economic inducements by either party during the campaign period. In the employer's case, such inducements may take the form of wage increases or other beneficial changes in terms or conditions of employment.[1] The union may similarly attempt to influence the employees' choice by offering to waive or reduce regular initiation fees and dues or by compensating employees for participating in campaign-related activity.

None of these actions alone necessarily constitutes election interference. There must be some basis for concluding that the action was undertaken for the purpose of influencing votes or that it was carried out in such a way that it naturally tended to impair the voters' freedom of choice before it can properly be deemed objectionable. The problem for the Board in this area has been to formulate guidelines which will prevent the parties from using their economic positions for such improper ends without unduly interfering with their ability to make necessary and proper adjustments to meet changing economic conditions during the campaign period. As we shall see, this task has proved particularly difficult for the Board.

EMPLOYER GRANTS OF BENEFITS

The advent of an organizing campaign should not preempt or interfere with the employer's right periodically to adjust

---

[1] See American Freightways, 124 N.L.R.B. 146, 148, 44 L.R.R.M. 1302 (1959), holding that a change in the employer's emergency leave policy was "a beneficial change in the terms and conditions of employment" and, therefore, the same as an economic benefit. But cf. National Waterlift Co., 175 N.L.R.B. 849, 71 L.R.R.M. 1074 (1969), holding that a change in the employer's cafeteria policy, opening it fifteen minutes earlier before the start of each shift, was of minimal significance and not likely to interfere with the employees' free choice.

104

employees' wages and benefits as conditions may dictate. The
Board, at least nominally, recognizes this principle. It is quick
to state that the employer is not prohibited from implementing
changes which had been decided upon earlier or which are necessitated by conditions beyond his control. Thus, the Board has
said that the employer is free to do what he normally does
during this period.[2] If he is confronted with an organizing
campaign, he should proceed to grant or withhold benefits as
he would if the union were not in the picture. Only if his
course of action is prompted by the union's presence, the Board
maintains, will it find that he has interfered with the election.[3]
Elsewhere, the Board has restated this principle in stricter
terms: it is the employer's *legal duty* to proceed as he would
have done had the union not been campaigning.[4]

During the Pre-election Period

It is often difficult or impossible to determine if in fact the
employer acted without regard to the union's presence, or if a
change initiated by the employer was motivated by the presence
of the union. Faced with this difficulty, the Board has resorted
to a form of presumption based on the timing of the employer's
action.[5] If the grant of benefits occurs during the pendency of
an election petition, the Board, in effect, presumes an unlawful
purpose or effect. It then imposes the burden on the employer
to show that established past practice, justifiable economic
considerations, or independent industry or corporate policy served
as the basis for the change in employee benefits.[6]

The employer's burden in such cases is a heavy one. It is
not sufficient simply to show that the grant was not specifically
intended to influence the voters or that it actually did not have
such an effect. For, as the Board's decision in *American Freightways Co., Inc.* stated, "The test is whether the employer engaged

---

[2] Famous-Barr Co., 174 N.L.R.B. 770, 70 L.R.R.M. 1307 (1969).

[3] Ayr-Way Stores, A Division of L.S. Ayres and Co., 205 N.L.R.B. No.
111, 84 L.R.R.M. 1127 (1973).

[4] Dynatronics, 186 N.L.R.B. 978, 75 L.R.R.M. 1568 (1970).

[5] WCAR, Inc., 203 N.L.R.B. No. 181, 83 L.R.R.M. 1440 (1973).

[6] International Shoe Co., 123 N.L.R.B. 682, 684, 43 L.R.R.M. 1520, 1521
(1959).

in conduct which, it may reasonably be said, tends to interfere with the free exercise of employee rights under the Act."[7] In effect, an objective test is applied against the employer's action, thereby eliminating the necessity to ascertain and prove intent to interfere and avoiding the need for proof of actual restraint and interference of employee free choice.

In 1964, the Supreme Court in the *Exchange Parts* case, considered whether Section 8(a)(1) of the National Labor Relations Act prevented an employer from conferring unconditional economic benefits shortly before the representation election, absent any further alleged restraint or coercion, where the employer's stated purpose was to affect the outcome of the election.[8] This case represented a substantial challenge to the approach which the Board had been taking in the past. It would have required the Board to prove the existence of actual interference with the employees' rights. The Court, however, upheld the Board's approach, making the now-famous statement:

> The danger inherent in well-timed increases in benefits is the suggestion of a fist inside the velvet glove. Employees are not likely to miss the inference that the source of benefits now conferred is also the source from which future benefits must flow and which may dry up if it is not obliged.[9]

The decision of the Court received much comment and criticism because it emphasized that substantial weight be given to the timing of economic benefits and diminished the need for proof of actual interference or coercion. *Exchange Parts* appears to encourage a *per se* rule of interference in cases involving well-timed benefit increases.

Board decisions do not actually acknowledge any *per se* rule. Such an approach would violate the Board's pronouncement in *United Screw & Bolt Corp.*[10] that the timing of an increase alone is not sufficient to show interference with the election. The Board indicated that it would be critical of changes in benefits coinciding with an election when: (1) the announcement of benefits does not follow a request by the employees and at the time is wholly unexpected by them; (2) the benefits

---

[7] 124 N.L.R.B. 146, 147, 44 L.R.R.M. 1302 (1959).

[8] NLRB v. Exchange Parts Co., 375 U.S. 405, 55 L.R.R.M. 2098 (1964).

[9] *Id.* at 409, 55 L.R.R.M. at 2100.

[10] 91 N.L.R.B. 916, 26 L.R.R.M. 1596 (1950).

while decided earlier are not announced until just before the election and no credible explanation for the delay is given; and (3) the announcement substantially differs from the customary time to grant benefits. On the facts of the *United Screw & Bolt* case, however, the Board upheld the employer's claim of past practice as a defense against the charge of election interference. The evidence showed that the election campaign had lasted four months. Approximately five weeks before the election the employer increased wages and benefits in the insurance program. The company showed a consistent policy, dating back for six years, of conforming the wage rate at the plant in question to that of another plant, and to the prevailing rates within the industry. Although *United Screw & Bolt* illustrates that an employer may be able to justify a grant of benefits during a campaign where his action is supported by clear evidence of conformity with an established practice, the decision offers scant comfort to the employer whose past actions in regard to benefits have not followed a consistent pattern. In that situation he may be hard pressed to produce tangible evidence to justify his decision, even though it was in fact based on legitimate considerations.

The standard imposed by the Board seems to tighten, moreover, when the employer's action occurs closer to the actual day of balloting. The Board's attitude toward the timing of the employer's action can be seen in the *Bata Shoe Co.* case.[11] Here, the employer had decided one year earlier to grant an increase in vacation time, but he announced the decision only one week before the election. The employer had given vacation increases the year before at this same time. The increases in question were allegedly in conjunction with the firm's fifteenth anniversary, and, therefore, they extended only the vacation time of those employees with fifteen or more years of service. The Board found that the mere fact that the employer had announced vacation increases the year before did not constitute sufficient past practice. The Board felt the increase should have been timed earlier than the crucial period preceding the election. The dissent brought out a significant aspect which had been dismissed by the majority. The vacation increase affected only ten out of the 1,133 employees. In addition, the Board did not discuss the promotional aspect of the increased

---

[11] 116 N.L.R.B. 1239, 38 L.R.R.M. 1448 (1956).

benefits which had been timed to coordinate with the anniversary date. The Board seems to have reacted purely out of concern for the timing of the vacation increase so close to election day, and ignored the question of interference and restraint in the election.

The Board evidenced a more lenient approach to an employer who affected an increase in the overtime rate for Sunday work approximately three weeks before the election.[12] The employer asserted that there was an existing company policy behind the action. There was a minimum of evidence presented to support the employer's argument. One witness indicated that he had been offered the increased overtime rate one month earlier, but he had not accepted the work. The Board felt that the employer met the burden of proving the change was not timed to interfere with the election. The decision may be explained on the basis that other violations by the employer were present in this case, and, therefore, the Board treated this particular charge lightly because the timing of the increase was not proximate to election day, or because the increase in the overtime rate was insignificant. However, the latter reason merely lends support to the dissenting opinion in the Bata Shoe case.

Two recent cases involving benefit increases, which were considered by the employer prior to the start of the union organization campaign and were announced during the election period, indicate a developing minority approach to the issue of timing. In Hineline's Meat Plant [13] the formulation of a profit sharing plan had been initiated prior to the campaign. The employer had sent it to the Internal Revenue Service for approval four days before the start of the critical period of the election. He announced the plan eleven days before the election. Likewise, the H-P Stores, Inc. case [14] deals with a pension plan which the employer began considering before the start of union activity. The plan was adopted during the election period. The employer waited thirteen days and then announced it four days before the election. In both cases the majority of the Board found that there was interference with the election because the employer had failed to meet the burden of proving that timing was moti-

---

[12] American Molded Products, 134 N.L.R.B. 1446, 49 L.R.R.M. 1373 (1961).

[13] 193 N.L.R.B. 867, 78 L.R.R.M. 1387 (1971).

[14] 197 N.L.R.B. No. 63, 80 L.R.R.M. 1539 (1972).

vated by legitimate considerations. Chairman Miller, dissenting in both cases, took the stand that where the decision has been reached legitimately by the employer to confer the economic benefits, the employees have the right to be informed of the benefits accruing to them in spite of unionization attempts or other union activity. Miller sees no policy reason which compels that predetermined benefits be hidden from employee view.[15]

Chairman Miller's argument is effective in its policy reasoning. In the industrial environment it is inevitable that the employer may be faced with conditions or factors over which he has no control, yet which may have a direct impact upon the decision to institute an increase in employee benefits. The Board, which is concerned with restraints upon the employees' freedom of choice, should not penalize the employer in such situations. One recent decision appears to follow with this view. In *Domino of California, Inc.*[16] the Board held that an announcement by the company of the decision to implement a profit-sharing plan did not violate Section 8(a)(1) and did not constitute election interference. The Board emphasized that the decision to institute its plan had been made before the start of the election campaign. It also noted that inclusion into the plan of the unit involved in the election had been dictated by tax considerations and advice by the Internal Revenue Service. The Board overruled the Administrative Law Judge who had based his finding solely on the timing of the announcement of the plan.

Unfortunately, however, the Board generally has only sporadically been receptive to the conditions faced by the employer in such cases. In *North American Aviation, Inc.*[17] a wage increase was announced by the employer five days before the election. Timing of the announcement was dependent upon approval of the National Aeronautics and Space Administration. The Board upheld the increase, but only after emphasizing that wages had been a major subject of the campaign. The decision seems to imply that the employer lawfully could not have made

---

[15] More recently Chairman Miller in Union Camp Corp., 202 N.L.R.B. No. 144, 82 L.R.R.M. 1765 (1973), indicated he would not find as objectionable employer conduct which granted increased holiday benefits on the day before the election, since the employer's initial effort at improving holiday benefits predated the union's campaign.

[16] 205 N.L.R.B. No. 123 (1973).

[17] 162 N.L.R.B. 1685, 64 L.R.R.M. 1232 (1967).

the announcement at that time if the subject of wages had not been a major campaign issue. This suggests an undue emphasis upon the issue of timing which disregards the employer's relationship with a third party.

In *Havatampa Cigar Corp.*[18] a new pension plan could only be implemented upon approval by the corporate Board of Directors. They met purely by coincidence on the day before the election. Upon approval of the plan, notification was sent out by mail to the employees at the plants not facing an election, and the directors' decision was posted on the bulletin boards in the working areas of the employees who faced the election. The majority of the NLRB held that there was no violation since the announcement was made in a routine fashion, the plan was adopted without regard to the election by the Board of Directors, and the employer was not obligated to withhold the announcement of the plan's adoption. Member Brown, nevertheless, dissented on the basis that the employer notified employees at other plants by *mail* and used the *bulletin board* to announce the news locally. He interpreted this to be a timing of the announcement by the employer intended to interfere with the election. However, it was established that the announcement of the plan's adoption had been given to the local press on this same day.

Another case decided by the Board and upheld by the circuit court of appeals also deals with a wage increase controlled by factors outside the reach of the employer.[19] The employer announced a wage increase two days before the election because of an industry-wide increase announced at that time. The employer's past practice had been to follow the industry's lead. In fact, the Board found that the employees would have expected him to do so. Therefore the Board claimed there was no interference on this point. On the other hand, the employer also at the same time announced an extra holiday, which had not been industry initiated. The Board rejected the employer's explanation that it was only natural to incorporate the two benefits into one announcement. Analysis of this case suggests that the Board is reluctant to accept third party influence as justification for an increase in employee benefits where the timing of the in-

---

[18] 175 N.L.R.B. 736, 71 L.R.R.M. 1037 (1969).

[19] J.P. Stevens & Co. v. NLRB, 461 F.2d 490, 80 L.R.R.M. 2609 (4th Cir. 1972).

crease is critical to the election. No suggestion is made in the opinion that the employees knew that the wage increase was industry-wide and that the holiday was locally initiated. Given their ignorance of this distinction, no justification exists for the Board's finding in this case, except the desire to pursue a near *per se* approach to the issue of timing.

Several cases have raised the charge that raffles or contests offering free give aways, which were organized by the employer, constituted unlawful inducements to the employees and thereby interfered with the election. Commonly, these election "gimmicks" have included raffling off television sets or groceries to those employees who voted in the election. For the most part the Board has permitted such conduct by the employer. In *Austin Concrete Works, Inc.*[20] the Board approved of a raffle because its sole stated purpose was to encourage the employee vote, and it was not conditioned upon one party receiving the vote.[21] The Board in *Hollywood Plastics*,[22] commenting upon the effect of a raffle of groceries valued at $82, said "[T]he raffle was conducted for the purpose of electioneering propaganda, and any inducement of employees to exercise their statutory right to vote in the election was purely incidental to that purpose."[23] The Board further stated that the use of a raffle was not interference *per se*, but that it would consider the value of the prize to see if it would create an obligation on the part of the employees to vote against the union.[24]

On certain occasions the circumstances may exist such that the raffle will constitute interference. In *Olympic Products Inc.*[25] the employer was going to give away groceries valued at an equal amount to the annual dues the employees would pay if the union won the election. The Board set aside the election not because of the comparison made between the

---

[20] 132 N.L.R.B. 184, 48 L.R.R.M. 1330 (1961).

[21] *See also* Tunica Mfg. Co., Inc., 182 N.L.R.B. 729, 76 L.R.R.M. 1535 (1970); Elgin Butler Brick Co., 147 N.L.R.B. 1624, 56 L.R.R.M. 1439 (1964).

[22] 177 N.L.R.B. 678, 71 L.R.R.M. 1397 (1969).

[23] *Id.* at 681, 71 L.R.R.M. at 1398.

[24] *But see* Tunica Mfg. Co., at note 21, *supra*, where the Board approved the raffle of a color television valued in excess of $300.

[25] 201 N.L.R.B. No. 64, 82 L.R.R.M. 1241 (1973).

groceries and the dues, but because the employer personally solicited the employees to vote and to participate in the raffle in violation of the agreed-upon procedures for bringing the employees to the polls. Apparently the Board felt these solicitations may have induced an obligation to vote against the union in order to participate in the raffle. In *Tunica Mfg.*[26] the employer held a rummage sale of his merchandise one week before the election. The Board did not view this conduct as similar to permissible electioneering propaganda. The prices offered for the goods constituted a significant bargain which had never been available before. The Board held that the sale was a benefit intended to induce employee votes against the union.[27]

Certain Board members have objected to the occurrence of such "gimmickery" during the election period. Member Zagoria dissented in both *Hollywood Plastics*[28] and *Buzza-Cardozo, A Div. of Gibson.*[29] His expressed view was:

> A Board-sponsored election is a serious governmental function conducted by agents whose responsibilities are sufficiently numerous without the additional burden of policing games-of-chance. The introduction of the raffle into the election creates a carnival-like atmosphere, transforming the employee from voter into contestant, and diverting his attention from the issue being decided to the possibility of winning a prize.[30]

Chairman Miller also has expressed his unwillingness to approve of such conduct for the same reasons as Zagoria.[31] These objections, while rightfully defending the overall propriety and seriousness of the election procedure, do not appear to focus upon the actual question of restraint and coercion. It may be posited that employees voting in an election are motivated to do so by several reasons apart from the ultimate question of union representation. However, these situations in general are insufficient grounds for directing a rerun election. The prohibition of raffles

---

[26] At note 21, *supra.*

[27] The Board viewed this conduct together with acts of interrogation and threats of plant closure. It said the rummage sale was part of the overall conduct calculated to interfere with the election.

[28] At note 22, *supra.*

[29] 177 N.L.R.B. 589, 71 L.R.R.M. 1390 (1969).

[30] *Id.* at 590, 71 L.R.R.M. at 1391.

[31] Electro-Voice, Inc., 191 N.L.R.B. No. 96, 77 L.R.R.M. 1436 (1971) (Miller, concurring for other reasons).

or other similar electioneering propaganda during the representation election campaign period should serve the limited purpose of insuring both reasoned and unrestrained voter choice.

Benefits Granted After the First Election

Similar problems and often additional ones face the employer who considers an increase in economic benefits after the first election, when objections have been raised to that election and there exists the possibility of a rerun election.

> As for the grant of benefits subsequent to the election, it is generally recognized that the Act, as construed by the Board and the courts, places the employer in a rather difficult position when he is impelled by bona fide economic considerations to revise his wage structure while a representation proceeding is pending.[32]

As a result of current NLRB rules, the employer will know within five days if the first election has been challenged by the union. His considerations then become complex: Is the timing of an increase still important and, if so, what is the "crucial period?" What is the likelihood of the Board directing a second election, and, if so, is this a significant factor in the decision to grant an increase? Will possible violations prior to the first election have an effect upon what he does now?

In *Ambox, Inc.*[33] the Board held that a wage increase announcement the week after the first election was calculated to influence the employees' free choice in the second election. It relied upon the employer's earlier unlawful conduct, his knowledge that union objections to the election were still pending, and his knowledge that there was a possibility that a second election would be directed. The *Dow Chemical Co.* case [34] involved the grant of a wage increase and a transfer of the employees from an hourly wage basis to a salaried status immediately after the results of the first election became known. The offer of these two benefits had been an element of the company's campaign platform during the first election period.[35] The union lost the

---

[32] Brearley Co., 163 N.L.R.B. 637, 643, 64 L.R.R.M. 1474 (1967) (Trial Examiner's Opinion).

[33] 146 N.L.R.B. 1520, 56 L.R.R.M. 1113 (1964).

[34] Case No. 20-RC-10516 (April 17, 1973).

[35] The Board held that the offer of increased wages and a transfer to salary status interfered with the first election. The company argued that the regional director had used the actual grant of the benefits as a basis for setting

second election and alleged the grant of the benefits as interference with this election. The Board agreed despite the employer's contention that

> [A]s the Board and all parties were aware of the wage increase when they proceeded to a second run-off election such conduct should not be treated as having occurred during the critical period for such election.[36]

It stated in reply that the "objectionable conduct occurring within the critical period is a basis for setting aside an election even if the parties are aware of the conduct at the time the election is directed." [37]

The *Tennessee Handbags* case [38] indicated that the uncertainty of a second election could be reason to give the employer the freedom to announce and implement benefit changes after the first election. This case was silent on the significance of employer violations before the first election. On the other hand in still another decision, *General Industries Electronics Co.*,[39] the Board upheld a wage increase between the first and second election. In conjunction with the increase the employer conducted personal interviews with the employees to explain the increase to them. The union appeared to possess a valid argument that the wage increase combined with the interviews exceeded the permissible bounds of campaign conduct. However, the Board disagreed and listed the following reasons for its decision: (1) the presence of past history showing similar scheduled wage interviews with employees; (2) the increase had been announced four months earlier; (3) the interviews began before the second election date

---

aside the first election, and, therefore, it could not be the basis for setting aside the second election. The Board agreed that the regional director's opinion on the objections raised to the first election used "inartful language," thereby creating confusion as to his specific reasons for setting aside the first election, but it concluded:

> A careful reading of his Report establishes that . . . the Regional Director recommended setting aside the first runoff election only because of the promises of benefits as he specifically found that the granting of benefits did not occur until after the polls were closed (at a time when the conduct could not have been the basis for setting aside the election as it was after that election) (p. 3 of the decision.)

[36] Case No. 20-RC-10516, p. 3.

[37] *Id.* at 3-4.

[38] 179 N.L.R.B. 1045, 72 L.R.R.M. 1576 (1969).

[39] 152 N.L.R.B. 1029, 59 L.R.R.M. 1238 (1965).

was announced; (4) there was a total lack of mention of the union and the election by the employer during the interviews; and (5) the interviews continued after the second election. The Board was especially impressed by the lack of campaigning by the employer during the interviews. The Board in this case even overlooked the fact that the employer systematically conducted 90 percent of the interviews before the second election, when he could have continued them afterwards.

Dynatronics [40] illustrates the often precarious position of the employer during the period between elections. The employer announced in April that an annual wage survey would be conducted and that the results would be ready on June 1. At this point objections to the first election were still pending. Subsequent to the employer's survey announcement a second election was ordered and set for June 5. On June 3, two days before the election the employer spoke to the employees and indicated he would not make any announcement concerning the survey results at that time. The day before this the employer had sent out a letter to the employees urging them to reject the union. The letter referred to the company's policy of periodic wage and benefit reviews, listed the benefits of the past year, and stated that the policy of increasing benefits and wages demonstrated that the union was unnecessary. It urged a "NO" vote and had a graphic representation of a ballot at the bottom of the letter with an "X" in the "NO" box.

The Board held that the employer interfered with the election because: (1) the employer did not normally announce to the employees when reviews were in progress or when to expect the results; (2) the "letter was an attempt by the Employer to link increased benefits and wages to the periodic surveys, thus implying that the results of the current wage survey would prove equally beneficial to the employees"; and (3) by withholding the results of the survey the employer attempted to place responsibility for such action upon the union and thus disparge it in the eyes of the employees and thereby discourage membership in the union.[41] The Board also said that the "strategic placement of the partial

---

[40] 186 N.L.R.B. 978, 75 L.R.R.M. 1568 (1970).

[41] *Id.* at 979, 75 L.R.R.M. at 1569.

sample ballot carries the suggestion that the effect of the current survey depended upon a 'NO' vote by the employees." [42]

The dissent by Chairman Miller emphasized that when the employer announced the survey in April and stated that the results would be given on June 1, he had no way of knowing the election would be scheduled a few days after that date. The employer's subsequent statement was an attempt to maintain credibility with the employees. The majority's reasons for setting aside the second election require further scrutiny. It said the employer did not normally announce to the employees that a survey was forthcoming. It had been shown, however, that the annual wage survey was an established past practice. Therefore a verbal announcement of a survey should have had a minimal effect upon the employees. They expected it as a matter of right and probably could have estimated when the results would be ready. The announcement alone, therefore, could not have constituted interference. The letter of June 2 by itself constitutes nothing more than permissible electioneering as is commonly contained in campaign literature. The connections which were alleged to exist between the letter and the speech seem rather strained in logic. The Board no doubt reacted strongly to the timing of the employer's speech only two days before the election and proceeded to take the separate facts of the case, which were independently harmless, and to merge them in order to support a charge of interference based upon a "totality of conduct" notion.

As the *General Dynamics* case demonstrates, the Board's decisions regarding increases in benefits during the interim period between elections do not afford employers any clear guidelines in governing their conduct in such circumstances. Although the Board refers to such factors as the relationship between previous illegal conduct and current actions by the employer, the likelihood of a second election, and the significance of past practice, its decisions to date have not indicated the relative weight to be given these factors or precisely how they will be applied. In view of the prolonged period which may intervene between elections if objections to the first election are litigated and appeals pursued, the need for clarification of the employer's rights and obligations during this period is particularly compelling.

---

[42] *Id.*, 75 L.R.R.M. at 1569.

Postponement of Benefits Until After the Election

An employer who is faced with a representation campaign may have legitimate reasons for announcing increases in benefits prior to the campaign, but he may hesitate to do so because of the fear of being charged with election interference. He may further realize that to withhold all benefits during this period may work to his disadvantage, since the employees would quickly support a labor organization promising increased benefits. In order to protect himself, the employer may announce to the employees during the election period that he intends to postpone any increases until after the election. The Board closely scrutinizes such situations.

The employer should not attempt to manipulate the postponement into a form of bribery or punishment since this is clearly interference with the employees' protected rights. Election interference, however, may arise under less explicit circumstances. In the *Great Atlantic & Pacific Tea Co.*[43] the employer sent a letter to the employees which stated that salaries of employees at the employer's other stores were being raised, but that they would not receive the increase because of a pending union representation election. He said he was not permitted under the law to do so at that time. The Board found that there was interference with the election:

> This announcement was coupled with a plea to the employees to vote against representation in the forthcoming election, but it did not make clear that the withheld increase would be granted, regardless of the result of the election.[44]

The Board seems somewhat narrow in its approach by insisting that before an employer may postpone benefit increases, he must make it affirmatively clear to the employees that their votes in the election will not have any effect upon the benefit.[45] The lack

---

[43] 101 N.L.R.B. 1118, 31 L.R.R.M. 1189 (1952).

[44] *Id.* at 1121, 31 L.R.R.M. at 1191.

[45] *See* Sonoco Products Co. v. NLRB, 399 F.2d 835, 69 L.R.R.M. 2037 (9th Cir. 1968), *denying enforcement on other grounds to* 165 N.L.R.B. 619, 65 L.R.R.M. 1405 (1967), where the court upheld the Board's finding that the employer in a speech, discussing the postponement of benefits, interfered with the election because he "made no mention of a desire to avoid charges of vote-buying . . ." 399 F.2d at 838, 69 L.R.R.M. at 2039. The court indicated it accorded the Board broad discretion in its finding, but that the case was a close one and the Board probably had come to the limit of its discretion.

of explicit threats by the employer could convey the same assurances to the employees.

One employer announced he was postponing wage increases until after the election since it would not be fair to grant them before the election.[46] In sustaining the election results the Board relied on the employer's neutral attitude. It did, however, ensure that there were economic reasons for the postelection benefits. The Board also held in favor of an employer who assured the employees that he would continue to pay the prevailing rates when he announced the postponement of the wage increase.[47]

The *Conolon Corp.* case[48] presents an issue similar to the above cases. Prior to an election the employer announced wage increases as a result of a wage survey. At that time he said another survey would be made after the first of the year, after the election. If necessary, wage rates would be changed again. Later, in defense against charges of election interference, the employer argued to the Board that the second survey was necessitated by the new federal minimum wage increase due to go into effect at that time. The employer said he had not included this increase with the first wage increase because he thought it would have been too much out of the ordinary (in amount) so close to the election. The Board found this to constitute interference, since the announcement of the second survey to be held after the election could only have been interpreted to convey to the employees the expectation of a further increase. The Board in this decision apparently ignored the legitimate economic reason for announcing the second survey and the total absence of threats by the employer making the second survey dependent upon the outcome of the election. Query whether the employer would have satisfied the Board if he had told the employees that he was postponing an additional wage survey until after the election because of the fear of creating an above-average wage increase prior to the election.

The courts have indicated a reluctance to follow the Board's application of its policy in cases involving the employer's announcement of the postponement of increases and have criticized the Board for its ambiguity and inconsistency in directing the appropriate course for the employer to take when he decides to

---

[46] Louisiana Plastics, 173 N.L.R.B. 1427, 70 L.R.R.M. 1019 (1968).

[47] UARCO, Inc., 169 N.L.R.B. 1153, 67 L.R.R.M. 1341 (1968).

[48] 175 N.L.R.B. 27, 70 L.R.R.M. 1465 (1969).

hold benefits or wage adjustments in abeyance because of a fear of violating Section 8(a)(1). In *NLRB v. Dorn's Transportation Co.*[49] the court charged the Board with placing the employer in a "damned if you do, damned if you don't" position. It suggested the Board should be limited in finding election interference to those cases where it could be shown that the employer was illegally motivated. In a later case, *Newberry Co. v. NLRB,*[50] the court said that although the Board did not seem to feel bound by the principles announced in *Dorn's Transportation* it would not be able to seek enforcement of its own policy by that court. The *Newberry* case points out even a futher employer dilemma. The employer was attempting to determine the appropriateness of postponing periodic wage reviews, where the reviews were fairly regular, and wage increases based on those reviews, which were discretionary.

In the *Big Three Industrial Gas*[51] case the Court of Appeals for the Fifth Circuit overruled a Board decision which set aside an election as the result of an employer's letter to the employees stating that wages would be "frozen" for an indefinite period of time because of the union's election petition. The court rejected the Board's view that the word "frozen" had a coercive interpretation, and it also said that while the letter was not the best statement of the employer's legal position with respect to the representation election proceedings, the legality of the words must be evaluated in the context of the circumstances of the election. In *Big Three Industrial Gas* the employer had been responding to a union letter which had asked, "How much longer must we wait for a wage increase?"

These court decisions call for a more flexible application of the objective test for determining election interference as the result of postponed increases in employee benefits. Board policy should undergo this change. Not only does employer motive deserve more consideration than the Board has given it, but also the Board's underlying presumption of the likelihood of interference arising from the announcement of a postponed benefit is highly questionable.

---

[49] 405 F.2d 706, 70 L.R.R.M. 2295 (2d Cir. 1969).

[50] 442 F.2d 897, 77 L.R.R.M. 2097 (2d Cir. 1971).

[51] NLRB v. Big Three Industrial Gas Co., 441 F.2d 774, 77 L.R.R.M. 2120 (5th Cir. 1971).

EMPLOYER OFFERS OF BENEFITS

The Board's concern in protecting the employees' interests by regulating employer increases in economic benefits during the campaign period must be balanced by the need to safeguard the freedom of the employer to conduct his business and to formulate his personnel programs. The Board's regulation of *offers* of employee benefits made during the election period similarly must be influenced by the interest in protecting employer free speech and in providing for a healthy and vigorous campaign. In practice these conditions have not always been met.

In each case the Board tries to determine if the offer of increased employee benefits was made contingent upon the employees' vote or upon the results of the election, or if it was calculated to influence employee union activity. Offers made during the campaign period, which are pursuant to a legitimate business purpose or to past practice, or which have been decided upon prior to union activity, are unobjectionable.[52]

> Just as an employer is free to rehearse for employees the benefits which they have previously received from the employer without a union, in order that they may evaluate the employer's past performance, so should an employer be permitted to notify employees of efforts in progress to improve the lot of the employees.[53]

In most cases they are closely related in substance to actual grants of benefits. The Board has indicated that it is immaterial whether the coercive statements (offers) made during the election period are direct or indirect, as long as the employees have reasonable cause to believe that a statement is a promise provoked by union activity. The Board generally has distinguished between explicit and implied offers.

Explicit Offers

The promise of a benefit made to an employee which is found to be *expressly* contingent upon the outcome of the election, or upon the employee's vote constitutes an explicit offer interfering

---

[52] American Dredging Co., 180 N.L.R.B. 800, 73 L.R.R.M. 1113 (1970); Danadyne, Inc., 182 N.L.R.B. 174, 74 L.R.R.M. 1022 (1970).

[53] Tommy's Spanish Foods, 187 N.L.R.B. 235, 238, 76 L.R.R.M. 1001, 1003-04 (1970) (Chairman Miller, dissenting). The Ninth Circuit relied upon the reasoning expressed in the dissent in denying enforcement to the Board's ruling, NLRB v. Tommy's Spanish Foods, Inc., 463 F.2d 116, 80 L.R.R.M. 3039 (9th Cir. 1972).

with the election. Usually such cases provide the clearest examples of election intereference. In *Paterson Fire Brick Co.*[54] a laid-off employee was asked to vote "NO" and promised a job if the union lost the election. In another case, an election was set aside when the employer promised increased insurance benefits if the union was defeated.[55]

The *Paterson* case additionally indicated that the Board feels it unnecessary to determine whether the explicit offer was effective in accomplishing the intended results. Such a viewpoint has led to several cases where the Board has found election interference on the basis of arguably general statements rather than offers. In *Anchor Coupling Co., Inc.*[56] the employer asked during the campaign to be given "another chance" and also promised "some different changes around here." He later stated, "If the union doesn't get in . . . we would find mostly anything for you girls to do." The Board said that these remarks, when considered in the context in which they were made, could only be interpreted as promises of economic benefits to the employees if the union lost the election. The Board apparently never asked itself if the statement was a "bona fide" offer, rather than employer campaigning, and if the requisite element of contingency upon the election results was present. Similarly, in an earlier case an election was set aside where the employer said shortly before the election:

> Wouldn't it be nice to come in here and vote "NO" on Election day and come back on Thursday and let me announce a similar package to the one I gave last year.[57]

The Board said that this was an offer in the form of a rhetorical question which carried with it the implied threat that the employees could be assured of a Christmas bonus and year-end raise only if they voted against the union. More recently, in *Borden Mfg. Co.*[58] the employer during the campaign emphasized that the union could give the employees nothing and that all benefits derived from him. The company stated that it would

---

[54] 93 N.L.R.B. 1118, 27 L.R.R.M. 1548 (1951).

[55] Wytheville Knitting Mills, 78 N.L.R.B. 640, 22 L.R.R.M. 1251 (1949).

[56] 168 N.L.R.B. 218, 66 L.R.R.M. 1275 (1967).

[57] Kent Plastics Corp., 107 N.L.R.B. 157, 33 L.R.R.M. 1090 (1953).

[58] 193 N.L.R.B. 1028, 78 L.R.R.M. 1498 (1971).

be more generous in granting benefits if the union were not there. The Board set aside the election. The dissenting Board member argued there was no interference since the employer was merely responding to union assertions that unless it became the employees' representative all benefits would be lost.

The *F.B. Rogers Silver Co.*[59] case illustrates the Board's inability to distinguish between offers of permanent benefits and temporary ones. A rumor was circulating that the employees would get a long weekend off if the union lost the election as had previously happened. The origin of the rumor was uncertain, but it was found that employer representatives had lent credence to the rumor. In setting aside the election the Board attributed responsibility for the rumor to the employer and said that he should have made a general statement discrediting the possibility of such a benefit. In reviewing the case, it seems difficult to believe that the employees would accept or reject a bargaining representative on the basis of one extra day off.

The Board rightfully should prevent explicit attempts to sway employee votes by means of economic benefits offered contingent upon the union's defeat in the election. However, the Board exceeds the limits of sound regulatory policy when it sets aside elections on the basis of statements or offers, which are not contingent upon the election outcome, but which are mere campaign statements or replies to union assertions. It becomes apparent that in many instances it is a misnomer to label the unlawful conduct an "express" offer.

Implied Offers

The election may be set aside if the Board determines that an offer or promise of benefit would lead the employees to believe that the offer was conditioned upon the results of the election when there has been no explicit conditioning of the offer upon the vote or results of the election. Here the Board's policy has developed under a twofold dilemma. The question of what is an offer again arises, and secondly, the Board must decide in each case what factors are likely to have made the offer contingent upon the election. In one situation the offer of financial assistance by an employer constituted election interference, since it was made simultaneously with a solicitation to vote against

---

[59] 94 N.L.R.B. 205, 28 L.R.R.M. 1019 (1951).

the union.[60] The Board said the timing of the statements would reasonably have led the employees to conclude that they were being offered an economic benefit conditioned upon their voting in a manner desired by the employer. In another case, *Maine Fisheries Corp.,*[61] the timing of an employer's statement on election day was considered to be an important factor. On the day of the election the employer in a speech indicated to the workers that he was considering new arrangements to provide more work. The Board said this was an implied promise of economic benefits, either as a reward for voting against the union or as an inducement for the employees to abandon their organization activities. The timing of the speech was such that they "could only have understood [the] words as expressing an implied promise of more work." [62] Another case involved similar language, but the timing of the announcement was one week prior to the election.[63] The employer's letter stated that in keeping with its progressive policy it was working on a formula for improving wages. The Board held this to be at most:

> [A] vague suggestion of the possibility that at some indeterminate date the Employer might evolve a formula whereby these benefits could be increased.[64]

Timing was apparently the factor distinguishing these two similar employer statements. The Board's reasoning is open to criticism not only because there is questionable significance in the five day difference between the timing of these two statements, but also because ambiguous statements should not be transformed into objectionable offers constituting election interference simply as a result of their timing.

It is interesting to note that in a subsequent *Maine Fisheries* case [65] the Board rejected a regional director's decision that there had been an implied reiteration of the earlier promise

---

[60] The Univis Lens Co., 82 N.L.R.B. 1390, 23 L.R.R.M. 1679 (1949).

[61] 99 N.L.R.B. 604, 30 L.R.R.M. 1101 (1952). *See also* The Paymaster Corp., 162 N.L.R.B. 123, 63 L.R.R.M. 1508 (1966).

[62] *Id.* at 606, 30 L.R.R.M. at 1102.

[63] American Laundry Machinery Co., 107 N.L.R.B. 511, 33 L.R.R.M. 1181 (1953).

[64] *Id.* at 513, 33 L.R.R.M. at 1182.

[65] Maine Fisheries Corp., 102 N.L.R.B. 108, 31 L.R.R.M. 1278 (1953).

of benefits. This same employer sent a letter to the workers prior to the second eelction mentioning the statement (promise) made before the first election. The Board said that at most the letter was a reminder of past benefits granted.

Additional alleged employer implied offers, couched in general or ambiguous terms, have led to inconsistent Board determinations of election interference. One employer said:

> I won't make you a lot of promises, but I can promise . . . you a year round job with a year round pay envelope, and you won't have to pay anybody to get it, or to keep your job.[66]

The Board compared this statement against a previous one (a prediction about the uncertainty of full-time work if the union won) and said:

> The juxtaposition of these two thoughts served to emphasize to the employees the substance of the second statement, namely, that they would benefit by rejecting the Petitioner.[67]

In other instances this employer's speech would have been found to be permissible election campaigning. The Board in *Coverall Rental Service, Inc.*[68] rejected the union's claim that the employer had implied a promise to provide a profit-sharing plan. The Board emphasized the fact that the employer's reference to the consideration of such a plan did not mention any "specific improvement of any substantial nature" and it was not even suggested as a "distinct probability." [69] In *Byrne Dairy, Inc.*[70] the employer said, "you can move ahead faster here, stay on our team, it will pay in the long run." The Board said this was an implied promise of benefit, while a dissenting member found the statement too ambiguous to characterize. *Byrne* conflicts with an earlier case, *Crown Food Products* [71] where the statement, "Your expressions of friendship and confidence are

---

[66] Coca Cola Bottling of Louisville, 118 N.L.R.B. 1422, 1423, 40 L.R.R.M. 1390, 1391 (1957).

[67] *Id.* at 1424, 40 L.R.R.M. at 1391.

[68] 205 N.L.R.B. No. 140, 84 L.R.R.M. 1072 (1973).

[69] *Id.*, 84 L.R.R.M. at 1073.

[70] 176 N.L.R.B. 312, 71 L.R.R.M. 1243 (1969), *enforced*, 431 F.2d 1363, 75 L.R.R.M. 2168 (2d Cir. 1970).

[71] 118 N.L.R.B. 1123, 40 L.R.R.M. 1324 (1957).

greatly appreciated and we are not going to forget them," was not found to be a promise of benefit. The Board declared this statement to be somewhat vague in meaning.

Evaluating employer election statements on the basis of implied promises of benefits constituting election interference inherently involves subjective interpretations of individual cases and the conditions under which the statements were made. As a result, Board decisions have resulted in a truly "case-by-case" analysis and do not fulfill the necessary purpose of providing guidance to the parties.

UNION INDUCEMENTS

The earlier discussion relating to the competing interests which the Board was required to deal with in formulating and administering the policy of regulating employer election conduct equally applies to an analysis of the regulation of union inducements made during the election campaign period. Generally, while the Board seeks to safeguard the same employee interests, it accords the union a different status in the campaign. In *NLRB v. Golden Age Beverage Co.*[72] the Court affirmed the Board's view that:

> An employer in an unorganized plant, with his almost absolute control over employment, wages, and working conditions, occupies a totally different position in a representation contest than a union, which is merely an outsider seeking entrance to the plant.[73]

While such a viewpoint of the current industrial environment is questionable and subject to criticism, nevertheless, it is directly reflected in the Board's evaluation of restraint and coercion arising from union inducements made during the election period.

The *Primco Casting Corp.*[74] case offers a good example of the Board's refusal to view a union's action during the campaign as analagous in principle to that of an employer. Two unions were competing for representation rights at the company. The incumbent union for six years had been receiving payments for its strike fund from deductions from the employees' pay.

---

[72] 415 F.2d 26, 71 L.R.R.M. 2924 (5th Cir. 1969), *enforcing*, 167 N.L.R.B. 151, 66 L.R.R.M. 1016 (1967).

[73] *Id.* at 30, 71 L.R.R.M. 2926-27.

[74] 174 N.L.R.B. 244, 70 L.R.R.M. 1128 (1969).

The employees always disliked this assessment. After the competing union filed an election petition, the incumbent union quickly decided to discontinue the strike fund assessments and to return a recent reduction to them (one week before the election). The Board held that there was no election interference by the incumbent.

> [W]e do not regard the [union's] action here in question as analagous in principle to that of an employer who, with a purpose to defeat a union, grants to employees a benefit he would not normally have granted. . . . A union's attempt to make itself more attractive to employees can scarcely be viewed by the employees as a warning that, if the union is not obliged, the employees may be made to suffer later. For, as the employees are aware, if the union is not obliged—that is, if it loses the election—it can have no effect on the employees in the future whatsoever. No element of coercion is therefore present.[75]

The above pronouncement of general policy by the Board ignores the crucial issue of the case. The change in the strike fund assessment program and the refund of the deduction implemented by the incumbent may have affected the ability of the competing union to campaign effectively, and arguably it had an influence upon the employees when the time came for them to choose between the competing unions. The dissent strongly urged that the union's change fairly induced the employees to vote for the incumbent union.

In contrast to the regulation of employer conduct, the promise of improved benefits and working conditions made by the union, contingent upon its victory in the election, is seen as permissible pre-election propaganda.[76] The promises are considered to be dependent ultimately upon successful collective bargaining. The Board's policy in such cases assumes that there were no misrepresentations or other restraints introduced by the union when it made the promises. The minority opinion in a more recent Board decision suggested a reconsideration of this general attitude concerning the limited effect of union promises of economic benefits. In *Smith Co.*,[77] the union promised, contingent upon its victory in the election, certain benefits, such as pension and dental plans,

---

[75] *Id.* at 245, 70 L.R.R.M. at 1129-30.

[76] Burson Plant of Kendall Co., 115 N.L.R.B. 1401, 38 L.R.R.M. 1078 (1956); Shirlington Supermarket, Inc., 106 N.L.R.B. 666, 32 L.R.R.M. 1519 (1953).

[77] 192 N.L.R.B. No. 162, 78 L.R.R.M. 1266 (1971).

certain work rules, job specialization, job security, tickets to Frontierland (an amusement park) at a discount, a blood bank, a credit union, and discounts on tires, cars, and appliances. The majority of the Board said the union's statements did not exceed the bounds of privileged campaign propaganda since the employees understood that the union could not obtain the benefits automatically by winning the election. The dissenting Board member, Chairman Miller, emphasized that the offer of certain benefits such as the blood bank, credit union, and discount prices constituted election interference, since these benefits derived solely from the union and they had been offered expressly contingent upon the union's victory.

Recently, a court affirmed a Board finding that there was no interference in a union promise that, if certified, it would establish a strike fund.[78] Although the fund was solely within the union's power to create and manage, at best it was considered to be protection against a possible future liability and consequently remote and uncertain. The Board noted also that such benefits normally followed from unionization.

The majority of Board cases involving union inducements alleged to be election interference deal with the waiver of initiation fees and union compensation made to employees for campaign related activity.

The Waiver of Initiation Fees

The union offer to waive initiation fees for all nonmember employees prior to the election was recognized at an early point by the Board as a legitimate recruiting and campaign technique.[79] However, the policy governing such offers has undergone changes over the years. The current Board rule had not received uniform acceptance by the circuit courts, and as we shall. see, the Supreme Court recently resolved the conflict by rejecting the NLRB's position.

The initial rule was formalized in the *Lobue Bros.* case.[80]

---

[78] NLRB v. Muscogee Lumber Co., Inc., 473 F.2d 1364, 82 L.R.R.M. 2849 (5th Cir. 1973).

[79] The Root Store, 88 N.L.R.B. 289, 25 L.R.R.M. 1316 (1950).

[80] 109 N.L.R.B. 1182, 34 L.R.R.M. 1528 (1954). *See also* Gruen Watch Co., 108 N.L.R.B. 610, 34 L.R.R.M. 1067 (1954).

[A] preelection offer of reduced initiation fees is objectionable
when the promised benefit is "contingent on how the employees
voted in the election or on the results of the election." [81]

Subsequent to the *Lobue* decision the Board narrowly construed the rule until it was ultimately overruled. There was no
published Board decision after *Lobue* in which the Board found
that the facts of the case warranted application of the rule.
In *General Electric Co.*,[82] where the facts were similar to the
Lobue case, the Board said there was no interference from the
union offer that "not one single person who votes for the IUE
in this election will be required to pay an initiation fee. . . ."
In spite of the express contingency of the offer, the Board said
it would not set aside the election because the union was re-
butting a rumor regarding the amount of the fee, and because
there was a state right-to-work law in effect.

In one case, however, the Court of Appeals for the Fifth
Circuit [83] refused to enforce a Board order upholding an election
where the union, in order to counteract a rumor regarding the
amount of the fee, waived fees for all those currently employed
at the time of the election in the event the union won the
election. The Board had distinguished this case from *Lobue*
on the ground that there the waiver had been contained on
cards circulated among employees, whereas here there were no
cards. The court said "this is a distinction without a difference,"
and it applied *Lobue*.

The union in *Bronze Alloys Co.*[84] told the employees that if
they joined the union before the election, initiation fees would
be reduced, whereas applications for membership after the election would be more costly and would require unanimous approval
of the full membership body. The Board said these statements
were made to persuade the employees to join the union before
the election, and the benefits were not contingent on the employees' vote or on the outcome of the election.[85] However,

[81] *Id.* at 1183, 34 L.R.R.M. at 1529.

[82] 120 N.L.R.B. 1035, 42 L.R.R.M. 1116 (1958).

[83] NLRB v. Gilmore Industries, Inc., 341 F.2d 240, 58 L.R.R.M. 2419 (5th
Cir. 1965), *denying enforcement to* 142 N.L.R.B. 781, 53 L.R.R.M. 1145
(1963).

[84] 120 N.L.R.B. 682, 42 L.R.R.M. 1047 (1958).

[85] *See also* A.R.F. Products, Inc., 118 N.L.R.B. 1456, 40 L.R.R.M. 1398
(1957); Orleans Mfg. Co., 120 N.L.R.B. 630, 42 L.R.R.M. 1016 (1958).

it appears that the Board failed to consider the alternative consideration that an employee persuaded to join the union before the election because of reduced fees would not likely vote against the union in the election. In that event, the offer would be an inducement likely to affect the election outcome. The Board extended the rationale of *Bronze Alloys* even further in *Weyerhauser Co.*[86] Four days before the election the union told the employees that it would reduce the initiation fees from $75 to $25 if all the employees came in as a group. The election was upheld since the waiver applied to all employees, regardless of how they voted, and was not contingent on how individual employees voted.

During this period before the *Lobue* rule was explicitly overruled, the Board in several cases upheld union waivers of initiation fees which were included on authorization cards distributed by the union to the employees. In *Gordea, Perez & Morrell S. En C.*[87] the Board held that such a waiver is harmless if it only buys membership cards and not votes. The cards did not specify that they would only be used to obtain an election. The waiver was not considered to be an interference since it applied both to those who joined at that time and to any others joining before a collective bargaining agreement was signed. A dissenting Board member felt that the practice of waiving initiation fees in return for signatures on authorization cards constituted the buying of votes. However, this case was overruled by the court of appeals [88] on the grounds that the union waiver of the fee was a misrepresentation since the union had not regularly imposed a fee.

In another case the Court of Appeals for the Second Circuit approved a waiver included on authorization cards.[89] The court admitted that the waiver was an inducement to the employees to sign the card but equated the offer to a union promise to better working conditions if it obtained majority status. The court also said:

---

[86] 146 N.L.R.B. 1, 56 L.R.R.M. 1116 (1964).

[87] 142 N.L.R.B. 475, 53 L.R.R.M. 1048 (1963).

[88] NLRB v. Gordea, Perez & Morrell, 328 F.2d 679, 55 L.R.R.M. 2586 (1st Cir. 1964).

[89] Amalgamated Clothing Workers of America v. NLRB, 345 F.2d 264, 59 L.R.R.M. 2228 (2d Cir. 1965).

Employees otherwise sympathetic to the union might well have been reluctant to pay out money before the union had done anything for them. Waiver of the payment would remove this artificial obstacle to their endorsement of the union.[90]

The waiver also was deemed proper because it clearly stated it was effective until the union executed a collective bargaining agreement. A concurring opinion raised the question whether the workers in this case (Puerto Ricans) would necessarily pick up the distinction that they did not have to join the union now instead of after the election in order to benefit from the waiver offer. The broader question should have been asked whether the employees would feel free to vote against the union once they have signed the cards containing the waiver, and they have joined the union.

The Board overruled *Lobue* in the *DIT-MCO, Inc.*,[91] stating that union offers to waive or reduce initiation fees were legitimate campaign techniques and did not affect the election results. The Board felt that such a reduction or waiver does not constitute a promise of benefit which improperly induces or coerces employees to vote for the union. "A full analysis of the circumstances convinces us that when these employees thereafter vote by secret ballot, their choice will be completely free of objectionable interference." [92] The amount of the initiation fee was not considered to be crucial to an employee's decision to join a union. The Board also stated that "[a]n employee who did not want the union to represent him would hardly be likely to vote for the union just because there would be no initial cost involved in obtaining membership." [93] The *DIT-MCO* rule has been upheld by the Eighth Circuit [94] and by the Ninth Circuit.[95] The Eighth Circuit held that the new policy was within the

---

[90] *Id.* at 268, 59 L.R.R.M. at 2231.

[91] 163 N.L.R.B. 1019, 64 L.R.R.M. 1476 (1967).

[92] *Id.* at 1021, 64 L.R.R.M. at 1477.

[93] *Id.* at 1022, 64 L.R.R.M. at 1478.

[94] NLRB v. DIT-MCO, Inc., 428 F.2d 775, 74 L.R.R.M. 2664 (8th Cir. 1970).

[95] NLRB v. G.K. Turner Associates, 357 F.2d 484, 79 L.R.R.M. 2932 (9th Cir. 1972).

Board's discretionary powers to regulate the conditions under which an election could be held.[96]

In a recent case, *NLRB v. Savair Mfg. Co.*,[97] the Sixth Circuit refused to enforce a Board order applying the *DIT-MCO* rule. The union had offered, contingent upon an election victory, to waive the initiation fee for all employees who executed authorization cards prior to the election. The substance of the court's opinion was:

> We simply refuse to believe that the waiver of initiation fees, contingent upon the outcome of an election, whether it is referred to as a fine, an assessment, or a waiver of initiation fees, is not coercive in the context of a union election.

The court felt *Lobue* and its own decision in *NLRB v. Gilmore Industries* [98] were sound rulings, and it concluded that the Board abused its discretion in declining to follow *Gilmore* and by overruling *Lobue*. Because of the conflict in views between the circuits, the Supreme Court granted certiorari to the *Savair* case.[99] Below we shall discuss the Supreme Court's decision affirming the position of the Sixth Circuit in *Savair*.

Shortly after the *DIT-MCO* decision, the Board announced a limitation in the application of the rule. In *Wagner Electric Corp.*[100] the Board said that *DIT-MCO* does not apply to the offers of "tangible economic benefits" which are made contingent upon a union victory. During the campaign the union mailed to the employees a certificate of group insurance providing $500 life insurance, up to $1,000 accidental death, and $100 funeral expenses. The union argued this came automatically with union membership. The Board said that there is a substantial distinction between the gift of life insurance coverage and a waiver of initiation fees. Where there is a waiver of initiation fees, there is no enhancement of the employees' economic position but merely an avoidance of a possible future liability. The gift of insurance is akin to an employer grant of a wage increase in anticipation of an election. It subjects the donees to a constraint to vote for the donor.

---

[96] 428 F.2d at 779, 74 L.R.R.M. at 2667.

[97] 470 F.2d 305, 82 L.R.R.M. 2085 (6th Cir. 1972).

[98] At note 83, *supra.*

[99] 411 U.S. 964 (May 7, 1973).

[100] 167 N.L.R.B. 532, 66 L.R.R.M. 1072 (1967).

The *Wagner* opinion has been applied to variety of situations in later cases. In the *Primco* case [101] the Board decided that the refund of a recent pay deduction for the strike fund by the union was not an economic benefit, but was incident to the change in the deduction policy which thereby resembled the "rebate of an unused premium." The disent felt that a precipitate distribution of money to the employees seven days before the election constituted a tangible benefit. In *Hughes & Hatcher, Inc.*[102] the former incumbent union offered the employees a credit for the $4 per month dues paid voluntarily to it during its period of nonrecognition. The Board said this was not an economic benefit like *Wagner*, but an offer to waive initiation fees as in *DIT-MCO*. "It is not likely that an employee would vote . . . to avoid future dues payments for a brief period when it could eliminate such payments altogether by voting against any union." [103] *Andal Shoe, Inc.* [104] involved a union offer to waiver a reinstatement fee for more than one-half of the affected employees. The Board applied the *DIT-MCO* rule to this waiver. The dissent, however, felt that this was a waiver of a previously accrued debt—a legally enforceable one, and therefore, it was an improper inducement.

Recently in *Loubella Extendables, Inc.*,[105] the Board held that a union offer to waive the initiation fee and back dues for four newly hired employees amounted to a grant of financial benefit, and thereby constituted interference since it was conditioned upon the union's victory in the election. The Board distinguished this case from *Andal Shoe* on the basis that there all of the employees were granted the waiver, that it pertained to a different employer, and could not have been an employment requirement with the new employer. In *Loubella* the waiver of fees and accrued dues "related to an obligation incurred by the four employees . . . with their present Employer." [106] The Board "deemed the four newly hired employees to be obligated under the contract to pay their initiation fees and delinquent dues and the employees could rea-

---

[101] At note 74, *supra.*

[102] 176 N.L.R.B. 1103, 71 L.R.R.M. 1375 (1969).

[103] *Id.* at 1105, 71 L.R.R.M. at 1377.

[104] 197 N.L.R.B. No. 131, 80 L.R.R.M. 1618 (1972).

[105] 206 N.L.R.B. No. 24, 84 L.R.R.M. 1210 (1973).

[106] *Id.*, 84 L.R.R.M. at 1211 n.6.

sonably have expected the Union to demand payment thereof." [107]

In 1973, the Supreme Court ruled that NLRB's policy of permitting union waiver of dues or fees was an abuse of discretion which permitted "the Union to buy endorsements and paint a false portrait of employee support during its election campaign." [108] The Court felt that the buying of endorsements constituted interference because this support may "serve as a useful campaign tool in the Union's hands to convince other employees to vote for the Union," and induce employees to feel obligated to vote for the union although they were not legally so bound. Since authorization cards may be used to show a union majority, the Court stated that "the latent potential of that alternative use of authorization cards cautions us to treat the solicitation of authorization cards in exchange for consideration of fringe benefits granted by the union as a separate step protected by the same kind of moral standard that governs elections themselves."

Although this issue remains unresolved, tentatively the Supreme Court's rejection of the *DIT-MCO* rule applies only to waivers during the period ending with the election. A union could conceivably waive initiation fees, contingent upon the election outcome, by extending the offer beyond the election period. Such a limited application of this ruling, however, seems unlikely to gain acceptance of a Court that rejected the NLRB's reasoning in *DIT-MCO*.

Compensation for Campaign-Related Activity

The Board has allowed payment to employees for time spent at campaign meetings. Such payments may not be excessive, may not be contingent upon the outcome of the election, and may not serve as inducements as to how to vote. Union payments to employees for expenses incurred as car pool drivers were upheld although there was no positive way of safeguarding against excessive payments. [109] The Board was influenced by the union's express disclaimer made to the employees of any intent to influence voting. Another election was upheld where payments were understood by the employees to be reimbursement, they were made in accord with

---

[107] *Id.*, 84 L.R.R.M. at 1211.

[108] NLRB v. Savair Mfg. Co., No. 72-1231 (U.S. Dec. 17, 1973).

[109] Federal Silk Mills, 107 N.L.R.B. 876, 33 L.R.R.M. 1245 (1954).

established policy, and they were not disproportionate in amount.[110] The Board has further held that it is permissible to offer prizes at union meetings to those employees who attend,[111] but when gifts are provided to the employees who do not attend the meeting, they are considered inducements to vote for the union.[112] The Board considers it legitimate for the union to encourage employee attendance, to generate a kindly feeling toward itself, and to make it more attractive as the bargaining agent by offering gifts only to those who attend union meetings.[113]

The NLRB has no formula for determining when union payments are excessive, but rules on a case-by-case basis. In *Teletype Corp.*[114] two competing unions conducted meetings before the election and compensated the employees on a straight time basis for attending. The rates paid increased as a result of the competition between the unions so that, "at one point, employees at a three-hour IBEW meeting were paid an amount equal to 8 hours at their regular hourly rates." [115] The Board set aside the election, and it characterized the activity by both unions as "outrageous conduct." [116]

The *Teletype* case was cited in *Collins & Aikman Corp. v. NLRB* [117] where the election was set aside because an employee was promised seven times his regular pay rate to act as the union observer, even though subsequently he was paid only three and one-half times his wage. While it was not determined that such union conduct actually influenced the employee or the other workers the court felt the conduct undoubtedly had the tendency to influence the election results.

A change in policy in regulating excessive union payments has been suggested by Chairman Miller in *Quick Shop Markets.*[118] In

---

[110] Commercial Letter, Inc., 200 N.L.R.B. No. 90, 82 L.R.R.M. 1220 (1972).

[111] Bordo Products Co., 119 N.L.R.B. 79, 41 L.R.R.M. 1045 (1957).

[112] General Cable Corp., 170 N.L.R.B. 1682, 67 L.R.R.M. 1635 (1968).

[113] Jacqueline Cochran, Inc., 177 N.L.R.B. 837, 71 L.R.R.M. 1395 (1969).

[114] 122 N.L.R.B. 1594, 43 L.R.R.M. 1341 (1959).

[115] *Id.* at 1595, 43 L.R.R.M. at 1341.

[116] 122 N.L.R.B. at 1595, 43 L.R.R.M. at 1342.

[117] 383 F.2d 722, 66 L.R.R.M. 2280 (4th Cir. 1967).

[118] 200 N.L.R.B. No. 120, 81 L.R.R.M. 1594 (1972). *See also* Plastic Masters, Inc., 206 N.L.R.B. No. 105 (1973) (Chairman Miller, dissenting).

this case payment to employee observers was twice their usual pay. The majority of the Board held this not to be grossly disproportionate to their usual pay. Miller, however, said it was bad practice to allow payments of reimbursement for time lost from work at an amount substantially in excess of the employees' regular rate of pay.

> In my view, any time an employer or a union offers an observer an extra payment over and above reimbursement at his regular rate of pay plus expenses, there is a lurking danger that, no matter how pure the heart of the payor, such payments will be regarded by the recipient as a form of monetary inducement. . . .[110]

Prohibiting all compensation in excess of normal wages would provide uniform regulation in an area where the exact impact of such conduct upon employee free choice cannot be determined.

CONCLUDING REMARKS

The Board has admitted to the different treatment accorded to employer and union inducements. The wisdom of its distinction is questionable especially when one begins to consider the economic benefits which may result from certification of the union as the bargaining representative, and which may arise independently of the collective bargaining process. One should also question the Board's unwillingness to attribute significance to union promises of future "bargaining gains." In every case the balance of power between management and the union must be clearly assessed.

The Board is overly protective of employee interests when it considers employer offers and grants of benefits during the election period. The Board expresses its concern in allowing the employer to function normally during this time, but it nevertheless restricts his managerial discretion by overlaying certain presumptions of illegality about decisions which are implemented during the campaign period. The lack of clarity in the Board's position has a compounding effect when the employer, uncertain about the lawfulness of implementing new benefits, announces his decision to postpone them until the question of representation has been resolved.

The Board should clarify the distinction between general campaign statements and specific promises made contingent upon the election results. It should also consider more closely the differ-

---

[119] 200 N.L.R.B. No. 120, 81 L.R.R.M. at 1596.

ence between longlasting benefits and temporary rewards. It is highly questionable whether the promise of a holiday, contingent upon a union's defeat, will affect the employee vote, when union representation offers a long-term relationship. In light of this attitude it is likewise inconsistent to maintain that union waivers of fees and offers of various benefits can have no impact upon the employees. The issue of the lawfulness of initiation fee waivers has been a long-standing problem, hopefully it has been resolved by the recent Supreme Court decision. The Board likely will be faced with the task of interpreting the *Savair* case in the situations where the union extends the waiver beyond the election period. Its approach to the resolution of this question should be guided by the application of the reasoning the Court developed in its opinion in rejecting the Board's rule.

CHAPTER VI

Reprisals And Threats Of Reprisals For Nonallegiance

An earlier section of this study dealt with election objections arising from campaign statements which were phrased as economic predictions, opinions, and statements of position, but which were alleged to constitute implied or veiled threats of reprisal or economic injury for failure to support a party to the election. The particular problem for the Board in those cases was to draw the distinction between legitimate expression of views and unlawful restraint or coercion, in accord with Section 8(c) of the Act. Related conduct requiring a separate analysis involves actual reprisals and direct threats of reprisal against employees resulting from their nonallegiance to the employer or to the participating union.

The reprisals which may serve as the basis of objections challenging the outcome of an election almost exclusively consist of discriminatory treatment or discipline by an employer. The reprisal may take the form of a discharge, or some other action affecting the terms and conditions of employment. The Board evaluates these cases by attempting to determine the employer's motive for the alleged unlawful conduct. It may rely on several factors in making its analysis. Generally, where there are legitimate economic or managerial reasons supporting the particular discipline or treatment of the employee, there is no election interference, and the employer has the opportunity to provide a defense or justification for his conduct. Union reprisals, for the most part, are limited to affecting the employees' union membership status, and they rarely are raised as objections in representation election proceedings. A few reasons become readily apparent: if the union is the outsider seeking certification as the bargaining representative, the privileges and obligations of membership have not yet been established, and the union lacks the power to act; if it is the incumbent representative, understandably it may be reluctant to alienate employee support by outward reprisals.

On the other hand, threats of reprisal for employee nonsupport may originate with union agents or adherents who may suggest physical violence or other retaliation against workers who fail to aid their cause. As we shall see, the Board does not consider the union to be in a position to coerce employees by means of threats of economic reprisal. A difficult subject of analysis, from the standpoint of clear and consistent policy, concerns threats by rank-and-file employees or other persons which are not directly attributable to the union. Statements also may come from company representatives which threaten to discharge, discriminate against, or impose more onerous working conditions on employees who support the union.

The primary problem for the Board in this general area is not one of reconciling its holdings with Section 8(c), since this provision of the Act specifically exempts threats of reprisal or force from protection. Rather, the problem in most instances is to determine when such threats have become serious enough to warrant setting aside an otherwise valid election. We must remember that labor relations are not maintained in a tearoom environment and that a certain amount of rough language and intimidation is both expected and unavoidable. At times the suggestion has been raised that the secrecy of the voting booth offers protection to a worker from these less than "laboratory conditions." [1] To void every election wherein threatening remarks have been exchanged would be both impractical and unnecessary.

Accordingly, the Board has adopted a general policy of voiding elections on the basis of campaign threats of reprisal only when it finds that the threats have created an "environment of tension or coercion" precluding the exercise of employee free choice.[2] In determining whether particular threats approach this standard, the Board may consider several factors: the content of the statement; the means of communication; the person who made the threat; the number of employees affected; and the timing of the threat in relation to the election. As with other election standards, the Board applies these factors on a case-by-case basis, and consequently, no precise formula exists for determining how much weight any one factor should be accorded. An understanding of the Board's regulation of conduct in these situations can only come from a review and comparison of many decisions.

---

[1] Stern Brothers, 87 N.L.R.B. 16, 25 L.R.R.M. 1061 (1949).

[2] NLRB v. Zelrich Co., 344 F.2d 1011, 59 L.R.R.M. 2225 (5th Cir. 1965). Monroe Auto Equipment Co., 186 N.L.R.B. 90, 75 L.R.R.M. 1340 (1970).

EMPLOYER REPRISALS

The freedom of choice necessary to employees in a representation election can be effectively destroyed by employer reprisals for nonallegiance. These actions constitute interference when they occur during the critical election period. The Board's task becomes one of separating legitimate disciplinary or remedial action from discrimination against union supporters. Of great significance to the protection of employee rights and to the regulation of this type of conduct is the fact that such retaliatory measures also violate Section 8(a)(3) of the Act. As a result, the Board quite often has entertained representation election objections in the context of an unfair labor practice proceeding.[3]

A reprisal represents a completed act rather than the threat of one, but, in many cases, discriminatory treatment displaying anti-union animus may indicate to other workers supporting the union that they too may face the same treatment.[4] However, because of the close relationship between the 8(a)(3) violation and election interference in the majority of the cases, the Board has not been compelled to provide sufficient and clear-cut guidelines to be used in evaluating the impact of particular employer actions upon the election results. The accepted patern of Board reasoning is that conduct which violates Section 8(a)(3) *a fortiori* interferes with the election.

The error in this logic was demonstrated in *Ablon Poultry & Egg Co.*,[5] where the Board held that there was an 8(a)(3) violation because an employee was discharged for leading a walkout to protest working conditions at the company. His conduct was found to be protected concerted activity under Section 7 of the NLRA. In addition to its disposition of the unfair labor practice charge, the Board set aside the election. However, the discharge had not been an action directed against the union or in response

---

[3] As indicated earlier, most election objections alleging acts of reprisal are raised by the union. This study does not attempt to evaluate all of the considerations and factors which have been raised in the many Board decisions dealing with employer 8(a)(3) unfair labor practices. For more detailed analysis within this area, see Comment, *Proving An 8(a)(3) Violation: The Changing Standard*, 114 U. PA. L. REV. 866 (1966); Getman, *Section 8(a)(3) of the NLRA and the Effort to Insulate Free Employee Choice*, 32 U. CHI. L. REV. 735 (1965).

[4] *See* Morehead City Garment Co., Inc., 94 N.L.R.B. 245, 28 L.R.R.M. 1038, *enforced*, 191 F.2d 1021, 29 L.R.R.M. 2023 (4th Cir. 1951).

[5] 134 N.L.R.B. 827, 49 L.R.R.M. 1297 (1961).

to its campaign activities. Furthermore, it was shown that the employer had not associated this employee with the organizing activities of the union during the election period.[6] Apparently, the Board was influenced by the fact that the discharge took place two days before the election. The implied reasoning of the decision appears to be that the discriminatory conduct was a restraint upon the free and fair election, even though it was unrelated in substance or by intent to the representation election campaign activities. The relationship between the reprisal for individual concerted activity and the employees' expression of free choice in the election by no means was evident.

In contrast to *Ablon Poultry*, the *E. J. Kelly Co.* case [7] held that the employer did not interfere with the election by hiring three new employees while an employee on strike had requested and had been denied reemployment. The Board said that the incident did not permit an inference that employee free choice had been affected. A major factor in support of the decision was that there was no unfair labor practice in the case since the striker had been permanently replaced. The sounder approach in such cases would emphasize the relevancy of the unlawful activity to the interests and issues related to the election campaign period itself.

The *Union Twist Drill Co.*[8] indicates that the employees must be aware of the existence of the reprisal at the time of the election. Therefore, it would seem reasonable to assert that absent knowledge by the workers of an 8(a)(3) violation, the existence of the unfair labor practice would not justify setting aside an election unless the Board were relying upon implied or constructive knowledge. It would also follow that consideration must be given to the *de minimis* effect of discriminatory reprisals involv-

---

[6] The Board said that this was not a necessary element of its decision. However, in several cases the Board has used employer knowledge of employee prounion activity as a factor in establishing the employer's unlawful motive. See The Faulhaber Co., 191 N.L.R.B. No. 49, 77 L.R.R.M. 1690 (1971); Associated Mills, 190 N.L.R.B. No. 8, 77 L.R.R.M. 1133 (1971); Park Edge Sheridan Meats, Inc., 146 N.L.R.B. 289, 55 L.R.R.M. 1296 (1964). See also The Bama Co., 145 N.L.R.B. 1141, 55 L.R.R.M. 1108 (1964), wherein the Board said that an indispensable element in the matter of a discriminatory discharge was whether the employer had knowledge of the employee's activities.

[7] 99 N.L.R.B. 791, 30 L.R.R.M. 1130 (1952).

[8] 124 N.L.R.B. 1143, 44 L.R.R.M. 1610 (1959).

ing only one or a few employees. The Board, however, has not paid direct attention to these points.

As noted earlier, discriminatory reprisals may take several forms. A discharge or suspension is quite common.[9] Further types of discriminatory treatment include demotion,[10] transfer between jobs,[11] denial of overtime,[12] refusal to hire union adherents,[13] and assignment to disagreeable tasks.[14] In every case, the Board seeks to ascertain the employer's motive to determine if the specific treatment of the employee was a discriminatory reprisal in response to union campaign activity. The employer may defend his conduct by raising economic or business reasons as a justification for his actions. In most cases, a variety of factors are combined in establishing an employer's unlawful motive in his treatment of an employee. Essentially it is a matter of weighing the proferred evidence and resolving the competing assertions. A specific purpose to thwart unionization does not have to be demonstrated. Instead, the Board may accept evidence of disparate employee treatment,[15] employer knowledge of employee

---

[9] Nebraska Bag Processing Co., 122 N.L.R.B. 654, 43 L.R.R.M. 1172 (1958); The Bama Co., 145 N.L.R.B. 1141, 55 L.R.R.M. 1108 (1964).

[10] The Faulhaber Co., 191 N.L.R.B. No. 49, 77 L.R.R.M. 1690 (1971).

[11] Associated Mills, 190 N.L.R.B. No. 8, 77 L.R.R.M. 1133 (1971). The Board concluded that the transfer was for the purpose of isolating the employee from the other workers. The employee was a known leader of the union drive.

[12] Buddy Schoellkopf Products, Inc., 164 N.L.R.B. 660, 65 L.R.R.M. 1231 (1967).

[13] Morehead City Garment Co., Inc., 94 N.L.R.B. 245, 28 L.R.R.M. 1038 (1951). The Board held that the employer interfered with the election by guaranteeing that only antiunion persons would thereafter be employed, thereby, exerting to that extent a degree of control over the election.

[14] United Moving & Storage, Inc., 151 N.L.R.B. 1413, 58 L.R.R.M. 1625 (1965). The employee was discharged for refusing to work with another employee. The Board found there was no interference because of earlier discharges upon similar grounds. The dissent felt the employer made no attempt to accommodate the employee's wishes.

[15] Big Three Industrial Gas, 181 N.L.R.B. 1125, 73 L.R.R.M. 1620 (1970); *accord*, NLRB v. Fashion Fair, 399 F.2d 764, 68 L.R.R.M. 2964 (6th Cir. 1968). *See* Ely & Walker, 151 N.L.R.B. 636, 58 L.R.R.M. 1513 (1965), where the Board also said that a discriminatory motive otherwise established is not disproved by the employer's showing that he did not weed out every union adherent.

prounion activity,[16] employer's expressed hostility to the union,[17] and the timing of the particular action.[18] The significance of these elements individually cannot be determined adequately, since, in each case, the factual situation requires an appropriate examination of the charges which often integrate several alternative allegations. The charging party must establish a *prima facie* case before the burden of justifying his conduct shifts to the employer. Again, there is no standardized composition for the *prima facie* case.

The employer in his defense may assert an employee's poor performance,[19] his misconduct,[20] or particular economic or business conditions [21] as reasons for the discipline or other treatment of the worker. In a relatively recent case, *Great Southwest Warehouses, Inc.*,[22] the Board rejected an employer's claim of misconduct as the basis for the discipline of a worker. He had been discharged for allegedly threatening and intimidating other employees for failure to join the union. The employee was informed in writing of the basis for the discharge, and apparently he acknowledged the stated reasons without protest. Shortly after the discharge and prior to the election, the employer posted on the company bulletin board a letter citing the specific reasons for the discharge. In addition, the employer declared that any employee could engage in lawful union activity, but that all future

---

[16] *See* cases cited at note 6, *supra.*

[17] Rish Equipment Co., 150 N.L.R.B. 1185, 58 L.R.R.M. 1274 (1965). *See also* Sarkes Tarzian, Inc., 157 N.L.R.B. 1193, 61 L.R.R.M. 1513 (1966), where the employer's hostility was established by repeated violations of the Act.

[18] The Bama Co., 145 N.L.R.B. 1141, 55 L.R.R.M. 1108 (1964). The discharge was one month before the election. In Bryan Mfg. Co., 94 N.L.R.B. 1331, 28 L.R.R.M. 1202 (1951), a four-month interval between employer interrogation of a worker and that individual's discharge was insufficient to establish a discriminatory motive.

[19] Radio Corp. of America, 90 N.L.R.B. 1989, 26 L.R.R.M. 1416 (1950). A legitimate reason included work spoilage by the employee.

[20] Harvey Radio Laboratories, Inc., 63 N.L.R.B. 892, 17 L.R.R.M. 33 (1945). *Cf.* Bryan Mfg. Co., 94 N.L.R.B. 1331, 28 L.R.R.M. 1202 (1951), where the discharge was approved dispite intermittent enforcement of a rule.

[21] California Cedar Products Co., 99 N.L.R.B. 341, 30 L.R.R.M. 1073 (1952). A demonstrated lack of work supported employee layoffs at the time of the election.

[22] 183 N.L.R.B. No. 75, 74 L.R.R.M. 1479 (1970).

conduct involving threats and intimidation would be handled in a similar fashion. The union raised objections to the election and filed unfair labor practice charges as a result of the discharge of this worker. At the Board hearing, three employees testified that they had been threatened by the worker. However, the individual denied making the threats. The Board credited his testimony, and as a result it set aside the election. Both the discharge and the posting of the letter were found to constitute unlawful interference since they were based on the unfounded allegations of threats.

This case illustrates a substantial weakness in the Board's policy of setting aside representation elections on the basis of alleged employer reprisals. Whether or not the discharge in this case was a lawful one should not have been dispositive of the election interference charge. The unfair labor practice could have been resolved by means of the normal employee reinstatement remedy. The employer's conduct during the election period did not evidence or suggest an antiunion motive designed to affect the outcome of the election.[23] Even though the discharged employee was found to have been a moving force in the campaign, the facts indicated that the employer took disciplinary action only after three employees had complained of intimidation and threats. Also, he clearly informed the entire work force of the reason for the discharge and assured them that legitimate prounion activity would be respected. The fact that the Board subsequently discredited the testimony of the complaining workers should not have been a basis for determining that employee free choice had been interfered with as a result of the discharge.

UNION DISCIPLINE

The Act makes it an unfair labor practice for a union to take action against an employee in reprisal for the exercise of his statutory rights.[24] It is also a violation of the NLRA for a union "to cause or attempt to cause an employer to discriminate against

---

[23] While it would be mere conjecture to attribute reasons for the employee's silence at the time of discharge, the failure to protest would have served to reinforce the employer's reasonable belief of the employees' charges, and it could have led the workers to evaluate on its face the published reasons for the discharge, as stated in the letter.

[24] 29 U.S.C. § 158 (b) (1) (A) (1970).

an employee. . . ." [25] However, a proviso in Section 8(b)(1)(A) of the Act expressly acknowledges the right of the union to regulate its internal membership affairs and discipline.

Unlawful union reprisals against its employee-members may occur under a variety of factual situations. Such conduct, however, has been an infrequent basis for employer objections charging the union with election interference. Certain practical considerations, suggested earlier, provide a degree of explanation for the absence of litigation upon this issue. However, there is a relationship, which has received little attention by the Board, which exists between certain cases of union discipline of its members occurring during the election period and the maintenance of the requisite "laboratory conditions" in that period.

A number of cases have been reported where the union has taken disciplinary action against an employee for filing a decertification petition. The question of a union unfair labor practice under Section 8(b)(1)(A) most often has been the only issue raised in those proceedings. However, in *United States Steel Corp.*[26] the Board stated that there was no significant distinction between employee conduct directed toward decertifying a union and conduct directed toward replacing the incumbent union with another one. This analogy is important because the decisions reached in these cases and the policy considerations they raise, under appropriate circumstances, would prevail in a representation election proceeding where the discipline was alleged as election interference.

The general rule is that a union does not violate the Act by suspending or expelling an employee for filing a decertification petition[27] since this constitutes permissible union discipline in accordance with the proviso to Section 8(b)(1)(A).[28] In *Smith-*

---

[25] *Id.* at § 158(b)(2).

[26] 189 N.L.R.B. No. 108, 77 L.R.R.M. 1027 (1971).

[27] This issue is clearly distinguishable from the case where the union takes disciplinary action against an employee because he has filed unfair labor practice charges against the union. The Supreme Court in NLRB v. Marine & Shipbuilding Workers, 391 U.S. 418, 68 L.R.R.M. 2257 (1968), upheld a Board rule that such union conduct was an unfair labor practice.

[28] Pittsburg-Des Moines Steel Co., 154 N.L.R.B. 692, 60 L.R.R.M. 1008 (1965); Tawas Tube Products, Inc., 151 N.L.R.B. 46, 58 L.R.R.M. 1330 (1965).

Lee Co.[29] the Board extended protection to the act of firing an employee from the union shop committee and barring him from union office for having filed a decertification petition. The lawfulness of these disciplinary measures has been justified by the Board on the basis that the union is merely defending its status as the bargaining representative. A distinction from the above rule was drawn in *Blackhawk Tanning Co.*,[30] where the Board held that the union committed an unfair labor practice when it fined an employee for circulating a decertification petition. The majority held that the act of fining was a punitive measure designed to discourage its employee-members from seeking access to the Board's process. Their reasoning was that the union had not improved its defensive posture by imposing the fine, since the dissident worker could still campaign against the Union while remaining a member of the organization. This would suggest that a fine accompanied by suspension or expulsion might be lawful.[31] The more persuasive argument was presented in a concurring opinion to the case by Member Brown, who stated that expulsion (or suspension) would have no effect upon an employee seeking to eliminate the very presence of the union in the company, and, thus, would be lawful. However, a fine imposed upon that employee was a "meaningful restraint" upon the exercise of his rights because it was a legally enforceable claim against him.[32] This reasoning perhaps could be used as the basis for disallowing a fine imposed concurrently with a suspension (or perhaps expulsion) of a member.

All of these cases have dealt with decertification election situations, and more importantly they have exclusively entertained the question of union discipline as an unfair labor practice. They have not provided substantial guidelines for arguing by analogy

---

[29] 182 N.L.R.B. No. 129, 74 L.R.R.M. 1201 (1970). *See also* Printing Pressmen, Local No. 481 [Westvaco Corp.], 183 N.L.R.B. No. 125, 74 L.R.R.M. 1698 (1970).

[30] 178 N.L.R.B. No. 25, 72 L.R.R.M. 1049 (1969), *enforced sub nom.* NLRB v. Molders, Local 125, 442 F.2d 92, 77 L.R.R.M. 2067 (7th Cir. 1971).

[31] In Pittsburg-Des Moines Steel Co. at note 28, *supra*, the original complaint included both a union imposed fine and suspension, but the fine was withdrawn by the union and the Board stated that the fine had not become an operative factor in the case.

[32] The dissenting Members Fanning and Jenkins unpersuasively argued that there was no distinction between a fine and expulsion. They would have imposed upon the employee the duty of resigning from the union prior to or shortly after engaging in decertification activity.

the impact of discipline of an employee upon the results of an election. *Tawas Tube Products, Inc.*[33] is the case which served as the foundation in the formulation of the Board's policy dealing with the lawfulness of union discipline. The case is even more important for our purpose because it involved a charge of election interference raised against the union, rather than of an unfair labor practice.

The employer's objection to the outcome of the decertification election in *Tawas Tube* was based upon the expulsion from the union of two employees for having filed a decertification petition and having actively supported the decertification movement. The complaint alleged that the conduct of the union restrained and coerced the other employees in the unit during the election. The regional director felt that the disciplinary action against the two workers inhibited the other employees from supporting the decertification cause, and consequently ordered that the election results should be set aside. The Board disagreed and held the expulsions did not constitute election interference, but rather they were a matter of internal union discipline and did not affect the individuals' employment interests. The Board continued by saying that the ground for the expulsions related to a mater of legitimate union concern—its continued existence as the bargaining representative—and one which properly constituted a subject matter of internal discipline. The Board felt that it would be difficult for the union to carry on an election campaign if the two employees, as members, retained their rights and privileges in the organization.

The Board correctly recognized in its opinion that any permissible union discipline must not affect the employment interests of the workers.[34] However, it did not elaborate on the scope of these "interests." Likely, they would include discharge, transfer, recall, etc. It is submitted, however, that the case offers a shortsighted view to the question of employment interests and to the conclusion that expulsion of these workers from the union did not possess a restraining effect upon the voters' free choice. The significance of union membership does not consist simply of affiliation with an organization which is serving as the bargaining representative. More importantly, there may be specific property interests arising from membership in a union which may become

---

[33] 151 N.L.R.B. 46, 58 L.R.R.M. 1330 (1965).

[34] Presumably, this would have to be the case under a union security clause in the collective bargaining agreement.

inseparable from "employment interests." [35]   These may include pension, medical, disability, death, and other economic benefits. One writer commenting on their significance remarked, "These rights, which are in the nature of insurance, frequently do have substantial value, and in practically all unions the expelled member forfeits all rights to benefit payments." [36]   This statement was made over twenty years ago, and since that time the composition of union-sponsored benefits has been greatly expanded.

The effect of the Board's opinion could be to force the workers, who are unhappy with an incumbent bargaining agent, to face the potential loss of their benefits in order to exercise their full rights under the Act. For example, the decision to sponsor a decertification petition may not indicate a total rejection of the principle of unionization, but it may evidence a desire to change representatives, or to inspire reforms by the incumbent. However, under the concept of majority selection of the bargaining agent, workers who organized the drive, who were expelled by the union, and who were in the minority in the election could find themselves permanently deprived of certain benefits, even though they were willing to abide by the reaffirmed desires of the majority.

A greater weakness in the Board's decision in the *Tawas Tube* case lies in its application of the standards applicable to an 8(b)(1)(A) unfair labor practice charge to evaluate the appropriateness of the disciplinary measures taken against the two employees and the effect of the action upon the election. In other areas, the Board's long stated policy has been that conduct may be found to have interfered with an election even if it did not constitute a basis for an unfair labor practice charge.[37]   To be consistent, instead of reaching the decision that the expulsions were proper forms of internal union discipline, not in violation of Section 8(b)(1)(A), and using that conclusion as the basis for rejecting the election interference charge, the Board should have focused on the separate question of the potential affect of the

---

[35] In dealing with a different issue, one court stated that "an improper expulsion has been viewed as a violation of a member's contract with his union . . . or as a deprivation of the member's property rights in the assets of the union." Hurwitz v. Directors Guild of America, Inc., 364 F.2d 67, 71, 62 L.R.R.M. 2653, 2656 (2d Cir. 1966).

[36] Summers, *Legal Limitations on Union Discipline*, 64 HARV. L. REV. 1049, 1052 (1951).

[37] General Shoe Corp., 77 N.L.R.B. 124, 21 L.R.R.M. 1337 (1948).

expulsion of the two workers upon the other employees' ability to make a free and reasoned choice in the election. The workers may have been unwilling to vote against continued representation by the incumbent union in light of the action taken against the two employees.

> The number of discipline cases, however, cannot fully measure the impact of union discipline. Far greater is the repressive effect it may have on all other members of the union who witness its use. A few well-placed, severe penalties can mark the danger lines which cautious union members will not dare to cross. Expulsion of a rebellious leader can demoralize an entire faction.[38]

While the above statement specifically relates to unlawful discipline by a union, it also suggests that union conduct, protected by the proviso to Section 8(b)(1)(A), nevertheless may have a substantial impact upon employees in an election who may not appreciate the specific legislative intent of the proviso to Section 8(b)(1)(A).

EMPLOYER THREATS

One of the employer's strongest bargaining weapons is his economic strength. During the representation election period the employer may draw upon this power in formulating campaign proposals or in making replies to union campaign assertions. This aspect of employer conduct was discussed earlier in the section dealing with promises and predictions.[39] We also considered the employer's use of his economic position under the subject "Offers and Inducements."[40] Employer threats of reprisal for employee nonallegiance relate to a more basic exercise of economic power. The question of the privileged expression of opinions and views is not at issue; the Board's sole concern is to ascertain the relevant circumstances which may have led to a restraint upon free choice.

In essence, the threat of reprisal is not a campaign tool, but rather it is a display of power in the attempt to chill individuals' desires to support or assist the union. The most common threat is to discharge the employee for his activities.[41] Other

---

[38] Summers, at 1050.

[39] *See* Chapter III at pp. 63-68, *supra*.

[40] *See* Chapter V at pp. 104-128, *supra*.

[41] Playskool Mfg. Co., 140 N.L.R.B. 1417, 52 L.R.R.M. 1260 (1963). In Union Aluminum Co., 116 N.L.R.B. 1331, 38 L.R.R.M. 1470 (1956), the

examples of proscribed conduct may include threats of harder
working conditions,[42] black-listing workers,[43] enforcing discriminatory work rules,[44] and eliminating part-time jobs.[45]

Certain employer statements because of their ambiguity or
insignificance must be summarily dismissed as alleged violations.
In commenting upon this point, one court suggested that the
substance of an alleged threat should not consist of "mere words
of interrogation or perfunctory remarks not threatening or intimidating in themselves . . . standing naked and alone." [46] The
Board has indicated there must be some indication that the employer will use his economic power.[47] Thus, it dismissed as unobjectionable the statement, "I feel sorry for young married couples
with children if the union gets in." In an early case the Board
held there was no interference when a foreman told an employee,
who had been a representative to two shop organizing committee meetings, that he should "stick close to his machine and keep
his nose to the grindstone." [48]

In *Field Container Corp.*[49] the remark, "that's your opinion,
you know what you are doing?" after an employee had expressed

employer threatened employees with discharge for failure to wear badges
bearing the words, "I'm Voting No." In setting aside the election the Board
said the threat was not diminished by the fact an employee did not wear
the badge. *See also* Murray Ohio Mfg. Co., 156 N.L.R.B. 840, 61 L.R.R.M.
1146 (1966), where the employer issued the threats in order to prevent
the wearing of prounion buttons.

[42] GTE Automatic Electric, Inc., 196 N.L.R.B. No. 134, 80 L.R.R.M. 1155
(1972). The employer threatened to make the employees paint floors and to
ride them so they would quit.

[43] South Bay Daily Breeze, 160 N.L.R.B. 1850, 62 L.R.R.M. 1252 (1966).

[44] *Id.*

[45] Low Bros. National Market, Inc., 180 N.L.R.B. 592, 73 L.R.R.M. 1101
(1970). It is noteworthy that the employer's statement was to the effect that
in a discussion with a union official he was told the union would have no
need for part-time workers if it became the representative of the employees.
This constituted interference and an 8(a)(1) violation.

[46] National Can Corp. v. NLRB, 374 F.2d 796, 806, 64 L.R.R.M. 2607, 2615
(7th Cir. 1967).

[47] Barber Colman Co., 116 N.L.R.B. 24, 38 L.R.R.M. 1184 (1956).

[48] S&S Corrugated Paper Machinery Co., Inc., 89 N.L.R.B. 1363, 26 L.R.R.M.
1112 (1950).

[49] 178 N.L.R.B. 536, 72 L.R.R.M. 1156 (1969).

a desire to be a union election observer, was held by the Board not to constitute an improper threat of reprisal. The trial examiner in that case had reasoned oppositely, stating that the remark was an implied threat that the employer in the future might not treat him as well. The distinction between unlawful threats of reprisal and mere expressions of rebuke or intimidation comes down to a matter of judgment. It is more easily demonstrated by example than expressed as an objective standard.

There are several factors which have been recognized to be of relevance in the determination of election interference. One court suggested that these elements would include the employer's history of hostility to the union, his objection to collective bargaining in principle, the absence of other threats or reprisals, and any reassurances by the employer to the employees of their freedom to vote as they choose.[50] In addition the Board has indicated on a few occasions that the position of the official making the statement may be a pertinent consideration.[51] In another case, *International Mfg. Co., Inc.*,[52] the Board stated that not the number of instances of threats or the number of employees involved, but rather the likelihood or reasonableness of interference resulting from the statements was the determinative factor.

The reasoning in policy as expressed by the *International Mfg. Co.* case has led to situations where the Board has ignored the *de minimis* effects of particular instances of employer threats in reaching their ultimate determination that the election should be set aside. An early case, *Threads-Inc.*,[53] involved the statement by an employer that he "could see why a company might be a little hesitant in hiring a person or his wife when it is well known that he has shown union tendencies, as that would be another vote for the union." [54] The Board held the statement to be a thinly veiled threat of probable economic retaliation. There was other conduct, including interrogation, additional coercive remarks, and the threat of blackballing used in support of the decision to set aside the election. Despite an argument that the

---

50 National Can Corp. v. NLRB at note 46, *supra*.

51 Threads-Inc., 124 N.L.R.B. 968, 44 L.R.R.M. 1553 (1959).

52 167 N.L.R.B. 769, 66 L.R.R.M. 1156 (1967).

53 At note 51, *supra*.

54 124 N.L.R.B. at 978, 44 L.R.R.M. at 1556.

employer's statement may have been sufficiently vague as to the likeliehood of action on his part, the greater criticism arises from the fact that only seven of 508 workers were found to have been coerced. The Board based its decision to set aside the election on its wide degree of discretion in ensuring employee free choice.

A greater tendency to conclude that employer threats have affected the election arises when election objections are accompanied by unfair labor practice charges. In *Playskool Mfg. Co.*,[55] decided in 1963, the the Board, citing the *Dal-Tex* rule held there was an 8(a)(1) violation and election interference. There was evidence of threats of discharge, economic loss, and the imposition of additional job burdens. Also, the employer told one worker, "better watch your step. . . . I hate to see you get fired." The trial examiner found that an unfair labor practice had occurred, but he reasoned that there was no election interference since only three employees of an approximate force of 228 had been confronted with the threats, and there was no evidence to suggest an awareness by the other employees of these events. Without evidence to the contrary, the Board overruled the trial examiner stating that conduct in violation of the Act was *a fortiori* election interference.

A later decision by the Board, *M&W Marine Ways, Inc.*,[56] followed the same approach. The employer made a statement to the effect that many things could happen to change the union's chances for victory and that employees who supported the union would be discharged if the union won. The trial examiner held the employer had violated Section 8(a)(1), but he felt there were insufficient grounds to set aside the election since the violation had involved a single worker and had occurred one and one-half months before the election. There was no indication that the knowledge of the threat had been circulated among the other sixty employees. The Board again disagreed with the trial examiner and said that the threat "was made in the context of an election campaign charged by [the Employer's] openly expressed opposition to the Union." [57] Lacking additional evidence, the Board also rejected the conclusion that the other employees were not aware of the unlawful conduct.

One further case, *Tennessee Handbags*,[58] lends a point of com-

---

[55] 140 N.L.R.B. 1417, 52 L.R.R.M. 1260 (1963).

[56] 165 N.L.R.B. 191, 65 L.R.R.M. 1334 (1967).

[57] *Id.* at 191, 65 L.R.R.M. at 1336.

[58] 179 N.L.R.B. 1045, 72 L.R.R.M. 1576 (1969).

parison to this area because the Board dismissed election interference charges in spite of the presence of an 8(a)(1) violation.
After reviewing the facts it determined that a supervisor had
threatened one employee with discharge or layoff as a result of
his campaigning activities. The Board held that the event was
too isolated within a work force of over four hundred employees
to constitute interference.

Without undertaking a complete reevaluation of the facts of these
cases in an attempt to point out all the inconsistencies and weak-
nesses of the Board's reasoning, we would call specific attention
to the Board's unwillingness or failure to assess carefully the
likelihood of interference arising from threats of reprisal.

UNION THREATS

In its policy of regulating union conduct, the Board has
adopted certain presumptions relating to the force and effect of
union actions. We have noted in previous chapters that the Board
does not consider employers and unions to be adversaries of equal
strength. Because of its position as an outsider seeking to gain
bargaining rights for the workers, the union is generally presumed
to lack any economic stronghold over the workers. As a result,
the Board is less likely to infer added or hidden implications from
statements made on the union's behalf.

The types of union threats commonly raised as objections to a
representation election proceeding include threats of bodily harm,
violence, intimidation, and economic injury. The scope of union
economic threats generally has been limited to matters involving
job security. The overall difference in the substantive nature of
union threats suggests that different considerations may be appropriate in assessing their impact upon the employees. The
Board has not done this in all cases. Arguably, physical threats
and intimidation by co-workers and union agents may have a
deeper, lasting, and more personal effect because of the close day-
to-day working relationships involved. There may be limits to the
protection offered by the secrecy of the polling booth in some
instances. Although these and other theories are difficult to
verify, it seems that in light of the Board's current administration of its "laboratory standards," these considerations should
have been fully deliberated.

An area of particular concern exists where threats have been
issued by rank-and-file workers or union adherents, and the issue

of interference is raised. Only rarely will the Board set aside an election based on such conduct. In general, however, the Board has determined that prounion conduct not directly attributable to the union should be accorded less weight in terms of potential restraint and coercion.[59] The Board's approach in this regard provides an interesting contrast with its reasoning regarding antiunion conduct not directly attributable to the employer, a subject discussed in a later chapter.[60]

Economic Threats

As previously indicated, the most common economic threat made by a union suggests to the employees that they will lose their jobs or suffer decreased job security if they fail to support the union. The Board generally has evaluated such statements on the basis of the union's power to carry out its threat. The alleged statement must not be ambiguous.[61] In order to constitute election interference, the Board has said that the threat of job loss normally must be accompanied by some indication of the union's ability to take positive measures to carry it out. The Board's application of this rationale, however, has wavered at times.

The union in *Globe Motors Inc.*[62] stated that if it won the election there would be a closed shop and all nonsupporters of the union would lose their jobs. Here the Board said there was no threat, since the employees were capable of evaluating the assertions and the statements were not within the union's jurisdiction. However, in *Knapp Sherill Co.*,[63] the union told employees that if they did not support the union and it won, they would lose their jobs or have subsequent difficulties with the employer in their jobs. The Board found that the statements were "clear threats" that the union was proposing to discriminate against those employees in its role as the bargaining representative.

---

[59] Orleans Mfg. Co., 120 N.L.R.B. 630, 42 L.R.R.M. 1016 (1958).

[60] *See* "Third Party Interference" at Chap. IX, *infra*.

[61] Electric Wheel Co., 120 N.L.R.B. 1644, 42 L.R.R.M. 1244 (1958). The Board found ambiguous the statement to an employee that he would find himself "out on the street," or "on the outside looking in." An additional circumstance of the case was that the employee was friendly with the union committee member who made the remark.

[62] 123 N.L.R.B. 30, 43 L.R.R.M. 1365 (1959).

[63] 171 N.L.R.B. 1547, 68 L.R.R.M. 1286 (1968).

Elsewhere, the Board has suggested that if the substance of a statement implies the need for employer acquiescence, the Board will not regard it as a threat standing alone.[64] Thus, where the union said that if it did not win the election the employer would lay off the workers, the Board said this was at most "an accusation against the Employer."[65]

Although the ultimate authority to hire and fire employees rests with the employer, certain statements by the union may carry indicia of control so that the Board may find that they constituted threats interfering with employee free choice. In one case the union told the employees that if they did not vote for the union it would cause the employees of another company, also represented by that union, to refuse to handle this employer's products.[66] The Board found the statement to be a threat affecting the election outcome because the employees reasonably could have believed that the union was capable of carrying out its threat of a boycott, and that such a boycott could have adversely affected the employees' job interests. The Board further indicated that attempts by the company to dispel the effect of such statements were ineffective since "it was not in a position to control the actions of the [union] or its members"[67] at the other company.

In two cases, *Hurwitz Electrical Co., Inc.*[68] and *Sperry Rand Corp., Vickers Inc. Div.*,[69] the unions threatened to process disciplinary measures against those employee-members who did not support it in the election. Although the nature of the alleged union proceedings was not elaborated upon, the implied consequences were expulsion from the union and subsequent loss of jobs. The Board found such statements to be threats which interfered with the election. It was felt, apparently, that the employees could have believed that if union charges were brought, vari-

---

[64] Shoreline Enterprises of America, 114 N.L.R.B. 716, 37 L.R.R.M. 1048 (1955).

[65] Otis Elevator Co., 114 N.L.R.B. 1490, 1493, 37 L.R.R.M. 1198, 1199 (1955).

[66] Superior Wood Products, Inc., 145 N.L.R.B. 782, 55 L.R.R.M. 1042 (1964).

[67] *Id.* at 784, 55 L.R.R.M. at 1042.

[68] 146 N.L.R.B. 1265, 56 L.R.R.M. 1032 (1964).

[69] 152 N.L.R.B. 793, 59 L.R.R.M. 1196 (1965).

ous penalties might be imposed upon them, even though, in fact, the NLRA would have protected their job security.

The courts on several occasions have disagreed with the Board's disposition of election interference charges arising from union economic threats. The Court of Appeals for the Tenth Circuit in *NLRB v. Sanitary Laundry, Inc.*[70] in effect treated union threats on the same basis as employer threats. It overruled a Board decision, which held that the employer interfered with the first election by threatening strikes and economic hardships, and yet decided that the union did not interfere with the second election by threatening the employees with the loss of jobs.

The Ninth Circuit[71] held a union's threat to be cause for a rerun election where the union business agent telephoned an employee the evening before the election, asked him how he was going to vote, and mentioned that a supervisor did not like him and that "he had better watch himself." The court called this "veiled advice, carefully unexpressed as a threat, [which] could well be interpreted as coercive in view of all the circumstances surrounding it, and its particular timing."[72] There had been additional instances of intimidation and physical threats on which the court relied. The Board's decision in dismissing them also was overruled. In the decision, the court openly stated its impression that the Board had created a "double standard" in evaluating union and employer threats of reprisal.

In *NLRB v. Janler Plastic Mold Corp.*[73] the Court of Appeals for the Seventh Circuit said there should have been a hearing on the employer's objections to the election alleging union threats of job losses. The Board had dismissed the charges because there was no indication of the union's ability to carry out the threats, and because a secret ballot was deemed to have protected the workers from the impact of the threat. The court disagreed and said, "the allegations of threats of loss of jobs were sufficiently serious to call for a hearing and, if made close to the time of election, would furnish grounds for setting aside the election."[74]

---

[70] 441 F.2d 1368, 77 L.R.R.M. 2359 (10th Cir. 1971).

[71] Sonoco Products Co. v. NLRB, 443 F.2d 1334, 77 L.R.R.M. 2589 (9th Cir. 1971).

[72] *Id.* at 1337, 77 L.R.R.M. at 2591.

[73] 82 L.R.R.M. 2174 (7th Cir. 1972).

[74] 82 L.R.R.M. at 2176.

The Eighth Circuit also refused to accept the Board's conclusions on charges of union interference. In *Wilkinson Mfg. Co.
v. NLRB* [75] the union representative told an employee at an open
meeting that if the union got in it had ways of getting rid of
nonunion employees. Another worker was told to "shut up"
or she would lose her job. The Board held that the first statement was intended to mean the union could accommodate itself
to the presence of nonunion employees. It said that the second
incident was only a conditioned threat spoken out of irritation.
The court rejected these conclusions and emphasized that there
had been extensive discussions among the employees over the
first incident. This court also felt that the Board took a less
than even-handed approach in regulating the parties' conduct.
This was the second election since the first had been set aside
because of employer interference.

As the foregoing cases demonstrate, the Board places great
emphasis on the necessity of demonstrating that union threats
possess indicia of control and convey a likelihood of being carried out. There is an ever lingering presumption that, since the
union cannot hire and fire workers without the employer's cooperation, the employees will assess union threats dealing with
job security with that knowledge in mind. This is, of course,
another area in which the basis of the Board's approach is an
assumption about the probable mental processes of prospective
voters, which the Board has neither the objective data nor expert credentials to support. Recent court disagreement with the
Board's holdings in this area has focused on the existence of a
"double standard" in dealing with employer and union threats
of reprisal. There is no reason to expect that the courts would
object to a less restrictive approach to vague and expansive campaign "threats" by unions if they could be given some basis to
believe that the Board would apply such a lenient approach
equally to campaign statements made by employers.

Intimidation, Bodily Harm, or Violence

In addition to a restraint upon free choice, threats of personal
injury or violence, and intimidation may instill personal fear in
the employees' minds. The election procedures in those cases may
provide insufficient protection to dispell such fears, but the Board
has said that some threats "will not suffice to impeach an elec-

---

[75] 456 F.2d 298, 79 L.R.R.M. 2682 (8th Cir. 1972).

tion where the balloting is secret." [76] There have not been a substantial number of cases where the element of fear arising from union threats has been discussed at length. Consequently, the Board has not provided meaningful statements of its policy.

In an early case, *G. H. Hess, Inc.*,[77] an employee was threatened with economic reprisal and bodily harm if she appeared at the polls to vote. On the basis of the two statements the Board held that the union had engaged in election interference. The concurring opinion voiced a much stonger and more explicit reaction to the second threat. "[T]hreats calculated to keep employees from coming to the polls to exercise the franchise may never be tolerated by this Board, whatever the source and whatever their effect." [78] The Board's acceptance of this view at best is uncertain. In a subsequent opinion, *Mallinckrodt Chemical Works*,[79] the Board dismissed similar threats made against an employee. The worker had been ostracized by other employees since the time of an earlier election for having failed to support the union. At this time he was told they would treat him as "one of the gang" if he did not vote, but if he did vote, they would make him "so miserable on his job that he would be glad to get out." In addition, he was visited at home on the evening before the election and again was told that he would be treated as "one of the men" if he did not vote. The Board concluded that there were no threats of reprisal of the type normally affecting freedom of choice. It is true some of the threats had come from fellow employees, but the union's business agent also had been involved in the conduct involving this employee. The only apparent, although unpersuasive reason for the Board's decision was that the threats suggested ostracism rather than explicit injury or violence.

In order to support objections, threats of violence must be reasonably clear, and they must directly relate to events or issues surrounding the election. The point was brought up in *The Great Atlantic and Pacific Tea, Inc.*[80] A union representative in response to an employee's question about the union's attitude

---

[76] Stern Brothers, 87 N.L.R.B. 16, 19, 25 L.R.R.M. 1061, 1062 (1949).

[77] 82 N.L.R.B. 463, 23 L.R.R.M. 1581 (1949).

[78] *Id.* at 466, 23 L.R.R.M. at 1582.

[79] 86 N.L.R.B. 662, 24 L.R.R.M. 1674 (1949).

[80] 177 N.L.R.B. 942, 71 L.R.R.M. 1554 (1969).

toward strike breakers stated that workers could cross picket lines, but that "Most anything could happen. You could get your arm broke." Charges of interference were dismissed because the statement at most referred to a future period in time "after the election, namely, at a time after the [union] was selected, as bargaining representative. . . ." [81] In another case, *Kennametal, Inc.*,[82] the Board held there was no threat affecting the election from the publication by the union of articles dealing with strike violence and other alleged strong-arm-tactics used by union representatives against its members. The incidents of violence did not refer to the current campaign.

The Board has determined on occasion that union threats of violence or intimidation aimed at the parties to the election instead of the employees can serve as the basis for election interference. In *Gabriel Co. Automotive Division* [83] one union employed threats and strong-arm tactics against the officials of the competing union in order to impede its campaign effectiveness. The Board found that the conduct had violated the "atmosphere of free choice" in the election. In a more recent case the Board dealt with alleged threats, harassment, and intimidation of management representatives during the election period.[84] The conduct could not be attributed to the union and consequently the majority concluded there were insufficient facts to justify directing a second election. The Board did agree, in part, with the dissent by Chairman Miller that such threats could constitute election interference.[85]

THREATS BY UNION ADHERENTS

Traditionally the Board has been reluctant to set aside representation elections on the basis of threats issued by union adherents, which cannot be attributed directly to the union. Commonly, the individuals engaged in this conduct are employees sup-

---

[81] *Id.* at 942, 71 L.R.R.M. at 1555.

[82] 119 N.L.R.B. 1236, 41 L.R.R.M. 1267 (1958).

[83] 137 N.L.R.B. 1252, 50 L.R.R.M. 1369 (1962).

[84] Apcoa Division—ITT Consumer Service Corp., 202 N.L.R.B. No. 5, 82 L.R.R.M. 1588 (1973).

[85] Chairman Miller would have directed an evidentiary hearing to determine if the alleged conduct was attributable to the union.

porting the union. The Board's attitude on such matters has been summarized in the following terms:

> While the Board will consider conduct not attributable to any of the parties in determining whether an election should be set aside, the Board accords less weight to such conduct than to conduct of the parties. The Board believes that the conduct of third persons tends to have less effect upon the voters than similar conduct attributable to the employer who has, or the union which seeks control over the employees' working conditions. Furthermore, were the Board to give the same weight to conduct by third persons as to conduct attributable to the parties, the possibility of obtaining quick and conclusive election results would be substantially diminished.[86]

To be sure, expeditious resolution of representation issues normally will benefit all of the parties concerned. One can argue further that it may be unfair to penalize a victorious union in an election by forcing it to incur the added expense of a rerun election as the result of conduct by individuals who are not subject to its control, and who are not subject to the provisions and prohibitions of Section 8(b) of the Act. However, the Board's policy is subject to question on certain points. For one thing, the Board seems to discount these considerations when evaluating objections based on third party conduct in *opposition* to unionization.[87] Further, the Board has not acknowledged the probability that threats suggesting injury and violence may be less dependent upon the status of the speaker as an election party than threats of an economic nature. One may question whether the recipient of a threat of the former type is any less likely to feel intimated simply because the speaker does not officially represent one of the parties.

When alleged threats have occurred during the election period, they should be evaluated pursuant to a common standard, regardless of the identity of the parties responsible for the conduct. The Board in dealing with employee threats has taken a different approach, as demonstrated by its decision in *Diamond State Poultry Co., Inc.*[88] holding in cases where threats were made during the campaign period by individuals who were not agents of either party, the test for determining this interference

---

[86] Orleans Mfg. Co., 120 N.L.R.B. 630, 633, 42 L.R.R.M. 1016, 1017 (1958).

[87] *See* Chapter IX, *infra.*

[88] 107 N.L.R.B. 3, 33 L.R.R.M. 1043 (1953).

was whether the election created "a general atmosphere of confusion and fear of reprisal."

The Board, by requiring this condition before it would overturn an election, arbitrarily created a standard of measuring conduct during the election period different from the "laboratory conditions" standard, which has been applied in other election cases. Arguably, the *Diamond State Poultry* test represents a less protectionist approach toward employees freedom of choice because it presents a more stringent evidentiary burden for the complaining party to satisfy thereby resulting in more dismissed election objections. Proof of such an "atmosphere" impliedly requires a showing of subjective reactions of fear and coercion whereas the "laboratory conditions" standard is measured by objective criteria, weighing events according to their presumed likelihood of interference. This analysis is not intended to call for an expansion of Board regulation of the conduct of union adherents. Rather, we note the inconsistency of the Board's approach because it casts doubts on the validity and necessity of the Board's requirement of the "laboratory standards" in regulating the conduct of the parties themselves. If a less stringent standard is acceptable in cases of third persons' conduct, why is it necessary to endure the expense and inefficiency of so many rerun elections as a result of marginal conduct by the parties themselves?

The judiciary has been critical of the creation of this double standard, and in many cases involving employee threats it has refused to enforce the Board's orders. A general comment on this problem was made by one court:

> It would seem to us, however, that the Board should apply a *single* standard against which it will measure the campaign conduct of *all* parties who might have interfered with employee free choice, weighing the conduct of each individual party according to the particular power he might possess. Such a test makes adequate allowance for setting aside an election whether, in a given context, either the employer or the union is the dominant party. Moreover, it permits an election to be set aside where neither is at fault, but where the Board agent or some outside party has interfered.[89]

Although we emphatically agree with the court that a single standard should be applied, it is submitted here that, contrary to the result suggested by the court in the above quoted decision, the

---

[89] Foremost Dairies of the South v. NLRB, 416 F.2d 392, 396-97 n.9, 71 L.R.R.M. 2663, 2666 (5th Cir. 1969).

standard applied should not be the "laboratory conditions" standard. Instead, there should be a uniform standard emphasizing voter self-reliance, which would make election results final and binding in all except the most glaring cases of interference, regardless of the source. The Board's rulings on objections to conduct by prounion individuals, therefore, warrant close examination since they seem to imply a more realistic view of the appropriate scope of agency regulation of campaign conduct than the Board's decisions in other areas indicate.

The *Diamond State Poultry* decision failed to provide adequate guidelines for evaluating future cases involving threats by union adherents. Subsequently, the Board generally had stated that "[t]he question of whether or not such an atmosphere existed . . . does not turn on the election results, but rather upon an analysis of the character and circumstances of the alleged objectionable conduct." [90] However, the opinion did not mention factors which would suggest the existence of a coercive atmosphere, or which likely would create the conditions leading to an "atmosphere of fear and reprisal." A general understanding exists that the types of threats referred to are those suggesting the likelihood of violence and personal injury.[91] Economic threats made by union adherents have not been sufficient to warrant a new election.[92]

The decision in *Poinsett Lumber & Mfg. Co.*[93] typically is cited as an example of the Board's application of *Diamond State Poultry* to a set of facts where the conclusion was reached that employer threats had created "an atmosphere of fear and reprisal . . . and that a free election was thereby rendered impossible." [94] This case is significant in that it provides a greater

---

[90] Central Photocolor Co., 195 N.L.R.B. No. 153, 79 L.R.R.M. 1568, 1569 (1972).

[91] *See* Al Long, Inc., 173 N.L.R.B. 447, 69 L.R.R.M. 1366 (1968), involving anonymous phone calls, threats of physical injury, bomb threats, property damage, and strike violence; General Truckdrivers Union, Local 980, 177 N.L.R.B. 579, 72 L.R.R.M. 1126 (1969), when acts of sabotage against the company were found to have created the fear of injury and death.

[92] *See* Allied Plywood Corp., 122 N.L.R.B. 959, 43 L.R.R.M. 1231 (1959). *Cf.* White's Uvalde Mines, 110 N.L.R.B. 278, 34 L.R.R.M. 1640 (1954), where an employee had been threatened with imprisonment. In many cases, however, threats of economic reprisal have been issued along with other threats.

[93] 116 N.L.R.B. 1732, 39 L.R.R.M. 1083 (1956).

[94] *Id.* at 1739, 39 L.R.R.M. at 1085.

understanding of *Diamond State Poultry.* The earlier decision
would seem to indicate that the Board openly acknowledged that
employee threats could interfere with an election, and that in
every case it would determine whether the specific threats created
conditions leading to an atmosphere of fear and confusion.

Poinsett Lumber, on the other hand, suggests that unusual circumstances in a case are necessary to prompt the Board to consider employee threats from the standpoint of election interference. The decision to direct a new election was reached as the
result of express manifestations of fear by certain employees
prior to the election. In discussing the threats of violence which
had occurred, the Board specifically noted that awareness of these
threats had spread throughout the plant, and that some workers
in fear had requested and had received police protection during
the election period.

What emerges from a review of the Board's subsequent decisions dealing with threats by union adherents is the understanding that extraordinary circumstances necessarily must be present
in those cases where the Board likely will find an interference
with the election. However, in *Trade Winds Co. v. NLRB* [95] the
Board apparently ignored such conditions. The employer challenged the results of the election alleging several threats against
employees' homes, families, and their lives. In addition, it was
shown that one woman had obtained a police escort to work, and
on election day one employee, whose voting eligibility was challenged by the union, swallowed his ballot when requested by the
Board agent to hand it over to him. The Board had refused to
conduct a hearing to investigate the employer's charges. The
court overruled this decision and said that a hearing was necessary to evaluate the merits of the case.

In placing the emphasis upon specific subjective reactions or
outward manifestations of fear by the workers, the Board de-
parts significantly from the approach it follows in cases where
statements by the parties themselves are in issue. Indeed, the
Board's rulings establish a virtual presumption that conduct
absent union authority has no effect upon the voters.[96] Thus,
although the results reached in such cases may represent a realistic approach to the Board's role as an election regulator, they

---

[95] 413 F.2d 1213, 71 L.R.R.M. 3033 (5th Cir. 1969), *rehearing den.,* 424 F.2d
549, 74 L.R.R.M. 2112 (5th Cir. 1970).

[96] *See, e.g.,* White Knight Mfg. Co., 195 N.L.R.B. No. 195, 79 L.R.R.M.
1638 (1972).

cannot logically coexist with the Board's insistence upon "laboratory standards" elsewhere. For, clearly, the Board's differentiation of cases on the basis of the "authority" of the speaker does not withstand scrutiny.

In *Urban Telephone Corp.*[97] an employee, acting as a self-appointed union campaigner, on several occasions threatened workers with injury, violence, and other reprisals. The Board dismissed the complaint because the employee was not an agent for the union and, therefore, possessed no authority. The dissenting opinion by Chairman Miller raised the question, which had not been discussed by the majority, of the effect of this conduct upon the overall atmosphere of the election. He was not willing to dismiss the complaint simply because of the absence of union authority. He pointed out that the union victory had been close (17 to 15), and that the employee had a reputation for violence. The majority had not even raised these points.

A similar attitude was demonstrated recently in *Dixon Distributing Co.*[98] The majority dismissed a request for a hearing on employer election objections and held there was no interference. The Board relied in part on disavowals of the employee threats by the union business agent. However, Member Kennedy, dissenting, elaborated on the conditions which he argued were pertinent to this case. The voting unit consisted of only seven employees; there was evidence of several threats of physical violence; and the employee engaging in the conduct was a leader of the union organizing drive rather than an ordinary worker. Kennedy summarized the reason for his dissent by saying that the central issue which the majority had focused on was the culpability of the union and not whether an atmosphere of fear and coercion had been created by the employee. He also felt that it was improper to theorize on the effectiveness of the union's disavowal without a hearing.

A more thorough understanding of the regulation of employee conduct comes from a reading of court opinions reviewing the Board's actions. Fundamentally, there is a difference of opinion concerning the potentiality for restraint and coercion arising from employee threats. In *Cross Baking Co. v. NLRB*[99] the First Circuit said:

---

[97] 196 N.L.R.B. No. 6, 79 L.R.R.M. 1625 (1972).

[98] 204 N.L.R.B. No. 159, 83 L.R.R.M. 1491 (1973).

[99] 453 F.2d 1346, 78 L.R.R.M. 3059 (5th Cir. 1971).

The question, however, is not the culpability of the union but whether an atmosphere of fear and coercion was created in fact. . . . It does not follow that fear would be less effective if it had an unofficial origin. Indeed, we can visualize situations where it might be more effective.[100]

Other circuit courts of appeals have taken similar stances on this question.[101]

The judiciary has been instrumental in pressing for an identifiable and consistent framework for evaluating cases of employee threats. In *Foremost Dairies of the South v. NLRB*[102] the court told the Board on remand to consider conduct cumulatively rather than as isolated incidents and to evaluate subjective evidence when appropriate. "The courts have usually applied an objective test to determine whether interference with an election is sufficient to set it aside. Subjective evidence of fear and coercion, however, may carry the day as well."[103] In *Cross Baking Co. v. NLRB*[104] the court said, "When fear and threats of violence are present, the employees' state of mind is precisely the question at issue."[105]

The Board, in turn, has expressly admitted subjective evidence in evaluating election interference charges. Recently, in *Steak House Meat Co., Inc.*,[106] there was evidence of threats made by two adult employees against a sixteen year old part-time worker. The boy's life was threatened and other reprisals were intimated. On one occasion a knife was brandished at him. The Board concluded that an atmosphere of fear and coercion was present in the case and set aside the election. The Board said:

> In the instant case, threats of bodily harm and reprisals were directed at a 16-year-old employee with the obvious aim of influencing him to vote for the Union or to abstain from voting. *As a result of these threats, he chose the latter course.*[107]

---

[100] *Id.* at 1348, 78 L.R.R.M. at 3059 (footnotes omitted).

[101] NLRB v. Southern Paper Box Co., 473 F.2d 208, 82 L.R.R.M. 2482 (8th Cir. 1973); Foremost Dairies of the South v. NLRB, 379 F.2d 241, 65 L.R.R.M. 2681 (5th Cir. 1967).

[102] At note 101, *supra.*

[103] 379 F.2d at 244, 65 L.R.R.M. at 2683.

[104] At note 99, *supra.*

[105] 453 F.2d at 1348, 78 L.R.R.M. at 3060.

[106] 206 N.L.R.B. No. 3, 84 L.R.R.M. 1200 (1973).

[107] *Id.*, 84 L.R.R.M. at 1200 (emphasis added).

Clearly, the Board relied upon subjective evidence of this one employee's reaction. Its decision was appropriate when it is noted that the employee unit consisted of eight workers and the election results were four to three in favor of the union.

In other cases the Board has applied the subjective test and has used it to support a decision to dismiss election objections. In *Foremost Dairies of the South* [108] the Board acknowledged that one employee had been restrained and coerced, but it said his vote could not have affected the election outcome. In *Monroe Auto Equipment Co.*[109] the Board found that only seven of 647 employees had been threatened. It also noted that four had indicated they voted according to their convictions. The Board also mentioned there was no evidence suggesting that the knowledge of these threats passed among the rest of the workers, and it concluded there was no interference.

It is noteworthy that the court in *Foremost Dairies* accused the Board of one-sided treatment in applying the subjective evidence test to employee threats. As the court saw it the Board had taken subjective evidence into account, but then had overruled the employer's objections by determining on an objective basis that the election outcome could not have been affected. The court referred to "the objective [or inferential] conduct impact appraised method" mentioned by the Board in the *International Mfg. Co.* case,[110] which held that a numerical analysis of the unlawful conduct and the number of employees affected would not be determinative of election interference. The court emphasized that the objective and subjective methods of evaluation were not mutually exclusive. The point raised by the court in *Foremost Dairies* indicates that the split in opinion between it and the Board concerning the effects of employee threats upon an election still exists.

---

[108] 172 N.L.R.B. 1242, 68 L.R.R.M. 1478 (1968).

[109] 186 N.L.R.B. 90, 75 L.R.R.M. 1340 (1970).

[110] 167 N.L.R.B. 769, 66 L.R.R.M. 1156 (1967).

CONCLUDING REMARKS

The natural problem of balancing the inevitable hostility between the competing parties to a representation election against a healthy appraisal of the impact upon the election outcome of reprisals and threats exchanged between the parties and their supporters continually emerges in this analysis of Board decisions. In certain instances the Board has been guided by antiquated preconceptions of the union's status in an election and its potential economic reputation among the workers. A serious weakness in the Board's overall policy exists as a result of the improper relationship struck between unfair labor practice charges and election interference complaints. The treatment of employer reprisals is overly dominated by a tie-in which has been made with Section 8(a)(3) of the Act. As a result, the relevance of specific actions to the election laboratory conditions has been lost. On the other hand, in dealing with union reprisals, the reverse effect has been created. The Board has relied on the proviso of Section 8(b)(1)(A) to ignore the relevance of union discipline to the protection of the voters' free choice.

The other major consideration brought out in this chapter has been the lack of consistency in the standards applied by the Board in evaluating objections based upon alleged threats made by or on behalf of unions, as compared with the standards the Board has applied elsewhere. Measuring the coerciveness of prounion threats according to the authority of the speaker or the ability of the union to carry them out ignores the question which the Board has viewed as central in related areas—*i.e.* how the employees perceived the threat. The indicia of control standard is based on an outdated appraisal of the union's strength in most plant situations, and the disparate treatment of conduct not directly attributable to a party cannot be reconciled with the Board's usual stringent standards in regulating campaign conduct.

CHAPTER VII

Questioning, Polling, And Surveillance

During the representation election campaign period the employer's efforts are centered upon winning employee support. In conjunction with this activity the employer may try to obtain information concerning the nature and extent of union sentiment among the employees, the union's campaign program, and the identity of union and employee campaign leaders. This conduct can be viewed as the natural reaction of an employer faced with a union organization movement in his company, and as a necessary element of the planning, organization, and execution of his own campaign. Depending upon how it is conducted, however, such an inquiry by the employer may provide grounds to invalidate the election if the union loses, and may even result in an unfair labor practice finding.

Although employees are entitled to organize without interference, restraint, and coercion, the employer should also be free to wage a noncoercive countercampaign. The problem for the Board is to devise standards that will adequately protect the former interest without unduly interfering with the latter. As we shall see, however, the Board's traditional attitude has been that there are few, if any, justifications for the employer's possession of information about the employees' union activities, and the union's campaign. The Board's decisions in this area approach a rule that there is an absolute right to privacy accompanying the employees' exercise of their rights under the National Labor Relations Act.

During representation election proceedings, the Board focuses its scrutiny upon the means by which the employer seeks to obtain information. The methods which he has commonly employed have been categorized as questioning or interviewing, polling, interrogation, and surveillance. Each category implies a different means of obtaining information, and it may be accompanied by separate employer objectives. The first three are closely related. Questioning or interviewing normally occurs in a personal meeting with individuals or small groups for the purpose of conferring on some point, and talking and questioning so as to elicit statements, facts, or opinions usually. of a general nature. Interrogation has the more limited purpose of obtaining answers to specific questions and it may be conducted in a formal, less personal manner. Polling involves the soliciting and recording of responses to a question or series of questions. An analysis of Board decisions suggests that the Board is not always precise in identifying specific factual situations with the appropriate category of conduct. The act of asking an employee about the general climate of unionization feelings at the plant should not be labeled summarily an interrogation. To do so would be to overlook the substance and purpose of the action and to pay insufficient attention to the different impact upon the employee of each of these forms of conduct.

Board decisions prohibit not only incidents or conduct which force the employee to disclose his views, but also conduct which causes the employee to feel that he has disclosed his views to the employer, or which creates the impression to the employee that he has been observed and identified by the employer as a participant in the unionization movement. The Board feels that, as a general proposition, if employees believe their employer knows who the organizers and union supporters are, they will fear that he will make reprisals against them. The Board and some courts have stated that this type of conduct has the "natural tendency to instill in the minds of employees fear of discrimination." [1] The Board views such conduct as inherently coercive, either because of an assumption that such questioning is likely to be followed by reprisals, or because of the difficulty in proving the presence of a good faith motive for obtaining the information about the campaign.[2] In addition, the Board has said that questioning employees about their union sentiments is not protected by Section 8(c), since "the purpose of the inquiry is not to express views but to ascertain those of the person questioned." [3]

---

[1] NLRB v. West Coast Casket Co., 205 F.2d 902, 32 L.R.R.M. 2353 (9th Cir. 1953).

[2] *See* Kleeb, *Taft-Hartley Rules During Union Organizing Campaigns*, 55 L.R.R.M. 114, 115 (1964).

[3] Struksnes Construction Co., 165 N.L.R.B. 1062, 65 L.R.R.M. 1385 (1967).

MEETINGS AND INTERVIEWS

Meetings and interviews conducted by the employer may be held with individual employees, small groups, or large groups. The employer's usual purpose is to present his views on the selection of a bargaining representative, to urge the employees to vote against the union, and to ascertain the employees' feelings about the current conditions of employment and possible improvements. The employer's conduct may include both campaigning or the expression of opinion, and the attempt to gather information from the employees. The dividing line is often unclear, and the Board does not seem concerned with analyzing the conduct on this two-pronged basis. Such an approach has detracted from the formulation of a sound and balanced policy of determining election interference.

An early Board decision in *General Shoe Corp.*[4] established the policy which has served as the basis for subsequent decisions. The general manager and personnel manager interviewed employees in their office individually and in small groups of ten to twelve and in turn urged them to reject the union. The statements were found to be temperate in nature. The Board, in setting aside the election, said:

> When rank-and-file employees are brought to the company offices in small groups, they do not deal in an "arms length" relationship with the company officials they are directed to see. Anti-union opinions, and the suggestion that the employees reject the union, when uttered in that locus of final authority in the plant, take on a meaning and significance they do not possess under other circumstances.[5]

Three significant points emerge from this decision. First, the Board firmly established the "locus of authority" principle as the significant determinant of restraint or coercion arising from employer-employee meetings.[6] The Board has given less emphasis to the identity of the speakers or interviewers, although they normally are managers, supervisors, and executives.[7] Sec-

[4] 97 N.L.R.B. 499, 29 L.R.R.M. 1113 (1951).

[5] *Id.* at 502, 29 L.R.R.M. at 1114.

[6] *See also* General Shoe Corp., 77 N.L.R.B. 124, 21 L.R.R.M. 1337 (1948).

[7] In Supreme Trailer Co., 115 N.L.R.B. 962, 37 L.R.R.M. 1448 (1956), the speaker was the employer's labor counsel. He was considered a responsible agent of the employer.

ondly, the Board spoke more in terms of campaigning conduct rather than information gathering. It would seem that the "locus of authority" principle only has true validity where the employee is being questioned or interviewed. When the principle is applied to temperate antiunion campaign statements, it serves as an undue restraint upon employer campaigning in the plant. Lastly, the Board indicated that the nature of the employer's comments or statements was not significant in the determination of election interference. "[W]ithout regard to precisely what was said at the meetings with the employees, the manner in which these meetings were conducted interfered with a free choice by the employees and warrants setting aside the election." [8]

The Board was implicitly overruling an earlier decision, *Mallinckrodt Chemical Works*,[9] which sustained the results of the election because the employer's comments made to the employees individually in the plant manager's and personnel director's offices were "temperate in content and tone." As a result of *General Shoe* the Board's thrust is to scrutinize the narrow procedural aspects rather than the substantive elements of the employee meetings and interviews. Although generally the Board makes note of the fact that the employer's statements were antiunion or that he was seeking to elicit antiunion sentiments from the employees, it rarely seeks to determine if the statements alone were coercive.[10] The Board focuses upon the place of the meeting and the size of the employee group. The importance placed on *where* something was said or asked rather than on *what* was said is inappropriate, especially since *General Shoe* and subsequent cases focus only upon employer campaign statements.

The *General Shoe* holding provides an illustration of agency regulation based upon pure speculation dispensed under the banner of "expertise." Although the Board predicated its conclusions upon an assessment of the psychological impact on the voters of a complex set of circumstances and relationships, it offered nothing but its *ipse dixit* to support the conclusion that intimidation would result. As indicated earlier the credentials of the Board's

---

[8] 97 N.L.R.B. at 502, 29 L.R.R.M. at 1114.

[9] 79 N.L.R.B. 1399, 22 L.R.R.M. 1514 (1948).

[10] However, in Arizona Television Co., 121 N.L.R.B. 889, 42 L.R.R.M. 1469 (1958), the employer's statements were a reply to last minute union propaganda and accusations, and they were found to be temperate and not beyond the scope of the accusations. The results of the election were upheld.

members, past and present, scarcely qualify them to make such elaborate psychological judgments without, at the very least, referring to some expert opinion or empirical data for support.

After *General Shoe* the Board was faced with the necessity of defining the "locus of managerial authority" under differing circumstances and facts. The apparent result of the sequence of these cases has been the broad extension of this principle. A critical element underlying the Board's theory was identified to be the "isolation" of the employee or employees from the rest of the workers.[11] The typical case would involve meetings held in the employer's private offices.[12] In *Peoples Drug Stores, Inc.*[13] the Board's theory was defined further:

> The very fact that employees were summoned by management representatives to a place, removed from their work stations, which has been selected for that purpose by management representatives imparts to the place selected its character as "the locus of final authority in the plant." [14]

The specific facts of the case illustrate the expansionary nature of the Board's decision. The employer had interviewed the employees at retail stores in the backrooms and basements. He argued to the Board that because of the nature of the business there was no other practical method of meeting with the employees, individually or in groups. The majority of the Board in a three to two decision indicated the employer should have met with them at their work stations during work hours, or during their off duty time. Both dissenting Board members emphasized that practical considerations fully supported the employer's method of holding the interviews. Member Jenkins prophetically stated the Board had created " 'a roving situs' for 'the locus of final authority.' " [15] In addition both he and Member Rodgers

---

[11] Mead-Atlanta Paper Co., 120 N.L.R.B. 832, 42 L.R.R.M. 1053 (1958).

[12] *See* Qualiton, 115 N.L.R.B. 65, 37 L.R.R.M. 1238 (1956), where the meeting was in the plant owner's office; Supreme Trailer Co., at note 7, *supra*, where the interview was in a separately located plant office; in Phelps Dodge Corp., 177 N.L.R.B. 531, 71 L.R.R.M. 1385 (1969), the supervisor's truck was considered the "locus."

[13] 119 N.L.R.B. 634, 41 L.R.R.M. 1141 (1957).

[14] *Id.* at 636, 41 L.R.R.M. at 1142.

[15] 119 N.L.R.B. at 642, 41 L.R.R.M. at 1143.

argued that the test for interference should focus on the substance of the statements.

Shortly after the *Peoples Drug* decision, the Board in *Mead-Atlanta Paper Co.*[16] added to the definition of "locus" the aspect of foreignness:

> When the employees are gathered to hear the views of company representatives respecting the election in open areas of the plant, where they are not unaccustomed to find themselves, there results free and open discussion with both management employees enjoying the confidence and assurances which are normal aspects of collective and group activities.[17]

Mead-Atlanta's conference room was not found to be the "locus." In a later case the nursing director's office was held to be a permissible location for interviews because it often was used for training sessions for the employees.[18] A plant manager's office also was approved by the Board since it was a customary meeting place for the workers, and it was located adjacent to the production area and separated from it only by glass doors.[19] From these cases it would appear that an employer would follow the safest course by establishing common-rooms in the plant and using these areas for interviews and other activities. However, this alternative generally would be feasible only to the large employer who could afford to allocate such space for nonproductive purposes, and it would preclude interviews or meetings with small groups or individual employees in other locations when the common-rooms would be inconvenient because of their size or location.

The Board lays heavy stress upon the size of the group of employees involved in the meeting or interview. Its decision in *Mead-Atlanta* was influenced somewhat by the fact that eighty employees had been gathered in the conference room. It appears safe to theorize that large groups do not tend to feel isolated or to be restrained by strange surroundings. In *Tuttle & Kift*[20] groups of employees, twenty-eight to forty-eight, were considered too large to have been coerced during their meetings. When the employer interviews his employees individually or in very

---

[16] At note 11, *supra.*

[17] 120 N.L.R.B. at 834, 42 L.R.R.M. at 1053.

[18] Three Oaks, Inc., 178 N.L.R.B. 534, 72 L.R.R.M. 1159 (1969).

[19] Marshall Durbin & Co., 179 N.L.R.B. 1027, 72 L.R.R.M. 1563 (1969).

[20] 122 N.L.R.B. 848, 43 L.R.R.M. 1210 (1959).

small groups, the Board more readily concludes that there was election interference. In these cases the Board has extended the principle of the "locus of managerial authority."

An early case, *Lakeshore Motors, Inc.*,[21] involved individual interviews of all twelve employees in the unit. The private interviews were held in the vice president's car, the employees' homes, and a manager's office. The Board said the conduct constituted interference "regardless of the noncoercive tenor of [the] employer's actual remarks."[22] There was no attempt to distinguish between the different locations for the meetings.[23] The significant element of the employer's conduct probably was the systematic interviewing of each employee in the unit on a personal basis. The Board did not consider the likelihood that in small bargaining units individual meetings between managers and employees may be a common way of handling relations with employees and, therefore, not coercive in nature. In *Economic Machinery Co.*[24] the employees were interviewed individually to acquaint them with the company's personnel policies and practices. The employer at this time also indicated his disapproval of the union as the potential bargaining agent and urged each of the workers to vote in the election. He did not specifically suggest a vote "against the union." The Board glided over the general purpose of the interviews and focused on the antiunion statements in setting aside the election.

The "locus of authority" was expanded in *Hook Drugs, Inc.*,[25] where the employees were individually interviewed at the store manager's desk in a location well traversed by the other employees. The Board said the "locus" did not have to be privately enclosed. The Board supported its finding of interference by looking to the employer's method of conducting the interviews:

---

[21] 101 N.L.R.B. 89, 31 L.R.R.M. 1017 (1952).

[22] *Id.* at 90, 31 L.R.R.M. at 1017. *See also* General Cable Corp., 117 N.L.R.B. 573, 39 L.R.R.M. 1293 (1957).

[23] Interviews in employee's homes are rigidly scrutinized and often constitute election interference. *See* Peoria Plastic Co., 117 N.L.R.B. 545, 39 L.R.R.M. 1281 (1957). In Mrs. Baird's Bakeries, Inc., 114 N.L.R.B. 444, 36 L.R.R.M. 1608 (1955), some of the employees were company drivers, and a few of the unlawful interviews also were conducted on the drivers' routes. The effect upon the employees was considered the same.

[24] 111 N.L.R.B. 947, 35 L.R.R.M. 1617 (1955).

[25] 117 N.L.R.B. 846, 39 L.R.R.M. 1331 (1957).

each employee was called individually by the employee interviewed before him, both the store manager and personnel manager were present, and a substantial number of employees (ten to twelve out of a unit of twenty-nine) were involved. In another case, *National Caterers of Virginia, Inc.*,[26] the company interviewed individual employees in the storeroom of its cafeteria. The manager's desk was located in the storeroom, but the interviews were conducted in a location away from the desk. The Board said:

> The unusual act of setting up two chairs in a corner of the storeroom which also contains the manager's desks for the purpose of conducting private interviews by a management official, in our opinion, reasonably led employees to believe that the location was a locus of managerial authority.[27]

It is possible that the employer may have set up the chairs in order to avoid subjecting the employee to the "locus of authority" at the manager's desk.

The *Great Atlantic & Pacific Tea Co., Inc.*[28] case illustrates how the Board's focus on the employer's technique of interviewing employees may lead it to set aside the election without adequately considering the effect of the conduct upon the election. The bargaining unit consisted of sixteen stores and approximately 120 employees. Prior to the election the area supervisor visited four stores and in the process interviewed five employees. They were singled out individually and taken away from their workplaces. The discussions related to the merits of unionization. The regional director dismissed the union's objections to the election because the remarks were not coercive, and because only five employees had been interviewed. The Board disagreed and set aside the election. It readily dismissed the argument that the conduct had a *de minimis* effect:

> Individual interviews took place in 25 percent of the total number of stores in the unit. This is hardly an isolated number of interviews, and it is not unreasonable in the circumstances to infer, as we do, that the ramifications of the interviewing technique extended beyond the employees immediately involved.[29]

---

26 125 N.L.R.B. 110, 45 L.R.R.M. 1070 (1959).

27 *Id.* at 112, 45 L.R.R.M. at 1071.

28 140 N.L.R.B. 133, 51 L.R.R.M. 1570 (1962).

29 *Id.* at 135, 51 L.R.R.M. at 1571.

The inference of the majority was based on the closeness of the vote against the union (52 to 60). However, the dissent emphasized that allegedly objectionable conduct should be evaluated on the merits rather than on the tally of the votes. The employer's conduct included singling out the few employees away from their workplaces. On this point the dissent forcefully stated:

> I, for one, cannot subscribe to a theory which is grounded in the assumption that all areas of a plant or store, except the employees' "work stations" are permeated with a subtle presence which strikes fear in the hearts of the employees causing words of discussion or persuasion to be transformed into words having the force and effect of threats or promises.[30]

The test of interference arising from employee meetings continues to include an analysis of the "locus" of the activity and the "technique" employed by the employer. Interviews at the employees' workplace generally will not constitute interference,[31] even if the employer urges the employees to vote against the union.[32] However, in other cases where the conduct occurs away from the work area, the employer is forced to select a meeting place carefully, and to avoid singling out and interviewing the employees individually. Little emphasis is given to the subject of the employer's campaigning or to the object of his questions.

INTERROGATION

The act of interrogation directly places the employee in the position of disclosing to the employer information about the campaign, or his specific views and preferences concerning the election. Normally the employer's goal is to gather information rather than to exchange views with employees as in an interview. An employee interrogation may occur on an individual basis, or it may be conducted systematically involving the entire work force or a majority of the employees. The appropriate test for determining interference with the representation election should attempt to measure the degree of pressure or coercion

---

[30] *Id.* at 137 n.12, 51 L.R.R.M. at 1571.

[31] American Sugar Refining Co. [Domino Bag], 123 N.L.R.B. 207, 43 L.R.R.M. 1394 (1959).

[32] Mall Tool Co., 112 N.L.R.B. 1313, 36 L.R.R.M. 1190 (1955). *See also* Bryant Electric Co., 118 N.L.R.B. 232, 40 L.R.R.M. 1158 (1957).

placed upon the employee in each situation. Factors which should be evaluated include the type of information sought by the employer, the purpose for the conduct, and the statements made during the interrogation. It will be seen that although the Board and the courts have formulated factors to assist in determining interference arising from systematic interrogations, the criteria to be used in cases of individual or isolated questioning are unclear.[33] Also, it can be said that the NLRB consistently has taken a restrictive regulatory approach to interrogation of employees.

The early Board rule was that interrogation of employees was *per se* unlawful.[34] In certain cases the Board recognized conduct having a *de minimis* effect upon the results of the election.[35] The reasoning in support of the *per se* rule of interference was discussed at length in *Syracuse Color Press, Inc.*[36] It was felt that an interrogation automatically brought out the employees' apprehensions of reprisal. The conduct also was seen as a direct infringement upon the employees' rights under the Act.

> [I]nherent in the very nature of the rights protected by Section 7 is the concomitant right of privacy in their enjoyment—"full freedom" from employer intermeddling, intrusion or even knowledge.[37]

The Board further said that interrogation was a specialized form of surveillance. The direct suggestion was made in *Syracuse Color Press* that there were extremely narrow limits to an employer's legitimate or good faith purpose for an interrogation. This viewpoint has prevailed in the Board's decisions.

---

[33] MORRIS, THE DEVELOPING LABOR LAW, 102 (1971).

[34] Standard-Coosa-Thatcher Co., 85 N.L.R.B. 1358, 24 L.R.R.M. 1575 (1949); General Shoe Corp., at note 6, *supra.*

[35] Fulton Bag & Cotton Mills, 89 N.L.R.B. 943, 26 L.R.R.M. 1064 (1950), where one employee one week before the election was asked how she was going to vote. The one instance of interrogation, but not the time period factor, was found insufficient basis to set aside the election. *See also* The Liberal Market, Inc., 108 N.L.R.B. 1481, 34 L.R.R.M. 1270 (1954), where the Board looked to the overall vigor of the campaign when three or four employees of a unit of seventy were interrogated.

[36] 103 N.L.R.B. 377, 31 L.R.R.M. 1473 (1953), *enforced,* 209 F.2d 596, 33 L.R.R.M. 2334 (2d Cir.), *cert. denied,* 347 U.S. 966, 34 L.R.R.M. 2143 (1954).

[37] *Id.* at 379, 31 L.R.R.M. at 1474 (citing Standard-Coosa-Thatcher Co., at note 34, *supra*).

During this period the courts were reluctant to follow the Board's strict approach. The Fifth Circuit held that the employer's conduct must bear some relationship to coercion or restraint of the employees' statutory rights.[38] The Seventh Circuit said that there must be some other evidence of the employer's antiunion hostility in order to reasonably establish the threat of reprisal.[39] The Second Circuit stated that interrogation was not unlawful if there were no threats, intimidation, or promises of benefits.[40] This court in another case also indicated that additional factors to consider in each situation would be the time and place of the interrogation, the person asking the questions, and the information sought.[41]

The Board reversed its policy and abandoned the *per se* rule of interference in *Blue Flash Express, Inc.*[42] It said that a finding of election interference from employee interrogation required an evaluation of all of the circumstances of the case. The specific conduct at issue in *Blue Flash* was an attempt by the employer to determine how many employees had signed authorization cards so that he would know how to respond to the union's claim of majority status. The interrogation was done on an individual basis in the employer's office, and the employer prefaced it by saying it was immaterial to him whether or not the employees were union members. In response to the union's objections to the results of the election, the Board said there would be no interference if (1) the employer communicated his purpose for the interrogations to the employees, and it was a legitimate one; (2) he assured them of no reprisal; and (3) the interrogation occurred in an overall background free of antiunion hostility.

In summary, *Blue Flash* on its face repudiated the *per se* rule of interference applicable to employer interrogations and established the three factors or guidelines for determining permissible employee questioning. However, an important question was left unanswered regarding the legitimate purposes which could serve

---

[38] NLRB v. Tennessee Coach Co., 191 F.2d 546, 28 L.R.R.M. 2334 (6th Cir. 1951).

[39] Max Sax v. NLRB, 171 F.2d 769, 23 L.R.R.M. 2191 (7th Cir. 1948).

[40] NLRB v. Montgomery Ward & Co., 192 F.2d 160, 29 L.R.R.M. 2041 (2d Cir. 1951).

[41] Syracuse Color Press, Inc. v. NLRB, at note 36, *supra.*

[42] 109 N.L.R.B. 591, 34 L.R.R.M. 1384 (1954).

as the basis for an interrogation. In addition *Blue Flash* recognized an employer's good faith desire to assess the union's claim of majority status and thereby altered to a small degree the long-standing presumption that the employer did not have the right to question employees about their union activities. Yet, the case did not indicate how much weight was to be given the "overall circumstances of the case," when evaluating an election interference charge. Later cases, however, illustrate the inconsistences on this issue. Finally, the Board failed to deal with the problem of individual or isolated interrogations by not making the guidelines applicable to such cases.

The spirit of the *Blue Flash* rule did not receive full consideration by the Board in subsequent cases involving employee interrogation. In the 1950's the Board applied uneven or insufficient weight in assessing the overall circumstances of each case and followed strict and narrow guidelines in evaluating the legitimacy of the employer's purpose with little attention given to the substance of the employer's questions. In *San Diego Glass & Paint Co.*[43] the employer asked each of his employees for their choice in the upcoming representation election. The Board said that the act of questioning the employees interfered with the election despite the fact that the employees were not required to answer. The Board may have been influenced by the size of the unit (four employees) and by the timing of the interrogation (two days before the election). However, the dissent argued that the case provided no evidence of threats or offers of benefits by the employer. In *Veeder-Root, Inc.*,[44] which cited *San Diego Glass & Paint*, the employer asked most of his employees if they were going to vote for the union. The Board said the interrogations interfered with the election even though they occurred at the employees' work stations. Other factors which may have influenced the Board were that practically all of the employees were systematically interviewed, and that additional interference was found from interviews occurring at a foreman's desk. It is interesting that the Board did not accord the "workplace" the significance as a protective shield to employee questioning as it did in the interviewing cases.

In later decisions by the Board in the 1960's the treatment of employee interrogations continued to be restrictive with respect

---

[43] 117 N.L.R.B. 59, 39 L.R.R.M. 1165 (1957).

[44] 120 N.L.R.B. 967, 42 L.R.R.M. 1083 (1958).

to the scope of permissible employer conduct. The two recognized legitimate purposes were to verify a union's claim for majority status, and to investigate facts in the preparation of a defense to union unfair labor practice charges.[45] The Board held in the *Charles V. Weise Co.*,[46] that an employer who made available anti-union campaign badges to be worn by the employees interfered with the election. The regional director had stated that merely making them available, even if not urging the employees to wear them, was unlawful conduct. The Board further agreed with his view that the employer was "in effect providing a means by which employees would be placed in a position of making an open declaration of preference." [47] This action was considered the same as if the employer had interrogated the employee concerning his preference. In *Standard Products Co.*,[48] asking an employee who else had joined the union was found likely to create the fear of reprisal. The *Phelps Dodge Corp.*,[49] case held that asking the employees if they had been approached by the union was coercive interrogation on the grounds that it would cause the employee to admit "that he did or did not support the Union, or [to provide] information as to the activities of the other employees." [50]

The Board set aside an election in *Abex Corp.*[51] where the employer asked workers who the union organizer was, and they merely laughed and did not reply. The trial examiner dismissed this union's objection because he did not find the interrogation coercive, but the Board overruled him saying, "The fact that such interrogation is made in a casual manner during a friendly conversation does not lessen its unlawful effect." [52] Since no apparent consideration was given to the ultimate impact upon employee free choice in the election from "casual" statements made in a "friendly" manner, the decision seems to reintroduce a *per se* rule of

---

[45] Johnnie's Poultry Co., 146 N.L.R.B. 770, 55 L.R.R.M. 1403 (1964).

[46] 133 N.L.R.B. 765, 48 L.R.R.M. 1709 (1961).

[47] *Id.* at 766, 48 L.R.R.M. at 1710.

[48] 159 N.L.R.B. 159, 62 L.R.R.M. 1421 (1966).

[49] 177 N.L.R.B. 531, 71 L.R.R.M. 1385 (1969).

[50] *Id.* at 532, 71 L.R.R.M. at 1386.

[51] 162 N.L.R.B. 328, 64 L.R.R.M. 1004 (1966).

[52] *Id.* at 329, 64 L.R.R.M. at 1005.

interference. Another case, *General Automation Mfg.*,[53] decided shortly after *Abex*, also said that an interrogation made in a casual manner during a friendly conversation in an informal context did not lose its unlawful effect upon the employee. In this case there was only one instance of interrogation, involving one employee, which was an inquiry into the identity of the signers of union authorization cards.

The courts, however, have refused to accept the restrictive approach taken by the Board in apparent disregard of the *Blue Flash* decision. The Second Circuit in *Bourne v. NLRB*[54] disagreed with the Board in its finding of unlawful interrogation. The court said interrogation, which is not threatening, is permissible,[55] and listed certain factors to be considered in each case: (1) the background of employer hostility; (2) the nature of the information sought; (3) the identity of the interrogator; (4) the place and method of interrogation; and (5) the truthfulness of the employee's reply. This case was given limited application in a subsequent Board decision, *Zayre Corp.*,[56] when the trial examiner suggested that the five factors listed by the court applied to systematic polling but not necessarily to other kinds of interrogation such as individual instances of questioning.[57] The rationale for this distinction was not given, and no basis appears for making it. The points raised by the court place an emphasis upon the evaluation of the overall circumstances of a case in determining election interference.[58] Cases involving individual interrogations also

---

[53] 167 N.L.R.B. 502, 66 L.R.R.M. 1084 (1967), *enforced*, 408 F.2d 380, 71 L.R.R.M. 2047 (6th Cir. 1969).

[54] 332 F.2d 47, 56 L.R.R.M. 2241 (2d Cir. 1964).

[55] *Cf.* Charlotte Union Bus Station, Inc., 135 N.L.R.B. 228, 49 L.R.R.M. 1461 (1962), where the Board said unlawful interrogation need not contain threats of reprisal or promises of benefit.

[56] 154 N.L.R.B. 1372, 60 L.R.R.M. 1222 (1965).

[57] Gruber's Food Center, 159 N.L.R.B. 629, 62 L.R.R.M. 1271 (1966), the Board used an employee's false answers during an individual interrogation as evidence of coercion.

[58] *See also* Griffith Ladder Corp., 159 N.L.R.B. 175, 62 L.R.R.M. 1383 (1966), where the Board listed the guidelines for permissible systematic employee interrogation. The employer must (a) communicate to the employee the purpose of the questioning, (b) assure him that no reprisal will take place, (c) obtain his participation on a voluntary basis, (d) put his question in a context free from hostility to union organization, (e) put questions not of themselves coercive in nature, and (f) restrict his questions to the necessities of the legitimate purpose of the interrogation.

should be scrutinized closely in order to minimize the disruption with the election process.

The Board has not been consistent in its handling of cases where the conduct arguably is of a *de minimis* nature. In *West Texas Equipment Co.*[59] three incidents of simple interrogation and conversation with employees four months before the election were dismissed as being isolated and insubstantial. Also in *Ortronix, Inc.*,[60] four instances of interrogation involving three employees out of a bargaining unit of over three hundred employees and occurring five months before the election were considered remote in time and of no effect because of the small number of workers involved.[61] The practical and policy reasons supporting such decisions are obvious. However, in other cases presenting similar circumstances the Board has set aside the election results. The *Intercontinental Mfg. Co., Inc.*[62] case involved the interrogation of six employees out of 730 eligible voters during the week before the election. A few were asked how they intended to vote and they were urged to vote "no"; one employee was questioned about the campaign buttons they were wearing. The hearing officer dismissed the case because of the limited instances of interrogation. The Board set aside the election on the grounds that "employer interrogation and threats concerning union activity, particularly in an industrial plant and during a preelection campaign, are likely to receive prompt and wide circulation." [63] It said that the number of employees involved or instances of interrogation did not serve as determinative factors in weighing the likely effect of coercive conduct. The Board failed to specify the factors which it did rely on and stated that the test was whether the conduct reasonably tended to interfere with the election.

Applying similar reasoning the Board set aside the election in *Standard Knitting Mills, Inc.*,[64] where four employees were inter-

---

[59] 142 N.L.R.B. 1358, 53 L.R.R.M. 1249 (1963).

[60] 173 N.L.R.B. 385, 70 L.R.R.M. 1109 (1968).

[61] *See also* National Bookbinding Co., 171 N.L.R.B. 219, 68 L.R.R.M. 1038 (1968), where a single instance of employee interrogation did not warrant setting aside the election. In a recent decision, Globe Shopping City, 203 N.L.R.B. No. 36, 83 L.R.R.M. 1059 (1973), the Board said that interrogation of two employees in a unit of about 122 was a technical violation but insufficient to set aside the election. The employer had also provided assurances that all employees were free to vote as they wished.

[62] 167 N.L.R.B. 769, 66 L.R.R.M. 1156 (1967).

[63] *Id.* at 770, 66 L.R.R.M. at 1156.

[64] 172 N.L.R.B. 1122, 68 L.R.R.M. 412 (1968).

rogated and threatened with plant closure and a loss of benefits. Both the regional director and hearing officer felt the misconduct was *de minimis* since the total work force was almost three thousand. The Board disagreed and set aside the election because of the likelihood that news of the statements and the conduct would have circulated among the other employees. The Board attempted to support its decision by emphasizing the timing of the conduct, the content of the statements, and the identity of the employer's agents. However, the Board's reasoning here and in *Standard Knitting Mills* suffers from its reliance on the presumed circulation of the information throughout the unit, and from its assumption that the other workers would be coerced by it. There should be a requirement for specific evidence in support of such a conclusion.

Recent decisions of the present Board suggest little if any change in the policy regulating employee questioning. In *Gabriel Mfg. Co., Inc.*[65] the Board said that asking the employees why they wanted a union constituted coercion, since the questioning was in an area of no concern to the employer. It is noteworthy that the Board's finding of coercive interrogation was reached through an analysis of the individual circumstances of the case: (1) the employees were Spanish speaking and, therefore, presumed to be less familiar with their rights under the NLRA; (2) they were all called into the president's office; and (3) the action took place three days before the election. The decision in *Isaascon-Carrico Mfg. Co.*[66] held that the coercive effect of an interrogation was not mitigated by the fact that it came from a friend. However, the case may be distinguished from *Abex Corp.*[67] because the questioning was not conducted in a similar casual manner.[68] The superior had asked the employees about the details of a recent union meeting, the identity of union organizers, the substance of the union's promises, and the reasons why they wanted a union. The Board concluded in *Globe-Union, Inc.*[69] that an employee

---

[65] 201 N.L.R.B. No. 151, 82 L.R.R.M. 1733 (1973).

[66] 200 N.L.R.B. No. 116, 82 L.R.R.M. 1205 (1972).

[67] At note 51, *supra*.

[68] *See also* Great Atlantic & Pacific Tea Co., Inc., 192 N.L.R.B. No. 83, 77 L.R.R.M. 1895 (1971), where questioning employees on what they thought of the coming election constituted unlawful interrogation; Birdsall Construction Co., 198 N.L.R.B. No. 20, 80 L.R.R.M. 1580 (1972).

[69] 194 N.L.R.B. No. 181, 79 L.R.R.M. 1149 (1972).

had been coerced when the plant manager spoke to him about union campaign stickers and signs which had been put on the company bulletin board. The employer's request that the employee used his influence to put a stop to this practice was considered to be an interrogation. The dissent pointed out the fact that the employee had been the chairman of the organization committee, and, therefore, he was the logical person to request assistance from in controlling the union's use of the company's bulletin board.

In summary, the Board has been reluctant to depart significantly from the early *per se* rule of interference concerning employee interrogations. At present the Board still seems to recognize only two legitimate purposes for questioning employees—verification of a union's claim of majority and investigation of charges of unfair labor practices. The Board's strict approach arises from the belief that the employee possesses an almost absolute right of privacy in the exercise of his Section 7 rights. But the determination of whether interrogation interferes with a representation election should involve a consideration of the particular circumstancs of each case; there should be evidence of restraint of coercion, and not just a bare showing that the employees were questioned. The judiciary has specified certain guidelines and factors it feels should be used in evaluating each situation, but the Board has applied them primarily to cases involving systematic interrogation. There appears to be little rationale for treating cases of individual interrogations on a separate basis.

POLLING

Employee polling essentially is a systematic form of interrogation. The conduct similarly is intended to obtain specific answers from the employees pertaining to the unionization movement. The guidelines to be used in the determination of election interference in the context of systematic employee interrogation cases were discussed earlier, and for the most part they have equal application in this discussion.[70] Usually an important feature of employee polling is the recording or tabulation of the employees' responses. The poll then assumes a similarity to the representation election

---

[70] Blue Flash Express, Inc., at note 36, *supra*, while repudiating the *per se* rule of interference from interrogations during the election period, specified the three aforementioned conditions for permissible employee polling; Johnnie's Poultry Co., at note 45, *supra*, indicated the legitimate purposes for polling employees; Griffith Ladder Corporation, at note 58, *supra*, listed six guidelines for systematic interrogations.

itself, and it raises additional questions about the restraining impact upon the employees, and the permissible purposes for the poll. The Board generally has been unwilling to permit such employer conduct during the representation election period.

The employer in *Offner Electronics, Inc.*[71] conducted a poll or straw vote during the election period. He distributed questionnaires asking the workers to indicate their preference for "No Union" or "Union." The employees were told not to put their name on the ballot. Approximately ninety-eight ballots were issued, twenty were not returned and seven or eight were returned unmarked. The results of the poll were not made known to the employees until after the Board election was completed. The Board set aside the election because of the employer-conducted poll.

> We are of the opinion that after the Board directs a representation election, or the parties agree to a Board-conducted election, the responsibility to conduct a secret ballot election for the resolution of the question concerning representation rests solely with the Board, and any secret balloting or polling of the employees on the representation issue by the parties, or by others on a party's behalf, is an intrusion upon the Board's responsibility and an interference with the Board-conducted election and may be utilized by an innocent party as a basis for setting aside the Board election.[72]

The opinion does not address itself to the question of restraint or coercion of the employees; consequently, it leaves unanswered the general significance of the use of ballots and of the measures taken by the employer to ensure the secrecy of the balloting. The dissent in *Offner* analyzed the case from the standpoint of restraint and coercion of the employees rather than preemption of the Board's responsibilities.

> It appears to me that employees, like potential voters in political elections, if polled for their views in what is obviously a "dry run" or "opinion poll," are well able to make up their own minds as to how to vote both then and when the official balloting takes place.[73]

The majority opinion can be criticized on the grounds that the election results should have been set aside only upon a finding that the employees were not able to freely express their choice. It is interesting to note that the results of the poll were 16 to 54

---

[71] 127 N.L.R.B. 991, 46 L.R.R.M. 1136 (1960).

[72] *Id.* at 992, 46 L.R.R.M. at 1137.

[73] *Id.* at 993, 46 L.R.R.M. at 1137.

against unionization, and the results of the Board election were 35 to 53 against.

The *Offner* case reached the Board a second time in an unfair labor practice proceeding.[74] The Board held that the secret poll was an 8(a)(1) violation.[75] This time the issue of restraint and coercion was discussed.

> Respondent, however, chose this particular time to intrude by raising new issues and new solutions, such as whether the employees might prefer to be represented by an independent union, or by any union other than the Petitioner. . . . The polling was therefore neither legitimate nor harmless, but was rather an unwarranted inquiry into the state of its employees' desire for union representation which was reasonably calculated to intimidate and coerce them.[76]

The Board indicated that the employer could have conducted a poll in this manner to ascertain the union's majority status.[77] Member Rodgers dissented on the same grounds as he did in the earlier *Offner* case. In summary, the purpose of the poll was the basis for the violation. However, the Board did not indicate what factors were used in support of its conclusion of employee restraint and coercion.

In *Daniel Construction Co., Inc.*[78] the employer had conducted three or four secret polls to determine whether the employees were for or against the union. The Board said this constituted election interference and an 8(a)(1) violation. The reasons given were: (1) there was no legitimate purpose for the employer to determine the union's strength in the plant; (2) the employer had instructed the foremen to ascertain union sympathy and the employees' desires; (3) the polls were conducted in a hostile atmosphere; (4) there were employer unfair labor practices during the campaign; (5) the three or four polls were timed just prior to the election. In effect the Board was applying the three-pronged test mentioned in *Blue Flash Express*.[79]

---

[74] Offner Electronics, Inc., 134 N.L.R.B. 1064, 49 L.R.R.M. 1307 (1961).

[75] It is noteworthy that the two members voting in the majority disagreed on the source of the unlawfulness. One member found the poll unlawful in the context of other coercive conduct, and the other member found the poll coercive without regard to the existence of other violations.

[76] 134 N.L.R.B. at 1066, 49 L.R.R.M. at 1307-08.

[77] *Id.*, 49 L.R.R.M. at 1307.

[78] 145 N.L.R.B. 1397, 55 L.R.R.M. 1162 (1964).

[79] At note 42, *supra*.

During this period there was certain judicial disagreement with the adequacy of the *Blue Flash Express* guidelines in the polling cases.[80] The D.C. Circuit in 1965, in effect, told the Board that *Blue Flash Express* should be revised.[81] On remand from the court, the Board in *Struksnes Construction Co.*[82] expanded the guidelines for determining when an employee poll was lawful. It listed five safeguards which the employer was required to preserve:

> (1) the purpose of the poll is to determine the truth of a union's claim of majority, (2) this purpose is communicated to the employees, (3) assurances against reprisal are given, (4) the employees are polled by secret ballot, and (5) the employer has not engaged in unfair labor practices or otherwise created a coercive atmosphere.[83]

These factors compare closely with the guidelines for interrogations as stated in *Griffith Ladder Corp.*[84] However, only one legitimate purpose for a poll is recognized, and the requirement for a secret ballot is included. The exact procedures an employer must follow in taking such a secret ballot have never been specified by the Board.

In *Glamorise Foundations, Inc.*[85] the union charged that a contest sponsored by the employer in which the employees were invited to guess the number of votes against the union interfered with the results of the election. The regional director and the Board held that this conduct constituted a polling of employee sentiment as to the outcome of the election, which was in violation of

---

[80] *See* NLRB v. Lorben Corp., 345 F.2d 346, 59 L.R.R.M. 2184 (2d Cir. 1965), where the court said failure to explain the purpose of the poll and to provide assurances of nonreprisal was too narrow a basis upon which to base an unfair labor practice. However, in Operating Engineers, Local 49 v. NLRB, 353 F.2d 852, 60 L.R.R.M. 2353 (D.C. Cir. 1965), the court said the Board was unwarranted in finding no 8(a)(1) violation because the employer made no assurances of nonreprisal and did not explain the purpose of the polls. The court also said it was wrong to dismiss the fact that the employer had a permanent record of the employees' votes.

[81] Operating Engineers, Local 49 v. NLRB, 353 F.2d 852, 60 L.R.R.M. 2353 (D.C. Cir. 1965).

[82] 165 N.L.R.B. 1062, 65 L.R.R.M. 1385 (1967).

[83] *Id.* at 1063, 65 L.R.R.M. at 1386.

[84] At note 58, *supra*.

[85] 197 N.L.R.B. No. 108, 80 L.R.R.M. 1433 (1972).

the rule established in *Offner*. The employer argued his conduct amounted to a raffle intended to stimulate interest in the election and was permissible according to the general policy regulating raffles during the election.[86] The Board rejected this argument and held that the conduct of the case most closely paralleled the *Offner* situation. "Although the conduct herein was not a poll of the individual voters preferences, it did nonetheless call for an estimate by voters of the number of 'No' votes they thought would be cast in the election. . . ."[87] One of the dangers the Board saw in the employer's conduct was that the poll or raffle would have created comment or speculation concerning the way the workers would vote. Apparently this constituted a restraint or coercion upon the election.

The question of the effect of employee polling by parties other than the employer has been raised recently. In *Springfield Discount Inc.*[88] the employer argued that polling of the employees by the union prior to the election was grounds for election interference under the *Offner Electronics* doctrine. In a brief reply the Board said that polling by employers was clearly distinguishable from such activity by unions. Although the basis for this distinction was not fully set forth here by the Board, the reviewing court, upholding the decision, cited for support an earlier Board case, *Plant City Welding and Tank Co.*[89] which discussed this situation in depth:

> [T]here is a substantial difference between the employment of the technique of individual interviews by employers on the one hand and by unions on the other. Unlike employers, unions often do not have the opportunity to address employees in assembled or informal groups, and never have the position of control over tenure of employment and working conditions which imparts the coercive effect to systematic individual interviews conducted by employers.[90]

Although here the Board was dealing with interviews and union visits to employees' homes, the rationale was clearly held to be

---

[86] *See* Chapter V, pp. 111-113.

[87] 197 N.L.R.B. No. 108, 80 L.R.R.M. at 1433.

[88] 195 N.L.R.B. No. 157, 79 L.R.R.M. 1542, *enforced*, 82 L.R.R.M. 2173 (7th Cir. 1972).

[89] 119 N.L.R.B. 131, 41 L.R.R.M. 1014 (1957).

[90] *Id.* at 133-34, 41 L.R.R.M. at 1015.

applicable to polling.[91] This familiar premise, criticized elsewhere in this study, is no more warranted in this context than in others. The concurring opinion by Chairman Miller in *Springfield Discount* suggested that all acts of employee polling alone should not constitute election interference. He would invalidate the election only if the polling were shown to have been used "as an instrument of illegal employer interference." Although this less restrictive viewpoint appears better suited to the goal of protecting employee rights without unduly interfering with legitimate employer conduct, it has not yet been adopted by the Board.

A recent case, *Finfrock Motor Sales*,[92] dealt with the company's complaint that a voting study conducted by a group of researchers before the election precluded a free choice in the election. The employees were interviewed and asked to indicate their voting preferences.[93] Their answers and other data were recorded for subsequent tabulation and analysis by the research team. The Board overruled the regional director's recommendations that the election be set aside, and it said that while the employees had been questioned in depth, there was no evidence that the interviewers or the questions coerced or prejudiced the employees.

The policy for regulating polling activity during the election period does not differ significantly from other forms of interrogation. Quite often employer conduct is interchangeably called systematic interrogation and polling. More precisely, however, polling should refer to a procedure whereby the employees record their responses. The employer must be careful to avoid duplicating the function of the representation election. The purpose of polling must be restricted to determining the union's majority status. Finally, employee polls must ensure the secrecy of the ballot in order to avoid the creation of a threat of reprisal.

SURVEILLANCE

The Board early held that surveillance of employees while they are engaging in the exercise of their rights under the Act is unlawful conduct by an employer or his agents.[94] Over the years

---

[91] *See also* Louis-Allis Co. v. NLRB, 463 F.2d 512, 80 L.R.R.M. 2864 (7th Cir. 1972).

[92] 203 N.L.R.B. No. 130, 83 L.R.R.M. 1130 (1973).

[93] For a detailed description of the voter study see Getman and Goldberg *The Myth of Labor Board Expertise*, 39 U. CHI. L. REV. 681 (1972).

[94] Consolidated Edison v. NLRB, 305 U.S. 197, 3 L.R.R.M. 645 (1938).

there have been innumerable cases involving a variety of factual situations and patterns of conduct, finding that employer surveillance constitutes an 8(a)(1) violation. Also, surveillance occurring during the representation election campaign period may serve as the basis for setting aside the election. Union objections to the results of the election rarely allege surveillance as the sole basis for interference. In practice, it normally emerges as only one element of the overall pattern of employer campaign conduct.

Surveillance suggests close scrutiny or supervision, or clandestine activity in the nature of spying with the purpose of obtaining and recording information. The Board seeks to prohibit conduct which will restrain or coerce the employees. No doubt a major basis for the policy of setting aside elections upon a showing of employer surveillance is the inherent threat of reprisal felt by employees. The Board's premise that the employer can have no legitimate cause to investigate employee participation in unionization activities has equal application to these cases. In addition, a significant factor underlying its reasoning, although not always specifically verbalized, is the element of uncertainty which affects employees who have been subjected to surveillance. They may wonder what the employer is seeking, what he obtained in the process, and, importantly, at what other times, unknown to them, have they been observed. Commonly, the surveillance cases involve the presence of management representatives at or near union meetings; the taking of photographs, bugging, or eavesdropping; the use of informers to obtain information; [95] and conduct creating the "impression" of surveillance.

The mere presence of the employer or his agents at union meetings or gatherings would not constitute surveillance. The Board's regulatory policy takes into account the location of the meeting, the conduct of the employer at this time, and other factors. In *Atlanta Gas Light Co.*[96] the union meeting took place at a bowling alley. The presence of the property manager did not constitute interference:

> [M]ere presence, without more specific evidence that it was not for a legitimate purpose, or that it was for the purpose of observing the meeting, establishes neither surveillance of the meeting by him, nor a reasonable basis for an impression of surveillance in the minds of employees in attendance at the meeting.[97]

---

[95] Bourne v. NLRB at note 54, *supra*.

[96] 162 N.L.R.B. 436, 64 L.R.R.M. 1051 (1966).

[97] *Id.* at 438, 64 L.R.R.M. at 1052.

Nothing extraordinary took place in the encounter. The meeting was held in the bowling alley playroom; the manager was seen looking into the room; he was invited to come in; he did so briefly, and then he left to bowl. This was the only alley in the area, and the manager was an occasional customer. The Board indicated that the manager, even if aware of the meeting, was free to bowl, either as an old or new customer. In *Patz Co.*[98] the regional director found there was no surveillance or election interference from the presence of two supervisors at a meeting since the union invited anyone to attend, the union made no attempt to eject the men and raised no protest, and the two representatives did not engage in any threatening or coercive conduct directed at the employees. The legitimacy of the employer's purpose and the reasonableness of the conduct in both of these cases was supported no doubt by the acquiescence or lack of objection by the union during the meeting. Although this factor may be relevant as evidence of lawful employer conduct, the Board has not ruled that failure of the union to object to the presence of employer agents at its meetings at that time constitutes a waiver of the right to raise later objections to the results of the election.

The employer's presence at a meeting was held to have interfered with the election in *Gallaher Drug Co.*[99] The Board emphasized the deliberateness of the conduct: [100] the supervisor came uninvited, and in the presence of the employees he insisted to be allowed to stay. The unlawful purpose to the conduct was derived further from the fact that the supervisor gave to his superiors the names of some of the employees who were present at the meeting.[101] The Board found that it was not an accident or mere coincidence that the employer in *Shovel Supply Co.*[102] parked his car near the place of the union activity and sat in it. Despite the fact that he did not speak to any employees and did not attend the meeting,

---

[98] Case No. 18-RC-5743, 55 L.R.R.M. 1360 (1964).

[99] 115 N.L.R.B. 1379, 38 L.R.R.M. 1057 (1956).

[100] *See also* Intertype Co. v. NLRB, 371 F.2d 787, 64 L.R.R.M. 2257 (4th Cir. 1967), where the court emphasized that the supervisor's appearance at the location of the meeting was not accidental—he went to see how many employees attended the meeting and who they were.

[101] Similar conduct subsequent to a union campaign meeting was emphasized by the Board in Lloyd A. Fry Roofing Co., 142 N.L.R.B. 673, 53 L.R.R.M. 1130 (1963).

[102] 118 N.L.R.B. 315, 40 L.R.R.M. 1189 (1957).

the Board found that the conduct was open surveillance. No plausible explanation by the employer was given to rebut the presumption that his presence was for the purpose of obtaining information about employee union activities. Under similar circumstances in *Murray Ohio Mfg. Co.*,[103] where the supervisor drove around the union hall during the meeting, the Board found election interference. In *Gallaher Drug* the Board rejected the company's argument that there was no election interference because its conduct affected only a few employees. It was held that the surveillance by its very nature not only affected the employees subjected to the surveillance, but also was calculated to and potentially did restrain all of the employees in the plant. The Board apparently was willing to assume the existence of substantial interference absent specific proof.

Photographing employees engaged in campaign activities often is considered to be unlawful surveillance. A photograph quite clearly serves as a means of recording and identification, and, therefore, the Board closely scrutinizes the employer's purpose for engaging in this conduct. In an early case, *Calmes Engineering Co.*,[104] the employer took photos of employees engaged in the distribution of campaign leaflets and union literature. The employer asserted he was obtaining evidence of possible union trespass. The hearing officer rejected this contention. The Board said that openly taking photographs of the employees, regardless of the motive, had the clear effect of "intimidating" the workers. A dissenting member sought evidence of intimidation. In *American Greetings Corp.*[105] the employer's attorney took a picture of an active advocate of the union. There was no interference in this case because the incident lasted only a few minutes, and there was no dramatic attempt to single out this employee. Recently, in *General Electric Wiring Devices, Inc.*[106] the Board said that the sudden unexplained appearance of a helicopter hovering over the voting area for several minutes and the taking of photographs by persons inside the aircraft interfered with the election. The significant factors in this decision probably were that the activity took place in the voting area, and that there was no ostensible justification for the

---

[103] 156 N.L.R.B. 840, 61 L.R.R.M. 1146 (1966).

[104] 90 N.L.R.B. 771, 26 L.R.R.M. 1271 (1950).

[105] 116 N.L.R.B. 1622, 39 L.R.R.M. 1057 (1956).

[106] 182 N.L.R.B. 876, 74 L.R.R.M. 1224 (1970).

conduct. This case can be contrasted with *A.D. Julliard and Co.*,[107] where the employer examined the voting list in the voting area for several minutes, but he made no attempt to record the names of those voting. The Board found no interference because there was no evidence indicating that the employees believed their actions had been recorded.

An election may also be set aside on the basis that the employer has created the "impression" of surveillance, even though no actual observation or recording of employee activity was present. In *Phelps Dodge Corp.*[108] the Board said the employer created such an impression when, in asking employees if they had been approached by the union, he said he knew they favored the union, but he did not tell them the source of his knowledge. An earlier case, *E-Town Sportwear Corp.*,[109] evidences similar reasoning where employees were questioned about the circulation of union campaign literature and visits by union campaigners. The Board said the employer's questions gave the workers the "feeling" they were under surveillance. The Board's thesis is that by creating the impression that he is concerned about union activity and anxious to find out who is involved, the employer may make employees reluctant to engage freely in such activity for fear of reprisals.

Prevention of conduct which creates the "impression of surveillance" raises problems of definition for the Board. It may be difficult for an employer to determine, based on the Board's decisions in this area, precisely what he may and may not do during a campaign without running afoul of the "impression of surveillance" ban. Similarly, it has been difficult for the Board, in cases where it has found such conduct, to compose an acceptable cease and desist order covering it. A simple ban against creating the impression of surveillance was held overly vague by the First Circuit in *NLRB v. Simplex Time Recorder Co.*[110] The court modified the order to prohibit only "willful conduct and a justifiable impression." It would serve the interests of clarity and fairness if the Board would similarly qualify the language of its election case rulings in this area. Thus, the prohibition would be limited

---

[107] 110 N.L.R.B. 2197, 35 L.R.R.M. 1401 (1954).

[108] 177 N.L.R.B. 531, 71 L.R.R.M. 1385 (1969).

[109] 141 N.L.R.B. 480, 52 L.R.R.M. 1365 (1963).

[110] 401 F.2d 547, 69 L.R.R.M. 2465 (1st Cir. 1968). *See also* NLRB v. Rybolt Heater Co., 408 F.2d 888, 70 L.R.R.M. 3159 (6th Cir. 1969).

to deliberate conduct reasonably calculated to coerce, and the Board and the parties would be spared the chore of speculating upon what "impression" might have been created by unintentional conduct.

CONCLUDING REMARKS

The Board has maintained a strict posture on the issue of the employer's right to possess information about employee and union campaign activities. The basic assumptions by the Board have been that the employees have an inherent right of privacy in the exercise of their rights, and that information obtained by the employer will be used in reprisal against them. The Board controls the employer's possession of information by regulating closely his attempts to obtain it.

Although Board decisions nominally differentiate between interviews and meetings, interrogation, polling, and surveillance, they show insufficient sensitivity to the differences and potential impact of these forms of conduct upon the employees. Employee interviews and meetings serve two purposes. They are part of the employer's campaign effort and they provide him feedback on the strength of the union's effort. By failing to recognize the legitimacy of these objectives, the Board has restricted the ability of the employer to campaign among small groups and individual employees. The Board substitutes broad presumptions based on the location where a meeting took place and how many employees were involved for any reasoned analysis of the impact of the meeting based upon what actually transpired. Moreover, the Board's intuitive presumption that all meetings in the "locus of managerial authority" are likely to have a coercive impact is unsupported by any tangible evidence, and rests entirely upon a psychological generalization which the Board can claim no expertise to make.

With respect to interrogation and polling by employers, the board has been reluctant to depart significantly from its initial policy of *per se* prohibition. Under judicial pressure it has formulated certain guidelines used to evaluate cases involving systematic interrogation, but generally it has not applied them to instances of individual employee interrogation. Any acceptable test must attempt to assess the degree of coercion or pressure placed upon the employee; the only reliable method is to look to the statements made, the people involved, the place and method of interrogation, and the overall background of the employer-employee relationship. The Board has failed to follow this approach consistently.

Comparable Board regulation of union activity has been conspicuously lacking. As we have seen, the Board lightly dismisses the possibility that questioning or polling of employees as to their voting preferences could have as much potential for coercive impact when conducted by a union as by an employer. Thus, without reference to any empirical evidence, the Board perpetuates the notion that employees in general harbor an instinctive fear of reprisal from management that will automatically cause them to infer a threat in any show of concern by their employer over the appearance of prounion sentiments. By contrast, the Board refuses to impute any potential coerciveness to union inquiries unless accompanied by actual threats. It is hoped that the Board will reexamine these fundamental presumptions in light of nonavailable empirical data on employees' voting behavior, and that the disparate treatment of employer and union campaign activities will be replaced with a more evenhanded policy.

CHAPTER VIII

Employer Favoritism Or Assistance Of Participating Union

The relationship of the parties to a representation election does not suggest by nature that a participating union would receive assistance from the employer. Yet, in many election cases, the Board has found that employer solicitations on behalf of a union, or preferential treatment accorded to it, has interfered with the results of the election. Commonly, these situations arise when two or more unions are competing for certification as the bargaining representative. The Board's policy is designed to protect the employees' expression of a free and, especially, reasoned choice in their voting. A major concern is that employer assistance to one union will mislead the voters into believing it is the more qualified agent for collective bargaining, thereby undermining the election prospects of the other union. Another fear is that the employer may seek to preserve an attractive relationship with an incumbent union whose certification is being challenged. Still another possibility is that the employer may attempt to shift employee sentiment between the competing organizations in the hope of achieving no union representation. In short, the Board does not want the voting alternatives, as perceived by the employees during the election period, to be distorted or biased through company intervention, or to be affected by direct or indirect economic pressures from management.

The Board early established the requirement of employer neutrality during the election period. In *Joshua Hendy Iron Works* [1] the basic policy was expressed:

> Since the selection of bargaining representatives is the exclusive concern of the employees, the Board requires that an employer during and before an election shall observe a policy of scrupulous neutrality and shall refrain from any action which may be interpreted as favoring any contestant to the election. [2]

---

[1] 53 N.L.R.B. 1411, 13 L.R.R.M. 174 (1943).

[2] *Id.* at 1418, 13 L.R.R.M. at 174.

This policy is founded upon Section 8(a)(2) of the NLRA which designates employer domination or interference "with the formation or administration of any labor organization" an unfair labor practice. Although this provision of the Act focuses upon the integrity of the day-to-day employer-union relationship, it will be seen that this section may also have a direct bearing upon representation election proceedings, for if the employer is found to have violated Section 8(a)(2) and the union receiving a majority of the votes is found to be an illegally-assisted organization, the employer's conduct may also serve as a basis to set the election aside.

Application of the principle of "strict neutrality" does not preclude all forms of employer conduct which may incidentally benefit one of the competing unions. The employer must, for example, be able to maintain uninterrupted labor relations with an incumbent union during the election campaign period, even though to do so may tend to strengthen the incumbent's election prospects. This may include administration of the contract, negotiations over the terms and conditions of employment, and grievance processing. Also, the Board has stated that:

> [A]n employer may urge its employees to vote, provided it does not tell them how to vote or otherwise interfere with the exercise of their free choice in the matter.[3]

In another decision, the Board held that an employer was free to express a preference for one of the competing labor organizations as long as his statements did not coerce the employees or indicate the promise of benefits.[4] The line dividing permissible speech from objectionable promises and threats is not always clear.

As the foregoing discussion suggests, the general principle of strict employer neutrality is subject to many exceptions, and for a real understanding of the Board's policies in this area an analysis of its decisions is necessary. For convenience, the relevant cases have been categorized according to the specific type of employer conduct involved: preferential treatment, unlawful support, declaration of preference, contract negotiation and execution, and pro-union solicitation by a supervisor.

---

[3] Pennsylvania Power & Light Co., 66 N.L.R.B. 1391, 1393, 17 L.R.R.M. 420, 421 (1946).

[4] Repcal Brass Co., 110 N.L.R.B. 193, 34 L.R.R.M. 1617 (1954).

PREFERENTIAL TREATMENT AND SUPPORT

As indicated earlier, Section 8(a)(2) of the Act has served as a foundation for regulation of the type and degree of permissible assistance to a union during the election period. It is not necessary, however, to find an 8(a)(2) violation in order to set aside an election. The nature of the employer's conduct which constitutes the unfair labor practice extends beyond the breach of the requirement of neutrality. The essence of the statutory violation has been described as follows:

> A labor organization is considered dominated within the meaning of Section 8(a)(2) if the employer has interfered with its formation or has assisted or supported its administration to such an extent that the organization must be regarded as the employer's creation rather than the true bargaining representative of the employees.[5]

Section 8(a)(2) cases primarily involve employer assistance which subjugates the union in its position and role as the certified bargaining representative. On the other hand, when charges of preferential treatment or unlawful assistance are raised as objections to a representation election, a mere showing of disparate treatment during the election period affecting one of the labor organizations or its supporters may suffice for a finding of election interference. The assistance may involve: (1) the employer's discriminatory grants of privileges to one union designed to influence the employees to vote for the employer's choice; (2) direct support of one of the parties in an attempt to undermine or to restrict the campaign effectiveness of the other union or; (3) express employer declarations of preference for one of the competing parties.

Discriminatory Treatment

An employer may seek to aid one union by denying its competitors equal opportunities to campaign. Initially, the Board must determine whether actual discrimination has taken place. In *LaPointe Machine Tool Co.*[6] the Board said that the granting of requests to one competing union does not constitute unlawful assistance unless the other union requests and is denied the same treatment or privileges. Absent such requests for equal treatment, it might be reasoned that no "privilege" in fact was granted. A slightly different focus is apparent in *X-Ray Mfg. Corp. of*

---

[5] 27 NLRB ANN. REP. 99 (1962).

[6] 113 N.L.R.B. 172, 36 L.R.R.M 1273 (1955).

America [7] where the Board held that there was no interference if the competing union was given similar but not identical campaign rights. The employer refused to allow one union, as he earlier had the other, the privilege of holding a campaign meeting in the plant during the employees' lunch hour. Instead, the union was permitted to electioneer at the loading platform on the company premises at times when the employees were present. The Board stated in response to the complaint of disparate treatment, "[I]t cannot be said that the mere denial of equality in one of the available means of communication created such an imbalance as would warrant our setting aside the election." [8] The dissent basically disagreed with the majority's finding that these were similar conditions for electioneering.

In other cases, unlawful employer assistance takes the form of discriminatory treatment of the employees supporting the disfavored union. The discrimination may relate to campaign activities, employee benefits, or terms and conditions of employment. The concern is that this conduct will have an immediate impact on the workers and will influence their support of the union. In *The Murray Co.* [9] the Board set aside the election when AFL supporters were allowed to wear campaign pins, while the employees favoring the CIO were asked to remove their pins. [10] The Board found in *Red Ball Motor Freight, Inc.* [11] that the employer had provided unlawful assistance to one union by denying overtime to some employees in order to encourage their support for that union. The employer also made a general offer of preferential overtime to the supporters of the union.

The company in *Humble Oil & Refining Co.* [12] interfered with an election by maintaining a retirement plan which conditioned the benefits upon the continued representation of the employees by the incumbent union. The Board reached its decision by analogiz-

---

[7] 143 N.L.R.B. 247, 53 L.R.R.M. 1287 (1963).

[8] *Id.* at 250, 53 L.R.R.M. at 1288.

[9] 49 N.L.R.B. 1225, 12 L.R.R.M. 212 (1943).

[10] Additional conduct mentioned in the case, although not required in support of the decision, included direct support by supervisors during the campaign—*i.e.* distributing union application cards and campaign pins.

[11] 157 N.L.R.B. 1237, 61 L.R.R.M. 1522 (1966), *enforced,* 379 F.2d 137, 65 L.R.R.M. 2309 (D.C. Cir. 1967).

[12] 160 N.L.R.B. 1088, 62 L.R.R.M. 1593 (1966).

ing this case to one where the employer had maintained a pension plan whose benefits were conditioned on the absence of union representation in the plant.[13] In this latter case the employer's conduct constituted an 8(a)(2) violation.

Preferential Treatment to One Union

In contrast to the cases cited above, the employer may attempt to provide assistance directly to one of the organizations seeking to represent the employees with the expectation that the employees ultimately will be led to favor that union.[14]

In *Atlas Imperial Diesel Engine Co.*[15] the employer engineered support for one union in the course of hiring employees. When the workers came to the plant and registered for employment, they were sent to the union and requested to sign a voluntary dues checkoff form. The employer did not attempt to dispel the suggestion that this procedure was necessary in order to receive a work assignment. The Board said that this conduct interfered with the subsequent election because the company union was not authorized to require membership and the procedure of clearance "accorded unlawful preferential treatment to the [union] in the assignment or transfer of employees to the can manufacturing plant."[16] The Board's reasoning can be compared to a more recent case, *American Beef Packers, Inc.*,[17] where it was found that the employer did not unlawfully assist the incumbent union during the election period by furnishing new employees with dues checkoff forms. The Board relied on the employer's practice of emphasizing that the workers did not have to join the union. At the same time, it rejected the trial examiner's broad assertion that election laboratory conditions "require an employer to take affirmative action to advise employees of a rival union's desire to represent employees." [18]

---

[13] Melville Confections, Inc., 142 N.L.R.B. 1334, 53 L.R.R.M. 1251 (1963), *enforced*, 327 F.2d 689, 55 L.R.R.M. 2241 (7th Cir.), *cert. denied*, 377 U.S. 933, 56 L.R.R.M. 2224 (1964).

[14] Dove Mfg. Co., 145 N.L.R.B. 1379, 55 L.R.R.M. 1154 (1964).

[15] 91 N.L.R.B. 530, 26 L.R.R.M. 1539 (1950).

[16] *Id.* at 532, 26 L.R.R.M. at 1540.

[17] 187 N.L.R.B. 1004, 76 L.R.R.M. 1797 (1971).

[18] *Id.* at 1004, 76 L.R.R.M. at 1798.

Employer support of an organization which constitutes election interference may closely approximate conduct in violation of Section 8(a) (2), or in fact it concurrently may serve as an unfair labor practice.[19] The *Edmont, Inc.* case [20] held that the Edmont Employees Committee had been unlawfully supported and assisted by the employer with the result that it was accorded a preferential status in violation of the Board's election procedure guidelines. The elements of the violation were: (1) the employer had been instrumental in activating the Committee at the outset of the election period; (2) he utilized it as an outlet for employee grievances; and (3) the Committee was used as a campaign tool against the competing union.[21]

Both the *Edmont* case and an earlier one, *Majestic Metal Specialties, Inc.,*[22] indicate that employer unlawful assistance does not have to be in support of a candidate to the representation election. In *Majestic Metal* the Board set aside the election where the employer had assisted an employees' "Council" in waging an antiunion campaign. The proposed alternative to the rejection of the union was the promise of increased employer relations with the "Council" after the election. In either of the situations presented by these two cases upon the question of support during the campaign, the employer violated the requirement of neutrality during the election period. Employer *domination* of the "Council" or the "Committee" also was a major basis for election interference in the Board's decision. In the latter case the factors the Board stressed were that the organization of the "Council" took place at the company and on company time, the organizers were paid while engaged in the activity, the employer furnished luncheons to the members, he provided stenographic help, and he donated the proceeds of the company vending machines for the group's use. The organization's structure reflected employer domination since supervisors served as "Council" members.

---

[19] For a general discussion of Section 8(a)(2) violations and the appropriate Board standards, see MORRIS, THE DEVELOPING LABOR LAW 125-49 (1969).

[20] 139 N.L.R.B. 1528, 51 L.R.R.M. 1534 (1962).

[21] *See also* Illinois Marble Co., Inc., 167 N.L.R.B. 1011, 66 L.R.R.M. 1235 (1967). The Board held that there was election interference, and an 8(a)(1) violation. It rejected the union's 8(a)(2) charge.

[22] 92 N.L.R.B. 1854, 27 L.R.R.M. 1332 (1951).

Section 8(a)(2) Violations and Election Interference

On certain occasions the Board has entertained the question of the effect upon the election of the presence on the ballot by a union which has been supported and dominated by the employer in violation of Section 8(a)(2). Where the complaint alleges both the unfair labor practice and election interference and the Board sustains the charges, it will set aside the election.[23] The Board indicated that the outcome of the election does not establish the union as the majority representative of the employees. Although it was not expressly stated, the Board's decision suggests that the presence of an 8(a)(2) violation during the election period automatically constitutes election interference.

The *Reliance Steel Products Co.*[24] case raised the issue of the propriety of setting aside the results of an election as a remedy for an unfair labor practice rather than as the result of objections to the representation election proceedings. An election was held in the company; subsequently, the losing union filed election objections which were rejected because they were untimely. Later on the same day it filed an 8(a)(2) unfair labor practice charge. The Board held that the employer had violated the Act and agreed with the trial examiner's prescribed remedy.

> Consequently, I must recommend that the standard remedial provision for a violation of Section 8(a)(2) be applied. Since this requires that the Respondent not recognize the unlawfully assisted union unless and until that organization shall have been duly certified by the Board, I must point out that this further means *certified after a valid* election. Under the circumstances present here, and in view of the unlawful assistance rendered Local 372, the election . . . must be held invalid and the results set aside.[25]

On appeal, the Fifth Circuit denied enforcement to the Board order.[26] It relied upon the fact that the union had filed its complaint after the five-day time limitation period for election objections past and claimed, "The Board may not achieve indirectly,

---

[23] Lunardi-Central Distributing Co., 161 N.L.R.B. 1443, 63 L.R.R.M. 1457 (1966); Midway Clover Farm Market, 175 N.L.R.B. 1065, 71 L.R.R.M. 1171 (1969).

[24] 135 N.L.R.B. 730, 49 L.R.R.M. 1559 (1962).

[25] *Id.* at 747 n.19 (trial examiner's opinion).

[26] NLRB v. Reliance Steel Products Co., 322 F.2d 49, 53 L.R.R.M. 2961 (5th Cir. 1963).

by way of the unfair labor practice charges, that which it could not achieve directly by way of objections to such election." [27] The general proposition that the unfair labor practice remedy to the 8(a)(2) violation could include setting aside the election was not challenged by the court's ruling.

In *Weather Seal, Inc.*,[28] the losing union in an election filed both unfair labor practices charges and objections to the representation proceedings. The same employer conduct served as the basis for both complaints. The Board determined that the employer had violated the Act by assisting the union, and that this had interfered with the election and directed a second election to be held. Since, the events found to be 8(a)(2) violations occurred before the election petition had been filed,[29] they could not have been used to support an objection to the conduct of the election. The Board resolved this argument by concluding:

> [i]t was the participation in the election of the unlawfully assisted union, not the unfair labor practices themselves, which rendered that election invalid. In the circumstances here, it is immaterial that the objections did not specifically rely on the assisted union's appearance on the ballot.[30]

The Board's reasoning no doubt was structured in such a way as to avoid another reversal by the circuit court.[31] Although the rule that the appearance of an unlawfully assisted union on the ballot is sufficient to constitute election interference, may often be a reasonable one, this case is not fully consistent with the policy of limiting collateral attack by the Board to the "finality" of representation elections. The employer's unlawful conduct clearly had preceded the election period. In fashioning the appropriate remedy, the Board should have investigated more deeply into the likelihood of a lingering restraining or coercive effect upon the employees during the critical period. The Board's decision to set

---

[27] *Id.* at 54, 53 L.R.R.M. at 2965.

[28] 161 N.L.R.B. 1226, 63 L.R.R.M. 1428 (1966).

[29] The Board indicated the conduct occurring during the election period was insufficient to constitute election interference.

[30] 161 N.L.R.B. at 1229, n.9, 63 L.R.R.M. at 1432.

[31] In a footnote to its conclusion in *Weather Seal, Inc.*, the Board said that although *Reliance Steel Products Co.* had been denied enforcement by the court, "insofar as we [the Board] concluded that the election therein could be set aside, we respectfully adhere to our view." 161 N.L.R.B. at 1229 n.9, 63 L.R.R.M. at 1432.

aside that election should be assessed on the basis of its potential failure to promote a primary objective of the NLRA—certainty.

Declaration of Preference

In contrast to the categories of employer assistance involving active employer patronage of a union, the Board also has found that employer statements declaring a preference in the choice of competing organizations may constitute election interference. As indicated earlier, the employer generally may urge the workers to vote, and he may endorse a particular union. The Board evaluates declarations of preference on the same basis as it does in cases involving employer promises and predictions concerning the effects of employee unionization. The Board examines the content of the statements to determine if an employer's endorsement suggest a promise of benefits for voting for a particular organization, or a threat of reprisal and loss of benefits by voting for the other. The question of the degree to which the employer may forcefully assert his preferences or views has not been dealt with adequately. Presumably, Section 8(c) of the Act protects the employer's right to express his approval or dislike for a particular union. However, approval or dislike, when expressed in strong terms, may be interpreted as carrying an implication that the employer would deal differently with the preferred union if elected than with the rival organization. This will result in election invalidation.

In *Boston Mutual Life Insurance Co.*[32] the Board was faced with rather strong employer language condemning one of the parties competing in the election. One letter to the employees emphasized "the dislike and contempt that your Company has for [the Union]."[33] A second letter by the employer mentioned that benefits came from the company; it continued by saying, "It should be obvious that no company in the exercise of good discretionary judgment would agree to arbitration procedure if it has no respect for the representatives of the union with which it is negotiating."[34] The Board concluded that the two letters implied an intention by the employer to provide better contract benefits if the employees chose the other union as its representative. The Board

---

[32] 110 N.L.R.B. 272, 34 L.R.R.M. 1636 (1954).

[33] *Id.* at 273, 34 L.R.R.M. at 1636 (emphasis omitted).

[34] *Id.* at 274, 34 L.R.R.M. at 1636 (emphasis omitted).

also indicated that each letter contained an element of the threat, but that either letter alone was not unlawful. The dissent objected to this merger of the two statements. The question which was unanswered was the significance and effect of the employer's strong comments against that union.

When the employer's endorsement remains simple in its content, the Board will not find election interference.[35] An employer was permitted to urge the employees to select job security instead of wage increases, and to mention specifically the unions identified with these campaign issues.[36] Statements which include a comparison of competing unions based on past activities or their previous bargaining practices are normally protected. There was no interference in a case where an employer compared the respective union wage rates, the strike records, and the initiation fees and assessments of the two organizations.[37] Also, the Board dismissed union objections to an employer's statement that the incumbent union was a better choice and would provide higher wages and a more favorable contract.[38] He had based his judgment on the incumbent's contracts with other companies.

The prediction of possible economic consequences to follow from the selection of one of the unions may be upheld by the Board. However, its practice in evaluating such statements has not been consistent. In *Rold Gold of California, Inc.*[39] the employer argued that the selection of one union could result in a loss of business because all of the competitors had contracts with the other union.

> If we have trouble with [the union] and our competitors can deliver in the Markets under Local 400, then our customers will go to other Companies—our competitors. If that happens, there will be no job for you. . . . Since all our competitors have contracts with Local 400, we have to be in the same business position, if we want to keep selling our products.[40]

The Board said there was no threat and this was merely an expression of preference. The substance of the statement in

---

[35] United Fur Mfg. Ass'n, Inc., 43 N.L.R.B. 369, 11 L.R.R.M. 38 (1942).

[36] Rheem Mfg. Co., 114 N.L.R.B. 404, 36 L.R.R.M. 1600 (1955).

[37] Clayton & Lambert Mfg. Co., 118 N.L.R.B. 1376, 40 L.R.R.M. 1387 (1957).

[38] Kinsman Transit Co., 78 N.L.R.B. 78, 22 L.R.R.M. 1165 (1948).

[39] 123 N.L.R.B. 285, 43 L.R.R.M. 1421 (1951).

[40] *Id.* at 286, 43 L.R.R.M. at 1421.

this case should be compared to *Benjamin Electric Mfg. Co.*[41] where the Board said that the employer interfered with an election by the threat of a plant removal if the union lost the election. His argument was based on economic grounds to the effect that the union label was necessary in the manufacture and successful sale of his product in that area.

The Board set aside an election in *Hudson Sharp Machine Co.*[42] where the employer defended the union he preferred in the face of certain rumors negatively affecting its position:

> We understand the statement has been made that unless the International Association of Machinists wins this election there will be no contract protection for the employees of Hudson Sharp. This is not true. The Company guarantees that if the Hudson Sharp Employees Association wins the election that it will negotiate a contract equal to or better than the one that presently exists.[43]

The Board said this employer created the impression of benefits to be gained from voting for the Employees Association over the International Association of Machinists. It said he merely should have denied the rumor.

As a comparison of these decisions indicates, the regulation of employer endorsements in favor of a particular union presents the same problem of analyzing speech on a case-by-case method as was demonstrated in the cases involving employer promises and predictions of the effects of unionization. Here, too, the interests of fairness and efficient administration would be better served if the Board would avoid detailed "postmortem examinations" of the precise wording of employer statements and instead adopt a policy which favored a free exchange of ideas, opinions, and preferences by all parties, and placed greater reliance on the employees to evaluate campaign statements for themselves.

CONTRACT NEGOTIATION AND EXECUTION

In addition to prohibiting preferential treatment of one of the competing unions during a representation election, the Board also maintains a policy making it unlawful for an employer

---

[41] 122 N.L.R.B. 1517, 43 L.R.R.M. 1332 (1959).

[42] 107 N.L.R.B. 32, 33 L.R.R.M. 1042 (1953).

[43] *Id.* at 33, 33 L.R.R.M. at 1043.

to execute a contract with any of the parties involved in the election.[44]

> Signing a contract with one of the two competing unions after an election has been directed accords a potent form of assistance to that organization and thereby prevents a free choice by the employees.[45]

The Board in the quoted case summarily dismissed the employer's claim that a new contract granting a wage increase was signed in order to maintain a parity between his wages and those of his competitors. The mere signing was sufficient enough to be considered interference. However, the employer may sign a contract covering other employees in the plant who are not involved in the election.[46] Quite obviously, the employer's neutrality or breach of it is not at issue in such a situation. The Board feels that an agreement reached before an election often is like a promise of future benefits to the employees to be derived from selection of that union, and thereby it accords recognition and prestige to the organization. Possibly, the execution of an agreement at this time creates a sense of futility in the employees' minds for voting for the alternate union.

The Board's policy is subject to the proviso that the election period should not dictate a lapse in the contractual relationship between the employer and the incumbent union. The union is entitled during this period to obtain from the employer all of the rights and benefits under the existing contract.[47] The Board has expressed this requirement of continuity in labor-management relations in the alternative by emphasizing that it would "give an undue advantage to the rival union by refusing to permit the incumbent union to continue administering its contract or processing grievances through its stewards."[48] Consequently, heavy emphasis is placed upon assessing proper administration of the contract by the parties and determining what prompted them to negotiate a contract or to make a new

---

[44] Johnson Transport Co., 106 N.L.R.B. 1105, 32 L.R.R.M. 1621 (1953).

[45] Id. at 1107, 32 L.R.R.M. at 1621.

[46] Emerson Electric Co., 106 N.L.R.B. 149, 32 L.R.R.M. 1211 (1953).

[47] The Coolidge Corp., 108 N.L.R.B. 3, 33 L.R.R.M. 1470 (1954).

[48] Shea Chemical Corp., 121 N.L.R.B. 1027, 1029, 42 L.R.R.M. 1486, 1487 (1958).

agreement. Mitigating factors in these cases may include business reasons and related contract provisions.

In *G & H Towing Co.*[49] the Board held that there was no interference when the employer and the union merely extended the termination date of their contract during the pre-election period. They engaged in no negotiations and did not make any changes to the agreement. The Board emphasized that the act of merely continuing existing benefits and conditions of employment until the representation issue was settled did not violate the employer's neutrality or accord the union a priority status. The Board upheld the results of another election where the specific provisions of the existing contract justified negotiations with the incumbent union while the election was pending. The decision indicates that there can be no interference or unlawful assistance if the parties have previously agreed to a contract and in fact were bound by its terms. Any influence upon the voters arising from such negotiations must be accepted as one of the natural disadvantages the competing union must face as a challenger to the incumbent union's position.

This principle was illustrated fully in *The Coolidge Corp.*[50] case where the parties renegotiated wages during the election period pursuant to a provision authorizing wage reopening during the life of the agreement. As the result of another provision creating the option of automatic renewal of the contract, the renegotiated wages became incorporated into the contract, which by the exercise of the parties' will was extended for an additional full year. The Board dismissed the challenging union's charge of election interference on the ground that the parties were merely applying the contract. It is interesting to note that in spite of the legal propriety of the parties' conduct, the employees were presented with increased economic benefits extending for a full new term during the period when they were faced with the choice of replacing their current bargaining agent. The legal requirement of employer neutrality quite easily could be a meaningless principle in this situation.

In *Traub's Market, Inc.*[51] the Board apparently applied certain limitations to agreements made by an employer and a

---

[49] 168 N.L.R.B. 589, 66 L.R.R.M. 1343 (1967).

[50] At note 47, *supra.*

[51] 205 N.L.R.B. No. 124, 84 L.R.R.M. 1078 (1973).

union in the face of a pending representation question. In this case the employer and the incumbent union were parties to an existing agreement. Prior to its expiration they bargained for a new contract and finally agreed upon the substance of the new contract. They did not formally execute it at this time. Subsequently, prior to the formal expiration of the existing collective bargaining agreement, the challenging union informed the employer that it represented a substantial portion of the employees and that the existing union was not the representative of the majority of the work force. It also requested a cessation of further collective bargaining with the incumbent. The challenging union then filed a representation election petition.

The employer executed the new compact with the incumbent union before the regional director was able to hold a hearing on the election petition. The Board concluded, quite affirmatively, that execution of the new contract with the incumbent occurred in the face of a pending challenge for certification as the bargaining agent. The NLRB emphasized that the election petition had been filed before the existing contract had expired, and before a new agreement had been reached. While not attempting to question the "timeliness" of the challenging union's petition for a representation election, one can raise the matter of the significance, if any, of the substantive oral agreement reached by the company and the incumbent union before the organizing attempts became evident. The employer's subsequent actions and their timing may have been subject to question, but the Board should have provided comment upon the effect of the oral agreement to a contract. In a literal sense collective bargaining had reached a material stage of accomplishment, but merely lacked formal execution. This consideration related to a challenge by an outside union merits closer attention than was evidenced by the Board in *Traub's Market*.

An example of business considerations justifying employer-union negotiations arose in *Tennessee Auger Co., Inc.*[52] The employer sought to increase the price of coal it sold to the Tennessee Valley Authority (TVA). However, pursuant to its contract with the TVA it was required to increase its employees' wages before increasing the sale price of its coal. As a result the employer and the union negotiated new wages during the election period. Relying on the conditions expressed

---

[52] 169 N.L.R.B. 914, 78 L.R.R.M. 1295 (1968).

in the contract with the TVA, the Board said there was no interference.[53]

The alleged unlawful conduct in many cases consists of negotiations and agreements which fall short of the formal execution of a collective bargaining agreement. The *Kiekhaefer Corp.*[54] case indicated that the act of continuing negotiations during the election period would interfere with the election.[55] The Board has continually held that a critical element of the interference arising in these cases is that the employees obtain knowledge about the agreement or any other resolutions reached during the negotiations.[56] In *Krambo Food Stores, Inc.*[57] the employer agreed to the union's general proposal to make any subsequent wage increase retroactive to a certain date. There was no bargaining on any specific contract proposals. At this time the union informed the employees about the agreement concerning retroactivity. The Board, upon objection by the losing union, set aside the election because of the restraining effect upon the voters created by the negotiation meeting and the public disclosure of the general agreement. The Board did not indicate whether the agreement would have been permitted absent publication of it by the union. In reaching its decision the Board rejected the employer's argument that the effect of the disclosure had been neutralized by his subsequent statement that he would be willing to negotiate on the question of retroactivity with whichever union won the election.

The Board gave undue significance to the disclosure of an agreement in *The Electric Auto-Lite Co.*[58] The employer and the incumbent independent union had initiated bargaining for

---

[53] The Board also mentioned that the increase was made to comport with prevailing industry rates; the question of the election at that time had not been fully resolved, and the competing union in its campaign had invited the employer to raise its wages.

[54] 120 N.L.R.B. 95, 41 L.R.R.M. 1442 (1958).

[55] However, this was not the sole basis for setting aside the election. For other grounds, see pp. 210-11, *infra*. *See also* Krambo Food Stores, Inc., 120 N.L.R.B. 1391, 42 L.R.R.M. 1188 (1958), which indicated that negotiating with the union was unlawful. The Board in this case also included other reasons for setting aside the election.

[56] General Steel Products Corp., 77 N.L.R.B. 810, 22 L.R.R.M. 1090 (1948).

[57] At note 55, *supra*.

[58] 116 N.L.R.B. 788, 38 L.R.R.M. 1366 (1956).

a contract renewal before the commencement of the election period. After the election had been directed, the old contract expired and the union went on strike. Three days later (fifteen days before the election) the employer and the union orally agreed upon a new contract and the strike ended. The employees became aware of this new agreement in the course of the incumbent union's campaign. The election was set aside because of the agreement reached during this period and because of the disclosure of it to the employees. The Board refused to consider the argument that the fact "that the Employer acted under duress [of the strike] would dissipate any assumption by the employees that the Employer was not neutral." [59] The employer's alternatives were an oral settlement of the dispute at that time or a continuing work stoppage for at least two more weeks. The Board seemed to ignore the fact that the union was bound by its responsibilities as bargaining agent for the workers to fight for a new contract. There was no evidence in this case that the strike or the settlement was a ploy to aid the union in its campaign. The employer was left with no lawful alternative to end the strike at that time since any settlement reached during that period to resume operations would have put the employees on notice of the existence of an agreement.

Processing grievances with the incumbent union during the election period generally does not constitute election interference.[60] The conduct no doubt lacks the appearance of preferential treatment to the union because it primarily administers the problem of the employees and makes a determination of their rights. For the most part relevant grievance procedures are specified by the collective bargaining agreement, and they are designed to play an on-going day-to-day role in employer-union relations.

Cases of interference arising from grievance processing occur when the employer joins in resolving a long-standing grievance and his timing is motivated by the pendency of the election.[61] There can arise a prejudicial effect against the challenging

---

[59] Id. at 790, 38 L.R.R.M. at 1366.

[60] The Electric Auto-Lite Co., 89 N.L.R.B. 1407, 26 L.R.R.M. 1126 (1950).

[61] See, e.g., Minnesota Mining & Mfg. Co., 61 N.L.R.B. 697, 16 L.R.R.M. 103 (1945).

union which compares to the grant or offer of benefits by the employer in an attempt to sway the employees against unionization. In *Kiekhaefer Corp.*[62] the employer settled four or five employee grievances on the morning of the election. The news of this spread to several other employees before the voting began. The Board categorized this conduct as a concession made in favor of the incumbent independent union.[63] In *Krambo Food Stores, Inc.*[64] the employer agreed with the current bargaining agent during the election period to continue the processing of grievances through the union stewards under the terms of the contract when the contract had been held by the Board not to be a bar to the election. The Board said this was an affirmative concession which, when disclosed to the employees, accorded the union an advantage and preferred status in the critical pre-election period. The more significant aspect of this case, which likely influenced the Board, was the questionable manner in which the incumbent union had gained recognition. However, the dissent argued that despite the alleged impropriety of earlier proceedings, the union had not lost its natural rights as the incumbent—including the right to process grievances.

The general policy of restricting the execution of a collective bargaining agreement during the election period has a firm foundation in the promotion of a fair and impartial election. The rule must be balanced by the consideration that the incumbent has the right to execute its responsibilities as the bargaining agent. Certain cases involving less than formal agreements or negotiations arising during the election period have been restrictive in their recognition of the mitigating circumstances inherent in the bargaining relationship. Disclosure of an agreement to the employees is an important factor in setting aside the election. The unlawfulness of grievance processing prior to the election is determined from the employer's express or implied motive for resolving the dispute and from the timing of the settlement.

---

[62] At note 54, *supra*.

[63] Also, the employer continued to negotiate for a new contract during the election period and made a proposal satisfying most of the Independent's demands.

[64] At note 55, *supra*.

SUPERVISOR'S PROUNION SOLICITATION

Solicitation of employee support for the union by supervisory personnel is a form of union assistance during an election which raises new issues on the question of election interference.[65]

> If supervisors actively encourage employees to vote for the Union, and the employer takes no known stance to the contrary, the supervisory conduct might well imply to the employees that the employer favors the Union. . . . The other conceivable effect of such supervisory activity is found in the implications of the continuing relationship between the supervisors and the employees.[66]

In cases of a union victory the employer may contest the results of the election on the basis of a misrepresentation of his position on the question of unionization or the creation of employee fear of harassment or discrimination by the supervisor in the event of a union defeat. In assessing these allegations of election interference the Board must weigh them against the consideration that the employer should not be allowed to assert his agent's wrongdoing as grounds for setting aside an election. The Board's policy in these cases has been to assess the issue of interference in conjunction with the employer's acquiescence in the

---

[65] *See also* Longchamps, Inc. d/b/a Steak and Brew, 205 N.L.R.B. No. 168, 84 L.R.R.M. 1113 (1973), where Chairman Miller in a lengthy dissent criticized the majority's dismissal of charges alleging employer prounion solicitation:

> It is difficult to see much practical difference, so far as the effect on employees is concerned, between direct supervisory solicitation of authorization cards and company-blessed solicitation by a union organizer on company time and property of such signatures, especially in an atmosphere where the employer . . . indicates that he approves of and supports the efforts of the organizer and thereafter grants voluntary recognition on the basis of signatures thus obtained. *Id.*, 84 L.R.R.M. at 1115.

In spite of the fact that the union was not competing against another organization for certification as the bargaining representative, Miller felt the employer's conduct prevented the employees' free choice, as expressed on the authorization cards. He summarized the impact of the actions:

> But for the 14 cards solicited on February 28 in the manner described above, the union would not have represented a majority of the employees on March 16 or at any other time. *Id.* 84 L.R.R.M. at 1115.

Following a card check the employer signed a collective bargaining agreement with the union which contained, *inter alia*, a union security provision and a checkoff clause.

[66] Stevenson Equipment Co., 174 N.L.R.B. 865, 866, 70 L.R.R.M. 1302 (1969).

supervisor's conduct and his attempts to disavow his actions.[67] On the matter of restraint and coercion of the employees as a result of supervisor solicitations, an important factor for consideration has been the role and authority of the supervisor with respect to the workers.

An initial determination must be made concerning the substance and significance of alleged prounion solicitation. The employer must offer evidence of affirmative solicitations by the supervisors. In *Brown-Dunkin Co.*[68] the supervisor's mere presence at two of five union meetings did not constitute prounion activity. Also, in *Boggs and Co., Inc.*[69] the appearance of a supervisor in the company of the union's business agent on occasion before the election and at the polls was not interference. In another case an employer's objections were dismissed where the conduct was found to be "in a spirit of levity" and the prounion statements were termed "innocuous." [70] More recently, the Board in *Pine Cone, Inc.*[71] said there was no interference where the supervisor merely described union benefits to the employees. It is noteworthy that the Board criticized, but it did not find unlawful, the supervisor's solicitation of authorization cards from the employees because they were already union members.

In most situations the Board requires the employer to disavow supervisors' actions or to dissociate himself from any prounion statements of which he is aware before it will allow him to ask for a rerun election on the basis of such conduct.[72] An effective disavowal, however, may be held to neutralize the effects of a supervisor's participation in a union pre-election campaign.[73] The

---

[67] Talladega Cotton Factory, Inc., 91 N.L.R.B. 470, 26 L.R.R.M. 1517 (1950).

[68] 118 N.L.R.B. 1603, 40 L.R.R.M. 1432 (1957).

[69] 122 N.L.R.B. 758, 43 L.R.R.M. 1182 (1958).

[70] NLRB v. Crest Leather Mfg. Corp., 414 F.2d 421, 71 L.R.R.M. 3022 (5th Cir. 1969), *enforcing,* 167 N.L.R.B. 1085, 66 L.R.R.M. 1240 (1967).

[71] 189 N.L.R.B. No. 88, 76 L.R.R.M. 1694 (1971).

[72] *See also* NLRB v. Air Control Products, Inc., 335 F.2d 245, 56 L.R.R.M. 2904 (5th Cir. 1964), were union solicitations by supervisory personnel *unknown* to the employer were cause for setting aside the election.

[73] Clauson's Garage Co., 107 N.L.R.B. 1499, 33 L.R.R.M. 1423 (1954).

employer must communicate his disavowal to the employees.[74] It is not sufficient to tell the particular supervisor to cease his activity. On the other hand, in *Robbins Tire & Rubber Co., Inc.*[75] the Board held that an employer's statement that "there would be no coercion of any kind" did not constitute an affective disavowal of previous coercive conduct by a supervisor. Although it was an expression of the employer's intent to maintain his neutrality, it did not dissipate the effect of the supervisor's activities. The employer had been unaware of the conduct, and, therefore, his pledge apparently was ineffective because it was considered to be a general campaign statement. No doubt the Board was influenced by the fact that the supervisor's conduct was coercive rather than simply partisan campaigning. In addition to knowledge of the solicitations, there must be sufficient opportunity for the employer to disavow them. In *Lamar Electric Membership Corp.*[76] the election was set aside because the employer only learned of the prounion campaigning by a supervisor the day before the election.[77]

The importance of the supervisor's position and the extent of his authority are two important factors in the regulation of supervisor conduct. They bear a direct relationship to the expected degree of restraint and coercion of the employees which may have occured as a result of the solicitation. In *Fall River House, Inc.*[78] one reason for dismissing the employer's objections was that the supervisor held a minor position. The Board also held that his conduct was of a *de minimis* nature. On the other hand, the election was set aside in *Sheraton Motor Inn*[79] where the individual was a major supervisor, and he engaged in active and outspoken support for the union. The two factors were used in support of the conclusion that the employees were coerced into

---

[74] Hadley Mfg. Corp., 106 N.L.R.B. 620, 32 L.R.R.M. 1512 (1953).

[75] 72 N.L.R.B. 157, 19 L.R.R.M. 1154 (1947).

[76] 164 N.L.R.B. 979, 65 L.R.R.M. 1199 (1967), *remanded from* 362 F.2d 505, 62 L.R.R.M. 2420 (5th Cir. 1966).

[77] *Compare* NLRB v. Piggly Wiggly Red River Co., Inc., 464 F.2d 106, 80 L.R.R.M. 3147 (8th Cir. 1972) *with* Pine Cone, Inc., at note 71, *supra.* The court in *Piggly Wiggly* indicated that the closeness of the election could be a factor in reaching a decision.

[78] 196 N.L.R.B. No. 17, 79 L.R.R.M. 1688 (1972).

[79] 194 N.L.R.B. No. 115, 79 L.R.R.M. 1040 (1971).

voting for the union because of the fear of subsequent retaliation. The Fourth Circuit has stressed the significance of the
supervisor's day-to-day authority stating in *NLRB v. Heck's,
Inc.*: [80]

> Such day-to-day authority over employees provided a basis for
> potential tyranny when improperly exercised by a supervisor
> thwarted in his aim to obtain union recognition, and an employee
> properly could doubt his ability to obtain protection by appeals to
> higher company authority.[81]

The elements of his authority included control of daily work
schedules and days off. Later in *Turner's Express, Inc. v.
NLRB* [82] the same court emphasized the supervisor's authority
to hire temporary employees, to recommend wage increases and
employee discipline, to impose certain discipline, and to assign
overtime.

Both of the above decisions by the Fourth Circuit suggest
that a supervisor's extensive authority over the employees takes
precedence over the employer's ultimate authority in the plant
and consequently restricts the ability of the employee to disavow
any threats of retaliation or prounion solicitation. In *Turner's
Express* the court stated:

> In industry an employee is more concerned about the attitude of
> his immediate supervisor than he is with the feelings of the com-
> pany president. This is similar to the Army where a private is
> more concerned with the attitude of his corporal or sergeant than
> he is with the colonel or general, since the corporal and sergeant
> control his day to day life.[83]

Furthermore, it stated that the supervisor's authority coupled
with prounion solicitations could make the employee fear for his
job security despite knowledge of his employer's antiunion position. The court's view provides an interesting departure from
previous Board decisions. The Board apparently has not yet
adopted this view of the dominance of the supervisor over the
employer in the industrial environment. Both views are subject
to criticism on the ground that neither the NLRB nor the judi-

---

[80] 386 F.2d 317, 66 L.R.R.M. 2495 (4th Cir. 1967).

[81] *Id.* at 322, 66 L.R.R.M. at 2498-99.

[82] 456 F.2d 289, 79 L.R.R.M. 2796 (4th Cir. 1972). *See also* NLRB v. Roselon
Southern, Inc., 382 F.2d 245, 66 L.R.R.M. 2036 (6th Cir. 1967).

[83] 456 F.2d at 292-93, 79 L.R.R.M. at 2798.

ciary has attempted to obtain evidence in support of their conclusions concerning the necessity or ability to disavow supervisors' prounion solicitations.

CONCLUDING REMARKS

When two or more unions are competing in an election for the right to represent the employees as the bargaining agent, the basic rule which the Board seeks to enforce is the employer's neutrality in regard to the support of one of the unions or opposition to the other. The voters must not be induced by implied or express promises of benefits or threats of retaliation in the event of the victory by one of the parties. Although there is a close relationship between election interference and the Section 8(a)(2) unfair labor practice, one does not have to prove domination of a union arising from support or assistance accorded to it in order to have the election results set aside.

An area of uncertainty is the propriety of employer declarations of preference. He may endorse one of the competing unions, but he may not threaten or coerce the employees as a result of his endorsement. The Board's rule suffers from the difficulty of attempting to regulate employer speech too closely on a case-by-case basis.

Additional considerations on the issue of interference emerge when one of the organizations is the incumbent bargaining agent. In certain respects the incumbent has an inherent advantage in the election. The Board seeks to minimize this condition by closely scrutinizing any negotiations or agreements between the employer and the union during the critical pre-election period. Even though administration of an existing contract or maintenance of the labor-management relationship is a right and an obligation of the two parties, some activities of this sort have been found to constitute election interference. The line dividing proper and improper action in this respect is also in need of clarification.

CHAPTER IX

Third Party Interference

In 1947 the Board set aside an election for the first time on the grounds that an antiunion campaign was conducted by independent, third parties.[1] The rationale for the decision was founded upon Board policy which guarantees every employee a right to a free and untrammeled choice of a bargaining representative.[2] In practice, a second election may be forced by a defeated union if it can show third part interference in the conduct of the election. A further showing of employer participation or approval of the third party's antiunion campaign, therefore, may not be necessary. As used throughout this chapter, the term "third party" is indicative of a class of persons other then the employer, union, or Board agent conducting the election. The misconduct by third parties may be either on an individual or a group basis and may include such diverse elements of the local citizenry as clergymen, police, newspaper editors, and businessmen. However, this discussion is further limited to alleged interference on the part of nonemployee, third persons.

THE NATURE OF THIRD PARTY INTERFERENCE

A factor common to most cases of third party interference is propaganda to the effect that unionization would cause the plant to shut down or move. The fears of plant closure or relocation are most prevalent in small communities where the plant is either a substantial or dominant factor in the local economy. As a result, almost all third party interference litigation is brought by the union, rather than the employer.[3] In order to ascertain

---

[1] P. D. Gwaltney Jr., and Co., Inc., 74 N.L.R.B. 371, 20 L.R.R.M. 1172 (1947).

[2] *Id.* at 379, 20 L.R.R.M. at 1174.

[3] Coercive conduct by employees in support of the union but without specific authority to act on the union's behalf was discussed in Chapter VI, *supra.*

the validity of the claimed third party misconduct, the Board makes the following inquiries: (1) can an agency relationship be established between the employer and the third party?; (2) and if so, did the employer attempt to disavow the activities of the third party; (3) has a general atmosphere of fear been created? One or more of these questions must be answered in the affirmative for the Board to call for a second election.

The Question of "Agency": Vicarious 8(a)(1) Violations By An Employer

Where a third party's electioneering efforts are of such a coercive nature that their propaganda content would otherwise constitute an 8(a)(1) violation, the Board will find that the employer, himself, has vicariously committed an unfair labor practice if it is shown that the misconduct of the third party can be attributed to the employer through a theory of agency.[4] As a result, an employer's coincident duty to disavow the activities of all third persons will depend upon whether they are deemed to possess the status and capacity as agents of the employer.[5]

Generally, an agency relationship is established when it is shown that one party (the agent) is acting on behalf of another (the principal) through some delegation of descretionary authority which is subject to the direction and control of the principal. Pursuant to the federal labor law, however, the Board is not limited to these strict common law concepts in finding that an agency relationship exists. Early constructions of the Wagner Act indicated that the legislative intent of Congress in fashioning the labor laws would not be frustrated by judicial restraints.

The Supreme Court in *I.A.M., Lodge No. 35 v. NLRB*,[6] outlined the concept of agency as reaching further than "technical concepts" in order to implement the "legislative policy to free the collective

---

[4] *E.g.*, H.I. Siegel, Inc., 165 N.L.R.B. 493, 494, 65 L.R.R.M. 1505, 1506 (1967).

[5] *See* Goodyear Clearwater Mill No. 2, 102 N.L.R.B. 1329, 1349, 31 L.R.R.M. 1447 (1953), wherein the Board approved the regional director's findings that the failure of the union to establish an agency relationship between the employer and third parties involved, negated any obligation of the company to disabow such activities.

[6] 311 U.S. 72, 7 L.R.R.M. 282 (1940).

bargaining process" from restraints.[7] Thus the Court indicated that agency could exist absent the usual master-servant relationship required under the rules of *respondent superior.*[8]

With the passage of the Taft-Hartley amendments, Congress wrote the principle of agency into the text of the Act,[9] with the legislative intent of bringing certain union representatives, as well as supervisors, within the purview of Board regulation.[10] To implement its intent, Congress defined the term "agent" in its broadest sense.[11] Subsequent interpretation of the agency provision has resulted in the Board's position that it will construe agency status by implication from the surrounding circumstances, irrespective of proof of employer authorization or ratification.[12] The result, of course, is that the Board is able to exercise review not only of alleged misconduct among the parties to an election, but also to examine the conduct of third parties.

The key element in establishing an agency relationship between third parties and the employer is economic in character and depends upon evidence of "an overlap of financial interests."[13] For example, where it can be shown that the alleged interfering third party has an interest in the land or plant of the company,[14] or substantial business interests fully dependent

---

[7] *Id.* at 80, 7 L.R.R.M. at 286; *accord,* NLRB v. General Metals Products Co., 410 F.2d 473, 475, 70 L.R.R.M. 3327, 3328 (6th Cir. 1969).

[8] 311 U.S. at 80, 7 L.R.R.M. at 286.

[9] *See* 29 U.S.C. § 152(2) (1970), wherein Congress defined an employer as "any person acting as an *agent* of an employer, directly or indirectly. . . ." (emphasis added).

[10] *See* 93 CONG. REC. 4561, 6608 (1947).

[11] 29 U.S.C. § 152(13) (1970), provides that:

In determining whether any person is acting as an "agent" of another person so as to make such other person responsible for his acts, the question of whether the specific acts performed were actually authorized or subsequently ratified shall not be controlling.

[12] NLRB v. General Metals Products Co., 410 F.2d 473, 475-77, 70 L.R.R.M. 3327, 3329-30 (6th Cir. 1969).

[13] Amalgamated Clothing Workers of America, AFL-CIO v. NLRB, 371 F.2d 740, 63 L.R.R.M. 2581 (D.C. Cir. 1966), *enforcing* Hamburg Shirt Corp., 156 N.L.R.B. 511, 61 L.R.R.M. 1075 (1966).

[14] *E.g.,* Henry I. Siegel, Inc., 165 N.L.R.B. 493, 65 L.R.R.M. 1505 (1967) (a development corporation sold stock in order to purchase land and con-

upon continued plant operations,[15] the Board will imply an
agency status by reason of the considerable stake in the venture
of the third parties. On the other hand, where the business
contact between company and third party is of a casual nature,
this relationship is insufficient to make the third party an agent
of the company.[16]

Of secondary importance is the necessity of the objecting union
to establish that the company had knowledge of the coercive
activities of its alleged third party agents. In this context,
the process of imputing knowledge of the third party activities
to the employer is closely analogous to procedural aspects of
the "ostensible" or "apparent" agent. Under common law, an
ostensible agent is one whose actions appear or can be implied
to be supported by the principal, either with the intentional
or negligent result of deceiving others into believing that the
agent is acting in behalf of his principal.[17] Again, at common
law, the principal may raise as a defense his unqualified disavowal of the unauthorized acts, or a repudiation of the authority under which the ostensible agent was assumed to act.[18]
Consequently, in the context of third party interference in a
representation election, an employer's duty to disavow the acts
of third parties can arise only if he has direct or constructive
knowledge of these acts.

Before the Board, the requisite showing of knowledge is quite
easily satisfied. For example, in *NLRB v. General Metals Products Co.*[19] the fact that the interfering third party was supplied

---

struct a plant that it leased to the employer); Mid-South Mfg. Co., Inc.,
117 N.L.R.B. 1786, 40 L.R.R.M. 1092 (1957) (individual owner of land and
plant which was leased to the employer).

15 *See* NLRB v. General Metals Products Co., 410 F.2d 473, 70 L.R.R.M.
3327 (6th Cir. 1969) (here a lawyer played a key role in persuading the
company to establish itself in the community where he was also chairman
of the board of the local bank, partner in a realty agency, part owner of land
upon which the plant was constructed, and financially interested in the construction company which built the plant).

16 *See* Goodyear Clearwater Mill No. 2, 102 N.L.R.B. 1239, 31 L.R.R.M.
1447 (1953) (business contacts limited to arms length transactions implicit
in the ordinary trade and usage within the community).

17 Black's Law Dictionary 85 (4th ed. 1951).

18 *Id.* at 549.

19 410 F.2d 473, 70 L.R.R.M. 3327 (6th Cir. 1969).

with the names of employees by company officials, who were both business as well as social intimates of the third party, was deemed to constitute constructive knowledge of his antiunion activities.[20] In another case, although the employer refused to assist the antiunion campaign of a third party, the mere fact that he had knowledge that it was taking place created in him a duty to disavow the third party's activities.[21]

Employer Disavowals

Once an agency relationship between an employer and a third party has been established, a duty arises on the part of an employer to disavow and disassociate himself from any coercive statements or conduct engaged in by third parties.[22] A problem of line drawing does exist, however, when the third party's campaign re-echoes the employer's campaign theme, thereby making the sincerity of any potential disavowal by an employer suspect. Faced with the problem of duplicate campaign activities, the Board in *Utica-Herbrand Tool Division of Kelsey Hayes Co.*,[23] set aside an election in which a massive campaign [24] conducted by third parties, reiterated and embellished upon the

---

[20] *Id.* at 476, 70 L.R.R.M. at 3329. In so holding, the court in *General Metals* reasoned that since company officials were aware of the activities, "their acquiescence must be construed as approval."

[21] H. I. Siegel, Inc., 165 N.L.R.B. 493, 494, 65 L.R.R.M. 1505, 1506 (1967).

[22] *Compare* H. I. Siegel, Inc., 165 N.L.R.B. at 494, 65 L.R.R.M. at 1506, (the employer's failure to disavow conduct violative of section 8(a)(1) engaged in by third parties caused the Board to set aside the election) *with* Stratford Furniture Corp., 116 N.L.R.B. 1721, 1724, 39 L.R.R.M. 1080, 1081 (1956) (the election was upheld where no showing of an agency relationship between the employer and third parties was forthcoming while the employer disavowed the claims of the third parties).

[23] 145 N.L.R.B. 1717, 55 L.R.R.M. 1223 (1964).

[24] Commenting upon the scope of the antiunion campaign, the Board stated:

> [The activities] of community officials, influential citizens, and others . . . through letters, home visits, leaflet distribution, radio newcasts and spot announcements, and newspaper editorials and advertisements, iterated and reiterated the themes that selection of the [union] would [produce] a distressed area, . . . cause the employer to move away, and . . . deprive employees of job opportunities. . . .

constituted coercive conduct on such a scale that even absent employer adoption of the third party efforts, a free election was impossible. *Id.* at 1719-20, 55 L.R.R.M. at 1225.

employer's own propaganda that a union victory would precipitate labor unrest. Where an employer has subsequently adopted the third party campaign theme as his own, without additional explanation, the Board has set aside the election.[25] Thus the question arises as to whether an employer may conduct any type of campaign in his own right where potential overlap with third party coercive conduct exists.

A partial answer was offered in *Claymore Mfg. Co.,*[26] where the Board divided over whether a company disavowal of interfering third party conduct was sufficient in order to conduct a similar campaign. In refusing to set aside the election, the majority based its conclusion on a company disavowal of third party conduct, the truthful context of the employer's message, and his stated intent to try his best to keep the plant open as distinguished from third party threats of closure.[27]

From this, we might conclude that an employer may conduct his campaign free from fear that the election will be set aside because of the activities of third parties, as long as his electioneering is noncoercive and he has disavowed the activities of third parties. Not so opined the dissent in *Claymore,* which would have set aside the election on the grounds that in such a situation, an employer's disavowal is ineffectual because of the "atmosphere of fear" which so permeated the election process.[28] Since the Board has never had the opportunity to instruct us further on the specific issue, the quite narrow holding of the majority is presumably the present standard. The alleged "atmosphere of fear" criterion, upon which the dissent in *Claymore* relied, however, is not unique. To the contrary, it affords the Board with an alternative avenue of resolution, should the employer be found in compliance with the agency and disavowal standards, so as to prevent the Board from setting aside the election on the vicarious 8(a)(1) violation.

---

[25] 165 N.L.R.B. at 493, 65 L.R.R.M. at 1506.

[26] 146 N.L.R.B. 1400, 56 L.R.R.M. 1080 (1964).

[27] *Id.* at 1402, 56 L.R.R.M. at 1084.

[28] *Id.* at 1403-1404, 56 L.R.R.M. at 1084-85 (Chairman McCulloch and Member Brown, dissenting).

Conduct of Third Parties Which Create a "General Atmosphere of Fear"

In *P. D. Gwaltney Jr., and Co., Inc.*[29] the Board set aside an election based on coercive conduct which could not be attributed either to the union or the employer, but rested squarely upon the acts of third parties. The contested election had been held among the predominantly black [30] employees of a packing plant in the small, southern town of Smithfield, Virginia. During the pre-election period, the townspeople had conducted a vigorous antiunion campaign, the thrust of which was primarily directed towards the unit's black employees. The local campaign was spearheaded by two individuals, one publisher of a weekly newspaper, and the other a local insurance agent.[31] Through various publications and a mass meeting of townspeople, they villified the petitioning union as an instrument of world communism and warned of Ku Klux Klan terriorism should a union be elected.[32] In addition, in various instances, citizens of Smithfield intimated to the union organizers that they might either be run out of town, thrown into the river, or lynched.[33] Although the Board found no merit in the union's contentions that the employer interfered with the election, the Board felt compelled to set aside the election because of the extraordinary viciousness and scope of the third party antiunion activities. In support of its determination, the Board reasoned that its primary concern over election conduct is whether the opportunity for free choice has been maintained. Consequently, the Board felt justified investigating allegations of misconduct on the part of third parties as well as that of the employer and union in achieving this goal. In a strongly worded conclusion, the Board

---

[29] 74 N.L.R.B. 371, 20 L.R.R.M. 1172 (1947).

[30] *Id.* at 372, 20 L.R.R.M. at 1172. Approximately 80 percent of the employees within the proposed unit were black.

[31] The tenor of the antiunion campaign is perhaps best illustrated by the statements of these individuals. According to their testimony, they had taken it upon themselves to spread "information and education of persons that did not have this faculty originally, through training," and called upon "all the preachers . . . and the various and sundry officials of the 'nigger' lodges and so forth" to "instruct them properly." *Id.* at 373, 20 L.R.R.M. at 1173.

[32] *Id.* at 375-76, 20 L.R.R.M. at 1173.

[33] *Id.* at 377-78, 20 L.R.R.M. at 1173.

stated that its determination that the employer had not violated
any standards of election conduct:

> . . . does not dispose of the case, which relates to the validity of
> a Board election, any more than would the fact that a hurricane
> or other Act of God could not be attributed to an employer neces-
> sarily lead to the conclusion that an election conducted in the
> atmosphere created by such a natural phenomenon must be upheld
> as a true expression of the employees' desires.[34]

In subsequent cases, the *P. D. Gwaltney* decision became the
cornerstone of Board policy in setting aside elections on the
sole basis of third party misconduct. The Board has attempted
to measure the probable impact of third party antiunion campaigns as to the extent they interfere with free choice.[35] The
yardstick utilized by the Board is whether the "fear of economic
loss so permeate[s] the atmosphere surrounding the election as
to render impossible the rational, uncoerced selection of a bargaining representative as contemplated by the Act." [36]

Since third party interference, based on the creation of an
atmosphere of fear, is a type of "no-fault" concept utilized by
the Board in setting aside elections, effective countervailing
arguments by an employer are severely limited. Theoretically,
an employer may meet these objections in two ways. First, he
may assert that a disavowal made by company officials has
served to negate the corecive impact of the third party's campaign. This argument is difficult to sustain on conceptual
grounds, since the employer would not be disavowing the acts
of individuals deemed to be his agents. Instead, the employer
is forced to argue that he effectively disclaimed any responsibility
for the acts of independent third persons, whose acts he has
no authority to control. In the few cases in which the employer
has attempted to raise this consideration, the Board has turned
an unsympathetic ear, dismissing the alleged disavowals as insufficient to negate the coercive impact of the third party's

---

[34] *Id.* at 379, 20 L.R.R.M. at 1174.

[35] *See generally* Universal Mfg. Corp., 156 N.L.R.B. 1459, 61 L.R.R.M. 1258
(1966) ; Benson Veneer Co., Inc., 156 N.L.R.B. 781, 61 L.R.R.M. 1137 (1966);
Utica-Herbrand Tool Division of Kelsey Hayes Co., 145 N.L.R.B. 1717, 55
L.R.R.M. 1223 (1964); Great Atlantic & Pacific Tea Co., 120 N.L.R.B.
765, 42 L.R.R.M. 1042 (1958).

[36] The Falmouth Co., 114 N.L.R.B. 896, 900-901, 37 L.R.R.M. 1057, 1058
(1955).

activities.[37] Although it is rarely considered, potentially an employer may also question whether the activities of third parties were in fact violative of the standard of conduct which precludes the possibility of holding a free election.[38] But, of course, there remains the question of whether the Board, in fact, has ever proved a relationship between third party communication and election results, or has the expertise to do so.

In the one area in which prounion third party misconduct prevails (anonymous threats), the "atmosphere of fear" standards are utilized to weigh their impact upon free choice.[39] Clearly, the Board is forced to fall back upon this test, since an anonymous threat by definition is incapable of being evaluated in terms of any agency test.

SPECIFIC TYPES OF INTERFERENCE BY THIRD PARTIES

When the typical sources of alleged third party interference are identified, it becomes apparent that the Board's administration of election standards often infringe upon important individual rights of the public. Significantly, certain first amendment rights may be severely limited. For example, although every citizen enjoys the rights of speech, assembly, and association, when a citizen's group or other community effort is mobilized in opposition to union entry, the Board may find that such activities amount to coercive conduct. This is true,

---

[37] *E.g.*, Monarch Rubber Co., Inc., 121 N.L.R.B. 81, 83, 42 L.R.R.M. 1294 (1958) (phone call by employer to newspaper publisher of antiunion advertisement disclaiming responsibility held ineffective); The Falmouth Co., 114 N.L.R.B. 896, 901, 37 L.R.R.M. 1057 (1955) (statement by employer in a speech supportive of one of two contending unions to affect that plant operations would be continued held insufficient to overcome "atmosphere of fear").

It should be noted that in this context, the Board has never been confronted with weighing the effects of a forthright, unencumbered employer disavowal of the activities of independent third parties.

[38] *See* James Lees and Sons Co., 130 N.L.R.B. 290, 47 L.R.R.M. 1285 (1961). In this case, the dissent argued that the third party propaganda was within the protected electioneering conduct standards of the Act, while questioning the implications of the majority opinion that "the employer had an obligation to disavow gratuitously the activities of the townspeople." *Id.* at 292, 47 L.R.R.M. at 1286 (Chairman Leedom and Member Rodgers, dissenting).

[39] *E.g.*, NLRB v. Tampa Crown Distributors, Inc., 272 F.2d 470, 45 L.R.R.M. 2109 (5th Cir. 1959); Monroe Auto Equipment Co., 186 N.L.R.B. 90, 75 L.R.R.M. 1340 (1970).

even though the townspeople may be legitimately concerned over the future economic welfare of their community.

Similarly, in finding that attacks by newspapers or other media are coercive, the Board engages in consideration over what restrictions on the freedom of the press are appropriate. In addition, regulating the extent to which the clergy or the police may intervene in the election process must be viewed in the light of the prevailing social mores of the community or in terms of protection of life and property. Finally, the impact of an anonymous threat of violence upon the recipient and his co-workers is not subject to any universal standard, but can only be approached on a case-by-case basis. This fundamental conflict between the Board's concept of a "free" election and the rights of third parties to address themselves to important local issues is a consistent background fixture of any Board resolution of claims of third party interference.

Interference By Various Townspeople

The organization of active opposition of any group of citizens towards unionization cannot be dismissed as mere artificial sentiment induced by an employer, but must be recognized as a genuine reflection of the community spirit. In most situations, the concern expressed by the local community is quite understandable, since the potentiality of strikes and plant closures or relocations, in the event of a union victory, presents an immediate and grave danger of economic reversal to the townspeople.[40] In small communities, the strong economic ties between populus and plant, coupled with the intimacy associated with small towns, may transform an otherwise run-of-the-mill representation election into a local *cause célèbre*. Logic is cast to the winds, while the townspeople emotionally react to an anticipated decline in the economy. These fears are not entirely without a basis in fact, since a shutdown or relocation may lawfully eventuate. Moreover, even if such action is taken unlawfully, during the interim period from the shutdown or relocation to a definite Board or court order, the citizenry may be deprived of their primary source of income. Although the Board has repeatedly held that it has the authority to remedy

---

[40] *See, e.g.*, Universal Mfg. Corp., 156 N.L.R.B. 1459, 61 L.R.R.M. 1258 (1966), wherein funds for the purchase of the plant site, as well as for the construction of the plant were obtained through a bond issue by the county government.

a runaway shop situation through a move back order, it has never actually utilized such an approach.[41]

The NLRB then must decide whether overanxious citizens have trespassed into the area of coercive conduct and expression preventing the Board from certifying the election as a free and fair reflection of the employees' desires. In order to reach this determination, the Board must consider the class of community interference, in addition to the familiar concepts of agency, employer disavowal, and "creation of a general atmosphere of fear," discussed *supra*. First, the antiunion campaign may be identifiable with mass participation by the entire community. Second, opposition may center upon the activities of a few, but influential, citizens. Finally, the source of the antiunion campaign may emanate from a local development corporation, which has a substantial investment in future plant operations.

When townspeople participate in an antiunion campaign *en masse*, the Board utilizes the "atmosphere of fear" standards in order to evaluate the impact of third party interference.[42] Generally, the more pervasive the instances of antiunion propaganda are, the more likely the Board is to set aside the election.[43] Thus, when the fear of a plant shutdown "confront[s] the employees at every turn,"[44] or is reinforced by frequent third party statements,[45] the Board has held that the requisite freedom of choice is lacking. Such factors as home visits by the local police and mayor as well as propaganda distributed at local banks,[46] threats of closure in the plant, at community retailers, and in the media,[47] as well as mass meetings,[48] have

---

[41] *See* Swift, *Plant Relocation: Catching Up With the Runaway Shop,* 14 B.C. Ind. & Comm. L. Rev. 1135 (1973), for an extensive discussion of the Board's policies and remedies utilized in the plant relocation situation.

[42] *E.g.*, James Lees and Sons Co., 130 N.L.R.B. 290, 291, 47 L.R.R.M. 1285, 1286 (1961).

[43] *See* Utica-Herbrand Tool Division of Kelsey Hayes Co., 145 N.L.R.B. 1717, 1719, 55 L.R.R.M. 1223, 1225 (1964).

[44] The Falmouth Co., 114 N.L.R.B. 896, 900, 37 L.R.R.M. 1057, 1058 (1955).

[45] 145 N.L.R.B. at 1717, 55 L.R.R.M. at 1225.

[46] *Id.* at 1717-18, 55 L.R.R.M. at 1225.

[47] 114 N.L.R.B. at 900-901, 37 L.R.R.M. at 1058.

[48] P.D. Gwaltney Jr., and Co., Inc., 74 N.L.R.B. at 375-76, 20 L.R.R.M. at 1173.

all been considered as inducive to the creation of an atmosphere of fear. Only when it appears that "opposition to an organizing drive has been limited to noncoercive campaigning and the employees eligible to vote are able to enter the polls without fear and cast their ballots freely" will the Board refuse to question the results of the election.[49]

When opposition to the union can be readily identified with an individual or small group effort, considerations of agency and employer disavowal are generally determinative of the issue. The Board will set aside an election where an agent of the employer [50] has indulged in coercive activities, absent an effective disavowal by the employer.[51] Moreover, the Board has held that it will set aside an election when it finds that a third party has made a speech concerning the election in violation of the *Peerless Plywood* rule.[52] On the other hand, the mere presence of allegedly antiunion employers in the plant immediately preceeding the election is of insufficient consequence to set aside an election when no evidence of electioneering by them is forthcoming.[53]

Because of the direct financial interest in the ongoing operation of an employer's plant by a local development corporation, the requisite showing of agency is easily established.[54] There-

---

[49] *Id.* at 378, 20 L.R.R.M. at 1173.

[50] *E.g.*, NLRB v. General Metals Products Co., 410 F.2d 473, 475-76, 70 L.R.R.M. 3327, 3329 (6th Cir. 1969); Goodyear Clearwater Mill No. 2, 102 N.L.R.B. 1329, 1349, 31 L.R.R.M. 1447 (1953). *See* discussion at pp. 218-21, *supra*.

[51] *E.g.*, Claymore Mfg. Co., 146 N.L.R.B. 1400, 1402, 56 L.R.R.M. 1080, 1083 (1964). *See* discussion at pp. 221-22, *supra*.

[52] Mid-South Mfg. Co., Inc., 117 N.L.R.B. 1786, 1787-88, 40 L.R.R.M. 1092, 1093 (1957). *Cf.* Benson Veneer Co., Inc., 156 N.L.R.B. 781, 61 L.R.R.M. 1137 (1966), wherein the Board adopted the regional director's finding that a speech by a group of local businessmen to an employee's meeting *within 24 hours of the election* to express vehement opposition to unionization, coupled with threats of reprisal, rendered the free choice of a bargaining representative impossible. *Id.* at 796, 61 L.R.R.M. at 1140. *See also* discussion in Chapter X, *infra*.

[53] *See* Encino Shirt Co., 117 N.L.R.B. 1687, 1688, 40 L.R.R.M. 1067, 1068 (1957).

[54] *But cf.* Stratford Furniture Corp., 116 N.L.R.B. 1721, 1723-24, 39 L.R.R.M. 1080, 1081 (1956). If a group of citizens denominate themselves as a "Development Association," without further proof of a substantial financial interest in the plant operations, substance over form will prevail to rebut the implication of agency.

fore, a Board determination to set aside the election is controlled by the issue of whether the employer has made a sufficient disavowal. Where an "overlap of financial interests" between employer and development group exists, the Board has held that the employer has an "obligation to disassociate itself" from the third party campaign since a failure to do so "warrants a finding that [he has] adopted and affirmed that campaign and thereby violated the Act." [55] On the other hand, the Board in *Electra Mfg. Co.*[56] held that "specific public disavowals of any intention to relocate" by an employer, coupled with supportive union propaganda to the same effect, "tended to neutralize any atmosphere of fear and confusion that otherwise might have been engendered by the . . . third party conduct." [57]

Interference by the Media

The Taft-Hartley amendments to the Wagner Act specifically provided for freedom of expression during the campaign period as long as it contained "no threat of reprisal or force or promise of benefit." [58] Thus the freedom of the press, so jealously guarded under the first amendment, must bow to the selective censorship imposed by the federal labor law. Media comment upon a representation election may take the form of a factual account, an editorial, or an advertisement. Where appropriate, the Board has rejected union claims of interference premised solely upon the basis of news articles, citing the "public interest" to be served in such accounts,[59] as well as the lack of any coercive element, which might be attributable to the employer.[60] Even news articles, however, are not totally exempt from Board strictures. When the NLRB determines that such accounts are slanted in such a manner so as to become part of the fabric of a larger,

---

[55] H.I. Siegel, Inc., 165 N.L.R.B. at 494, 65 L.R.R.M. at 1506.

[56] 148 N.L.R.B. 494, 57 L.R.R.M. 1054 (1964).

[57] *Id.* at 497, 57 L.R.R.M. at 1055.

[58] 29 U.S.C. § 158(c) (1970).

[59] *See* West-Gate Sun Harbor Co., 93 N.L.R.B. 830, 833, 27 L.R.R.M. 1474, 1476 (1951) (newspaper reports of pre-election organizing activity held noncoercive in light of 6-week old strike, picketing, and apparent general community interest therein).

[60] McGraw-Edison Co., 184 N.L.R.B. No. 95, 74 L.R.R.M. 1618 (1970).

antiunion campaign, it has found that the existence of third party interference is sufficient to set aside the election.[61]

It is in the area of editorials and advertisements, however, that the Board has found the majority of instances of interference by the media. On one hand, advertisements, being a species of commercial speech, have never enjoyed the same degree of first amendment protection as other forms of expression.[62] On the other hand, the Section 8(c) limitation upon freedom of expression, strikes directly at the preservation of the free exchange of ideas and information contemplated by the first amendment and exemplified by editorials. The Board has skirted potential charges of censorship in cases involving editorials through use of the "agency" rationale. The Board has held that although antiunion editorials are permissible,[63] where it is shown that the publisher is acting as an agent, and in effect, the "mouthpiece" of the employer, the editorial loses its protection under 8(c).[64]

The most blatant example of the use of a newspaper as an instrument of antiunion propaganda occurred in *Universal Mfg. Corp.*[65] In that case, the two local papers made full use of editorials, advertisements, and news stories to convey their opposition to the union. The editorials utilized a two-prong attack, predicting on one hand that a union victory would force the employer to relocate, creating severe economic hardships, while, on the other hand, injecting the issue of race into the campaign by identifying the locally unpopular civil rights movement with union contributions and support.[66] Similarly, advertisements, which reflect the community's fear of economic loss, warned that a union victory could only be detrimental. The ads had been sponsored by both an unidentified citizens' group and the editor himself, a member of the employer's

---

[61] Universal Mfg. Corp., 156 N.L.R.B. 1459, 1466, 61 L.R.R.M. 1258, 1260 (1966).

[62] *See generally* Note, Freedom of Expression in a Commercial Context, 78 HARV. L. REV. 1191 (1965).

[63] Vita Food Products, Inc., 116 N.L.R.B. 1215, 1218, 38 L.R.R.M. 1437 (1956).

[64] 156 N.L.R.B. at 1466, 61 L.R.R.M. at 1260.

[65] *Id.* at 1459, 61 L.R.R.M. at 1258.

[66] *Id.* at 1461-62, 61 L.R.R.M. at 1260.

community advisory board. The NLRB found that an implicit element of interference in both the editorials and the advertisements was the coincident refusal of the newspapers to run either prounion editorials or accept union ads.[67] Reviewing the probable impact of the third party's conduct, the Board concluded:

> By appealing to the employees' sentiments as civic-minded individuals, injecting the fear of personal economic loss, and playing upon racial prejudice, the full-page ads [and] the editorials . . . were calculated to convince the employees that a vote for the union meant the betrayal of the community's best interests.[68]

Interference By Clergy or Police

Another variety of potential interference arises when the position in the community of the third party is such that his status alone, being one of authority or respect, magnifies the seriousness of the alleged misconduct. Specifically, this issue gains material significance when the third party is either a member of the clergy or of a law enforcement body.

The Clergy. In *Balboa Pacific Corp.*[69] the union alleged, *inter alia*, that a letter, mailed to the employees by a member of the local clergy, had upset the possibility of conducting a free and untrammeled election because the letter misled voters into believing that a vote for the union would be futile. The clergyman, a member of the Catholic Labor Institute, had indicated to the employer that he wished to influence employees not to affiliate with the participating union because of alleged communist tendencies. To accomplish this goal, he composed a letter that was sent to all Spanish surnamed employees, urging them to vote against the union and organize an independent union with whom the employer would be willing to bargain.[70] The regional director had interpreted the letter as "containing an implication that the Employer would not bargain with the union if certified, but would bargain only with the employees' own

---

[67] *Id.* at 1461, 1463, 61 L.R.R.M. at 1258. The Board stated that "[w]hile a newspaper retains the right to refuse advertisements at will, the action might be a basis for setting aside an election if the union were thereby prevented from adequately communicating its message to the employees." *Id.* at 1461 n.5, 61 L.R.R.M. at 1258.

[68] *Id.* at 1466, 61 L.R.R.M. at 1260.

[69] 92 N.L.R.B. 85, 27 L.R.R.M. 1043 (1950).

[70] *Id.* at 87, 27 L.R.R.M. at 1044.

representative . . . group," thus constituting a promise of
benefit.[71] The Board, however, disagreed with the regional director that the employer was under an obligation to repudiate
the letter, on the grounds that it contained no promise of
benefit.[72] The Board's decision is interesting because it laid
down no rule regarding interference by the clergy, but rather
disposed of the case on the evidentiary finding of no promise
of benefit. At the time, the decision may have implied a reluctance on the part of the Board to regulate the conduct of
the clergy.

In view of recent social activism on the part of organized
religions, the potential for interference by the clergy has increased. For example, in a case heard by the Pennsylvania
State Labor Relations Board, an election among Catholic ele-
mentary school teachers was contested by the union on the
basis of a letter distributed by Cardinal Krol, which urged the
teachers to vote against unionization.[73] The cardinal's message
implied that a "no" vote was necessary in order to avoid any
threat to the continuance and special character of the schools,
and it charged that the election represented a dangerous intrusion by the state into the internal affairs of the church.[74]
In setting aside the election, the state labor board found that
the letter had "the effect of intimidating such voters by implying that if they voted for the union they were in agreement
that they had no interest in the religious training of the children
they were teaching." [75]

In an incident relating to the nationally publicized organizing campaign taking place at the Farah Manufacturing Company, a recent full-page advertisement sponsored by the Amalgamated Clothing Workers of America was inserted in the
New York Times. The advertisement prominently featured an
open letter from the Bishop of El Paso, Texas, addressed to all
other bishops in the United States urging support of the union's
efforts to organize the Farah workers. In addition the letter

---

[71] Id. at 88, 27 L.R.R.M. at 1044.

[72] Id., 27 L.R.R.M. at 1044.

[73] St. Joseph's Preparatory School, Case No. PERA-R-1060-E, CCH 49,
999.12 (1972).

[74] Id.

[75] Id.

accused Farah of blocking election efforts by the NLRB, equated standard union contract clauses as being in accord with concepts of "social justice," and finally urged a nationwide boycott of Farah products at both the retail and wholesale level.[76] It remains to be seen whether the company, in a like case, will claim third party interference and if so, what will be the Board's reaction.

The Police. It is quite likely that the presence of police officers during an election will not go unnoticed by the employees. Whether mere presence alone, however, is of significant consequence to direct a new election is another question which the Board has answered in the negative.[77] As long as "the police did not inject themselves into election issues nor speak to any employees or voters during the election," the Board will allow the results to stand.[78] Further, if these conditions are satisfied, the reason for the presence of police officers at the election is immaterial.[79] It is only when the conduct of the police has created a general atmosphere of confusion or fear of reprisal that the Board will set aside the election.[80] Thus, when the union's principal organizer was arrested by police for a technical violation of a city ordinance, in full view of a number of eligible voters and only minutes before the election was scheduled to start, the Board found that a free election had been rendered impossible.[81]

Anonymous Telephone Threats

The Board has long held that for it to overturn an election on the basis of anonymous telephone threats, such threats must be attributable to one of the participating parties under either

---

[76] N. Y. Times, Feb. 21, 1973.

[77] Louisville Cap Co., 120 N.L.R.B. 769, 42 L.R.R.M. 1064 (1958).

[78] *Id.* at 771, 42 L.R.R.M. at 1065.

[79] Vita Food Products, Inc., 116 N.L.R.B. 1215, 1219, 38 L.R.R.M. 1437, 1438 (1956).

[80] Great Atlantic & Pacific Tea Co., 120 N.L.R.B. 765, 42 L.R.R.M. 1042 (1958).

[81] *Id.* at 766-67, 42 L.R.R.M. at 1043.

an "agency" test,[82] or else must be conduct of such an aggravated nature that an atmosphere of fear has been created.[83] Of course, there is an underlying difficulty in any exact application of the "agency" test because of the very anonymity of the threat.[84] Nonetheless, the Fifth Circuit in *NLRB v. Tampa Crown Distributors, Inc.*[85] suggested that a showing of union agency might be *prima facie* sufficient when its officials do not take the stand and deny that the union was responsible or had knowledge of such threats. Subsequently, the Board in *Monroe Auto Equipment Co.*,[86] another case involving anonymous telephone threats, took the opportunity to comment upon *Tampa Crown*, pointing out that although its view was "somewhat different" from that of the Fifth Circuit, the Board would not reject outright a test of agency based upon the silence of union officials.[87]

The more practical resolution is based on the "general atmosphere of fear" standards. Under this rationale, the primary determination of whether this atmosphere existed, is accomplished by a consideration of the extent to which the threats pervaded the pre-election period. This approach may be implemented in two ways. First, the Board might look to the number of employees actually affected.[88] Accordingly, where the number of employees receiving threats were also sufficient in number to affect the results of the election, the probability of their votes being a product of fear serves to invalidate the election as a representative reflection of the employees' free choice.[89] Secondly, the Board may find that the anonymous calls were part of a pattern of coercive acts

---

[82] *See, e.g.*, NLRB v. Tampa Crown Distributors, Inc., 272 F.2d 470, 472, 45 L.R.R.M. 2109, 2111 (5th Cir. 1959) (citing cases).

[83] *Id.*, 45 L.R.R.M. at 2111.

[84] *Id.* at 473, 45 L.R.R.M. at 2111.

[85] *Id.* at 470, 45 L.R.R.M. at 2109.

[86] 186 N.L.R.B. 90, 75 L.R.R.M. 1340 (1970).

[87] *Id.* at 96, 75 L.R.R.M. at 1347.

[88] 272 F.2d at 473, 45 L.R.R.M. at 2111.

[89] *Id.*, 45 L.R.R.M. at 2111.

preceding the election. For example, in *Al Long, Inc.*[90] the Board held that where "[e]vents occurring during the critical period included extensive property destruction, anonymous telephone threats to eligible voters, the report of a bomb threat," and riotous conduct on the part of union pickets, the only possible conclusion was that an "atmosphere of fear" had been created which precluded free choice.[91]

The Board's approach to anonymous telephone threats as a condition sufficient to set aside an election has been particularly confusing. For example, in two cases wherein a unanimous opinion was delivered, two out of three members of the panel had heard both cases,[92] and issued the following statements. Setting aside an election in *Al Long, Inc.*, the Board stated that:

> It is not material that fear and disorder may have been created by individual employees or nonemployees and that their conduct cannot probatively be attributed either to the Employer or to the Union. The significant fact is that such conditions existed and that a free election was thereby rendered impossible.[93]

On the other hand, in *Monroe Auto*, the Board upheld an election, stating that:

> To set aside an election because of anonymous phone calls, except in the most compelling case, would render the election proceeding vulnerable to the acts of cranks, pranksters, and anyone else who for some reason wishes to sabotage an election.[94]

Since the statements are contradictory, the only apparent explanation is that the Board fears that anonymous threats might be used as a tool by the parties in an election to fashion an objection in advance if the results of the election are unfavorable. On the other hand, if the threats get out of hand or are made in conjunction with other coercive conduct, the Board will not hesitate to set the election aside.

---

[90] 173 N.L.R.B. 447, 69 L.R.R.M. 1366 (1968).

[91] *Id.* at 448, 69 L.R.R.M. at 1367-68.

[92] Board Members Brown and Jenkins.

[93] 173 N.L.R.B. at 448, 69 L.R.R.M. at 1368.

[94] 186 N.L.R.B. at 96, 75 L.R.R.M. at 1347.

PART FOUR

Regulation of the Time, Place, and Manner of Campaigning

CHAPTER X

"Captive-Audience" Speeches and the 24-Hour Rule

In regulating the time, place, and manner of compaigning, the Board historically has pursued two fundamental, often conflicting objectives. On the one hand, the Board has sought to assure employees access to all the information they need to make a rational choice concerning union representation by adopting rules designed to ensure that the parties participating in an election will have adequate channels through which to communicate their views to the employees. On the other hand, the Board has attempted to guarantee that the employees' choice may be made freely by preventing either party from utilizing methods of communication which, by their nature, are likely to give that party undue influence over the employees' decision. Nowhere has the conflict between these two basic objectives been more evident than in the area of pre-election speeches on company premises. Although a personal address to the employees before an election unquestionably can be an effective means of providing them with information, Board decisions have frequently reflected the fear that it may be too effective—that when used as a campaign technique in a highly partisan struggle, face-to-face exhortation carries such a potential for influencing the voters' choice that it may actually impair, rather than enhance the rationality of the election process.[1] In the case of pre-election speeches by employers, an additional factor which enters into the Board's deliberations, and which has at times in the Board's history been given controlling weight, is the coercive potential the Board has long found to be inherent in the employment relationship itself,

---

[1] For comprehensive studies comparing the effectiveness of various means of organizational communication see Note, 61 YALE L. J. 1066 (1953); Note, 14 U. CHI. L. REV. 104 (1947). *See also* HOVLAND, COMMUNICATION AND PERSUASION 20 (1953); DOOB, PUBLIC OPINION AND PROPAGANDA 460-61 (1948).

whereby an added impact is presumed to result from the employer's words and conduct because of his economic power over the employees.

DEVELOPMENT OF BOARD DOCTRINE

As we have noted, in its early decisions under the Wagner Act, the Board accorded great importance to the latter consideration and took the position that the Act obliged employers to maintain complete neutrality regarding their employees' decisions for or against union representation. Accordingly, the Board applied a strict rule that any pre-election antiunion speech by an employer would constitute an unfair labor practice and a ground for setting the election aside.[2]

The courts never fully accepted this broad limitation on the employer's freedom of expression,[3] and in 1941 the Supreme Court made it clear in *NLRB v. Virginia Electric & Power Co.*[4] that the employer retained the constitutional right to "take any side it may choose on this controversial issue" as long as the employer's statements were not coupled with actions making them coercive. Thereafter, the Board relaxed its position somewhat, in line with *Virginia Electric,* and began to judge employers' statements in light of the "totality of conduct" engaged in by the employer to determine whether they were a part of a coercive course of conduct.[5]

---

[2] *E.g.,* Rockford Mitten & Hosiery Co., 16 N.L.R.B. 501, 5 L.R.R.M. 244 (1939); Virginia Ferry Corp., 8 N.L.R.B. 730, 2 L.R.R.M. 525 (1938); Nebel Knitting Co., Inc., 6 N.L.R.B. 284, 2 L.R.R.M. 151 (1938); *see* 1 NLRB ANN. REP. 73 (1936). *See also* discussion in Chapters II and III, *supra.*

[3] *See, e.g.,* Press Co., Inc. v. NLRB, 118 F.2d 937, 7 L.R.R.M. 631 (D.C. Cir. 1940), *cert. denied,* 313 U.S. 595, 8 L.R.R.M. 458 (1941); NLRB v. Ford Motor Co., 114 F.2d 905, 7 L.R.R.M. 441 (6th Cir.), *cert. denied,* 312 U.S. 689, 7 L.R.R.M. 324 (1940); Continental Box Co. v. NLRB, 113 F.2d 93, 6 L.R.R.M. 824 (5th Cir. 1940). *But cf.* NLRB v. Federbush Co., Inc., 121 F.2d 954, 8 L.R.R.M. 531 (2d Cir. 1941); NLRB v. Falk Corp., 102 F.2d 383, 4 L.R.R.M. 642 (7th Cir. 1939).

[4] 314 U.S. 469, 9 L.R.R.M. 405 (1941).

[5] *E.g.,* Monumental Life Ins. Co., 69 N.L.R.B. 247, 250-51, 18 L.R.R.M. 1206, 1207 (1946); Oval Wood Dish Corp., 63 N.L.R.B. 1129, 1138, 16 L.R.R.M. 249, 251 (1945). *See generally* 11 NLRB ANN. REP. 34 (1946); *cf.* NLRB v. American Tube Bending Co., Inc., 134 F.2d 993, 12 L.R.R.M. 615 (2d Cir.), *cert. denied,* 320 U.S. 768, 13 L.R.R.M. 850 (1943).

Before long, however, by shifting its focus from *what* the employers said in their speeches to employees to *when* and *where* the speeches were made, the Board began to develop new rigid limitations upon the employer's right to express his views about unionization. In 1946, in the *Clark Brothers* case,[6] the Board announced a flat prohibition against so-called "captive-audience" speeches—that is, pre-election speeches given on company time and property at which employee attendance is required. The Board reasoned that even if the employer's words were not coercive, the use of employer's economic power to compel attendance at an antiunion speech constituted a prohibited interference with the employees' freedom of choice.

Congress responded a year later, in the Taft-Hartley amendments, by providing in Section 8(c) of the Act that "[t]he expressing of any views, argument, or opinion, or the dissemination thereof, whether in written, printed, graphic, or visual form, shall not constitute or be evidence of an unfair labor practice under any of the provisions of this Act, if such expression contains no threat of reprisal or promise of benefit." The legislative history of Section 8(c) left no room for doubt that one of Congress' purposes in adding this provision was to overrule the "captive-audience" doctrine set forth in the Board's *Clark Brothers* decision, and the Board soon formally announced its abandonment of that rule.[7]

It was not long, however, before the Board announced a new restriction aimed at controlling, at least to some degree, the use of the captive-audience speech as a medium for presentation of management views. Thus, in 1951, in *Bonwit-Teller, Inc.*[8] the Board formulated a doctrine of "equal opportunity" predicated upon what the Board viewed as the right of employees to "hear both sides under circumstances which approximate equality." Under the *Bonwit-Teller* rule an employer could deliver a captive-audience speech only if he then allowed

---

[6] Clark Bros. Co., Inc., 70 N.L.R.B. 802, 18 L.R.R.M. 1360 (1946), *enforced*, 163 F.2d 373, 20 L.R.R.M. 2436 (2d Cir. 1947). *See also* American Tube Bending Co., 44 N.L.R.B. 121, 11 L.R.R.M. 61 (1942), *reversed*, 134 F.2d 933, 12 L.R.R.M. 615 (2d Cir.), *cert. denied*, 320 U.S. 768, 13 L.R.R.M. 850 (1943).

[7] *See* Babcock & Wilcox Co., 77 N.L.R.B. 577, 22 L.R.R.M. 1057 (1948); Merry Brothers Brick & Tile Co., 75 N.L.R.B. 136, 21 L.R.R.M. 1008 (1947).

[8] 96 N.L.R.B. 608, 28 L.R.R.M. 1547 (1951).

the union an opportunity, on company time and premises, to reply.[9]

The *Bonwit-Teller* rule differed in operation from the repudiated *Clark Brothers* rule, but it reflected the same underlying concern of the Board—that compulsory, face-to-face speeches by the employer on company premises, carried an impermissible potential for undue influence over the employees' votes. This fundamental assumption was grounded solely upon the Board's own intuition, not on any objective data or expert opinion by psychologists or communications analysts. But the Board was apparently convinced of its own "expertise" on this subject. Thus, if it could no longer prohibit employers from using this too-effective channel of communication, as it had under *Clark Brothers*, then it would open the channel to both sides, apparently hoping that opposing pressures from the competing parties would tend to cancel out any improper influence.

THE *LIVINGSTON SHIRT* AND *PEERLESS PLYWOOD* RULES

The *Bonwit-Teller* rule was also short-lived. In 1953, following a change in its composition under the Eisenhower administration, the Board reexamined *Bonwit-Teller* and found it to be merely a revival of "the discredited *Clark Bros.* doctrine in scant disguise"; hence, an unwarranted impingement on the employer's freedom of expression.[10] Besides being contrary to the purpose expressed by Congress in Section 8(c), the Board majority announced that the "equal opportunity" doctrine had proved itself "unworkable in the arena of practical labor-management relations," since it implicitly encouraged *seriatim* speech-making by the election parties, with the validity of the election often hung on who was given "the last word." [11] For these reasons,

---

[9] The Board's decision in *Bonwit-Teller* was actually foreshadowed by language in the Second Circuit's opinion in NLRB v. Clark Bros. Co., Inc., 163 F.2d 373, 376, 20 L.R.R.M. 2436, 2438 (2d Cir. 1947), where the court said it would hesitate to hold that an employer could not express his views in a captive-audience speech "provided a similar opportunity to address them were accorded representatives of the union. . . ."

[10] Livingston Shirt Corp., 107 N.L.R.B. 400, 407, 33 L.R.R.M. 1156, 1158 (1953).

[11] *Id.* at 407, 33 L.R.R.M. at 1158. *But see* 107 N.L.R.B. at 418-20, 33 L.R.R.M. at 1165-66 (Member Murdock, dissenting).

and over the vigorous dissent of Member Murdock, the Board overruled *Bonwit-Teller* and established yet another set of standards for captive-audience speeches in its decisions, issued in tandem, in the *Livingston Shirt Corp.*[12] and *Peerless Plywood Co.*[13] cases.

Under the *Livingston Shirt* rule, an employer may make preelection speeches on company time and premises and deny the union's request for an opportunity to reply, so long as he does not bar the union from delivering its opposing views through traditional channels of communication by enforcing a broad nosolicitation rule. Viewing *Livingston* independently, one might have thought the Board had abandoned its long-held conviction that the captive-audience speech carried an inherent potential for coercion which set it apart from all other forms of pre-election communication, for the Board seemed now to be saying that other channels should be adequate to permit the union to neutralize any coercive effects of the employer's face-to-face talks. *Peerless Plywood* made it clear, however, that the Board still adhered to the intuitive belief that such speeches constituted a dangerous technique.

Although it felt compelled in *Livingston* by considerations of free speech and Section 8(c) to allow employers to make captive-audience speeches without granting the union company time and space to reply, the Board drew the line in *Peerless* at allowing such speeches by either side during the final 24 hours preceding the election. Reasoning—again, purely on the basis of intuition— that such last-minute captive-audience sessions "have an unwholesome and unsettling effect and tend to interfere with that sober and thoughtful choice which a free election is design to reflect," [14] the Board ruled in *Peerless Plywood* that "employers and unions alike will be prohibited from making election speeches on company time to massed assemblies of employees within 24 hours before the scheduled time for conducting an election." [15]

To avoid the Section 8(c) conflict which it had found in the *Bonwit-Teller* doctrine, the Board limited the effect of the *Peerless Plywood* rule to the election context: a violation will

[12] 107 N.L.R.B. 400, 33 L.R.R.M. 1156 (1953).

[13] 107 N.L.R.B. 427, 33 L.R.R.M. 1151 (1953).

[14] 107 N.L.R.B. at 429, 33 L.R.R.M. at 1151-52.

[15] *Id.* at 429, 33 L.R.R.M. at 1152.

result in invalidation of the election but will not sustain a Section 8 (a) (1) charge.[16] Further, the Board carefully defined the scope of the rule, specifying that it applies only to speeches within the final 24-hour period and not to any speeches, on or off company premises "if employee attendance is voluntary and on the employees own time."[17] The parties remain free, moreover, to engage in any other legitimate campaign activities, even during the final 24 hours.

The *Livingston Shirt* and *Peerless Plywood* rules evoked immediate and continuing criticism.[18] *Livingston Shirt* was attacked on the ground that it made the captive-audience speech, which had long been regarded as the single most effective instrument of campaign persuasion available exclusively to employers, and left unions to rely on lesser methods which could not be expected to restore balance to the campaign psychology. *Peerless Plywood* was criticized for its inconsistency with *Livingston*, and the 24-hour moratorium for which it provided was discounted as too short to be of real value. In this view, unions forced to rely on other media could not be expetced to respond effectively in the time remaining so as to neutralize the impact of captive-audience speeches delivered, for example, 25 hours before the election. Nevertheless, the *Livingston Shirt* and *Peerless Plywood* rules have survived the commentators' assaults, and the Board continues to apply them.[19]

---

[16] As noted earlier in this study, Section 8 (c) literally applies only to unfair labor practices. Accordingly, the Board has long taken the position that statements which may not be made the basis for finding a Section 8 (a) (1) violation may nevertheless constitute grounds for invalidating an election. *See* General Shoe Corp., 77 N.L.R.B. 124, 127, 21 L.R.R.M. 1337, 1340-41 (1948). Further, since the test for election interference is more stringent than the test under Section 8 (a) (1), the Board has held that conduct violative of Section 8 (a) (1) *a fortiori* invalidates an election. Dal-Tex Optical Co., 137 N.L.R.B. 1782, 50 L.R.R.M. 1489 (1962).

[17] 107 N.L.R.B. at 430, 33 L.R.R.M. at 1152.

[18] *See, e.g.,* AARON, EMPLOYEE FREE SPEECH: THE SEARCH FOR A POLICY, PUBLIC POLICY AND COLLECTIVE BARGAINING (Shister, Aaron & Summers ed., 1962) ; Christensen, *Free Speech, Propaganda and the National Labor Relations Act*, 38 N.Y.U. L. REV. 243 (1963) ; Wirtz, *Board Policy and Labor Management Relations: Employer Persuasion*, N.Y.U. 7th CONF. ON LAB. 79, 97 (1954). *See also* NLRB v. F.W. Woolworth Co., 214 F.2d 78, 34 L.R.R.M. 2293 (6th Cir. 1954).

[19] The Board was asked to reconsider the *Livingston Shirt* rule in General Electric Co. [McCulloch Corp.], 156 N.L.R.B. 1247, 61 L.R.R.M. 1222 (1966), but declined on the ground that it should wait until the practical effects on

Application of the Rules

Where Other Means of Union Access are Limited. Despite the apparent mechanical simplicity of the current rules, their application has given rise to some serious disagreements. In 1962, a majority of the Board, again reconstituted following a change of national administrations, held in *May Department Stores Co.*[20] that *Livingston Shirt* did not authorize an employer to make captive-audience speeches and deny the union's request for an opportunity to reply while the employer at the same time exercised its privilege as a retail establishment to prohibit solicitation on its selling floors during working and nonworking time.[21] Reviving, at least partially, the *Bonwit-Teller* doctrine of "equal opportunity," the Board held that even though the employer's no-solicitation rule was lawful and his pre-election speeches were not coercive in content, the denial of the union's request to respond, under the circumstances, was a violation because it created a "glaring 'imbalance in opportunities for organizational communication.' "[22] To the surprise of the dissenting members,[23] the majority concluded that neither *Livingston Shirt* nor the Supreme Court's decisions in the *Nutone* and *Babcock & Wilcox* cases[24] had overruled *Bonwit-Teller* insofar as it applied to retail establishments having broad but privileged no-solicitation rules. *Livingston*, the majority said, had expressly exempted such situations, and the Supreme Court's decisions in *Nutone* and *Babcock & Wilcox* (authorizing certain employer restrictions on organizational activities on company premises)

---

organizing of its decision in Excelsior Underwear, Inc., 156 N.L.R.B. 1236, 61 L.R.R.M. 1217 (1966), issued on the same day, were known. *Excelsior* established the rule requiring employers to supply petitioning unions with employee name-and-address lists to facilitate off-site communications prior to Board-conducted elections. See discussion Chapter XIV, *infra.*

[20] 136 N.L.R.B. 797, 49 L.R.R.M. 1862 (1962).

[21] For a discussion of the permissible limits upon union solicitation in department stores, see Marshall Field & Co., 98 N.L.R.B. 88, 90, 29 L.R.R.M. 1305, 1306 (1952). See also discussion at pp. 290-92, *infra.*

[22] 136 N.L.R.B. at 801, 49 L.R.R.M. at 1864.

[23] See 136 N.L.R.B. at 804-808, 49 L.R.R.M. at 1865-66 (Members Rodgers and Leedom, dissenting).

[24] NLRB v. United Steelworkers of America [Nutone, Inc.], 357 U.S. 357, 42 L.R.R.M. 2324 (1958); Babcock & Wilcox Co., 351 U.S. 105, 38 L.R.R.M. 2001 (1956). See also discussion at pp. 247-48, notes 36 & 37, *infra.*

did not reach this far, but were limited to those circumstances in which other sufficient channels of communication were available to afford the "balance in 'opportunities for organizational communication.' "[25] Emphasizing this concept of "balance," the Board flatly declared that other channels could not be deemed adequate unless they provide an opportunity for employees "to discuss the matter with their fellow employees *at their place of work.*"[26] Since the company's broad no-solicitation rule precluded such discussion by the May employees, "balance" could be maintained only by letting the union respond to the employers speeches on company time and premises.

Although the holding of *May* could technically be reconciled with *Livingston,* the rationale of the majority reflected a conviction that had not been expressed by the Board since the pre-*Livingston* days—the conviction that no amount of union exhortation away from the employees' immediate work station could restore the rationality of their decision-making processes after the psychological impact of a captive-audience speech. The dissenting members protested that the Board could not dismiss other channels as inadequate merely because the avenues open to the employer were superior, and insisted that the Board should make findings concerning "whether, by virtue of the location of the place of employment, the facilities and resources available to the union, and the relevant alternative channels available for communications, the union has an adequate opportunity for effectively reaching the employees outside the employer's premises through reasonable efforts."[27] Under the dissenters' approach, then, the proper test was not whether there had been a "balance" or "imbalance" in opportunities for communication, but whether the circumstances had afforded the union some *sufficient* means for getting its message to the employees.

On review, the Court of Appeals for the Sixth Circuit agreed with the dissenters. There was no "magic," the court held, to the word "imbalance"; rather, the test was whether the facts would support a finding "of non-accessibility amounting to a

25 136 N.L.R.B. at 800-802, 49 L.R.R.M. at 1864.

26 *Id.* at 802, 49 L.R.R.M. at 1864 (emphasis added).

27 *Id.* at 809, 49 L.R.R.M. at 1866.

handicap to self-organization." [28] In making such a finding, the Board should consider whether the employees, away from company premises, were removed or isolated from the "normal, usual communications." [29] The Board could not, the court said, simply dismiss all methods of communication other than working-time speeches to employees as "'catch-as-catch can,' ineffective methods." [30]

Although the Board subsequently expressed disagreement with the Sixth Circuit's decision and announced that it would adhere to its *May* rationale,[31] it has not, since the *May* case, actually ordered any employer to grant an opportunity for reply to a captive-audience speech without first making factual findings of the sort the court found lacking in the *May* case. Thus, in *Montgomery Ward*,[32] after declaring its reaffirmance of its *May* holding, the Board went on to state that "[t]he facts of the instant case are much stronger for finding a violation than in the *May* case," and pointed out that the no-solicitation rule involved was broader than that in *May*, since it prohibited solicitation not only on the selling floors, but anywhere in the store at any time.[33] On review, the Sixth Circuit distinguished *May* on this ground and held that, in this instance, the Board's findings were sufficient to sustain a violation.[34] In *S & H Grossinger's, Inc.*[35] the Board again made extensive factual findings concerning the physical inaccessibility of the employees off company premises, and used these findings as a basis for concluding that the employer's delivery of antiunion speeches during working hours, while precluding on-site union solicitation, violated Section 8(a)(1). The Second Circuit agreed that

---

[28] May Dept. Stores Co. v. NLRB, 316 F.2d 797, 801, 53 L.R.R.M. 2172, 2175 (6th Cir. 1963).

[29] *Id.*, 53 L.R.R.M. at 2175.

[30] *Id.* at 800, 53 L.R.R.M. at 2175.

[31] Montgomery Ward & Co., Inc., 145 N.L.R.B. 846, 55 L.R.R.M. 1063 (1964).

[32] *Id.*, 55 L.R.R.M. at 1063.

[33] 145 N.L.R.B. at 849, 55 L.R.R.M. at 1064.

[34] Montgomery Ward & Co. v. NLRB, 339 F.2d 889, 58 L.R.R.M. 2115 (6th Cir. 1965).

[35] 156 N.L.R.B. 233, 61 L.R.R.M. 1025 (1965).

the union had "[n]o effective alternatives [to on-site solicitation] in its organizational efforts" and sustained that part of the Board's order directing the employer to drop its ban against solicitation by nonemployees.[36]

It appears, then, that despite the Board's proclaimed adherence to its *May* position, it has, in effect, adopted the approach urged by Member Leedom in his dissent in *May*. That is, before the Board will find a violation based upon captive-audience speeches made in conjunction with a broad no-solicitation rule, it will examine the facts to see whether, "when all alternative channels of communication are considered, the ability of the union to carry its message to the employees has been truly diminished."[37] Accordingly, while there may still be unresolved disagreements regarding the proper theoretical approach in cases such as *May*, in light of the Board's actual practice, any such remaining controversy is essentially academic.

Remarks to Small Groups or in Informal Settings. Other controversies, more mundane perhaps but of greater current importance in the day-to-day administration of the Board's election policies, have arisen regarding the application of the *Peerless Plywood* 24-hour rule. A threshold question in any case of this sort, of course, is whether the speech or statement complained of amounts to a "captive-audience speech" as the Board uses that term. In general, the Board has sought to

---

[36] NLRB v. S & H Grossinger's, Inc., 372 F.2d 26, 29, 64 L.R.R.M. 2295, 2298 (2d Cir. 1967). Having thus removed the bar to adequate communication, the court found unnecessary the further provision of the Board's order granting the union equal opportunities to make captive-audience speeches, and it struck this portion of the order. *Id.* at 30-31, 64 L.R.R.M. at 2299. *See also* NLRB v. H.W. Elson Bottling Co., 379 F.2d 223, 65 L.R.R.M. 2673 (6th Cir. 1967). In two cases following *Grossinger's*, the Second Circuit has taken a more restrictive approach than the Board concerning the extent of access to employees to which nonemployees organizers are entitled. *See* NLRB v. New Pines, Inc., 451 F.2d 797, 81 L.R.R.M. 2423 (2d Cir. 1972), *denying enforcement to* 191 N.L.R.B. No. 144, 77 L.R.R.M. 1543 (1971); NLRB v. Kutsher's Hotel and Country Club, Inc., 427 F.2d 200, 74 L.R.R.M. 2394 (2d Cir. 1970), *denying enforcement to* 175 N.L.R.B. 1114 (1969). Recently, the Board itself has appeared more willing to permit restrictions against organizing by non-employees on company property, even if this means the union must resort to a variety of different communications techniques, none of which by itself would be sufficient to reach a significant portion of the work force. *See* Falk Corp., 192 N.L.R.B. No. 100, 77 L.R.R.M. 1916 (1971); Monogram Models, Inc., 192 N.L.R.B. No. 99, 77 L.R.R.M. 1913 (1971). *See also* discussion at pp. 286-90, *infra*.

[37] 136 N.L.R.B. at 809, 49 L.R.R.M. at 1866 (Member Leedom, dissenting).

define the coverage of the rule broadly. One of its purposes, after all, is to simplify the handling of election cases by eliminating much case-by-case evaluation of remarks made to employees within the final 24-hours. Still, the rule does not cover every statement made by one of the parties within the 24-hour period, and the Board's decisions do not always make it clear why some such statements are excepted and others covered.[38]

Peerless Plywood describes the object of its 24-hour prohibition as all "election speeches on company time *massed assemblies* of employees. . . ."[39] However, the Board has never adequately explained what is meant by "massed assemblies." There is no question that remarks made to individual employees are beyond the ambit of the rule.[40] But when it comes to statements made to small groups of employees, the Board's decisions become difficult to reconcile.

In *Independent Linen Service*[41] the Board overruled an employer's objection based on "electioneering speeches" made on behalf of the union to "employees in small groups" within the 24-hour pre-election period, stating that "such activities do not constitute speeches to massed assemblies of employees within the *Peerless Plywood* rule."[42] On the other hand, the Board has indicated elsewhere that the size of the group addressed is immaterial. Thus, in the *Great Atlantic & Pacific Tea Co.*[43] the Board

---

[38] Recently the Board majority rejected the contention of Chairman Miller and Member Kennedy in a dissenting opinion, that an employer had the right under a strict application of the *Livingston Shirt* rule to prohibit an employee from asking a question in response to a company captive-audience speech and to fire the employee when he wished that his question be heard. Prescott Industrial Products, 205 N.L.R.B. No. 15, 83 L.R.R.M. 1500 (1973).

[39] 107 N.L.R.B. at 429, 33 L.R.R.M. at 1152 (emphasis added).

[40] *See, e.g., William B. Patton Towing Co.*, 180 N.L.R.B. 64, 81, 75 L.R.R.M. 1522, 1523 (1969); American Sugar Refining Co., 123 N.L.R.B. 207, 43 L.R.R.M. 1394 (1959); Globe Motors, Inc., 123 N.L.R.B. 30, 31-32, 43 L.R.R.M. 1365, 1366 (1959); Montgomery Ward & Co., 119 N.L.R.B. 52, 40 L.R.R.M. 1444 (1957).

[41] 124 N.L.R.B. 717, 44 L.R.R.M. 1493 (1959).

[42] *Id.* at 719, 44 L.R.R.M. at 1493. *See also* Business Aviation Inc., 202 N.L.R.B. No. 151, 82 L.R.R.M. 1710 (1973) (*Peerless Plywood* rule held not applicable to "every minor conversation between a few employees and a union agent or supervisor"); Eagle-Picher Industries, Inc., 171 N.L.R.B. 392, 305, 68 L.R.R.M. 1570, 1571 (1968) (supervisor's statements to three employees held that it was not a captive-audience speech).

[43] 111 N.L.R.B. 623, 626, 35 L.R.R.M. 1537, 1538 (1955).

declared that the term "massed assemblies" is not "limited to all
or most of the unit employees, or to any certain proportion of
them, or to any assemblage of such employees whose votes would
[be sufficient in number to] affect the outcome of the election."
In accordance with this interpretation, elections have been set
aside on *Peerless Plywood* grounds where the "massed assembly"
addressed consisted of fewer than 2 percent of the employees in a
large unit,[44] and, in another instance, where the group addressed
consisted of only six of the 266 eligible voters in an election which
was decided by a 23-vote margin.[45] If, as it appears, these latter
decisions represent the prevailing Board policy, then some further
explication of that policy is needed, for it is difficult to understand how remarks to so small a portion of the eligible voters can
engender the sort of "mass psychology" the *Peerless Plywood* rule
was purportedly designed to prevent.[46]

Also in need of clarification is how the 24-hour rule applies to
election statements made to employees in informal settings or in
response to questions from the employees. In *Eagle-Picher Industries, Inc.*[47] the Board rejected an objection charging that a
supervisor had joined a group of employees on election day and
worked along with them for some 45 minutes, during which time
he "engaged in antiunion propaganda." No violation of the rule
was found, since the employees were apparently free to talk to
the supervisor and there was no evidence that the supervisor
"engaged in a long monologue." On these facts, the Board distinguished *Peerless Plywood* and found, even though the supervisor's remarks were partisan, that this was not the sort of session
which "tends to create a mass psychology which overrides arguments made through other campaign media."[48] A similar result

---

[44] *Id.*, 35 L.R.R.M. at 1538.

[45] Honeywell, Inc., 162 N.L.R.B. 323, 64 L.R.R.M. 1002 (1966). *See also*
Riblet Welding & Mfg. Corp., 112 N.L.R.B. 712, 36 L.R.R.M. 1076 (1955)
(separate meetings with three small groups of employees held about two hours
before the election constituted a violation).

[46] *See* 162 N.L.R.B. at 326-27, 64 L.R.R.M. at 1003-1004 (Members Fanning
and Jenkins, dissenting).

[47] 171 N.L.R.B. 293, 68 L.R.R.M. 1570 (1968).

[48] *Id.* at 305, 68 L.R.R.M. at 1571, *quoting from* Peerless Plywood Co.,
107 N.L.R.B. 427, 429, 33 L.R.R.M. 1151, 1152 (1953).

was reached in the Board's early decision in *National Petro-Chemicals Corp.*,[49] holding the 24-hour rule inapplicable to remarks made to employees by their plant manager in an informal "bull session" called by him to answer charges that the employer was opposed to one of the petitioning unions and to discuss labor relations in general.[50]

But any exception based on the informality of the remarks must be recognized as exceedingly limited. For despite the foregoing decisions, the Board has proclaimed broadly in other cases that the 24-hour prohibition is not confined to "a formal speech in the usual sense," but is designed to bar "absolutely" during the 24-hour pre-election period the use of company time for campaign speeches "in any form." [51] Thus, in *Honeywell, Inc.*,[52] the Board set aside an election because of the conduct of a supervisor who entered a room where a small group of employees was working about one and one-half hours before voting commenced, asked whether they had any questions about a "fact sheet" of company propaganda, and then talked and made comments about the sheet until the voting period began, answering questions which he solicited. In language plainly too sweeping to be reconciled with the *Eagle-Picher* and *National Petro-Chemicals* cases, the Board concluded that this session constituted a captive-audience speech, and that no "exception from the *'absolute'* prohibition of the *Peerless Plywood* rule is warranted." [53] Similarly, when confronted with pre-election meetings conducted on a strict question-and-answer format, the Board has rejected a narrow, literal approach and held that such sessions fall within the intent of *Peerless Plywood's* ban on captive-audience "speeches." [54]

---

[49] 107 N.L.R.B. 1610, 33 L.R.R.M. 1443 (1954) (ruling issued nearly three months after *Peerless Plywood*).

[50] *See also* Kenyon-Peck, Inc., 121 N.L.R.B. 780, 42 L.R.R.M. 1429 (1958) (antiunion "comments" to employees by the company's president within 24 hours of the election was held not a "speech" to a "massed assembly" of employees).

[51] Montgomery Ward & Co., Inc., 124 N.L.R.B. 343, 44 L.R.R.M. 1375, 1376 (1959); *accord*, Honeywell, Inc., 162 N.L.R.B. at 325, 64 L.R.R.M. at 102; Great Atlantic & Pacific Tea Co., 111 N.L.R.B. at 626, 35 L.R.R.M. at 1538.

[52] 162 N.L.R.B. at 325, 64 L.R.R.M. at 1002.

[53] *Id.*, 64 L.R.R.M. at 1003 (emphasis added).

[54] 124 N.L.R.B. at 344, 44 L.R.R.M. at 1376.

As a general matter, the Board has recognized that the *Peerless Plywood* rule applies in situations where employees have been "gathered together for the purpose of hearing the speech...." [55] The *Honeywell* decision is notable, however, because it found a violation of the rule even in the absence of any indication that the employees had been assembled specifically to hear management's views. In *Honeywell* it apparently was enough that the employees were together in the room where they worked when their supervisor undertook to address them, and were obliged to remain there while he spoke.[56] Thus, while a planned assembly of employees is the usual circumstance in captive-audience cases, it is not a necessary prerequisite. In keeping with this view, the 24-hour rule has been applied to union speeches broadcast by a sound truck stationed opposite the plant which could be heard by employees throughout their working hours on the day before the election.[57]

Peerless Plywood exempts from its prohibition election speeches that are "voluntary *and* on the employees own time." [58] Board decisions make it clear that this is a dual requirement and that both conditions must be met before a speech will be exempted. In *The Fluorocarbon Co.*[59] for example, a speech to employees within the 24-hour pre-election period was held to violate the rule even though employees were told in advance that their attendance would be voluntary and were advised again at the outset of the meeting that they need not remain and listen. The employees were compensated for their time, the Board pointed out, and "this single factor . . . suffices" to establish a transgression of the

---

[55] United States Gypsum Co., 115 N.L.R.B. 734, 735, 37 L.R.R.M. 1374, 1375 (1956).

[56] 162 N.L.R.B. at 325, 64 L.R.R.M. at 1002.

[57] 115 N.L.R.B. at 735, 37 L.R.R.M. at 1375. *But cf.* Crown Paper Board Co. Inc., 158 N.L.R.B. 440, 442-45, 62 L.R.R.M. 1041, 1042-43 (1966), where the Board, in a lengthy opinion, distinguished *United States Gypsum*, and overruled objections based upon a union's use of soundcar broadcasts which, the Board found, were directed at employees entering and leaving the plant at a shift change and only accidentally reached employees who were in the plant working. Since most of the employees exposed to the broadcasts were "not . . . together in a group in the plant during working hours," the Board held they were not a "massed assembly" within the rule. *Id.* at 443, 62 L.R.R.M. at 1042.

[58] 107 N.L.R.B. at 430, 33 L.R.R.M. at 1152 (emphasis added).

[59] 168 N.L.R.B. 629, 66 L.R.R.M. 1375 (1967).

rule.[60] By reverse token, the Board holds that a speech delivered on the employees *own* time violates the 24-hour ban if it is not made clear to the employees that their attendance is voluntary.[61] It is also interesting to note that, although the Board at times has indicated that speeches to employees at their place of work carry a special impact,[62] it applies the *Peerless* rule even to speeches *off* company premises, as long as they are delivered on company time.[63]

Relation of Remarks to the Election. Although the *Peerless Plywood* decision emphasizes that the vice of last-minute, captive-audience speeches lies in the circumstances of their delivery more than their content, questions regarding the content of such speeches do occasionally arise in the application of the 24-hour rule. Obviously, it must appear that the speech has something to do with the election before it can be a ground for setting the election aside.[64] Moreover, the speech must include something more than just a nonpartisan reference to the election. Speeches, for example, simply urging employees to vote, even if delivered in capitive-audience sessions, have been held not to violate the rule so long as the employees are not urged to vote in a particular manner.[65] This accords with the Board's basic position that its *Peerless Plywood* rule is simply an extension of its rules prohibiting *electioneering* near the polls.[66] Moreover, the rule is

---

[60] *Id.* at 656, 66 L.R.R.M. at 1376. *See also* Mid-South Mfg. Co., 117 N.L.R.B. 1786, 40 L.R.R.M. 1092 (1957).

[61] Robbins Packing Corp., 115 N.L.R.B. 1429, 38 L.R.R.M. 1092 (1956); H. & P. Mining Co., 114 N.LR.B. 1436, 37 L.R.R.M. 1183 (1955); Rock Hill Printing & Finishing Co., 114 N.L.R.B. 836, 37 L.R.R.M. 1046 (1955); Fuller Ford, Inc., 113 N.L.R.B. 169, 36 L.R.R.M. 1270 (1955).

[62] *See, e.g.,* 136 N.L.R.B. at 800-802, 49 L.R.R.M. at 1863-64.

[63] Hamilton Watch Co., 107 N.L.R.B. 1608, 33 L.R.R.M. 1449 (1954).

[64] *Peerless Plywood* defines the object of its prohibition simply as *"election speeches* on company time to massed assemblies of employees" within the 24-hour pre-election period. 107 N.L.R.B. at 429, 33 L.R.R.M. at 1152 (emphasis added).

[65] *E.g.,* Malone & Hyde, Inc., 115 N.L.R.B. 498, 37 L.R.R.M. 1327 (1956); John W. Thomas Co., 111 N.L.R.B. 226, 35 L.R.R.M. 1444 (1955).

[66] *See* 107 N.L.R.B. at 430, 33 L.R.R.M. at 1152. *Cf.* Patz Co., Case No. 18-RC-5743, 55 L.R.R.M. 1360 (1964), wherein the regional director held that an employer's remarks to employees on election day concerning a pre-existing insurance program, in which the employer referred to statements in a union campaign handbill, did not amount to a "campaign speech" in violation of the rule.

applicable only to speeches. Other forms of campaigning, such as solicitation, distribution of literature and posting of campaign propaganda are not affected by the *Peerless Plywood* ban, though they may be subject to other Board regulations.[67] Indeed, the Board has held it permissible for an employer to distribute within the final 24 hours printed copies of a captive-audience speech he delivered earlier.[68]

Measurement of the 24-hour Period. The one area where the Board has been most rigid in the application of the *Peerless Plywood* rule is the enforcement of its time provisions. The rule does not apply to speeches given at any time during the day preceding the election, but only those within 24 hours of the scheduled opening of the polls.[69] Thus, objections to captive-audience speeches the day before the election have been overruled where investigation revealed that the sessions were completed a few minutes more than 24 hours before the scheduled polling time.[70] The Board has been so strict in enforcing this time limitation, in fact, that it set aside an election based upon the employer's delivery of a captive-audience speech within 24 hours of the time when the election was *scheduled* to begin, although the election thereafter had to be rescheduled, because of the inadvertent failure of the Board's agent in charge to appear at the proper time, and voting did not actually begin until some 40 hours after the speech.[71] The rule was designed to enable parties to determine "the *exact* cutoff period," the Board stated, and to

---

[67] *See* Fisher Radio Corp., 123 N.L.R.B. 879, 44 L.R.R.M. 1015 (1959) (posting campaign signs); Doughboy Plastic Products, Inc., 122 N.L.R.B. 338, 43 L.R.R.M. 1122 (1958) (distribution of propaganda); Gallaher Drug Co., 116 N.L.R.B. 1263, 38 L.R.R.M. 1455 (1956) (solicitation). *See also* McKibbon Bros., Inc., 123 N.L.R.B. 1571, 44 L.R.R.M. 1187 (1959) (rule was not violated when the employer permitted a parade of employees to march through the plant wearing "vote no" helmets within the final 24 hours).

[68] Vita Food Products, Inc., 116 N.L.R.B. 1215, 38 L.R.R.M. 1437 (1956).

[69] National Bookbinding Co., 171 N.L.R.B. 219, 68 L.R.R.M. 1038 (1968).

[70] Peachtree City Warehouse, Inc., 158 N.L.R.B. 1031, 62 L.R.R.M. 1169 (1966) (speech was completed 24 hours and 20 minutes before the polls were scheduled to open); Verson Mfg. Co., 114 N.L.R.B. 1297, 37 L.R.R.M. 1152 (1955) (24 hours and 45 minutes before); Jewett & Sherman Co., 111 N.L.R.B. 534, 35 L.R.R.M. 1506 (1955) (25 hours and 15 minutes before).

[71] Hamilton Welding Co., 126 N.L.R.B. 138, 139-40, 45 L.R.R.M. 1285, 1286 (1960).

override the objection in these circumstances would allow the employer to gain through fortuitous circumstances a "competitive advantage . . . contrary to the purpose of the rule." [72] Strangely, however, the Board permitted an exception to the rule when it was charged that a speech planned to terminate precisely 24 hours before the scheduled voting time in fact extended some 5 minutes beyond the 24-hour limit. Since the employer was aware of the rule and any such intrusion was "accidental," the Board held, it did not warrant the invalidation of the election. [73]

EVALUATION OF THE CURRENT RULES: CONCLUDING REMARKS

In summary, the Board's present policies allow the parties to a representation election to make noncoercive pre-election campaign speeches in captive-audience sessions on or off company premises, subject to two basic limitations: (1) the employer may not make such speeches while at the same time applying a broad band against union solicitation on company property which denies the union sufficient access to employees to communicate its countervailing views; and (2) neither party may make such speeches within the final 24 hours before the scheduled opening of the polls.

The theoretical underpinnings of these rules are still subject to some dispute. [74] Moreover, the Board's fundamental assumptions about the potential impact of last minute appeals are dubious. As pointed out earlier, the Board's assumptions in this regard, like those underlying many of its other election rules, have been based entirely on its own intuition. The agency has neither conducted nor referred to any objective studies of the actual impact of particular forms of communication on prospective voters. Indeed, until recently no comprehensive studies of this sort had ever been made in connection with NLRB elections. The results of the one such study now available cast serious doubt upon many of the Board's long-cherished suppositions

---

[72] *Id.* at 139, 45 L.R.R.M. at 1286 (emphasis added).

[73] Granite State Veneer, Inc., 123 N.L.R.B. 1497, 44 L.R.R.M. 1154 (1959).

[74] *See* discussion at pp. 240-42, *supra*. *See also* MORRIS, THE DEVELOPING LABOR LAW, 80-81 (BNA Books, 1969) for criticism of the use of different standards in complaint cases arising under Section 8(a)(1) of the NLRA and representation cases arising under Section 9(c).

about the effects of campaign communications, for in fact there seems to be little correlation between particular forms of communication and changes in employees' disposition to vote for or against union representation.[75]

Nevertheless, the application of the *Livingston Shirt* and *Peerless Plywood* rules for nearly two decades has given them high seniority among Board doctrines. In general, putting aside the question of the need for such restrictions, the Board's approach has fairly effectively served the primary purpose of a mechanical policy; it has provided the parties with relatively certain guidelines as to permissible pre-election conduct, and it has fostered administrative efficiency in disposing of postelection objections. However, these objectives would be served more effectively if the Board were to exercise greater care in defining the grounds upon which certain pre-election statements to employees, apparently because of their form, format, setting, delivery or content, are found to fall outside the coverage of its captive-audience rules.

---

[75] Results of the study are published in three articles: Getman & Goldberg, *The Myth of NLRB Expertise*, 39 U. CHI. L. REV. 681 (1972); Getman, Goldberg & Herman, *The National Labor Relations Board Voting Study: A Preliminary Report*, 1 J. LEG. STUD. 233 (1972); Goldberg & Getman, *Voting Behavior in NLRB Elections*, 23 N.Y.U. CONF. LABOR 115 (1970).

CHAPTER XI

Electioneering and Other Conduct Near the Polls

In furtherance of its policy of protecting voters from the potential undue influence of last-minute campaign exhortation, the Board has also established rules barring electioneering or coercive conduct in polling areas while elections are being conducted. In effect, the Board closely scrutinizes the presence of union and employer agents in the polling area during this period of time. In this respect, the Board's function is similar to that of election judges in normal political elections where similar prohibitions are customary.[1] In either case, the ban on electioneering serves an overall purpose of maintaining order and equity in the election process.

> The Board's rule against electioneering at or near the polling place is designed to ensure an atmosphere free from pressure or influence of any sort at the time and place where the employees cast their ballots.[2]

Thus, as in the case of captive-audience speeches within the final pre-election hours,[3] the Board gives significant weight to its long-held assumption that last-minute tactics by any party may prevail in the voter's mind when he indicates his choice on the ballot. Such conduct, in the Board's view, may prove unfair to the party which did not have the last-minute advantage and may prevent the voter from making a free and reasoned choice in his selection of a representative. In practical terms, it must

---

[1] Indeed, in an early case applying its ban against electioneering near the polls, the Board indicated that it was following the requirements established by local law for political elections. The Board referred to the prohibition as "the usual rule in force in Ohio," the state in which the election in question was held. The Kilgore Mfg. Co., 45 N.L.R.B. 468, 469, 11 L.R.R.M. 139 (1942).

[2] Spartan Aircraft, 111 N.L.R.B. 1373, 1375, 35 L.R.R.M. 1679 (1955).

[3] See text at pp. 242-56, supra.

be recognized that campaigning must stop at some reasonable time and place during the election period.

In determining whether an election should be set aside because of alleged instances of either coercive election speech or conduct, the Board must make two preliminary inquiries: (1) does the speech or conduct in question actually constitute "electioneering" —*i.e.* is it propaganda designed to pressure or influence voters in casting their ballots; and (2) did it occur within the nonelectioneering zone surrounding the polling place. In making the former determination, the Board generally applies an objective test:

> It is well established that the Board will not attempt to evaluate the precise impact of improper conduct by one of the parties to an election upon the exercise by the voters of their freedom of choice. Rather it is sufficient that such conduct is reasonably calculated to have the effect of interfering with a free choice.[4]

In order to evaluate instances of alleged electioneering, in certain situations, as we shall see later, the Board has established a number of presumptions that are in effect, *per se* rules prohibiting particular types of conduct within the vicinity of the polls.

The determination of whether protested incidents of electioneering were sufficiently proximate to the voting area to invalidate the election has posed difficult problems for the Board. Generally, electioneering before the opening of the polls does not warrant setting aside an election, regardless of the proximity of the conduct complained of to the polling place.[5] But once the balloting has begun, the Board attempts to prohibit electioneering and other coercive activity "at or near the polls." Disputes inevitably arise which require a determination of what is "near the polls." Ideally, the Board agent or the concerned parties will stipulate the nonelectioneering zone. In many cases, however, no such stipulation is made and the parties and the Board are left to contend with ambiguous delineations determining permissible conduct. Consequently, the Board engages in a case-by-case analysis in establishing the nonelectioneering zone. The physical location of the ballot box often may determine the prohibited zone for electioneering. For example, if the

---

[4] 111 N.L.R.B. at 1375, 35 L.R.R.M. at 1679.

[5] Mutual Distributing Co., 83 N.L.R.B. 463, 24 L.R.R.M. 1114 (1949).

election is held on the third floor of a building, electioneering may be allowed on the other floors.

One Board decision indicates the clearest rationale used in defining the neutral zone. In *Alliance Ware, Inc.*[6] the union positioned a sound truck on a public highway and broadcasted electioneering material during the polling hours. Although the truck was approximately 340 feet from the polling place, the Board found that such electioneering interfered with the election.

> The determining factor is not the *linear distance* from the sound truck to the employee's entrance or the polling place, but the immediacy of the voice of the electioneering broadcaster to the eligible voters as they approached the polling place.[7]

Emphasis has also been placed on the fact that the conduct in question occurred in a location where the campaigner could talk to or be observed by employees while they were waiting to vote. In many cases this has meant the location where the employees were standing in line.[8] In other cases, the Board has said that the nonelectioneering zone included hallways and open areas through which employees passed in going to vote.[9]

The reason for establishing a nonelectioneering zone is quite legitimate. The Board, however, should not have to rely upon geography and estimation of voter impact in a case-by-case analysis. In the interests of consistency and clarity there is a need for either a standard rule delineating the nonelectioneering zone or a strictly enforced requirement that the Board agent, in cooperation with all parties, must stipulate the prohibited area in each case.

After having considered the general aspects of the electioneering rule, some attention to the specific types of conduct which violate the Board's rule is necessary. We shall consider them

---

[6] 92 N.L.R.B. 55, 27 L.R.R.M. 1040 (1950).

[7] *Id.* at 57, 27 L.R.R.M. at 1040 (emphasis added). *But cf.*, Higgins, Inc., 106 N.L.R.B. 485, 32 L.R.R.M. 1156 (1953).

[8] Sonoco Products Co., 179 N.L.R.B. 637, 72 L.R.R.M. 1417 (1969). *See also* Stevenson Equipment Co., 174 N.L.R.B. 865, 70 L.R.R.M. 1302 (1969).

[9] *E.g.*, Performance Measurement Co., 148 N.L.R.B. 1657, 57 L.R.R.M. 1218 (1964); Belk's Department Store of Savannah, Ga., Inc., 98 N.L.R.B. 280, 29 L.R.R.M. 1325 (1952). *See also* NLRB Field Manual, § 11326.5, specifying that there should be no "organized" electioneering "along the line of march between workplace and polls," whether the distance be "20 feet or 5 blocks."

in two categories: cases in which actual electioneering conduct near the polls is established, and those in which the presence or conduct of agents of a party in the vicinity of the polls is challenged even in the absence of specific evidence of electioneering. Finally, we will look at a recent rule established by the Board which attempts to standardize to some extent the permissible conduct by the parties in the nonelectioneering zone.

OVERT ELECTIONEERING NEAR THE POLLS

As noted above, in resolving cases where evidence of actual electioneering conduct is present, the Board looks at the facts of each case and determines whether interference was likely under the circumstances. The decision to set aside an election based upon such conduct typically is governed by the substantiality of the electioneering. Brief or isolated incidents may be dismissed as inconsequential. For example, where a union committee said to one voter "you might as well vote yes," the incident was found to be too insignificant to warrant setting aside the election.[10] When the temporary union president on two isolated occasions during the balloting period said "vote for the CIO, we've got it won," the Board found again that even though it was illegal conduct it was unlikely that the incidents could have affected the results.[11]

More persistent or sustained electioneering, on the other hand, will be found objectionable. During a one-hour polling period, an employer's supervisor for fifteen minutes urged newly hired employees to vote against the union. The Board considered conduct for such a period of time to be an interference and consequently set aside the election.[12] In that case, the Board also noted that the results of the election were very close (31 to 30 against the union) and the swaying of one voter would have made the difference. A union representative was electioneering near the entrance of the balloting area; he was asked to leave three times and yet he continued urging the employees

---

[10] Intertype Co., 164 N.L.R.B. 770, 65 L.R.R.M. 1235 (1967), *enforced*, 401 F.2d 41, 69 L.R.R.M. 2067 (4th Cir. 1968).

[11] Similarly, the wearing of union campaign buttons at the polling place has been held not to constitute a ground to set the election aside. La Plante-Choate Mfg. Co., Inc., 30 N.L.R.B. 56, 8 L.R.R.M. 32 (1941).

[12] Claussen Baking Co., 134 N.L.R.B. 111, 49 L.R.R.M. 1092 (1961).

to vote for the union. The Board said this conduct was sufficient interference to set aside the election.[13] It emphasized that he had electioneered for a substantial period of time. The Board gave no indication, however, as to the weight, if any, it accorded the agent's refusal to leave the area when requested.

MERE PRESENCE OF PARTIES NEAR THE POLLS WITHOUT OVERT ELECTIONEERING

The presence and conduct of the parties' agents in the polling area, when there is no specific evidence of electioneering, may also be cause for the Board to find interference with the election and to set aside the results. Ideally, the Board seeks complete protection from restraint or coercion for the voter, up to and during the election. It is for this reason that conduct other than electioneering is closely scrutinized. Cases of this sort can generally be broken down into two categories: those in which the mere presence of the agent is primarily an issue, and those in which some action by the agent, such as conversation, is alleged to be interference.

There is no doubt that the presence of an agent of one of the parties in the polling area may have a coercive influence upon the voter preparing to cast his vote. The employee may develop fears of reprisal at the last minute, or he may have certain fears reinforced at this time. On the other hand, neither party generally has any basic, compelling reason to have agents, other than its appointed election observers, present in the polling area. Accordingly, the NLRB agent and the observers normally are the only nonvoting personnel allowed in the neutral zone.

Exceptions do arise, however, and the Board recognizes them. Thus, in situations where an agent has a legitimate reason for his presence in the polling area the Board will not find interference with the election. In the *ITT Cannon Electric Co.* case,[14] for example, the Board accepted the presence of management personnel in the hallway where they could view the polling entrance and where the employees had to pass by for the reason that they were located at that place to prevent unauthorized

---

[13] Star Expansion Industries Corp., 170 N.L.R.B. 364, 67 L.R.R.M. 1400 (1968).

[14] Case No. 28-RC-1245, 1965 CCH NLRB ¶ 9366 (1965).

people from entering the polling area. Presence which cannot be justified by such reasons may nevertheless be excused if the interference is insignificant. Where a supervisor entered the voting area for a few minutes, the Board found such presence was i :sufficient to find election interference.[15]

The Board recognizes that in most cases the polling area will be located on the employer's premises in a location where the presence of supervisory personnel in the polling area may be impossible to avoid because of general practice or physical layout.[16] The Board, in fact, may go to great lengths to accommodate this situation. The *Covenant Club of Illinois* is a case in point.[17] Polling took place in rooms near the administrative offices of the employer and most employees had to pass by these offices in order to vote. The manager and assistant managers of the club traversed the corridor in the course of the day as part of their normal duties. On the day of the election the manager and his assistant questioned a few employees about their eligibility to vote. The employees nevertheless voted under challenge. The Board overruled the regional director and said that although the employer's actions in the corridor were not fully compliant with the procedural safeguards of the election, the presence of the agents was insufficient to set aside the election.

In addition to relying upon the physical layout of the polling area, the Board mentioned two other factors: the presence of the agents was not continuous, and no objections were raised to the Board agent by the union during the election. By emphasizing lack of immediate objections, the Board demonstrates that it will not allow parties to condone an objectionable situation when they have a chance to correct it by timely objection and then rely on that situation later to set the election aside if they are dissatisfied with the results. This approach has the laudable objective of making all parties cooperate to minimize the incidence of rerun elections.

The issue of an agent's presence in the polling area appears in several other Board cases. In *Belk's Department Store of Savannah, Ga., Inc.*,[18] the manager of the store and several

---

[15] Murray Ohio Mfg. Co., 156 N.L.R.B. 840, 61 L.R.R.M. 1146 (1966).

[16] Serv-Air, Inc., 183 N.L.R.B. No. 32, 74 L.R.R.M. 1284 (1970).

[17] Case No. 13-RC-10233, 1965 CCH ¶ 9365 (1965).

[18] 98 N.L.R.B. 280, 29 L.R.R.M. 1325 (1952).

supervisors stood in the area where the employees gathered while waiting to vote. The manager spent 70 to 80 percent of the polling time in this area. The Board held that the presence of the agents was interference, especially the manager's near-continual presence. Similarly, the Board found in *Performance Measurements Co.*,[19] that the "continual presence" of the company president near the door used by the employees to enter the polling place or seated at a table six feet away from the door was improper conduct. The Board felt that the likelihood of an atmosphere of fear of reprisal was great. The Board's decision does not indicate what weight was given the fact that the agent in question was the president of the company. In *Benson Veneer*[20] the Board made mention of the fact that the president and vice-president of the company had been present near the polls, but again, the Board did not indicate how significant it was that these were the company's top-level officers. While some weight justifiably can be given to the rank of the agent in question within the company or union hierarchy, this factor alone does not afford a reliable measure of the probable intimidating effect of his presence, and it certainly should not be dispositive of a case.

Situations in which an employer or union agent has conversed with an employee in the voting line or in the polling area have presented difficult problems. The Board dealt with such cases in an inconsistent manner, until, in a recent decision, it established strict standards for such situations. In an early case, *Detroit Creamery Co.*,[21] the union vice-president on the day of the election was on company premises talking among production employees. The nature and substance of his conversations were unknown. He was stationed at a point where employees leaving the production area to cast their ballots had to pass him on the way, and he remained there for almost thirty minutes. The Board found interference and set aside the election.

> While there is no evidence as to the actual substance of [his] conversations with the employees, we reasonably infer that the con-

---

[19] 148 N.L.R.B. 1657, 57 L.R.R.M. 1218 (1964).

[20] 156 N.L.R.B. 781, 61 L.R.R.M. 1137 (1966).

[21] 60 N.L.R.B. 178, 15 L.R.R.M. 221 (1945).

versations related to the election since there is no other explanation for [his] presence in the Company's plant during the election.[22]

A few years later in a similar factual situation, the Board reached the opposite decision.[23] A union's international representative sat in his parked car for some time in clear view of the polling place and in a position where employees passed by and talked with him on their way to vote. He was there approximately thirty minutes. There was no proof of specific acts of electioneering. The Board said it would not set aside the election, since his actions did not constitute improper conduct of such a character as to have affected free choice in the election. The Board did not discuss the possibility that it could infer electioneering from the circumstances, as it had in *Detroit Creamery*; yet the agent's presence at the company at that time was similarly open to question.

The Board's decision, however, was overruled by the Court of Appeals for the Fifth Circuit.[24] The court emphasized that the agent had remained in the area for a comparatively long time after the voting began, and it concluded that his activities had interfered with "a free and fair election." The court also noticed that a change of one vote might have changed the result of the election, and a change of two votes certainly would have done so.

The *Houston Shell and Concrete Division* case [25] held that the mere presence of union representatives at or near the polling place is not sufficient ground for setting aside the election, nor is the fact that such representatives conversed with the voters at or near the polls, absent any evidence of coercive statements. This holding clearly conflicted with *Detroit Creamery*; yet the Board did not refer to that decision. In a later case,[26] however, the Board made a turn back in the direction of *Detroit Creamery*. Here, two supervisors spent 10 to 15 minutes in the vicinity of the voting line, and the secretary of the company

---

[22] *Id.* at 180, 15 L.R.R.M. at 221.

[23] Southwestern Electric Service Co., 90 N.L.R.B. 457, 26 L.R.R.M. 1301 (1950).

[24] Southwestern Electric Service Co. v. NLRB, 194 F.2d 939, 29 L.R.R.M. 2552 (5th Cir. 1952).

[25] 118 N.L.R.B. 1511, 40 L.R.R.M. 1409 (1957).

[26] Intercontinental Mfg. Co., 167 N.L.R.B. 769, 66 L.R.R.M. 1156 (1967).

was near the polling place talking to employees waiting to vote. The Board set aside the election, finding significance in the fact that the secretary had engaged in interrogations and threats up to and including the day of the election.

THE *MILCHEM* RULE

It was against this variegated background that the Board, in 1968, undertook in *Milchem, Inc.,*[27] to eliminate the inconsistencies of its prior decisions and establish a standardized and strict rule of conduct for union and employer agents in the polling area. In *Milchem,* the Board was asked to determine whether conversations between an employer or union agent and an employee waiting to vote would void an election in the absence of any proof of actual coercion or electioneering. The Board summed up accurately the status of this issue at that time:

> In our prior decisions dealing with the effect of conversations between parties to the election and employees preparing to vote, we have not enunciated a clear standard against which to measure such conduct.[28]

In *Milchem,* the secretary-treasurer of the union stood for several minutes during the voting period near the voting line, engaged in conversation, apparently of a general nature, with the employees. The Board specifically overruled *Houston Shell* and announced a strict new rule prohibiting all conversations between a party agent and the voters while the latter are in a polling area waiting to vote. In ruling on objections to such conduct, the Board announced, there would be no necessity for inquiry into the nature of the conversations. The Board emphasized that "the final minutes before the employee casts his vote should be his own, as free from interference as possible."[29] This "blanket prohibition" did provide for the exclusion of trivial incidents:

> [T]his does not mean that any chance, isolated, innocuous comment or inquiry by an employer or union official to a voter will necessarily void the election. We will be guided by the maxim that "the law does not concern itself with trifles."[30]

---

[27] 170 N.L.R.B. 362, 67 L.R.R.M. 1395 (1968).

[28] *Id.* at 362, 67 L.R.R.M. at 1395.

[29] *Id.,* 67 L.R.R.M. at 1395.

[30] *Id.* at 363, 67 L.R.R.M. at 1396.

The Board acknowledged that this exception to the rule could be troublesome to interpret, and it urged that all parties involved in representation elections cooperate by complete compliance with the *Milchem* rule.

Most of the cases following the *Milchem* decision have been concerned with defining the "last few minutes" with which the *Milchem* rule deals. The Board has said that the rule applies only when the voters are in the polling area or in line waiting to vote [31] and when the polls are in fact open.[32] As these conditions were mentioned in the *Milchem* decision, the Board merely has been clarifying rather than retreating from its rule. Although the Board has not yet squarely faced the problem of trivial conversations between parties, it has said that the incidence of a chance "hello" greeting will not suffice to set aside an election, but that repeated conversations with voters would suffice.[33]

The *Milchem* rule appears to have generated a new minority view with respect to stricter standards of conduct during the voting period. Chairman Miller has dissented twice in cases in which he felt the majority of the Board failed to be consistent with the spirit of a strict rule of conduct in the voting area. In *Lach-Simking Dental Laboratories, Inc.*,[34] the union provided a luncheon of sandwiches and soft drinks for at least 15 to 20 of the 44 eligible voters while the election was in progress in another part of the same building. The majority of the Board found that there was no interference, since the luncheon was held outside of the immediate polling area, the employees were not compelled to attend, those who went had to go out of their way to get there, and the value of the drinks and food was not sufficient to constitute an improper inducement to vote for the union. But Chairman Miller cited *Milchem* and the emphasis which it had placed on the sanctity of the final minutes

---

[31] *E.g.*, Sonoco Products Co., 179 N.L.R.B. 637, 72 L.R.R.M. 1417 (1969); Marvil International Security Services, 173 N.L.R.B. 1260, 70 L.R.R.M. 1003 (1968); Harold W. Moore & Son, 173 N.L.R.B. 1258, 70 L.R.R.M. 1002 (1968).

[32] Lincoln Land Moving & Storage, 197 N.L.R.B. No. 160, 80 L.R.R.M. 1489 (1972).

[33] Modern Hard Chrome Service Co., 187 N.L.R.B. 82, 75 L.R.R.M. 1498 (1970).

[34] 186 N.L.R.B. 671, 75 L.R.R.M. 1385 (1970).

before the voter cast his ballot. He felt that a free luncheon created a problem similar to conversations with the voters.

I would find that where any party provided free refreshments during and immediately surrounding polling times and in this close proximity to the polling place, the election should be set aside.[35]

In a later case, Chairman Miller again felt that a strict approach by the Board was mandated by *Milchem*. In *Mead Corp.*[36] only one voter had been affected by the illegal electioneering conduct of the union, and one vote was not dispositive of the election. Miller, in dissenting, argued that since *Milchem* was a strict rule which prohibited such conduct, the Board should not ignore even the slightest violation but should set aside the election whether or not the violation of the rule would have a discernible impact upon the results of the election.

The difficulty with Chairman Miller's approach is that it overemphasizes strict compliance with the Board's election rules at the expense of finanlity in election proceedings. *Per se* rules can be a useful means of clarifying and simplifying the limits on election conduct, but they must be applied with a sense of flexibility in order to minimize the incidence of rerun elections. One of the benefits of a "blanket" rule such as the *Milchem* rule is that it eliminates the need for much case-by-case evaluation of conduct and thus expedites the election process. But this value would be substantially undermined if the Board were to begin applying its rule rigidly to insignificant and unintended violations.

---

[35] *Id.* at 672, 75 L.R.R.M. at 1386.

[36] 189 N.L.R.B. No. 36, 76 L.R.R.M. 1563 (1971).

CHAPTER XII

Visiting Voters' Homes

Unlike its current policies concerning captive-audience speeches and electioneering near the polls, which at least theoretically apply equally to conduct by either party, the Board openly applies different rules to campaign visits to voters' homes by unions and employers. In *Peoria Plastic Co.*,[1] the leading case on campaign visits by employer representatives, the Board determined that the technique of "calling upon [individual employees] at their homes to urge them to reject the union" amounted to "conduct calculated to interfere with the free choice of a bargaining representative regardless of whether or not the employer's actual remarks were coercive in character." [2] Accordingly, systematic home visits by an employer afford a ground for automatically invalidating the election, even if only a small portion of the electorate, insufficient in itself to affect the outcome of the election, has been visited.[3]

Home visits by union representatives, on the other hand, are considered unobjectionable as long as they are not accompanied by any actual threat or coercion.[4] Indeed, the Board's election policies actively encourage union representatives to call on employees at their homes as a means of getting the union's campaign message across to the voters. In *Excelsior Underwear, Inc.*[5] the Board announced the rule requiring employes in elec-

---

[1] 117 N.L.R.B. 545, 39 L.R.R.M. 1281 (1957).

[2] *Id.* at 547-48, 39 L.R.R.M. at 1282. *See also* F. N. Calderwood, Inc., 124 N.L.R.B. 1211, 1212, 44 L.R.R.M. 1628 (1959); Mrs. Baird's Bakeries, Inc., 114 N.L.R.B. 444, 36 L.R.R.M. 1608 (1955); General Shoe Corp., 77 N.L.R.B. 124, 126-27, 21 L.R.R.M. 1337 (1948).

[3] The Hurley Co., Inc., 130 N.L.R.B. 282, 47 L.R.R.M. 1293 (1961).

[4] General Shoe Corp., 123 N.L.R.B. 1492, 44 L.R.R.M. 1161 (1959); Orleans Mfg. Co., 120 N.L.R.B. 630, 42 L.R.R.M. 1016 (1958); Plant City Welding and Tank Co., 119 N.L.R.B. 131, 41 L.R.R.M. 1014 (1957).

[5] 156 N.L.R.B. 1236, 61 L.R.R.M. 1217 (1966).

tion proceedings to supply the petitioning unions with employee name-and-address lists specifically to facilitate the unions' communication with employees at their homes. The possibility that this would lead to intimidation or coercion by union organizers was brushed aside by the Board in *Excelsior*. "We cannot assume," the Board said, "that a union, seeking to obtain employees' votes, in a secret ballot election, will engage in [harassment and coercion of employees in their homes]; if it does, we shall provide an appropriate remedy." [6]

The Board set forth its rationale for this differing treatment of similar employer and union conduct in *Plant City Welding and Tank Co.*[7] in the following language:

> [T]here is a substantial difference between the employment of the technique of individual interviews by employers on the one hand and by unions on the other. Unlike employers, unions often do not have the opportunity to address employees in assembled or informal groups, and never have the position of control over tenure of employment and working conditions which imparts the coercive effect to systematic individual interviews conducted by employers. Thus, not only do unions have more need to seek out individual employees to present their views, but, more important, lack the relationship with the employees to interfere with their choice of representatives thereby.[8]

In short, the Board grants unions the privilege of campaigning at the voters' homes, but denies employers this privilege for two reasons: (1) it believes unions need this avenue of communication more than employers do; and (2) it also believes visits by employers are more likely to intimidate employees than visits by union agents, because the employers have an economic leverage that unions lack. The validity of each of these fundamental assumptions is open to serious question.

The fact that employers may have other media, not available to unions, for communicating their views to employees, affords no justification in itself for prohibiting employers from making home visits. Stripped of its verbiage, the Board's rationale in this respect comes perilously close to its old, repudiated "balancing" approach, whereby it sought to equalize "oppor-

---

[6] *Id.* at 1244, 61 L.R.R.M. at 1220, citing *inter alia*, Plant City Welding and Tank Co., 119 N.L.R.B. 131, 41 L.R.R.M. 1014 (1957). *But see* Lewis, *The NLRB Intrudes on the Right of Privacy*, 17 LAB. L. J. 280-84 (1966).

[7] 119 N.L.R.B. 131, 41 L.R.R.M. 1014 (1959).

[8] *Id.* at 133-34, 41 L.R.R.M. at 1015.

tunities for organizational communication."[9] But even if the establishment of such a "balance" were a proper function of the Board, it would be unrealistic to attempt to do so by a *per se* rule such as the ban on all home visits by employers. In many cases, the Board's rule may actually create a marked imbalance in favor of the petitioning union. Surveys of election behavior indicate that campaign techniques which single out individual voters for personal attention are by far the most effective.[10] The Board's rules foreclose virtually all such forms of campaigning to employers. Unions, on the other hand, can, and frequently do, capitalize on the theme that the union is interested in the employees *as individuals* but the employer is not, as evidenced by the union's visiting the employees personally, while the employer relies on impersonal mass meetings or written campaign materials. If the union can convey this message effectively, it is the employer, not the union, who will suffer from the lack of an adequate channel of communication, since the Board's rules leave him no means to address the employees on a personal basis and rebut the union's charge.

The Board has refused to modify its rule even in circumstances which make it clear that the opportunities for organizational communication are heavily weighted in the union's favor. In a case involving an election among oil drilling company "roughnecks" in the Permian Basin of West Texas,[11] the employer requested that the regional director either prohibit the union from making personal campaign calls on voters or allow the company representatives to make such calls also. The grounds for the employer's request were compelling: the election was to be conducted in accordance with the Board's *Hondo* formula for determining voter eligibility,[12] and, accordingly,

---

[9] May Department Stores Co., 136 N.L.R.B. 797, 49 L.R.R.M. 1862 (1962), *enforcement denied*, 316 F.2d 797, 53 L.R.R.M. 2172 (6th Cir. 1963); *see also* discussion at pp. 245-48, *supra.*

[10] ELDERSVELD, POLITICAL BEHAVIOR (Eulaus, Eldersveld and Janowitz, eds. 1956); DOOB, PUBLIC OPINION AND PROPAGANDA 460-61, 529 (1948); LAZARDFELD, BELDERSON & GAUDET, THE PEOPLES' CHOICE 150-52 (1944).

[11] Leatherwood Drilling Co., Case No. 16-RC-5051 (1969).

[12] Hondo Drilling Co., 171 N.L.R.B. 1399, 69 L.R.R.M. 1107 (1968); *enforced*, 428 F.2d 943, 74 L.R.R.M. 2616 (5th Cir. 1970). The *Hondo* formula, which applies only to oil well drilling company elections and is based on the unique pattern of operations and employment in that industry, provides in general that "roughnecks" who have worked at least 10 of the

a number of those eligible to vote in the election would be persons not currently working at any of the company's sites. Without home visits, therefore, there was no opportunity for the employer to contact these voters face-to-face. The regional director, nevertheless, denied the employer's request for modification of the usual rule, and the Board denied the employer's subsequent requests for review of the regional director's action. As a result, not only was the employer frustrated by the inability to communicate his views to the employees before they voted, but the employees were denied the full facts needed to vote intelligently.

The Board's refusal to permit employer home visits even in these unique circumstances belies its protestations of concern for the ability of the parties to communicate with eligible voters, at least where the party facing a communications handicap is the employer. Viewed in this context, the Board's references in *Plant City Welding* to the asserted greater need of unions for individual contact with employees must be regarded as an insubstantial makeweight, and not a valid justification for according different treatment to union visits.

The proposition that employer home visits are more likely than union visits to intimidate employees cannot withstand scrutiny. To be sure, employers have economic powers unions lack, making it possible for them to discharge or discriminate against employees in reprisal for nonallegiance. However, unions have significant powers of reprisal as well, ranging from physical violence and harassment to numerous forms of discrimination. The Board proclaims that employees cannot "deal in an 'arm's-length' relationship with the company officials" when the company singles them out for unaccustomed personal attention during a campaign.[13] But it may often be equally difficult, or even more so, for the employees to deal on an "arm's length" basis with unfamiliar agents of a powerful labor union, particularly if it has a reputation for tough organizing tactics. In either situation, the likelihood of actual intimidation depends upon how the employees themselves assess the probability that the party

---

last 90 days preceding issuance of the election notice and have not been terminated for cause or voluntarily quit prior to completion of the last job for which they were hired may vote in the election although not currently on the company's payroll.

[13] General Shoe Corp., 97 N.L.R.B. 499, 502, 29 L.R.R.M. 1113, 1114 (1951).

visiting them during the campaign will actually *use* its powers of reprisal against them if they make "the wrong choice" in the election. No concrete evidence has ever been cited to show whether retaliation by employers is actually more common than retaliation by unions, or, more importantly, that employees are more likely to expect retaliation from their employer than from the union. Yet the Board maintains, *ipse dixit*, that employees will automatically anticipate reprisals if their employer visits them at home, but that they will not fear retaliation from the union unless it makes overt threats.

As unions grow in size and strength and campaign practices on the part of both labor and management become more sophisticated, the Board's rationale for this disparte treatment of unions and employers becomes progressively less tenable. The Board would do well to reconsider, in light of present-day conditions, the view earlier suggested by Member Rodgers in *Plant City Welding* [14]—that neither the employer nor union visits to employees' homes are coercive *per se*, and that the Board should allow such visits by either party so long as no actual threats or coercion are shown. With this approach, the Board would expand the employees' access to relevant campaign information from both sides. At the same time, if either party behaved improperly, the Board could "provide an appropriate remedy." [15]

---

[14] 119 N.L.R.B. at 134 n.9, 41 L.R.R.M. at 1015.

[15] *See* text accompanying note 6, *supra.*

CHAPTER XIII

Permissible Restrictions On Campaigning On Company Property

An employer may be held to have interfered with the results of an election by unduly restricting the union's right to carry its campaign message to the employees on company time or company property. The same conduct may also be found to constitute an unfair labor practice under Section 8(a)(1) of the Act.[1]

To this point, in exploring the rules governing the time, place, and manner of organizational campaigning, we have been concerned chiefly with the Board's attempts to balance competing interests of the employees themselves—their interest in maximum exposure to relevant information on the one hand, and in protection from intimidation, coercion, and inflammatory pressures on the other. When we turn to the subject of union campaigning on company premises, however, another set of interests enters into the balance: the employer's interests in maintaining plant discipline and efficiency and protecting basic property rights. The Supreme Court has recognized that employers have an "undisputed right" to make rules and regulations necessary for the preservation of these basic interests.[2] But it has also described the employees' interest in organizational communication as "undisputed."[3] "Accommodation between the two must be obtained with as little destruction of one as is consistent with the maintenance of the other."[4] Accordingly, the Board has labored strenuously to determine what kinds of employer rules and restrictions are genuinely necessary to prevent union campaign

---

[1] For additional material concerning the subject covered in this section see Dereshinsky, *The Solicitation and Distribution Rules of the NLRB*, 40 U. CINN. L. REV. 417 (1971).

[2] Republic Aviation Corp. v. NLRB, 324 U.S. 793, 16 L.R.R.M. 620 (1945).

[3] *Id.* at 797, 16 L.R.R.M. at 622.

[4] NLRB v. Babcock & Wilcox Co., 351 U.S. 105, 38 L.R.R.M. 2001 (1956).

activities from interfering with production or intruding upon legitimate company property rights, and what kinds go beyond this necessary protection and constitute an unwarranted interference with employee organizational rights.

As might be expected, a balance between these conflicting, often ill-defined interests has been difficult to achieve in particular cases.[5] As in other areas of election regulation, there is much to be said for the desirability of clear-cut rules of broad applicability, which would give the parties in advance a definite, unwavering standard for judging how far the union can go in campaigning on company property and how far the employer can go in restricting campaign activities. Unfortunately, the Board has been hampered in the formulation of such rules by the Supreme Court's pronouncements condemning a "mechanical" approach. The Court's decision in the consolidated *Nutone* and *Avondale* cases[6] appears to interdict establishment of any *per se* rules in this area, and calls instead for an *ad hoc* evaluation of the circumstances in each case:

> No . . . mechanical answers will avail for the resolution of this non-mechanical, complex problem in labor-management relations. If by virtue of the location of the plant and of the facilities and resources available to the union, the opportunities for reaching the employees with a pro-union message, in spite of a no-solicitation rule, are at least as legally authorized expression of his anti-union views, there is no basis for invalidating these "otherwise valid" rules. The Board, in determining whether or not the enforcement of such a rule in the circumstances of an individual case is an unfair labor practice, may find relevant alternative channels available for communications on the right to organize.[7]

Mindful of this language, the Board has carefully qualified its holdings in this area to avoid the appearance of a *per se* approach. Nevertheless, because of the practical impossibility of assigning weight fairly to all the competing factors in each

---

[5] Much of the basic law in this area has its origin in unfair labor practice cases arising under Section 8(a)(1) of the National Labor Relations Act. The rules thus established are also applicable in the election context, of course, since the Board holds that conduct violative of Section 8(a)(1) is, *a fortiori*, conduct which will sustain election objections. Dal-Tex Optical Co., 137 N.L.R.B. 1782, 50 L.R.R.M. 1489 (1962). *See* discussion at pp. 243-44 & note 16, *supra*.

[6] NLRB v. United Steelworkers of America, 357 U.S. 357, 42 L.R.R.M. 2324 (1958).

[7] *Id.* at 364, 42 L.R.R.M. at 2327.

case, the Board has resorted to a number of broad *presumptions* which it invokes in dealing with particular types of employer regulations. Notwithstanding their arguable inconsistency with the approach mandated by the Supreme Court in *Nutone,* these presumptions have become quite well-established, and now, although always qualified and subject to exception, they at least provide a well-defined framework for the Board's *ad hoc* deliberations in each case.

In this section we shall seek to identify these basic presumptions and then to explore some of the difficulties encountered in their application in individual cases. Because of the distinction generally made between restrictions on the conduct by prounion employees themselves and restrictions on the activities of outside organizers, we shall deal with these two types of restrictions separately.

ACTIVITIES BY PROUNION EMPLOYEES

An employer is not free to place any restrictions he deems desirable upon the campaign activities of his prounion employees. Instead, the Board and the courts have long been engaged in "working out an adjustment between the undisputed right of self-organization assured to employees . . . and the equally undisputed right of employers to maintain discipline in their establishments." [8] Nonetheless, there has been general agreement, at least in principle, that the Act's guarantee to employees of freedom to "form, join or assist labor organizations" and engage in "concerted activities" [9] was not intended as a license to ignore their assigned job responsibilities.

Rules Against Solicitation and Distribution of Literature

Distribution of literature on company property introduces additional considerations. For one thing, handbilling on company premises often poses a danger of littering, with attendant hazards to production, health, and safety. These dangers are greatest, of course, when the literature is distributed in working areas within the plant. Another consideration is that campaign literature, unlike oral solicitation, is permanent in form; it can be received

---

[8] 324 U.S. at 797, 16 L.R.R.M. at 622.

[9] 29 U.S.C. § 157 (1970).

at one time and place and perused by the recipient at another. As a result, rules which limit distribution to particular times and places do not seriously impair its effectiveness as a campaign technique, as long as the union has *some* adequate opportunity to get its literature into the employees' hands.

Basic Presumptions. As the Board stated in its early *Peyton Packing Co.*[10] decision, "Working time is for work." Therefore, a rule prohibiting union solicitation during working hours will be "presumed to be valid in the absence of evidence that it was adopted for a discriminatory purpose."[11] On the other hand, the Board reasons that time outside working hours "is an employee's to use as he wishes without unreasonable restraint although the employee is on company property."[12] Hence, a rule prohibiting employees from soliciting for the union in the plant on nonworking time, such as regular lunch or break periods, is presumptively unlawful "in the absence of evidence that special circumstances make the rule necessary" for maintaining "production and discipline."[13]

It took the Board a number of years to settle upon an approach for dealing with no-distribution rules. At one point, the Board considered the employers' interest in promoting safety and order in the plant to be of overriding importance. It held that, in order to prevent littering, employees could lawfully forbid distribution on company premises at all times.[14] Later, the Board switched its focus and began to view such restrictions as an interference with the employees' interest in communication. The Board then declared that the burden was on the employer to justify any rule prohibiting distribution on nonworking time by showing that the rule was necessary for plant dis-

---

[10] 49 N.L.R.B. 828, 843-44, 12 L.R.R.M. 183 (1943), *enforced,* 142 F.2d 1009, 14 L.R.R.M. 792 (5th Cir.), *cert. denied,* 323 U.S. 730, 15 L.R.R.M. 973 (1944).

[11] 49 N.L.R.B. at 844, 12 L.R.R.M. at 183.

[12] *Id.,* 12 L.R.R.M. at 183.

[13] Republic Aviation Corp. v. NLRB, 324 U.S. 793, 803-804 n.10, 16 L.R.R.M. 620, 624 (1945). For a discussion of the type of showing of "special circumstances," an employer must make to justify a broader rule see McDonnell Douglas Corp. v. NLRB, 472 F.2d 539, 82 L.R.R.M. 2393 (8th Cir. 1973).

[14] Tabin-Picker & Co., 50 N.L.R.B. 928, 12 L.R.R.M. 244 (1943).

cipline.[15] Still later, the Board again reversed its approach and ruled that employers could prohibit distribution in the plant proper even during nonworking time, but could not apply such broad prohibitions elsewhere on company premises, such as in parking lots.[16]

This admittedly "checkered history"[17] of decisional doctrine was reexamined by the Board in the *Stoddard-Quirk Mfg. Co.* case in 1962, and the majority of the Board announced a position which, although it arguably represented yet another modification of the prevailing rule, has become excepted and fairly well-defined:

> [B]ecause distribution of literature is a different technique [from oral solicitation] and poses different problems both from the point of view of the employees and from the point of view of management, we believe that organizational rights in that regard require only that employees have access to nonworking areas of the plant premises.[18]

In general, no-solicitation rules are presumed valid if applicable only to solicitation during working time, but constitute unlawful interference if, on their face or in application, they extend to solicitation during nonworking time. Rules prohibiting distribution of literature may go further, and are now presumed valid unless they extend to activities on nonworking time and in nonworking areas. Broader restrictions are permissible in certain circumstances. For example, in retail department stores, oral solicitation may be prohibited on the selling floors even during nonworking time, because of the special dangers to business

---

[15] American Book-Stratford Press, Inc., 80 N.L.R.B. 914, 23 L.R.R.M. 1171 (1948).

[16] Monolith Portland Cement Co., 94 N.L.R.B. 1358, 28 L.R.R.M. 1204 (1951).

[17] *See* Stoddard-Quirk Mfg. Co., 138 N.L.R.B. 615, 618, 51 L.R.R.M. 1110, 1111 (1962), quoting from the opinion of the Court of Appeals for the District of Columbia Circuit in NLRB v. United Steelworkers of America [Nutone, Inc.], 243 F.2d 593, 597-98, 39 L.R.R.M. 2103, 2105 (D.C. Cir. 1956).

[18] 138 N.L.R.B. at 621, 51 L.R.R.M. at 1113. *Accord,* United Aircraft Corp., 139 N.L.R.B. 39, 51 L.R.R.M. 1259 (1962), *enforced,* 324 F.2d 128, 54 L.R.R.M. 2492 (2d Cir. 1963), *cert. denied,* 376 U.S. 951, 55 L.R.R.M. 2769 (1964). *But see* Republic Aluminum Co. v. NLRB, 374 F.2d 183, 64 L.R.R.M. 2447 (5th Cir. 1967); NLRB v. Rockwell Mfg. Co., 271 F.2d 109, 44 L.R.R.M. 3004 (3d Cir. 1959).

inherent in union solicitation in areas where customers are likely to be present.[19]

Restrictions which would otherwise be considered legitimate under the foregoing presumptions may nonetheless be found to constitute unlawful interference if the evidence shows they were adopted or applied in a discriminatory manner, since the justification for such rules is removed if the employer does not apply them uniformly. Thus, an employer who permits solicitation or distribution for other causes in the plant generally is estopped from claiming that similar activity creates an intolerable threat to production or discipline when it is undertaken on behalf of a union.[20] But the Board has not been constant in its views regarding the type of evidence that must be adduced to demonstrate unlawful promulgation or enforcement. For example, in *Star-Brite Industries* [21] the Board held that a valid no-solicitation rule could not be invalidated upon a showing that it had been promulgated until after a union organizing campaign had began and had been applied only as a bar to union solicitation. The Board stated:

> With respect to the timing of and the circumstances under which the rule was announced, we are unable to conclude that because the Respondent may not have formulated the rule prior to, but did so at the time of, the advent of the Union, that this alone necessarily evidences a "discriminatory purpose." It would be an anomaly to recognize that an employer may lawfully adopt such a rule, yet to hold that he may not do so when the occasion for its use arises.[22]

The Board indicated a disinclination to look behind the presumption of validity arising from the limitation of the rule on its face to conduct on "working time." To do so, it said in *Star-Brite*, "would render the presumption meaningless." [23]

---

[19] Meier & Frank Co., Inc., 89 N.L.R.B. 1016, 26 L.R.R.M. 1081 (1950); Goldblatt Bros., 77 N.L.R.B. 1262, 22 L.R.R.M. 1153 (1948); Marshall Field & Co., 34 N.L.R.B. 1, 8 L.R.R.M. 325 (1941), *enforced*, 129 F.2d 169, 10 L.R.R.M. 753 (7th Cir. 1942), *affirmed*, 318 U.S. 253, 12 L.R.R.M. 519 (1943).

[20] Walton Mfg. Co., 126 N.L.R.B. 697, 45 L.R.R.M. 1370 (1960), *enforced*, 289 F.2d 177, 47 L.R.R.M. 2374 (5th Cir. 1961).

[21] 127 N.L.R.B. 1008, 46 L.R.R.M. 1139 (1960).

[22] *Id.* at 1011, 46 L.R.R.M. at 1141.

[23] *Id.*, 46 L.R.R.M. at 1141.

The Board reversed its approach in 1964 in the *William H. Block Co.* case.[24] Specifically overruling *Star-Brite*,[25] the Board announced a new view which would place less reliance on the presumption and greater emphasis on the facts. Since the facts in *Block* showed that employees had, with management's knowledge solicited for a number of gambling pools, sold tickets for various functions, and collected money for gifts to supervisors, all during working time, the Board concluded that a ban on union solicitation during working time was unjustified. This approach continues to prevail, and the Board now imposes a heavy burden on the employer to justify any no-solicitation rule if the evidence indicates a disparity in its application to union and nonunion activities, or if the promulgation or initial application of the rule coincided with the advent of "intensive union activity." [26]

Problems of Application. The development of these basic presumptions has tended to standardize the law concerning no-solicitation and no-distribution rules to some extent. But the validity of a given rule in a particular case may still turn on the niceties of the Board's interpretation of certain key phrases. Disagreements have arisen, for example, over the meaning of "working" and "nonworking" time, and of "working" and "non-working" areas. In some cases, moreover, organizing activities have been difficult to classify as either "solicitation" or "distribution," and disputes have centered on which set of rules is applicable. The following discussion is illustrative, but certainly not exhaustive, of the kinds of problems encountered in connection with the application of Board doctrines concerning no-solicitation and no-distribution rules to specific fact situations.

Having proclaimed that "working time is for work," [27] the Board declined for several years to decide precisely what "working time" means. Several early cases presented the issue of whether informal, unscheduled break time for which employees

---

[24] 150 N.L.R.B. 341, 343, 57 L.R.R.M. 1531, 1534 (1964).

[25] *Id.* at 343 n.6, 57 L.R.R.M. at 1534.

[26] State Chemical Co., 166 N.L.R.B. 455, 65 L.R.R.M. 1612 (1967); Pepsi-Cola Bottlers of Miami, Inc., 155 N.L.R.B. 527, 60 L.R.R.M. 1356 (1965); Rose Co., 154 N.L.R.B. 228, 59 L.R.R.M. 1738 (1965); Ward Mfg., Inc., 152 N.L.R.B. 1270, 59 L.R.R.M 1325 (1965).

[27] Peyton Packing Co., Inc., 49 N.L.R.B. 828, 843-44, 12 L.R.R.M. 183 (1943).

are paid is immune from application of a no-solicitation rule, but the Board disposed of the cases on other grounds.[28] The Board, however, finally confronted the issue in *I. F. Sales Co.*[29] In this case, the foundry employees worked eight-hour continuous shifts with no regular lunch or break periods; they were to eat lunch at such times as would not interefere with their performance of critical job functions, and were paid for a full eight-hours. The employer applied a no-solicitation rule to prohibit union activities while the employees were briefly away from their machines to eat lunch, contending this was still "company time." The Board found a violation:

> The mere fact that an Employer compensates his employees for lunch and rest periods—however short, and whether or not regularly scheduled—during which they are free to leave their places of work and assemble to eat or talk, does not justify him in attempting to curtail their right to engage in concerted activities at such time.[30]

More recently, the Board indicated adherence to this view, reversing a contrary decision by its trial examiner, in a case presenting facts similar to *I. F. Sales*, although the Board again took the technical route of declining to pass on the issue.[31]

But if the Board has been slow to specify exactly what it means by "working time," it has shown little patience with employers' failures to be specific in using the term in formulating their no-solicitation rules. A rule reading "Solicitation by employees on company property during working time is prohibited" was ruled fatally ambiguous by the Board in the *Campbell Soup* case [32] on the theory that "working time" might be construed by employees as meaning all times when the plant was in operation. A similar result was reached in *Exide Alka-*

---

[28] *See* W.T. Smith Lumber Co., 79 N.L.R.B. 606, 22 L.R.R.M. 1426 (1948); North American Aviation, Inc., 56 N.L.R.B. 959, 962 n.2, 14 L.R.R.M. 172, 173 (1944).

[29] 82 N.L.R.B. 137, 23 L.R.R.M. 1531 (1949), *enforced*, 188 F.2d 931, 27 L.R.R.M. 2603 (5th Cir. 1951).

[30] *Id.* at 138, 23 L.R.R.M. at 1531.

[31] Canton Cotton Mills, 148 N.L.R.B. 464, 466 n.7, 57 L.R.R.M. 1033, 1034 (1964).

[32] Campbell Soup Co. [Swanson Div.], 170 N.L.R.B. 1547, 68 L.R.R.M. 1036 (1968). *See also* Campbell Soup Co. v. NLRB, 380 F.2d 372, 65 L.R.R.M. 2608 (5th Cir. 1967).

line Battery Division of ESB, Inc.,[33] and wherein the Board held that although company practice made it clear that the rule against solicitation on "working time" did not apply to scheduled coffee and lunch breaks, it was still defective because *other* instances of nonwork time were not clearly exempted. In particular, the company was found to have applied the rule unlawfully against employees who engaged in solicitation while standing in line waiting to punch out at the end of the day. Thus, under present Board law, in order to avoid a violation, no-solicitation rules must be clearly phrased to indicate that they do not apply to situations in which neither the employee doing the soliciting nor the employee solicited is immediately on-duty, even if the plant is in full operation.

Precise definition of "working" and "nonworking" *areas* may be even more difficult. The distinction so easily drawn by the Board in *Stoddard-Quirk Mfg. Co.*[34] in the case of an industrial plant with well-defined working zones often becomes blurred in other types of operations. For example, in *Willow Maintenance Corp.*[35] the Board considered the validity of a no-distribution rule applied in a "waiting room" which served dual functions as a lounging area for taxi drivers waiting to be dispatched and a work-place for the company's dispatcher and cashier. Finding that the *Stoddard-Quirk* distinctions "do not entirely fit this case," the trial examiner, with subsequent Board approval, resorted to a completely *ad hoc* balancing of the employer's interest "in anticipating disorder in the waiting room" against the employees' organizing rights.[36] In the Board's view, this approach was mandated by the Supreme Court's decisions in *Republic Aviation, Nutone,* and *Babcock & Wilcox*[37] and is the only recourse available when the usual presumptions are not decisive.[38] Applying such a balance in *Willow Main-*

---

[33] 177 N.L.R.B. 778, 71 L.R.R.M. 1489 (1969), *enforced,* 423 F.2d 663, 73 L.R.R.M. 2911 (4th Cir. 1970).

[34] 138 N.L.R.B. 615, 51 L.R.R.M. 1110 (1962), discussed at pp. 277-78, *supra.*

[35] 143 N.L.R.B. 64, 53 L.R.R.M. 1366 (1963), *enforced,* 332 F.2d 367, 56 L.R.R.M. 2258 (2d Cir. 1964) (per curiam).

[36] *Id.* at 67, 53 L.R.R.M. at 1367.

[37] Discussed at pp. 273-75, *supra.*

[38] 143 N.L.R.B. at 68, 53 L.R.R.M. at 1367.

tenance, the examiner concluded that the usual objections to distribution in a working area were not present in the company's waiting room, despite the functions of the dispatcher and the cashier there, and, therefore, found the company's rule unlawful.[39] The difficulty to the parties in ascertaining in advance what result the Board may reach when it decides to embark upon such a balancing venture needs no elaboration.

Willow Maintenance highlights yet another problem of definition that has recurred in the application of the Board's rules— the problem of applying the *Stoddard-Quirk* distinction between oral solicitation and distribution of literature in borderline cases. The "literature" distributed in *Willow* was a 3-by-5 inch union authorization card. The trial examiner hinted, without elucidation, that the handing out of small cards might not be regarded as creating the same sort of problems of littering as distribution of usual campaign leaflets or handbills.[40] The Board itself had equivocated on this issue in *Gale Products,*[41] declaring that an overly broad rule was invalid as applied to the distribution of authorization cards "whether [such action] be deemed to be solicitation or distribution of literature. . . ." In *Southwire Co.,*[42] the Board gave a somewhat clearer indication that it would apply no-solicitation principles to the "distribution" of authorization cards, since, in its opinion, such activity essentially amounts to "solicitation of an employee's signature to a union card." Finally, in *Farah Mfg. Co.,*[43] the Board squarely confronted this question and held that the distribution of such cards would be equated with other forms of *oral* solicitation, rather than the distribution of *written* campaign literature. Since the *Farah* determination was based on the unique nature of authorization cards, the Board's reasoning leaves unresolved the status of other forms of campaign activity which share

---

[39] *See also* Miller-Charles & Co., 148 N.L.R.B. 1579, 57 L.R.R.M. 1211 (1964) (employer violated the Act by prohibiting distribution at a bench, located near continuously operating machines, where employees gathered for rest and break periods).

[40] 143 N.L.R.B. at 67, 53 L.R.R.M. at 1367.

[41] Gale Products Div., Outboard Marine Corp., 142 N.L.R.B. 1246, 1248, 53 L.R.R.M. 1242, 1243 (1963).

[42] 145 N.L.R.B. 1329, 55 L.R.R.M. 1151 (1964).

[43] 187 N.L.R.B. 601, 76 L.R.R.M. 1100 (1970), *enforced,* 450 F.2d 942, 78 L.R.R.M. 2542 (5th Cir. 1971).

attributes of both solicitation and distribution, *e.g.*, distributing union buttons and requesting employees to wear them. Resolution of such issues presumably requires yet another resort to the process of balancing basic interests, and parties can only guess how the Board will rule in individual cases.

Rules Against the Wearing of Union Insignias

It is common during union organizing and election campaigns for employees to wear buttons or other emblems to work advertising their pro- or antiunion sentiments to their fellow employees. The practice has been upheld as a form of protected concerted activity,[44] and generally an employer may not prohibit it absent a showing of some substantial business justification for his action. The determination of whether a sufficient business reason exists to outweigh the employees' organizational rights again entails a delicate balancing of interests. Among the grounds that an employer may legitimately assert for banning or restricting the wearing of such insignias are: a demonstrable threat to plant discipline,[45] employee safety,[46] or product purity.[47]

Any rule that purports to restrict the wearing of union insignia also limits the on-premises campaign activities in which employees are permitted to engage. Thus, it must be carefully drawn so as not to exceed the employer's legitimate interest in prohibiting such forms of electioneering. In *Floridan Hotel of Tampa, Inc.*,[48] the Board held invalid a rule against the wearing of union badges by hotel employees on the ground that, in application, the rule extended to employees who had no contract with customers or guests. Hence, the rule exceeded the interest the employer had asserted in maintaining a "dignified appear-

---

[44] Republic Aviation Corp. v. NLRB, 324 U.S. 793, 16 L.R.R.M. 620 (1945).

[45] Such restrictions have been permitted where the threat to plant discipline is attributable to the animosity between competing factors of employees. Caterpillar Tractor Co. v. NLRB, 230 F.2d 357, 37 L.R.R.M. 2619 (7th Cir. 1956); Boeing Airplane Co. v. NLRB, 217 F.2d 369, 34 L.R.R.M. 2821 (9th Cir. 1954); United Aircraft Corp., 134 N.L.R.B. 1632, 49 L.R.R.M. 1384 (1961).

[46] Clover Industries Div. of GTI Corp., 188 N.L.R.B. No. 36, 76 L.R.R.M. 1366 (1971).

[47] Campbell Soup Co., 159 N.L.R.B. 74, 81-82, 62 L.R.R.M. 1352 (1966), *enforced as modified*, 380 F.2d 372, 65 L.R.R.M. 2608 (5th Cir. 1967).

[48] 130 N.L.R.B. 1105, 47 L.R.R.M. 1453 (1961).

ance" among its hotel staff. On review, the Court of Appeals for the Fifth Circuit disagreed, finding that the rule was limited by its terms to the wearing of badges "that may be seen by any customer or guest," and returned the case to the Board for a consideration of the legality of the rule as construed by the court.[49] The Board remained adamant, however, finding that since the badges in question were "small, neat and inconspicuous" and that there was no showing of discord among employee factions, the hotel's interests in maintaining its "dignity" had not been jeopardized, and, therefore, even with this narrow construction, the rule was justified.[50]

On the other hand, proper limitation of a rule may be an important saving factor if the Board concludes that some legitimate underlying employer interest is present. In *Andrews Wire Corp.*,[51] a rule prohibiting employees from affixing union stickers to their safety helmets was sustained, largely on the ground that it had been made clear to the employees that they could wear such stickers elsewhere on their clothing as long as they did not obscure the shiny surface of their aluminum "hard hats," which the employer claimed made the employees more visible, and thus safer, in dimly-lighted areas of the plant. The Board was obviously reluctant to second-guess management on a matter relating to employee safety, and it upheld the rule despite suspicious circumstances surrounding its promulgation.[52] On review, the Fourth Circuit upheld the Board.[53] It, too, was

---

[49] NLRB v. Floridan Hotel of Tampa, Inc., 300 F.2d 204, 49 L.R.R.M. 2780 (5th Cir. 1962).

[50] Floridan Hotel of Tampa, Inc., 137 N.L.R.B. 1484, 50 L.R.R.M. 1433 (1962), *enforced as modified*, 318 F.2d 545, 53 L.R.R.M. 2420 (5th Cir. 1963). *But see* Gimbel Bros., 147 N.L.R.B. 500, 56 L.R.R.M. 1287 (1964), holding that the wearing of flowers, unaccompanied by any legend, by some prounion employees in two large stores was properly subjected to employer prohibition, since it was not sufficiently identified with employee union sympathies to constitute protected activity.

[51] 189 N.L.R.B. No. 24, 76 L.R.R.M. 1568 (1971).

[52] The trial examiner had found that the rule was adopted for discriminatory purposes, pointing out, *inter alia*, that it was first announced at the height of a union organizing effort, that other types of stickers had been worn on the hard hats in the past without comment from management, and that one employee had even painted his hard hat black with the cooperation of a supervisor. *Id.*

[53] United Steelworkers of America v. NLRB, 79 L.R.R.M. 2164 (4th Cir. 1971).

suspicious of the manner in which the rule had been announced and applied, but, since the rule was limited so that the employees remained free to wear union insignia anywhere but on their hats, the interference with their organizational rights was viewed as minimal, and any doubts were resolved in favor of the possibility that the rule would promote plant safety.[54]

A related Board policy concerning campaign insigna also deserves attention in this context—the rule that an election will be set aside if the employer provides employees with antiunion buttons to wear during the campaign period. In *Charles v. Weise Co.*[55] the petitioning union objected to an election it had lost by a large margin on the ground that the employer had passed out buttons before the election reading, "Vote on the right side—Vote No." In support of its objections, the union alleged that the employer had unlawfully required employees to wear these buttons. The regional director, however, concluded that it was unnecessary to resolve the factual issue raised by the union's allegations because:

> . . . [b]y making available such badges, even if not urging employees to wear them, the employer was in effect providing a means by which employees would be placed in a position of making an open declaration of preference. If the employee accepted and wore the badge, it was tantamount to expressing an overt anti-union preference, while, on the other hand, if the employees refused to accept the badge, or did not wear it, he thereby indicated a pro-union sentiment, or, at the least, failed to indicate an anti-union sentiment.[56]

The employer argued that his conduct was no different from the distribution of campaign buttons by a union, which the Board has repeatedly rejected as a ground for invalidating elections.[57] But the Board disagreed, relying on the well-worn premise that

---

[54] *See also* Standard Oil of California, Western Operations, 168 N.L.R.B. 153, 66 L.R.R.M. 1276 (1967), sustaining a similar rule against defacement of hard hats, relying in part on the existence of a company color-coding system, whereby employees were identified by the color of their hats.

[55] 133 N.L.R.B. 765, 48 L.R.R.M. 1709 (1961).

[56] *Id.* at 766, 48 L.R.R.M. at 1710. *Accord*, Pepsi-Cola Bottling Co. of Miami, Inc., Case No. 12-RC-1237, 49 L.R.R.M. 1042 (1961).

[57] Delaware Mills, Inc., 123 N.L.R.B. 943, 946, 44 L.R.R.M. 1039 (1959); Timber Laminators, Inc., 123 N.L.R.B. 60, 62, 43 L.R.R.M. 1367 (1959); Furniture City Upholstery Co., 115 N.L.R.B. 1433, 1435, 38 L.R.R.M. 1093 (1956); J. J. Newberry Co., 100 N.L.R.B. 84, 86-87, 30 L.R.R.M. 1234 (1952).

"the Employer's control over the tenure and the working conditions of the employees involved" could render such an insignificant act as making antiunion buttons available coercive in effect.[58]

The Board's assumption is that if management puts employees in a position where they have an opportunity "to indicate antiunion sentiment" although it does not actively urge them to do so, they will inevitably infer that if they do not, the employer is likely to use its economic powers to retaliate against them through discharge or other discrimination. This assumption is applied regardless of any experience the employee in question might have had with his own employer that would tend to contradict such an inference. In contrast, union organizers, including outside agents working on the union's payroll and unknown to the employees, may not only pass out buttons, but actively "*instruct*" employees to wear them,[59] and yet the employees will be presumed not to fear any reprisal if they decline.

The Board's continued application of such presumptions, therefore, attaches an unrealistic weight to the employers' powers of economic reprisal and indicates a myopic view of present-day labor relations. Whatever the validity of such assumptions in the past, there is simply no basis now for concluding that the use of retaliatory tactics by union organizers as a class is any less a reality of current industrial experience than the use of such tactics by otherwise law-abiding employers.

ACTIVITIES BY NONEMPLOYEE ORGANIZERS

Employers may go considerably farther in restricting the campaign activities of nonemployee union agents on company property than they can in restricting employee activities.[60] It is the employees, not the union or its agents, whose rights are guaranteed under the Act. Accordingly, restrictions against non-employee campaigning are invalid only if they would result in an interference with the organizational rights of the employees

---

[58] 133 N.L.R.B. at 766, 48 L.R.R.M. at 1710. *Cf.* Gary Aircraft Corp., 193 N.L.R.B. No. 21, 78 L.R.R.M. 1535 (1971).

[59] Timber Laminators, Inc., 123 N.L.R.B. 60, 62, 43 L.R.R.M. 1367 (1959).

[60] NLRB v. Babcock & Wilcox, 351 U.S. 105, 38 L.R.R.M. 2001 (1956).

themselves.[61] The Board and the courts have construed the employees' rights under the Act as including a basic right to receive the union's campaign message; some channel of communication must be available to enable the union "to reach the employees."[62] The Supreme Court, however, has made it clear that as long as an employer's rules do not make it impracticable under all the circumstances for outside union agents to get the union's message across to the employees through "reasonable efforts," the employer may prohibit such agents from intruding upon his property.[63]

Inaccessibility of Employees Away from Company Premises

In order for an employer's rule against nonemployee campaigning on company property to constitute an unfair labor practice or election interference, it must be shown that the union faces some sort of unique handicap in communicating with the employees. The problem in this area is to define the circumstances that will suffice for such a showing.[64]

The instances are rare in which employees are totally inaccessible to outside union organizers. Lumber camps and company towns obviously present extreme problems of inaccessibility, and in these situations the employer's property rights have had to yield to permit the union some contact with employees.[65] A similar result was recently reached in a case in-

---

[61] *Cf.* Diamond Shamrock Co. v. NLRB, 443 F.2d 52, 77 L.R.R.M. 2193 (3d Cir. 1971), wherein the court, overturning the Board's contrary decision, held that an employer could lawfully exclude *off-duty employees* from all production areas of the plant, absent a showing that such plant access was essential in order for prounion employees to communicate with their coworkers.

[62] *Id. See also* NLRB v. United Steelworkers of America [Nutone, Inc.], 357 U.S. 357, 42 L.R.R.M. 2324 (1958).

[63] *Id.* at 362, 42 L.R.R.M. at 2327; 351 U.S. at 112, 38 L.R.R.M. at 2004.

[64] As noted p. 274 note 5, *supra*, most of the basic law in this area is found in unfair labor practice cases under Section 8(a)(1) of the Act. The rules developed in that context are relevant here, however, since they define the limits to which unions may utilize professional organizers in their preelection campaigns, and the extent to which they must rely on prounion employees within the prospective bargaining unit. Moreover, under the *Dal-Tex* rule, any restrictions held to be overly broad may result in election invalidation.

[65] *See* NLRB v. Lake Superior Lumber Corp., 167 F.2d 147, 150, 21 L.R.R.M. 2707, 2711 (6th Cir. 1948); *cf.* NLRB v. Stowe Spinning Co.,

volving towboat employees who lived on board the boats and were accessible only there during most of the pre-election period.[66]

The Board has long regarded resort hotels whose employees live on the premises as presenting a similar problem, but its view has recently met resistance in the courts. Initially, in *NLRB v. S&H Grossinger's, Inc.*,[67] the Court of Appeals for the Second Circuit sustained the Board's finding that employees of the Catskills resort hotel were sufficiently inaccessible to reasonable union organizing efforts to warrant an exception to the general rule allowing employers to exclude outsiders from their property. In subsequent cases, however, the court has indicated that the exception is narrowly limited. Thus, in recent cases involving two other New York state resorts, the Second Circuit overturned the Board's decisions and applied the *Grossinger's* rationale, on the ground that the unions involved had not made sufficient efforts to contact employees through other means to justify their claim that access off company premises was impractical.[68]

The Court of Appeals for the Third Circuit also recently overturned a *Grossinger's*-type Board decision in *NLRB v. Tamiment, Inc.*[69] The court indicated that before a union can legitimately claim that access to the employees off the premises is infeasible, it must first exhaust available organizing alternatives. Specifically, the court said, the union should have tried to reach employees off company premises, to the extent possible, at places where they congregated during off-duty hours; it also should have requested the right to post notices on the resort premises and should at least have asked the employer for an employee

---

336 U.S. 226, 23 L.R.R.M. 2371 (1949). *See also* Alaska Barite Co., 197 N.L.R.B. No. 170, 80 L.R.R.M. 1765 (1972) (Ore processing plant on a remote island accessible only by air or sea).

[66] Sioux City & New Orleans Barge Lines, 193 N.L.R.B. No. 55, 78 L.R.R.M. 1580, *enforcement denied*, 472 F.2d 753, 82 L.R.R.M. 2488 (8th Cir. 1973).

[67] 372 F.2d 26, 64 L.R.R.M. 2295 (2d Cir. 1967).

[68] NLRB v. New Pines, Inc., 468 F.2d 427, 81 L.R.R.M. 2423 (2d Cir. 1972); NLRB v. Kutsher's Hotel & Country Club, Inc., 427 F.2d 200, 74 L.R.R.M. 2394 (2d Cir. 1970).

[69] 451 F.2d 794, 78 L.R.R.M. 2726 (3d Cir. 1971), *cert. denied*, 409 U.S. 1012, 81 L.R.R.M. 2881 (1972).

mailing list.[70] The Board's petition for *certiorari* to review the Third Circuit's decision was denied by the Supreme Court.[71] Ironically, in overturning the Board's decision in *Tamiment*, the court of appeals relied in part on decisions of the Board itself in cases involving union demands for access to parking lots at manufacturing establishments.[72] For, in that context, particularly in recent cases, the Board has taken a much more restrictive view of the kinds of circumstances which will warrant an exception to the general rule permitting exclusion of outside organizers. In *Falk Corp.*[73] the Board held that a union was not entitled access to company parking lots because, even though personal contact with the employees elsewhere was difficult, the union could have utilized other means of organizing, including group meetings, home visits, telephone calls, and newspaper, radio, and television appeals, as well as making greater use of already sympathetic employees to carry its message to other employees. Public media advertisements have often been criticized as an impractical campaign technique for unions in large metropolitan areas where costs are high and no single station or publication would be likely to reach a substantial portion of the company's work force at any given time,[74] but the Board declined in *Monogram Models, Inc.*[75] (decided on the same day as *Falk*) to make any distinction on this basis, saying it does "not

---

[70] *Id.* at 798, 78 L.R.R.M. at 2729. *See* NLRB v. United Aircraft, Inc., 324 F.2d 128, 54 L.R.R.M. 2492 (2d Cir. 1963), *cert. denied*, 376 U.S. 951, 55 L.R.R.M. 2769 (1964), in which the Second Circuit commented at length on the relative ineffectiveness of such other channels of communication and the greater expense and effort to which the union would be put in order to utilize such methods, all of which it saw, in that case, as reasons for invalidating a company rule restricting on-site solicitation.

[71] 409 U.S. 1012, 81 L.R.R.M. 2881 (1972). *But cf.* H & G Operating Corp., 191 N.L.R.B. No. 110, 77 L.R.R.M. 1758 (1971), wherein the Board held it was a violation to exclude organizers from a private resort because access off the premises was limited and the employer "failed to establish . . . any necessity for the continued enforcement of its policy of absolutely excluding union representatives seeking to enter its compound. . . ."

[72] 451 F.2d at 797, 78 L.R.R.M. at 2729.

[73] 192 N.L.R.B. No. 100, 77 L.R.R.M. 1916 (1971).

[74] *See* NLRB v. United Aircraft, Inc., 324 F.2d 128, 130, 54 L.R.R.M. 2492 (2d Cir. 1963). *See also* Gould, *The Question of Union Activity on Company Property*, 18 VAND. L. REV. 73 (1964).

[75] 192 N.L.R.B. No. 99, 77 L.R.R.M. 1913 (1971).

believe it wise or proper to adopt a big city rule and a different small town rule." [76]

Dexter Tread Mills [77] illustrates the extent to which the Board now carries the presumption in favor of rules excluding outside organizers from manufacturing plant parking lots. In *Dexter Thread*, the only access to the plant was by automobile, through a single entrance to the parking lot from a four-lane, 60-mile-per-hour highway, and the employees' residences were dispersed throughout a densely-populated suburban area. Nevertheless, the Board upheld the company's right to exclude union organizers from its parking lot and relegate them instead to a "10-foot wide grassy tree-filled public easement" separating the parking lot from the highway. Access to the lot was not necessary, the Board concluded, since it would have been "relatively easy and safe" for the organizers to stand in the grassy area and copy license numbers of the cars entering the lot, then check the vehicles' registrations, and thereby compile a list of employees name and addresses. "From this, and through a greater utilization of sympathetic employees, the Union could have obtained a fairly complete list of employees for direct home contact or for distribution of literature through the mails." [78] The Board's shift in emphasis from earlier decisions is, therefore, exemplified by its observation in *Dexter Thread Mills* that the test in such cases is "not one of relative convenience." [79]

"Quasi-Public" Places

In 1968, in *Logan Valley Plaza,*[80] the Supreme Court considered the problem of a union's right of access to individual businesses located within a shopping center compound. The issue arose in the context of an action to enjoin union picketing on the shopping center grounds. The Court analogized the situation to that of a company town, stressing that the property in question had been

---

[76] *Id.*, 77 L.R.R.M. at 1914.

[77] 199 N.L.R.B. No. 113, 81 L.R.R.M. 1293 (1972).

[78] *Id.*, 81 L.R.R.M. at 1295.

[79] *Id.*, 81 L.R.R.M. at 1295.

[80] Amalgamated Food Employees, Local 590 v. Logan Valley Plaza, Inc., 391 U.S. 308, 68 L.R.R.M. 2209 (1968).

opened to the general public,[81] and held that the injunction violated the union representatives' right of free speech. To rule otherwise, the Court noted, would permit the rapidly increasing number of suburban retail establishments to immunize themselves from traditional forms of "on-the-spot public criticism" by creating a *cordon sanitaire* of parking lots around them.[82]

In a case decided shortly thereafter, *Solo Cup Co.*,[83] the Board interpreted *Logan Valley Plaza* as applying with equal force to an "industrial park" compound which employees entered exclusively by automobile from a heavily-traveled commuter thoroughfare.[84] The Court of Appeals for the Seventh Circuit, however, disagreed. Unlike a shopping center, the court pointed out, the industrial park in question had not voluntarily diluted its own property rights by holding out its premises as being open to the general public. Accordingly, the evidence did not support the Board's conclusion that the shared roadways and parking areas within the compound were "quasi-public" in nature. Hence, the employer's property rights prevailed.[85] The Supreme Court's subsequent decision in *Central Hardware Co.*[86] appears to resolve the issue in favor of the Seventh Circuit's interpretation of *Logan Valley* rather than the Board's. The Court made it clear that *Logan Valley* does not apply to all business premises isolated by expanses of privately-owned parking lots. Indeed, even if customers are allowed to use such parking lots, the employer retains his property rights as long as the area does not become the "functional equivalent" of a "normal municipal 'business block.' " [87] Unless the area has taken on such a character,

---

[81] *Id.* at 318, 68 L.R.R.M. at 2213; *cf.* Marsh v. Alabama, 326 U.S. 501 (1946).

[82] 391 U.S. at 324-25, 68 L.R.R.M. at 2216.

[83] 172 N.L.R.B. 1110, 68 L.R.R.M. 1385 (1968). *See also* Scholle Chemical Corp., 192 N.L.R.B. No. 101, 78 L.R.R.M. 1009 (1971), *enforced*, 82 L.R.R.M. 2410 (7th Cir. 1972).

[84] *Cf.* Priced-Less Discount Food Stores, Inc., 162 N.L.R.B. 872, 64 L.R.R.M. 1405 (1967).

[85] NLRB v. Solo Cup Co., 422 F.2d 1149, 73 L.R.R.M. 2789 (7th Cir. 1970); *See* Marshall Field & Co. v. NLRB, 200 F.2d 375, 31 L.R.R.M. 2073 (7th Cir. 1952).

[86] Central Hardware Co. v. NLRB, 407 U.S. 539, 80 L.R.R.M. 2769 (1972).

[87] *Id.* at 547, 80 L.R.R.M. at 2772.

the decision indicated, the union's right to access will depend upon the usual evaluation of whether the employees can be reached outside the premises by "reasonable efforts." [88] Presumably, then, the Board's current view of what constitutes "reasonable efforts" on the part of union organizers to reach employees, as reflected in the *Falk, Monogram Models,* and *Dexter Threads* decisions, will be determinative of their right to enter virtually all employer compounds except for full-scale shopping plazas or company towns.[89]

---

[88] The Court in *Central Hardware* remanded the case to the Court of Appeals for the Eighth Circuit to determine whether the Board's alternative finding—that "no reasonable means of communication with employees were available to the nonemployees union organizers other than solicitation in Central's parking lot"—was supported by substantial evidence. *Id.* at 548, 80 L.R.R.M. at 2772. On remand, the Eighth Circuit rejected the Board's finding. Central Hardware Co. v. NLRB, 468 F.2d 252, 81 L.R.R.M. 2468 (8th Cir. 1972).

[89] *But see* Visceglia d/b/a Peddie Buildings, 203 N.L.R.B. No. 27, 83 L.R.R.M. 1066 (1973); *and* Scott Hudgens, 205 N.L.R.B. No. 104, 84 L.R.R.M. 1008 (1973), in which the Board made it clear it will follow the principles of *Babcock & Wilcox,* rather than *Central Hardware,* in cases involving activity by *employees* in shopping malls and industrial parks.

PART FIVE

Regulation of the Board's
Election Process

CHAPTER XIV

Interference By Employer And Union

In addition to attempts to ensure a free and untrammeled choice of representatives through rules governing campaign conduct, the NLRB has also undertaken to enhance and to protect the election procedures by regulating the mechanics of compliance with the Board's own election process. For example, on its own initiative, the Board has promulgated a rule requiring full disclosure of employee names and addresses in order to facilitate the dissemination of campaign propaganda by the union. On the other hand, in order to protect the integrity of its own election processes, the Board has proscribed the use of official NLRB documents as campaign material. Furthermore, the Board has placed restrictions upon the use of observers by parties to an election, as well as regulating the conduct of the observers. Although the Board has universally stated that the legal bases for these rules are inherent in its mandate from Congress to determine questions of representation,[1] their thrust does not promote a speedy resolution of the representation issue. Instead, they establish certain rules of election conduct, which if violated, will cause the Board to set aside the election.

Much has been said about the unrealistic approach of the Board in attempting to regulate the compaign practices of the competing parties to an election. Nonetheless, when the Board's own processes are attacked, strict rules are necessary to preserve the appearance of Board neutrality. It is only when such rules, formulated under the guise of protecting the Board's integrity, serve to foster partisan advantage to either union or employer that their practical effect is open to criticism or suggested modification.

---

[1] *See* 29 U.S.C. §§ 153 (b), 159 (e) (1), (2) (1970).

EXCELSIOR: *THE "NAMES AND ADDRESSES" RULE*

In early 1966, the so-called "Kennedy Board," in the *Excelsior Underwear, Inc.*[2] case, annunciated a controversial rule that required an employer to prepare and to disclose a list of the names and addresses of its employees for the use of participating unions in a representation election. The *Excelsior* rule caused a deluge of litigation in the circuit courts of appeal, finally culminating in the Supreme Court case of *NLRB v. Wyman-Gordon Co.*,[3] wherein the plurality of the Court approved the doctrine as a matter of Board supervision of its own election procedures. Unlike other rules of election procedure, which profess to regulate the conduct of *both* parties in the hopes of insuring a freer election, the *Excelsior* rule is specifically limited to regulating *only* the conduct of the employer. It is not surprising then, that management has opposed the *Excelsior* doctrine from its inception.

Establishment of the Rule and Judicial Review

The gravamen of the issue presented in *Excelsior* was a claim by the union that the "employer's denial of its request for a list of employees' names and addresses so that it would have an opportunity to mail campaign material to those employees" constituted such misconduct as would justify the Board to order a second election.[4] The regional director had overruled the union's objections, resting his finding on the previously established principle regarding the disclosure of names and addresses. Prior to *Excelsior* the Board had required that an employer, shortly before the election, made available to the regional director for inspection by the parties a list of employees claimed to be eligible to vote in that election, without requiring that this list contain addresses in addition to names.[5] Prompted in part[6] by an article by Derek Bok, now President of Harvard

---

[2] 156 N.L.R.B. 1236, 61 L.R.R.M. 1217 (1966).

[3] 394 U.S. 759, 70 L.R.R.M. 3345 (1969).

[4] 156 N.L.R.B. at 1237, 61 L.R.R.M. 1217.

[5] *Id.* at 1239, 61 L.R.R.M. at 1217-18.

[6] As long ago as 1946, in a case before the Supreme Court, Justice Jackson had urged an election rule requiring the preparation of an eligibility list and its disclosure to all interested parties. NLRB v. A.J. Tower, 329 U.S. 324, 335-38, 19 L.R.R.M. 2128, 2133-34 (1946) (Justice Jackson, dissenting).

University, who advocated broader distribution of information
prior to an election as a means of promoting a reasoned choice,[7]
the NLRB declared it had determined that the employer's denial
of the union's request for names and addresses of employees
eligible to vote presented a question of substantial importance
in the administration of the Act.[8] After a hearing on the merits,
the Board promulgated the *Excelsior* rule, which states that:

> [W]ithin 7 days after the Regional Director has approved a con-
> sent-election agreement . . . , or after the Regional Director or the
> Board has directed an election . . . , the employer must file with
> the Regional Director an election eligibility list, containing the
> names and addresses of all the eligible voters. The Regional Direc-
> tor, in turn, shall make this information available to all parties in
> the case. Failure to comply with this requirement shall be grounds
> for setting aside an election whenever proper objections are filed.[9]

In support of this requirement, the Board reasoned that the
legal basis of the rule was founded upon Congressional legislation
that entrusted to the NLRB alone the regulation of the conduct
of elections. As a matter of discharging that trust, it is the
Board's function to conduct elections not only free from the interference violative of the Act, but also from other elements
that may prevent a free and reasoned choice. The Board posited
that among these elements that may impede a reasoned choice
is lack of information. Therefore, the Board concluded, the list
of employees' names and addresses to be furnished by the employer would permit a more effective selection process, since it
would remove a possible impediment to communication between
union and employees during the pre-election period.[10] In addition, the Board set forth the following considerations in support
of its reasoning:

> (1) Since the employer has such lists in his possession and may
> use them freely for campaign purposes, the *Excelsior* list
> should be supplied to the union to "maximize the likelihood
> that all the voters will be exposed to the arguments for, as well
> as against, union representation."

---

[7] *See* Bok, *The Regulation of Campaign Tactics in Representation Elections
Under the National Labor Relations Act*, 78 HARV. L. REV. 38, 46, 92 (1964),
cited at 156 N.L.R.B. 1240 n. 8, 61 L.R.R.M. 1218.

[8] 156 N.L.R.B. at 1238, 61 L.R.R.M. at 1218.

[9] *Id.* at 1239-40, 61 L.R.R.M. at 1218.

[10] *Id.* at 1240, 61 L.R.R.M. at 1218.

(2) The list should be prepared by the employer, since he is likely to have the most accurate information readily available.

(3) Similar to the ready availability of lists of registered voters in public elections, which are open to inspection and copying by the public, the Board saw no reason why analagous opportunities should not be afforded in a representation election.

(4) The Board asserted that the lists could also be used as a time-saving devise, which would allow unions to more readily investigate the eligibility of employees unknown to them without resorting to the practice of making blanket challenges which later must be resolved by the Board at a post-election hearing.[11]

Turning to the employer's arguments against the disclosure requirement, the Board chided the company for relying on an asserted infringement of *employee* rights, rather than relating its main arguments to any infringement of *employer* rights.[12] Because of the nature of the issue at hand, however, any arguments by the employer which were cosmetically acceptable were of necessity based on employee rights. The attractiveness of the *Excelsior* rule is that it bears all the trappings of accepted notions of fair play. Thus, the Board could argue from a position of strength that since addresses of employees were already available to an employer if he desired to use them to send campaign propaganda, fairness alone dictated that the union should also have a similar opportunity in its electioneering.

In view of the Board's "fairness argument," it is understandable why an employer would refrain from disputing the proposed doctrine in terms of its practical effect. Stripped of all verbiage, the import of management's opposition to *Excelsior* is that it is a one-sided, prounion decision, which requires the employer to surrender access to the lists of his employees, at his own expense, in order that the union is able to use these lists to its own partisan advantage. Thus, it may be argued that the primary effect of *Excelsior* is to foster unionization by granting union organizers an advantage which had previously been denied to them—access to the employees without the expenditure of union effort to locate them.

In *Excelsior*, the argument was also made that pursuant to the decisions of the Supreme Court in *NLRB v. Babcock &*

---

[11] *Id.* at 1241-43, 61 L.R.R.M. at 1218-19.

[12] *Id.* at 1243, 61 L.R.R.M. at 1220.

Wilcox Co.[13] and *NLRB v. United Steelworkers of America [Nutone, Inc.]*,[14] the Board could not require an employer to disclose the names and addresses of his employees unless, in the particular case involved, the union would otherwise be unable to reach the employees with its message. Rejecting this contention, the Board opined that the issues in *Excelsior* could be distinguished from those present in *Babcock* or *Nutone*. More importantly, the Board concluded that "even assuming the availability of other channels of communication to the employees which the union *might* possess, [the NLRB] may require employer disclosure so as to *insure* the opportunity of all employees to be reached by all parties in the period immediately preceding a representation election." [15]

After three years of extensive litigation involving the enforceability and substantive validity of the *Excelsior* rule,[16] the Supreme Court in *NLRB v. Wyman-Gordon Co.*,[17] granted *certiorari* to a Board appeal from a First Circuit decision in which the circuit court had refused to enforce an *Excelsior*-type subpoena. The basis of the First Circuit's [18] determination was that the Board, in promulgating the rule, disregarded the notice and hearing requirements of the Administrative Procedure Act (APA).[19] For our purposes, the significance of the court's refusal to enforce an *Excelsior* subpoena lay not in the narrow grounds of being violative of the statutory provisions of the APA, but rather in the fact that the court did not question the rationale or substantive validity of the rule. Indeed, at the out-

---

[13] 351 U.S. 105, 38 L.R.R.M. 2001 (1956).

[14] 357 U.S. 357, 42 L.R.R.M. 2324 (1958).

[15] 156 N.L.R.B. at 1244-45, 61 L.R.R.M. at 1220 (emphasis in the original).

[16] *See, e.g.*, McDonald, *The* Wyman-Gordon *Case: A Second Look at the NLRB's* Excelsior *Rule*, 20 LAB. L. J. 599, 602-607 (1969), for a broad overview of the appellate court litigation preceding *Wyman-Gordon*.

[17] 394 U.S. 759, 70 L.R.R.M. 3345 (1969).

[18] 397 F.2d 394, 68 L.R.R.M. 2483 (1st Cir. 1968).

[19] 5 U.S.C. § 553 (1970). The specific requirements of the APA, which the court stated were ignored by the Board, were: publication in the Federal Register of notice of proposed rule-making and hearing; opportunity to be heard by interested parties; a statement in the rule of its basis and purposes; and publication in the Federal Register of the adopted rule thirty days prior to its effective date.

set of its opinion, the court indicated that it was "not impressed
by the arguments challenging the wisdom of the *Excelsior*
rule." [20] Later, the court added it regretted that the controversy
had arisen "in connection with a rule to which [the court saw]
little or no objection and for which there is much to be said." [21]

Before the Supreme Court, six Justices agreed with the First
Circuit's contention that the Board, in announcing the *Excelsior*
rule, was fashioning its own rule-making procedure in violation
of the APA.[22] Four of these Justices, however, is what constituted the plurality opinion, held that although the Board's
prospective announcement of the rule requiring names and addresses in *Excelsior* was violative of the APA, the Board's order
in *Wyman-Gordon* was valid, since the subpoena was instigated
in response to an adjudiciatory proceeding.[23] In other words,
the *Excelsior* doctrine as a general rule was in violation of the
APA, but on a case-by-case basis, could be enforced as an aid
to Board investigation of a proposed representation election.
Therefore, regardless of the legal basis of *Excelsior*, as a practical matter, a total of seven Justices agreed that district courts
should enforce the Board's "names and addresses" subpoenas.

Although the substantive merits of the *Excelsior* doctrine
were not at issue before the Supreme Court in *Wyman-Gordon*,
it is almost a certainty that the Court's decision was greatly
influenced by its desire to save the *Excelsior* requirement of
employee lists. Absent this consideration, the Court's action in
reversing the First Circuit decision, while at the same time
declaring that the promulgation of the rule violated the APA,
would be inexplicable. Justice Fortas, speaking for the plurality,
noted that all the circuit courts of appeal, which had considered
the *substantive validity*, of the rule had upheld it.[24] Furthermore, the opinion pointed out that since it was a matter within
the discretion of the Board to establish procedures to insure
a fair and free choice at the polls, the NLRB possessed the
requisite authority to determine that the performance of this

---

[20] 397 F.2d at 396, 68 L.R.R.M. at 2484.

[21] *Id.* at 397, 68 L.R.R.M. at 2485.

[22] *See generally* 394 U.S. 759, 70 L.R.R.M. 3345 (1969).

[23] *Id.* at 766, 70 L.R.R.M. at 3347.

[24] *Id.* at 767, 70 L.R.R.M. at 3347.

duty outweighed objections by employees that their right to privacy had been violated.[25] In retrospect, it is clear that judicial review of *Excelsior,* from the inception of the names and addresses disclosure requirement to its culmination in *Wyman-Gordon,* was dominated by one principle—the necessity of permitting union access to the names and addresses of employees in representation elections, dictated in terms of the respective courts' equitable consciences that the doctrine involved a matter of fairness.

Possible Alternatives to Strict Application of the Excelsior *Requirement*

As a product of the numerous challenges to *Excelsior,* the Board's policy, as supported by the courts, crystallized very early, to the extent that proposed alterations in the rule have consistently been shunted aside as belonging to that class of objections which would threaten the very basis of the doctrine itself. Whether the Board will choose to continue its inflexible standards regarding the furnishing of employees names and addresses belongs to the realm of pure speculation, but several potentially valid alterations have been advanced which deserve consideration. These suggestions may loosely be categorized as attempts to vary the *Excelsior* rule through: (1) an *exception* whenever the employer can show that the union has adequate alternative means of communication or already possesses a complete list of employees; (2) an *extension* to require union assistance in the preparation of the list; and (3) a *modification* to prevent potential harassment of the employees by union organizers. In discussing these proposed alternatives we will proceed from the initial presumption, clearly the basis of the Board and court support of the doctrine,[26] that in order to upgrade the fairness of an election, it is desirable that the union have some means of access to the names and addresses of employees to enhance the possibility that each of the parties to an election will have an adequate opportunity to disseminate campaign propaganda.

---

[25] *Id.,* 70 L.R.R.M. at 3347.

[26] *See, e.g.,* NLRB v. Hanes Hosiery Division-Hanes Corp., 384 F.2d 188, 66 L.R.R.M. 2264 (4th Cir. 1967), wherein the court concluded that "fairness in the elective process demands here, as it does in public or corporate elections, the opportunity of contesting parties to communicate their respective positions to the electorate." *Id.* at 191, 66 L.R.R.M. at 2266.

The Exception. The proposed exception to the *Excelsior* doctrine, which would negate the disclosure requirement if the union had adequate alternative means of communication with the employees, was initially advanced by the employer in the *Excelsior* case. Thus, in subsequent cases,[27] the Board has disallowed this objection, citing its own language in *Excelsior*, which indicated that even if the union did possess avenues of communication through which it might reach all the employees, the Board's disclosure requirement is justified as an additional means of insuring the opportunity to communicate with the employees. Moreover, as the Board has properly pointed out, "we see no justification for permitting employers to decide for themselves in each case whether a 'need' for such a list exists [since] such a policy could result only in confusion and delay. . . ."[28]

Similarly, an alternative exception to *Excelsior*, which has been offered, would operate whenever an employer was able to prove that the union already possessed its own complete list of employee names and addresses. For example, in *NLRB v. Beech-Nut Life Savers, Inc.*[29] claimed that at the time of the election the union possessed a list of the names and addresses of all eligible employees,[30] the company asserted that it was improper for the Board to set aside the election on the ground that the company had not complied with the *Excelsior* order. The Second Circuit held that an employer was not entitled to refuse to comply with the *Excelsior* rule on this basis, since the alleged union list did not carry the same assurance of accuracy and completeness as a list obtained from the employers' records.[31]

Subsequent to the *Wyman-Gordon* decision, the Board in *Murphy Bonded Warehouse, Inc.*[32] rejected the contention of an employer that the Supreme Court's decision granted employers

---

[27] *E.g.*, Swift & Co. 163 N.L.R.B. 17, 64 L.R.R.M. 1241 (1967); Crane Packing Co., 160 N.L.R.B. 164, 165-66, 62 L.R.R.M. 1398 (1966).

[28] 163 N.L.R.B. at 17, 64 L.R.R.M. at 1241.

[29] 406 F.2d 253, 259-60, 69 L.R.R.M. 2846, 2850 (2d Cir. 1968), *cert.* denied, 394 U.S. 1012, 71 L.R.R.M. 2057 (1969).

[30] *Id.* at 260 n.5, 69 L.R.R.M. at 2850. Apparently the union had sent out literature to the employees stating that it possessed the names and addresses of the salesmen who composed the bargaining unit.

[31] *Id.* at 260, 69 L.R.R.M. at 2850-51.

[32] 180 N.L.R.B. 463, 72 L.R.R.M. 1609 (1969).

the right to litigate the issue of necessity upon a showing that the union already had in its possession the required names and addresses. In support of its decision, the Board reasoned that permitting such litigation would serve no practical purpose because the union's list is arguably less accurate than an employer's list. In addition, the evidence elicited would be inconclusive, because it would only reflect the situation as of the date of the hearing, while an *Excelsior* list is required seven days *after* the Board directs an election. Thus, the question of union need for a more current list, subsequent to the hearing and direction of election, would be left unresolved.[33] Moreover, pursuing such a line of inquiry could very well result in the impermissible examination of authorization cards by the employer, which is an administrative matter not subject to litigation.[34] The most telling argument, however, was that if the union does possess an accurate list of employees, then the employer's list may be used for corroborative purposes to insure a complete list, culled from two independent sources.[35] Subsequently, in similar cases, the Board has specifically adopted the *Murphy Bonded Warehouse* rationale as dispositive of the issue.[36]

The Extension. In a trilogy of cases involving an election among oil drilling company "roughnecks" in the Permian Basin of West Texas and New Mexico, the Fifth and Tenth Circuits have held that the *Excelsior* disclosure requirement of names and addresses does not impose any obligation on the part of a union to assist in the completion of an *Excelsior* list.[37] Because of "the nature of the employment in each instance, the union had been requested by the Board to "cooperate" with the employer and regional director in the preparation of the *Excelsior* list.

---

[33] *Id.* at 464, 72 L.R.R.M. at 1610.

[34] *Id.*, 72 L.R.R.M. at 1610. *Compare* O.D. Jennings & Co., 68 N.L.R.B. 516, 18 L.R.R.M. 1133 (1946); *with* Union Mfg. Co., 123 N.L.R.B. 1633, 44 L.R.R.M. 1188 (1959) (decertification proceedings).

[35] 180 N.L.R.B. at 464, 72 L.R.R.M. at 1610.

[36] *E.g.*, Martin Outdoor Advertising Co., 198 N.L.R.B. No. 156, 81 L.R.R.M. 1067 (1972); Piggly Wiggly West Monroe, Inc., 180 N.L.R.B. 576, 73 L.R.R.M. 1104 (1970).

[37] NLRB v. Moran Oil Producing and Drilling Corp., 432 F.2d 746, 75 L.R.R.M. 2304 (10th Cir. 1970); NLRB v. Rod-Ric Corp., 428 F.2d 948, 74 L.R.R.M. 2621 (5th Cir. 1970); NLRB v. Hondo Drilling Co., 428 F.2d 943, 74 L.R.R.M. 2616 (5th Cir. 1970).

In only one of the cases did the union supply any name and address information at all in response to this request, and even there it fell short of submitting its own complete list. In each instance, the employer sought to have the election set aside, alleging that the *Excelsior* rule had been violated.

In each case, the Board held that the union's failure to cooperate did not afford a ground for invalidating the elections and the courts upheld the Board's subsequent bargaining orders. The courts noted that "the Board's *Excelsior* rule does not by its terms apply to unions," and held that the Board, therefore, was not obligated to apply the requirement to unions. Moreover, since the Board had found that the unions had cooperated sufficiently by merely withholding information they had,[38] the courts apparently concluded that a contrary court decision would infringe upon the Board's discretionary authority in regulating representation elections.[39]

Whether the Board should continue to exempt unions from the *Excelsior* requirement presents a question of policy which the Board has not adequately answered. As the Board in *Excelsior* rationalized, its rule was designed to remove one of the impediments to a "free and reasoned choice"—lack of information— and thereby "*maximize the likelihood that all the voters will be exposed to the arguments for, as well as against, union representation.*" [40] Clearly, it is not unreasonable to argue that the *Excelsior* doctrine should cut both ways. The Board in *Murphy Bonded Warehouse, Inc.*,[41] rightly pointed out that the employer, as a reliable source of information, maintains records of eligible voters, which "include those on vacation, lay-off status, sick leave, leave of absence, military leave, and in appropriate

---

[38] Compare *Moran Oil*, 432 F.2d at 749, 75 L.R.R.M. at 2306; *and Rod-Ric Corp.*, 428 F.2d at 951, 74 L.R.R.M. at 2623 (the Board found that the unions did not possess the information requested); *with Hondo Drilling*, 428 F.2d at 948, 74 L.R.R.M. at 2620 (the Board found that the union had complied with its request to the best of its ability because it had furnished the NLRB with names and addresses appearing on authorization cards in its possession and corrected addresses on the original list furnished by Hondo).

[39] *E.g.*, NLRB v. A.J. Tower Co., 329 U.S. 324, 330, 19 L.R.R.M. 2128, 2131 (1946).

[40] 156 N.L.R.B. at 1241, 61 L.R.R.M. at 1218 (emphasis added).

[41] 180 N.L.R.B. 463, 72 L.R.R.M. 1609 (1969).

circumstances, economic strikers and their replacements." [42] In a similar manner, it is undeniable that unions also strive to maintain records of eligible employees through the available mediums of authorization cards, union membership lists, and withdrawal cards, as well as through contacts with sympathetic employees. These records are also of value for the "corroborative purposes" mentioned in *Murphy*, to improve the accuracy of the *Excelsior* list.

Although the purpose of the *Excelsior* rule was designed to provide a union with ability to communicate with employees, commensurate to that of an employer, an unintended side effect is that the union now has two sources of information to rely upon in its electioneering efforts. This qualitative difference may become significant in situations such as the Permian Basin drilling company elections, where either a substantial number of eligible employees are not employed during the election period, or the electorate is highly transient.[43]

The Modification. Whether an individual employee may have his name and address withheld from an *Excelsior* list at his option is an issue which has plagued the doctrine from its inception. In *Excelsior*, one of the grounds of employer opposition to the disclosure requirement was that in providing the union with information, which certain employees have chosen not to divulge, an employer would be compelled to interfere with the Section 7 rights of employees to refrain from union activity, or in the alternative, subject these employees to the dangers of harassment and coercion in their homes.[44] These two issues, as well as an employee's constitutional right to privacy, have been the subject of subsequent litigation.[45]

In *NLRB v. Hanes Hosiery Division-Hanes Corp.*,[46] the initial court review of the harassment issue was put to the test. Apparently, the Fourth Circuit saw little merit in the argument,

---

[42] *Id.* at 464, 72 L.R.R.M. at 1610.

[43] *See* Chapter XII, *supra*, wherein the ability of the union to engage in home visitation, and at the same time, insulate prospective voters from communications with the employer is discussed.

[44] 156 N.L.R.B. at 1244, 61 L.R.R.M. at 1220.

[45] *E.g.*, NLRB v. Delaware Valley Armaments, Inc., 431 F.2d 494, 74 L.R.R.M. 2973 (3d Cir.), *cert. denied*, 400 U.S. 957, 75 L.R.R.M. 2810 (1970).

[46] 384 F.2d 188, 66 L.R.R.M. 2264 (4th Cir. 1967), *cert. denied*, 390 U.S. 930, 67 L.R.R.M. 2632 (1968).

disposing of it with the singular observation "that every an-
noyance of the voters is shunned by the seasoned campaigner,
and unions are not novices in this area." [47] Subsequently, the
same circuit in *NLRB v. J. P. Stevens & Co., Inc.*,[48] reviewed
an appeal from the district court, granting enforcement of an
Excelsior subpoena,[49] in which a large number of the employees
in the prospective bargaining unit were permitted to intervene
in order to oppose production of the list. At the outset, the
intervenors contended that the earlier *Hanes* decision should
not control because it was the employees, themselves, in *J. P.
Stevens* who were claiming that their rights would be violated
if the union was given their names and addresses.[50] In summary,
the intervenors contended that since Section 7 of the Act granted
them the right to refrain from union activities, furnishing the
union with this information would force the employers to indirectly aid in the union's campaign efforts.[51] The court, however, indicated that merely affording the union with an opportunity to communicate with the eligible voters does not
encroach upon the right of these voters to remain neutral, since
they are not "required" to read union literature sent in the mail,
or speak to union representatives who may visit their homes.[52]
Moreover, the court indicated that in the context of a representation election, Section 7 rights are most effectively exercised by
voting for or against representation. Thus, the court concluded
that the *Excelsior* doctrine, designed to insure a "more fully
informed and reasoned choice" by employees in casting their

---

[47] *Id.* at 191, 66 L.R.R.M. at 2266. In light of the very recent strife
between the United Farm Workers and Teamsters Union over representation
among California agricultural workers, which has involved beatings as well
as homicide, the court's statement may involve, not a little, wishful thinking.
    Furthermore, in addition to the harassment issue, the court in *Hanes* also
rejected the employer's contention that the union could dispose of the information for commercial exploitation, pointing out that should any anticipated abuse occur, the Board could be relied upon to adopt preventative
sanctions. *Id.*, 66 L.R.R.M. at 2266.

[48] 409 F.2d 1207, 70 L.R.R.M. 3110 (4th Cir. 1969).

[49] 69 L.R.R.M. 2756 (D.C.N.C. 1968).

[50] 409 F.2d at 1209, 70 L.R.R.M. at 3111.

[51] *Id.*, 70 L.R.R.M. at 3111.

[52] *Id.*, 70 L.R.R.M. at 3111.

ballots, is not inconsistent with Section 7, but rather furthers its purpose.[53]

The harassment and right of privacy issues were dismissed in a similar manner. Basically, the court felt that the mere potential of harassment is far outweighed by the "public interest" in an informed electorate.[54] The difficulty in this approach lies in the ambiguity of whose "public interest" is involved. The logical answer, of course, is that as a matter of policy, the electorate is assumed to be unable to make their own choice and more likely to vote for the union if given the chance to be propagandized. Recent studies, however, have shown that only a small fraction of a given electorate is susceptible to influence by the content of an election campaign in which the electioneering of one of the parties is deemed so coercive that it constitutes an unfair labor practice.[55] Moreover, surveys of election behavior indicate that campaign techniques which single out individual voters for personal attention are by far the most effective.[56] Thus, the release of names and addresses permits a labor organization to allocate its time and resources toward making visits to the homes of undecided and adverse factions in the electorate. Although there is nothing improper in this campaign strategy by the union, the company is barred by the Board from making its own visits to the homes of its employees.[57] The result is that the union is given a special advantage in electioneering, denied to an employer, and calculated to have the greatest potential impact on the electorate. One may well question, therefore, whether the alleged "public interest" is synonymous with "fostering unionization."

Several alternatives, which would protect employees from having their names and addresses furnished to the union over their objections, while at the same time, afford substantial com-

---

[53] *Id.*, 70 L.R.R.M. at 3111.

[54] *Id.*, 70 L.R.R.M. at 3112 (citing cases).

[55] *See* Getman & Goldberg, *The Myth of Labor Board Expertise*, 39 U. CHI. L. REV. 681, 697 (1972).

[56] ELDERSVELD, POLITICAL BEHAVIOR (Eulas, Eldersveld and Janowitz ed., 1956); DOOB, PUBLIC OPINION AND PROPAGANDA 460-61, 529 (1948); BELDERSON & GAUDET, THE PEOPLES' CHOICE 150-52 (1944).

[57] *E.g.*, Plant City Welding and Tank Co., 119 N.L.R.B. 131, 41 L.R.R.M. 1014 (1957); Peoria Plastic Co., 117 N.L.R.B. 545, 39 L.R.R.M. 1281 (1957); *see also* Chapter XII, *supra*.

pliance with *Excelsior*, have been advanced. On the lower end of the compliance scale, the employer in *Montgomery Ward & Co.*[58] posted a notice informing his employees of its reasons for refusing to comply with the *Excelsior* requirement and furnishing the addresses of the two participating unions so that employees, who wished to do so, could communicate with them. A second tack, at a slightly higher level of compliance, was offered by the employer in *British Auto Parts, Inc.*[59] In that case, the employer proposed to satisfy the *Excelsior* rule by submitting the names of all eligible employees, but withholding their addresses, and providing them with an envelope addressed to the regional director, for the employees' use in submitting the additional information at their discretion. As the Board pointed out, these types of partial disclosures do not comply with the *Excelsior* doctrine, since it will still remain difficult for the union to communicate with a significant number of employees.

A potential compromise solution, which was dismissed without comment in a hearing before a regional director merits another look. In *Union Bleachery*,[60] the employer offered to submit the names and addresses of his employees to a third party who would, at the employer's expense, mail out any union literature. This procedure would have permitted the union to reach employees through the mail without the corollary effect of facilitating home visitation. Thus, the Board's refusal to consider this alternative in *Union Bleachery* can be read as a sign that in fact one of the Board's purposes was to promote union visits to employees' homes. Indeed, the argument that the disclosure rule fostered union visitation, had been initially raised and rejected in the *Excelsior* case itself, wherein the Board stated that although "employers are free to communicate with their employees in the plant, a union, as a practical matter, is severely limited in its efforts at inplant communications."[61] In effect, the Board was reaching back to the old "balancing" principle in establishing the *Excelsior* rule. But in attempting to achieve

---

[58] 160 N.L.R.B. 1188, 63 L.R.R.M. 1107 (1966).

[59] 160 N.L.R.B. 239, 62 L.R.R.M. 1591 (1966). *See also* NLRB v. Delaware Valley Armaments, Inc., 431 F.2d 494, 73 L.R.R.M. 2973 (3d Cir. 1970), wherein the employer, in preparation of an *Excelsior* list, requested of all his employees whether or not they wished their addresses released.

[60] Case No. 11-RC-2398, 63 L.R.R.M. 1208 (1966).

[61] 156 N.L.R.B. at 1246 n. 27, 61 L.R.R.M. at 1221.

the mean, the Board seemingly has pushed the union advantages too far, creating a marked imbalance.

Consequently, in order to restore some semblance of an even-handed approach to campaign practices under the *Excelsior* rule, the Board would seem to have to do one of two things: (1) permit employer as well as union visits to the voter's homes; or (2) restrict union access to mailing campaign literature through an intermediary. The first alternative would be consistent with the goal of maximizing the flow of information available to the electorate. However, it might be considered undesirable from the standpoint of the employees, since there is no reason to believe that employees who object to potential harassment by the union would be appreciative of a rule which permitted *both* unions and employers to camp on the employees' doorsteps. Thus, the second alternative, mailing campaign literature through an independent third party, might be regarded as more responsive to the purposes of *Excelsior* and the desires of the parties. The union would have a guaranteed channel of communications to prospective voters, the employer's handicap over home visitation would be lessened, and the employees, themselves, would possess the right to exercise their own discretion in deciding whether or not union organizers would be invited into their homes.

The Substantial Compliance Rule

Shortly after the Board had announced its *Excelsior* disclosure rule, in *Program Aids Co., Inc.*,[62] it was faced with a case in which an employer contended that an election should not be set aside even though he had not complied with all of the specific requirements of the *Excelsior* rule. The union had asserted that the employer breached *Excelsior* by filing the requisite list four days after the prescribed filing date. The employer answered that the tardy filing was permissible, since it was accomplished pursuant to an alleged agreement between parties, which carried the approval of the Board agent. Rather than make any determination as to whether such an agreement had in fact been reached, the Board stated that it found nothing in its *Excelsior* decision "which would require the rule stated therein be mechanically applied."[63] Instead, the standard to be used in de-

---

[62] 163 N.L.R.B. 145, 65 L.R.R.M. 1244 (1967).

[63] *Id.* at 146, 65 L.R.R.M. at 1244.

termining whether an employer had violated the *Excelsior* rule
is one of "substantial," as opposed to absolute compliance.[64]
Ever since the formulation of the "substantial compliance" rule
in *Program Aids*, the test of substantiality has been centered
around both the qualitative aspect of the list—*i.e.* errors and
omissions—and the timeliness of its submission.

Errors and Omissions in an Excelsior *List.* In general, the
Board will set aside an election because of an insubstantial failure to comply with the *Excelsior* rule if the defects are not
"attributable to gross negligence or an unwillingness on the employer's part to afford the union full access to all eligible employees." [65] Moreover, as a rule of thumb, the omission of the
names and addresses of employees is more likely to constitute
a fatal defect in an *Excelsior* list than will a number of inaccuracies. For example, the Board held in *Fontainbleau Hotel
Corp.,*[66] that even though fifty-six out of a possible three hundred
addresses were erroneous, the employer had made a good faith
attempt to furnish the requisite information and the errors did
not vitiate his substantial compliance with the *Excelsior* rule.
On the other hand, in *Gamble Robinson Co.,*[67] a smaller percentage of omissions in a list did justify the Board in finding that
the employer had failed to substantially comply with the *Excelsior* doctrine.

Furthermore, an *Excelsior* list may not be utilized as a vehicle to dispute the eligibility of certain employees by omission
or inclusion. Thus, in *Ponce Television Corp.,*[68] an election was
set aside for failure to satisfy the *Excelsior* requirements when

---

[64] *Id.,* 65 L.R.R.M. at 1245.

[65] Telonic Instruments, 173 N.L.R.B. 588, 589, 69 L.R.R.M. 1398, 1399
(1968). Whether or not the outcome of the election should be utilized as a
factor in determining substantial compliance is unsettled and has depended
upon a case-by-case analysis. *See* Rite-Care Poultry, Inc., 185 N.L.R.B. 41,
42, 75 L.R.R.M. 1212, 1213 (1970) (numerous errors and omissions in
Excelsior list coupled with close election results caused the Board to order
a new election).

[66] 181 N.L.R.B. 1134, 73 L.R.R.M. 1606 (1970). *See also* Lobster House,
186 N.L.R.B. 148, 75 L.R.R.M. 1309 (1970); Valley Die Cast, 160 N.L.R.B.
1881, 63 L.R.R.M. 1190 (1966) (in which the addresses, 16 and 15 percent
respectively, were erroneous).

[67] 180 N.L.R.B. 532, 73 L.R.R.M. 1049 (1970). *See also* Sonfarrel, Inc.,
188 N.L.R.B. No. 146, 76 L.R.R.M. 1497 (1971) (11 percent of addresses
omitted).

[68] 192 N.L.R.B. No. 20, 77 L.R.R.M. 1622 (1971).

certain names were omitted from the list in order to support the employer's position that these employees were ineligible. The Board pointed out that if the employer wished to contest the eligibility of certain voters, such purpose could be accomplished through the challenge procedures at the polls. Instead, the Board found that the employer's acts, in effect, "arrogated to [the employer] the Board's powers with regard to eligibility determinations in representation proceedings." [69] Similarly, the union may not challenge the substantive compliance with *Excelsior* where it claims that the names of alleged supervisors have been included on the list.[70]

Timeliness of Submission of Excelsior *List.* In accordance with the *Excelsior* rule an employer must file with the regional director, a list of names and addresses *within seven days* of the Board direction or stipulation for a consent election.[71] The Board, however, will not "mechanistically" apply the seven-day filing requirement to set aside elections when the effect of a tardy filing is *de minimis.*[72] Moreover, where extenuating circumstances for the delay are present and there is no evidence of employer bad faith in his late filing, the Board has held that such conduct is in substantial compliance with *Excelsior.*[73] Nonetheless, in the *Coca-Cola Co. Foods Division* [74] case, the Board set aside an election in which the union's tardy receipt of the *Excelsior* list was caused by a Board error in misaddressing the list. In upholding the union's objection, the Board based its findings on the prejudice suffered by the union, rather than failure to comply with the *Excelsior* requirements.[75]

---

[69] *Id.*, 77 L.R.R.M. at 1623.

[70] Stotts & Murphy Ford, Inc., Case No. 7-RC-7530, 64 L.R.R.M. 1396 (1967).

[71] 156 N.L.R.B. at 1239, 61 L.R.R.M. at 1218.

[72] *E.g.*, Singer Co., 175 N.L.R.B. 211, 212, 70 L.R.R.M. 1500, 1501 (1969) (large unit of over 1,100 voters where supplementary list of 30 was filed two days prior to the election); Program Aids Co., Inc., 163 N.L.R.B. 145, 146, 65 L.R.R.M. 1244, 1245 (1967) (relatively small unit of 50 employees where list was submitted four days late and union had it in its possession for ten days prior to the election).

[73] Taylor Publishing Co., 167 N.L.R.B. 228, 229, 66 L.R.R.M. 1049 (1967) (employer's submission of list one day late was inadvertant and employer attempted to cure this defect by asking for a one day postponement).

[74] 202 N.L.R.B. No. 123, 82 L.R.R.M. 1724 (1973).

[75] *Id.*, 82 L.R.R.M. at 1725.

Concluding Remarks

The *Excelsior* doctrine is one of many products of the Kennedy Board's paternalistic attitude toward unionism as the most desirable means of protecting employee rights from infringement by their employers. The rule imposes a duty of disclosure upon the employer for the benefit of the union's campaign efforts. In so doing, however, the Board has subjected employees to the same potentiality of surveillance and interrogation by the union, which it has condemned on the part of employers.[76] Suggested modifications of *Excelsior* that would protect employees from such abuse have been ignored.[77]

For 30 years prior to *Excelsior*, elections without the benefit of the disclosure requirement were successfully conducted. Indeed, the presumed inability of unions to effectively alert employees to the benefits of union membership is sharply contradicted by a phenomenal rate of growth—from three and one-half million members in 1935 to nearly 18 million members in 1966, the year of the *Excelsior* decision.[78] As one commentator has observed:

> [T]he [Kennedy] Board has persistently undercut employee freedom of choice and protection whenever in conflict with the growth of labor unions. The organizations whose rights are derivative have been favored over the source of those rights. The agents have been given precedence over the principles.[79]

Given current attitudes of Board and courts, it is unlikely that the disclosure requirement of *Excelsior* will be abolished—nor is that policy urged here. Nontheless, serious attention should be paid to employee objections to such disclosure. In the alternative, the Board might consider the employer's suggestion in *Union Bleachery*, to provide for dissemination of union literature through an independent intermediary such as a mailing house.

---

[76] *See* Chapter VII, *supra.*

[77] *See* discussion at pp. 305-309, *supra.*

[78] *U.S. Bureau of Labor Statistics, Dep't of Labor, Handbook of Labor Statistics* 300 (1968).

[79] McGuiness, The New Frontier NLRB 238 (Labor Policy Ass'n, Inc., 1963).

REPRODUCTION OF BOARD BALLOTS AND
OTHER DOCUMENTS

The nature of the propaganda distributed by parties prior to a representation election takes many forms. The Board has often stated that it will not take on the responsibility to police or censor campaign propaganda, but rather leave its interpretation to the good sense of the voters and charge the opposing parties with the task of correcting inaccurate or untruthful statements.[80] As we have seen, however, this general rule is subject to a large number of exceptions. One such exception was formulated in *Allied Electric Products, Inc.*,[81] wherein the Board stated that:

> . . . it will not permit the reproduction of any document purporting to be a copy of the Board's official ballot, other than one completely unaltered in form and content and clearly marked sample on its face, and upon objection validly filed, will set aside the results of any election in which the successful party has violated this rule.[82]

The significance of the doctrine lies in the concern that the participants may attempt to trade on the official status or prestige of the Board itself, to give the employees the impression that the interfering party is the Board's choice. In the extreme situation (*e.g.*, a claim such as "four out of five Board members interviewed recommend XYZ Union as the voters' choice"), the notion of preventing participants in an election from passing off on the Board's prestige is a reasonable guideline for maintenance of the integrity of the Board's election procedures. Under the *Allied Electric* doctrine, however, a violation may be grounded in what is more a matter of form than substance, even though the rather drastic measure of setting aside the election is the remedy.

Over the years, the Board has extended the *Allied Electric* rule to the reproduction of all Board documents, while at the same time trying to define the scope of just what is a purported copy of a Board document. The litigation following *Allied Electric*, insofar as either violations or exceptions are concerned,

---

[80] *See, e.g.*, Stewart Warner Corp., 102 N.L.R.B. 1153, 1158, 31 L.R.R.M. 1397, 1399 (1953); *cf.* Linn v. Plant Guard Workers, 383 U.S. 53, 60, 61 L.R.R.M. 2345, 2347 (1966).

[81] 109 N.L.R.B. 1270, 34 L.R.R.M. 1538 (1954).

[82] *Id.* at 1272, 34 L.R.R.M. at 1539.

appears to comprise both the flagrant and the frivolous. For convenience, the following material analyzes the development, formulation, and application of the *Allied Electric* rule to cases involving ballot alterations before discussing the exceptions and extensions of the rule into all areas of Board documents utilized to communicate with employees.

The Allied Electric Products *Rule*

Arguing "that no participant in a Board election should be permitted to suggest either directly or indirectly to the voters that [the NLRB] endorses a particular choice," the Board in *Allied Electric Products, Inc.,* [83] formulated a broad rule encompassing the use of copies of sample ballots for partisan purposes. The rationale for the doctrine was to prevent any tendency of altered copies of the official ballot to suggest that the material appearing thereon bears the Board's approval.[84] Prior to the *Allied Electric* decision, four factors had been considered determinative of the legality of the use of altered sample ballots: (1) whether the ballots bore the word "sample" upon them; (2) whether they contained the signature of the regional director; (3) whether they contained campaign propaganda; and (4) whether the boxes on the ballot were marked to indicate the selection of any party.

In the first case involving objections to the use of sample ballots as campaign material, *Sears, Roebuck and Co.,*[85] the Board held that the word "sample" must appear across the face of any facsimile official ballot distributed to the employees as campaign propaganda. In this decision, the NLRB laid the theoretical foundation upon which the entire structure of the doctrine prohibiting the misuse of Board documents rested. In *Sears,* the Board originated the idea that there was an inherent danger in allowing the distribution of marked facsimile ballots which might be construed by employees as implied support by the Board of the party indicated on the altered ballot. Logically, the Board could have formulated the *Allied Electric* rule directly from *Sears* because, although the ballot may be overprinted with the word "sample", the fact that it is also marked

---

[83] *Id.,* 34 L.R.R.M. at 1538.

[84] *Id.,* 34 L.R.R.M. at 1539.

[85] 47 N.L.R.B. 291, 11 L.R.R.M. 247 (1943).

in favor of one of the participants would of necessity, tend to mislead employees into believing that the Board supported that party by the means of distributing sample ballots indicating its choice.

Instead, the Board proceeded slowly, upon a circuitous path, first finding and then discarding each of the preceeding factors as the sole determinative of the issue. For example, in the *Am-O-Krome Co.*[86] case, a sharply divided Board held that a facsimile ballot, which included the name and title of the regional director, that had been distributed by the union was *per se* misleading and, therefore, improper. In reaching this conclusion, the Board reasoned that by including the regional director's name and title on a ballot, which urged the employees to vote for the union, the plain implication was that he endorses the union in the election.[87] This implication could not be cured by the simple device of including the word "sample" on the ballot. The majority countered the dissent's argument that the word "sample" printed on the face of the ballot indicated that the document is not an official notice of the Board in an ingenious manner. It noted that the ballot on the official notice of election is also overprinted with the word "sample"; thus, the ballot distributed by the union constituted a copy of an official Board document.[88]

In a subsequent case, *Anderson Air Activities*,[89] the Board held that a sample ballot, purported to be a facsimile of the Board's official ballot, which had been modified to include union propaganda, wrongfully created the impression that the Board endorsed the union's propaganda claims. The Board allowed that although it had privously permitted parties to distribute marked sample ballots in order to show their partisans how to vote at the election, their license did not extend to the distribution of falsified ballots under the guise of true copies of official ballots used in elections.[90]

---

[86] 92 N.L.R.B. 893, 27 L.R.R.M. 1182 (1950).

[87] *Id.* at 894, 27 L.R.R.M. at 1182.

[88] *Id.* at 894 n.3, 27 L.R.R.M. at 1182.

[89] 106 N.L.R.B. 543, 544, 32 L.R.R.M. 1486 (1953).

[90] *Id.* at 545, 32 L.R.R.M. at 1486.

Thus, on the eve of the *Allied Electric* decision, the state of the law regarding the use of facsimile ballots for campaign purposes was that the ballot could be altered to indicate a choice between participants only if it had been overprinted with the word "sample," did not contain the name or title of any Board official, and had not been modified by the inclusion of partisan propaganda. The purpose of the Board in annunciating the *Allied Electric* rule was based on precluding the use of Board documents entirely in campaign propaganda. Addressing itself to this point, the Board stated:

> As there are many legitimate methods available to the parties for disseminating campaign propaganda which clearly do not entail an apparent involvement of the Board or its processes, we believe it is unnecessary to permit unlimited freedom to partisans in election cases to reproduce official Board documents for campaign propaganda purposes.[91]

An argument for permitting the use of sample ballots was set forth in the dissent in the *Am-O-Krome* [92] case. Briefly stated, the dissent reasoned that the average employee is sufficiently sophisticated in the use of campaign literature and propaganda that he would not infer Board support of a marked ballot. This sophistication has been brought about by the participation of employees in state and national elections where circulation of a sample marked ballot is a well-known technique of American politics. Furthermore, sample political ballots contain the name and title of the election commissioners, a situation comparable to the inclusion of the name and title of the regional director.[93] There is no evidence that such ballots mislead voters.

Nevertheless, it remains true that a ban on the use of marked facsimile ballots anticipates speculation over whether the employees were in fact misled. Since utilization of such ballots is nonessential because of all the alternative methods of electioneering, the prohibition is inconsequential in regard to the total campaign picture. Moreover, since the Board is the government agency charged with the responsibility of conducting elections, it must remain neutral in all phases of the election. This neutrality is particularly important when one considers that the Board's

---

[91] 109 N.L.R.B. at 1272, 34 L.R.R.M. at 1539.

[92] 92 N.L.R.B. 893, 27 L.R.R.M. 1182 (1950).

[93] *Id.* at 895-96, 27 L.R.R.M. at 1183.

duty to conduct elections is also coupled with its authority to act as a forum for labor disputes. As the ultimate source of the Board's authority to obtain the compliance of the parties with its orders is based on their confidence in the fairness of its procedures, the Board's stance in *Allied Electric* is justifiable as an attempt to protect its own integrity.

Electoral Interference Under the Allied Electric *Rule*

The history of the *Allied Electric* rule has been liberally sprinkled with the attempts of both unions and employers to test the Board's firmness in setting up the rule. Because the Board's statement in *Allied Electric* was an unambiguous announcement of a total ban on the distribution of documents purporting to be a copy of the Board's official notice other than one completely unaltered in form and content and clearly marked sample upon its face, it is difficult to understand why any participant, other than one in complete ignorance of the rule,[94] would act contrary to the Board policy to its own detriment.[95]

The critical policy consideration, which has held the fabric of the *Allied Electric* rule together, is that the intent of the offending party, as well as the extent to which any alteration may have lead employees to believe in fact that the Board favored the violator, is irrelevant. Thus, the Board has held that any alteration which falls within the purview of the doctrine constitutes a *per se* violation.[96] This is because, unlike so many situations in which the Board is concerned with protecting the right of employees to exercise a fair and free choice, the rule is aimed at preventing a participant from appropriating the prestige of the Board to its own partisan advantage. In effect, the Board is trying to deter election parties from claiming to be protégés of the Board by a blanket policy which eliminates any potential gain from the use of the technique.

In applying the *Allied Electric* rule, the Board has rejected obviously specious attempts to limit it, such as the claim that the rule only applied to sample ballots distributed but not

---

[94] *See, e.g.,* The De Vilbiss Co., 114 N.L.R.B. 945, 37 L.R.R.M. 1061 (1955).

[95] 109 N.L.R.B. at 1272, 34 L.R.R.M. at 1539. As the Board in *Allied Electric* stated, it "will set aside the results of any election in which the *successful* party has violated this rule."

[96] 114 N.L.R.B. at 947, 37 L.R.R.M. at 1062; *accord,* Superior Knitting Corp., 112 N.L.R.B. 984, 36 L.R.R.M. 1133 (1955).

posted,[97] or that it was limited to cases in which only one union, not two, participated.[98] In addition, any election material which might accompany the distribution of an altered ballot does not cancel its tendency to mislead or neutralize the effect of an altered ballot so as to justify its use.[99] Finally, the fact that the altered ballot is not an exact copy of the Board's official ballot, but has been modified to a limited extent, is of no consequence, since the *Allied Electric* rule has been held to apply to alterations of any ballot *purporting* to be an official Board document even though it is not an exact reproduction.[100]

The adamance with which the Board applies the concept that it will not inquire into the extent that an altered ballot may have had upon the voting tendencies of the employees is clearly indicated by the nature of its decisions. For example, in *Wallace & Tiernan, Inc.*,[101] the Board set aside an election pursuant to the *Allied Electric* rule even though the altered sample ballot had been sent by the offending union *fully one month before the date of the election.* In another case, an attempted "retraction" of a prior altered ballot upon the discovery that it was in violation of the *Allied Electric* rule was considered insufficient by the Board to overcome the deleterious effect caused by the alteration.[102] Finally, in an ingenious attempt to skirt the doctrine, the Board in *United States Gypsum Co.*[103] set aside an election in which one of the contestants had attached its campaign buttons to the "Yes" square of the sample ballot. Aside

---

[97] Certain-Teed Products Corp., 173 N.L.R.B. 229 n.2, 69 L.R.R.M. 1485 (1968).

[98] Wallace & Tiernan, Inc., 112 N.L.R.B. 1352, 36 L.R.R.M. 1189 (1955).

[99] *Compare* Boro Wood Products Co., Inc., 113 N.L.R.B. 474, 36 L.R.R.M. 1325 (1955); Bachman Uxbridge Worsted Corp., 110 N.L.R.B. 1195, 35 L.R.R.M. 1211 (1954) (each ballot was accompanied by instructions for voting); *and* Hughes Tool Co., 119 N.L.R.B. 739, 41 L.R.R.M. 1169 (1957); Wallace & Tiernan, Inc., 112 N.L.R.B. 1352, 36 L.R.R.M. 1189 (1955) (ballots accompanied by campaign propaganda); *with* Arlen House, 187 N.L.R.B. 1030, 76 L.R.R.M. 1202 (1971) (no literature accompanying the altered sample ballot).

[100] *E.g.*, Custom Moulders of Puerto Rico, 121 N.L.R.B. 1007, 42 L.R.R.M. 1505 (1958).

[101] 112 N.L.R.B. at 1353, 36 L.R.R.M. at 1190.

[102] The De Vilbiss Co., 114 N.L.R.B. 945, 37 L.R.R.M. 1061 (1955).

[103] 124 N.L.R.B. 1026, 44 L.R.R.M. 1577 (1959).

from the originality exhibited by the union, the significance
of the case rests on its strict adherence to the *Allied Electric*
doctrine. The regional director had found that the pinning
of the button to the ballot was not an alteration as contemplated
by *Allied Electric* because the button was intended to be removed and worn. He concluded that it would be unreasonable
to assume that the button was considered part of the Board's
official ballot by the employees,[104] however, the Board disagreed.
Under *Allied Electric* there could be no reproduction of a Board
document other than one free from alteration and clearly marked
"sample." Here, the pinning of the button served to indicate
an intent to vote "Yes." Therefore, contrary to the regional director's finding that no evidence of any tendency to mislead the
voters was derived from the act of the union, the Board restated the principle that it was the act of alteration itself,
and not whether the employees were in fact mislead by the
alteration, that constituted a violation of the *Allied Electric*
rule.[105]

Partial Reproductions: Exceptions to the Allied Electric *Rule*

When the Board formulated its *Allied Electric* rule, the focal
point of the doctrine was that it prohibited altered ballots which
"purported to be a copy of the Board's official document. Because of this requirement, a number of cases have arisen in
which the Board has found it necessary to determine the validity
of an objection on whether the altered document indeed purported
to be a copy of a Board's official ballot.

In *Phelps-Dodge Copper Products Corp.*[106] the Board concluded
that "the mere reproduction of three voting boxes enclosed by
dotted lines with markings indicating a proposed choice to the
voters, is not within the proscription of the *Allied Electric*
rule." [107] The Board reached this conclusion by reasoning that
the basis of the *Allied Electric* decision "was the . . . concern
that documents used for campaign purposes must not tend to
suggest that the Board approves of any material appearing in

---

[104] *Id.* at 1026-27, 44 L.R.R.M. at 1578.

[105] *Id.* at 1027, 44 L.R.R.M. at 1577.

[106] 111 N.L.R.B. 950, 35 L.R.R.M. 1616 (1955).

[107] *Id.* at 951, 35 L.R.R.M. at 1616.

the document." [108] Thus, where propaganda is limited to a mere instructional devise recommending which box to mark, without reference to the Board—the element of passing off which the *Allied Electric* rule was designed to prohibit is absent, since the imprimatur of the Board is lacking. By approving the use of altered partial reproductions, the Board has concluded that certain portions of the ballot do not reflect the authority of the Board; thus, they are severable and can be utilized for legitimate purposes of electioneering.

Through a distillation of the existing case law, it is possible to enumerate the permissible uses of material of which a partial reproduction is constructed. First, a reproduction which merely consists of copying the voting boxes and indicating a preference is clearly outside of the *Allied Electric* rule which requires that the alleged misuse purport to be an official Board document.[109] Further, the additional inclusion of the direction to mark an "X" in the square of the employees' choice,[110] the inclusion of the interrogatory of whether the employees wish to be represented for purposes of collective bargaining,[111] and indeed, the entire bottom section of the ballot may be reproduced and altered for campaign purposes.[112]

The unfortunate "tempest in a teapot" aspect which often plagues the decisions pursuant to the *Allied Electric* doctrine arose again very recently in the case of *Stedman Wholesale Distributors, Inc.*[113] In *Stedman*, one day prior to the election, the employer distributed a leaflet that urged the employees to vote in the election, to vote against the union, and also assured the voters that the Board would protect the secrecy of their ballots. Within the body of the leaflet was an oblong box, identical to the bottom portion of the ballot and introduced by

---

108 *Id.*, 35 L.R.R.M. at 1616.

109 *E.g.*, Kilborn-Sauer Co., 120 N.L.R.B. 804, 42 L.R.R.M. 1068 (1958); Lincoln Plastics Corp., 112 N.L.R.B. 291, 36 L.R.R.M. 1005 (1955); Phelps-Dodge Copper Products Corp., 111 N.L.R.B. 950, 35 L.R.R.M. 1616 (1955)

110 Stratford Furniture Co., 116 N.L.R.B. 1721, 39 L.R.R.M. 1080 (1956).

111 *Id.*, 39 L.R.R.M. at 1080.

112 Reflector Hardware Corp., 121 N.L.R.B. 1544, 43 L.R.R.M. 1042 (1958); Houston Shell and Concrete Division, 118 N.L.R.B. 1511, 40 L.R.R.M. 1409 (1957).

113 203 N.L.R.B. No. 31, 83 L.R.R.M. 1055 (1973).

the statement that it was a sample of the way the bottom of the official ballot would look. The "No" box contained an "X" mark.[114]

In a split decision, the majority of the Board, in disagreement with the regional director, who had found that the leaflet constituted an altered ballot in violation of the *Allied Electric* rule, refused to set aside the election.[115] Member Fanning, dissenting, argued that the leaflet was within the purview of the *Allied Electric* rule because the employer, himself, stated that the reproduction was a portion of the ballot to be used by the Board. Moreover, the reproduction was an integral part of a propaganda leaflet stating that the election would be supervised by the federal government. Therefore, Member Fanning argued that the alleged interference came fully under the doctrine, since the reproduction purported to be a copy of a Board document, it had been altered, and it was accompanied by partisan propadanda.[116]

On the other hand, the majority apparently based its decision on the grounds that no formal mention had been made in the handbill of either "United States Government," "National Labor Relations Board," "Official Secret Ballot," or "Board Agent." [117] Because of the absence of any references tying the sample to the auspices of the Board, the majority reasoned that there could be no tendency on the part of employees to view the handbill as carrying the endorsement of the Board.

As is apparent, the positions of neither the majority or dissent actually went to the issue that is to be decided under the *Allied Electric* rule. Instead, each was concerned with the cosmetics involved rather than the substance of the objection. Indeed, in consideration of the factors which the Board deemed persuasive, and their lack of relevancy, the decision could have easily gone either way.

---

[114] *Id.*, 83 L.R.R.M. at 1056.

[115] *Id.*, 83 L.R.R.M. at 1056.

[116] *Id.*, 83 L.R.R.M. at 1056.

[117] *Id.*, 83 L.R.R.M. at 1056. The "saving factors" enumerated by the majority constitute an extreme example of hair-splitting. Although it is true that the area within the sample ballot was free from their inclusion, the leaflet itself contained reference to "Federal Government" and "U.S. Government" in the immediately preceding paragraph.

It is unfortunate that the *Stedman* case is representative of the majority of cases involving altered sample ballots that arise under the *Allied Electric* doctrine. In consideration of the fact that the Board's decision-making capacity is a limited resource, faced with an ever increasing case load, the triviality and technicality of the *Allied Electric* doctrine, as applied to altered sample ballots, may no longer justify taxing the Board's time. Therefore, it may be that the time has come for the Board to reconsider the rule for a determination of whether the infraction is serious enough to justify setting aside an election on the sole grounds that one of the parties has distributed copies of an altered sample ballot.

Reproduction of Other Board Documents

Alleged interference with the Board's election processes caused by interference with official documents, other than the alteration of facsimile sample ballots, is also adjudicated on the basis of the *Allied Electric* rule. Unlike the case of altered ballots, however, the infractions in this area constitute a far more serious attempt to trade on the Board's prestige. A number of recent cases have dealt with the problem of preventing the politicization of official Board documents for electioneering purposes. The misuse of NLRB instructional material constitutes a serious attack on the Board's integrity. It is quite probable, as the opponents of the *Allied Electric* rule have argued, that the average voter possesses adequate electoral sophistication to recognize a marked sample ballot for the propaganda that it is. On the other hand, it is imperative that prospective voters have some unbiased, independent guidance available to them in order to exercise not only an unrestrained, but also an informed vote regarding the question of union representation. To that end, the Board has reserved to itself, the responsibility to inform employees of their rights and privileges under the Act.[118]

In the leading case of *Rebmar, Inc.*,[119] a divided Board held that a handbill, distributed by the union, which reproduced the section of the Board's standard notice entitled "Rights of Employees" on one side and contained an explanation in generalized terminology concerning the nature of a trade union,

---

[118] *See* Rebmar, Inc., 173 N.L.R.B. 1434, 70 L.R.R.M. 1018 (1968).

[119] *Id.* at 1434, 70 L.R.R.M. at 1018. The fact that the leaflet contained no reference to the participating union by name was deemed irrelevant.

its functions, and the significance of a collective bargaining agreement on the reverse side, constituted a breach of the *Allied Electric* doctrine. Disagreeing with the majority, the dissent argued that because the innocuous nature of the propaganda itself did not contain an inference that the Board recommended employees to vote one way or another, it should not be construed violative of *Allied Electric*. The majority rebutted this argument, stating that since the Board has the responsibility to fully inform employees of their rights and privileges under the Act, any duplications of an official Board notice and addition to it of a partisan message is an undesirable use of official Board documents, which have been designed for another purpose.[120]

Although the misconduct of the union in *Rebmar* may have been at most, a technical violation of the rule, as conceded to by the majority,[121] any attempt to base infractions on the relative seriousness of the violation would only invite litigation by various participants, motivated to test the Board's resolve to enforce the rule. Illustrative of this point are two contemporary cases in which the Board was urged to adjudicate infractions on the basis of their probable effect upon the participants. In the *Thiokol Chemical Corp.*[122] case, the company had mailed to its employees a purported copy of a Board document reproducing the Board's seal and certain other portions of an official handbook entitled, *A Layman's Guide to Basic Law Under the National Labor Relations Act* (1962 edition). On the title page of the *Layman's Guide,* the employer had added the caption, "Here's What the U.S. Govt. has to Say," and subscribed the document with the corporate name. A divided Board found merit in the union's claim that the employer's actions violated the *Allied Electric* doctrine.[123] The majority held that the reproduction of the purported Board document constituted interference not only because the company had appropriated it to its own partisan advantage, but also because the document reprinted was out of date and contained an inaccurate statement concerning the reinstatement rights of employees in the event of an

---

[120] *Id.* at 1434, 70 L.R.R.M. at 1019.

[121] *Id.* at 1434, 70 L.R.R.M. at 1019.

[122] 202 N.L.R.B. No. 57, 82 L.R.R.M. 1583 (1973).

[123] *Id.,* 82 L.R.R.M. at 1584.

economic strike. They reasoned that the crux of the issue was that the violator, under the cover of implied Board sanction, might have been able to create a false and misleading view as to his employee's reinstatement rights pursuant to the Act. This was particularly important in this case, since the employer's campaign theme had laid great stress on the possibility of a strike and its consequences. Thus, the majority found that the employer's use of the 1962 document in this context served to reinforce the tenor of its propaganda that in the event of an economic strike, the employees would lose their reinstatement rights—a result sanctioned by the United States government.[124]

In another case, *NLRB v. John S. Barnes Corp.*,[125] the Seventh Circuit denied enforcement of a Board certification order on the ground that the union had unlawfully altered an official Board document. Inexplicably, the Board in *Barnes* had affirmed the regional director's findings without comment, wherein he had held that although a Board document had been altered, such alteration had no tendency to mislead the voters into believing that the Board endorsed the union because the union's message merely proclaimed its success in obtaining an election.[126] Subsequent to a Board "Order Denying Motion" for stay of a second election, the union distributed a copy of this order, captioned "Now An Election Can Be Held As Promised!!!" Two days later, the union printed and distributed a second circular entitled, "IAM Wins Three Important Victories!!" In the body of this second leaflet, three points had been enumerated as union victories. First, the handbill stated that the Board's order meant that the government had denied the company's "frantic efforts to stall the election." Secondly, the union claimed that at an NLRB conference, it had succeeded in preventing the company from stopping the election, and hereafter its scheduling would be handled by the government. The final union claim, that it had maneuvered an election off company property, was irrelevant to the alleged interference. The conclusion of the leaflet

---

[124] Board and court decisions subsequent to the issuance of the 1962 booklet substantially enlarged the reinstatement rights of economic strikers. *See, e.g.,* The Laidlaw Corp., 171 N.L.R.B. 1366, 68 L.R.R.M. 1252 (1968), *enforced,* 414 F.2d 99, 71 L.R.R.M. 3054 (7th Cir. 1969), *cert. denied,* 397 U.S. 920, 73 L.R.R.M. 2537 (1970).

[125] 478 F.2d 1105, 83 L.R.R.M. 2052 (7th Cir. 1973).

[126] *Id.* at 1107, 83 L.R.R.M. at 2052.

stated, "When the Board Sets the Election Date—the Union Will Notify You Immediately." [127] Because of the closeness in the distribution dates of the two handbills, and the incorporation by reference of the Board's formal order into the second leaflet, the regional director considered both handbills as one, thereby rendering comment on the second circular as being reflective of the Board's "Order Denying Motion." [128]

On appeal, the court reacted strongly to the rationale adduced by the regional director that because the handbills merely added a message "proclaiming union success in obtaining an election," the alleged interference was insufficient to constitute a valid claim in order to set aside the election. Questioning the credulity of such a statement by an appeal to common sense, the court stated that:

> The contention that the handbills could in no manner be interpreted by the employees as an endorsement by the Board of the Union flies in the face of reason and experience. To conclude that the Union's messages merely proclaim that the Union was successful in obtaining an election lies in the same category. *It was more. It was a partisan statement, and we can only conclude it was added for a purpose which seems obvious.*[129]

Drawing substantially from the Board's prior decision in *Rebmar, Inc.*,[130] the court concluded that the result in *Rebmar* was the better rule and was dispositive of *Barnes sub judice*.[131]

One of the peculiarities of the body of law pertaining to the misuse of Board documents under the *Allied Electric* doctrine has been the shift in analysis. Initially, the controversy had centered on the probable effects of such violations upon the thinking of the employees. The perspective of recent Board cases, however, has emphasized an inquiry into the intent of the alleged violator to misuse Board documents. As a result, the doctrine is approaching a completely *per se* status. Indeed, a dogma, analogous to the common law principle that "one is presumed to intend the natural consequence of one's own actions" is coming to the fore. Under the initial thrust of the

---

[127] *Id.* at 1106-1107 n.1, 83 L.R.R.M. at 2052-53.

[128] *Id.* at 1107, 83 L.R.R.M. at 2053.

[129] *Id.*, 83 L.R.R.M. at 2053.

[130] 173 N.L.R.B. 1434, 70 L.R.R.M. 1018 (1968); *See* discussion at pp. 322-23, *supra*.

[131] 478 F.2d at 1107-1108, 83 L.R.R.M. at 2054.

Allied Electric doctrine the "natural consequence" factor was supplied in terms of policy. This has caused the recent shift in emphasis to an examination of intent. Consequently, in current cases, the primary defense put forth by the alleged violator has been based on the contention that in appropriating the documents, there was no intent to mislead.[132] In refusing to entertain argument on the question of intent, the wisdom, as well as the logic, of the majority viewpoint is the greater. Any attempt to weigh the intentions of the alleged interferer falls within the same category as the question concerning the actual extent of confusion produced by altered documents in the minds of the employees which was originally annunicated under the *Allied Electric* doctrine.

Concluding Remarks

Although the doctrine promulgated in the *Allied Electric* decision is a relative unknown when compared to its more famous counterparts in representation election law, its all-encompassing nature and ability to withstand attack render it a unique principle in a constantly changing body of law. The rule has weathered all but minor changes and exceptions for fully twenty years. Its rationale has remained the uncomplicated proposition that the continued integrity of the Board's election processes are dependent upon the Board's ability to remain neutral, and, therefore, the politicization of its own official documents must be prevented in order to safeguard the necessary neutrality. Yet for all of its strengths, the *Allied Electric* doctrine occupies the anomalous position of encountering increasing opposition and deterioration from its original position regarding sample ballots, while gaining increasing support as a Board sanction to protect the misuse of its notices to employees by participants in an election.

Although it is still too early to predict with certainty the future course of the *Allied Electric* doctrine, such indicators as the obviously withering effect of the *Stedman Wholesale Distributors, Inc.*[133] case on the extent of the doctrine's applicability to

---

[132] *E.g.*, Thiokol Chemical Corp., 202 N.L.R.B. No. 57, 82 L.R.R.M. 1583, 1584 (1973) (Chairman Miller, dissenting); Rebmar, Inc., 173 N.L.R.B. 1434, 1435, 70 L.R.R.M. 1018, 1019 (1968) (Members Brown and Jenkins, dissenting); *see also* NLRB v. John S. Barnes Corp., 478 F.2d 1105, 83 L.R.R.M. 2052 (7th Cir. 1973).

[133] 203 N.L.R.B. No. 31, 83 L.R.R.M. 1055 (1973).

sample ballots coupled with recent trends in its use in the area of Board communications to employees foreshadow its probable metamorphosis, for as we have already seen, the utility of the *Allied Electric* doctrine as applied to altered sample ballots is deteriorating in an age of an ever-expanding Board case load.

THE OBSERVER AND HIS CONDUCT

The Board has frequently stated that the parties to a representation election conducted pursuant to a Board order are not entitled to appoint observers "as a matter of right." [134] This principle does not constitute a total ban on the ability of the parties to select representatives of their own choice, but instead, subjects the appointment of observers to such limitations as the regional director will prescribe.[135] Thus, the Board has held that a total refusal of the regional director to permit representatives of the employer to be present for the purpose of challenging the eligibility of voters or any other purpose was not an abuse of discretion.[136] Moreover, the Board has held that a prospective observer who is "too closely identified with the employer," such as a personnel director [137] or company attorney,[138] is unqualified to serve as the employer's representative.

The union also has the power to veto an employer's choice of representatives at the polls. In *Marlin-Rockwell Corp. v. NLRB*,[139]

---

[134] *E.g.*, San Francisco Bakery Employers Ass'n, 121 N.L.R.B. 1204, 1206, 42 L.R.R.M. 1546 (1958); Eisner Grocery Co., 116 N.L.R.B. 976, 38 L.R.R.M. 1376 (1956); Simplot Fertilizer Co., 107 N.L.R.B. 1211, 1221, 33 L.R.R.M. 1357 (1954). *See also* cases cited at note 135, *infra*.

[135] *See* Wiley Mfg., Inc., 93 N.L.R.B. 1600, 1601, 27 L.R.R.M. 1623 (1951); Burrows & Sanborn, Inc., 84 N.L.R.B. 304, 305, 24 L.R.R.M. 1228 (1949).

[136] American Radiator Co., 7 N.L.R.B. 505, 506, 2 L.R.R.M. 293 (1938). This principle of permitting the regional director to pass upon proposed representatives of the company was the subject of intense litigation in the initial years that the Act was in force and has retained its validity to the present day. *See* Richfield Oil Co., 8 N.L.R.B. 428, 2 L.R.R.M. 95 (1938); Marlin-Rockwell Corp., 7 N.L.R.B. 836, 838, 2 L.R.R.M. 342 (1938); American France Line, 4 N.L.R.B. 1140, 1-A L.R.R.M. 189 (1938).

[137] Harry Manaster & Bro., 61 N.L.R.B. 1373, 1374, 16 L.R.R.M. 156 (1945).

[138] The Union Switch & Signal Co., 76 N.L.R.B. 205, 211, 21 L.R.R.M. 1169, 1170 (1948).

[139] 116 F.2d 586, 587, 7 L.R.R.M. 353, 355 (2d Cir. 1941).

the company objected to the conduct of the election, contending that the Board had abused its discretion in refusing to allow it to have a representative present at the election. The refusal was based upon Board policy which prohibits attendance by an employer's representative at elections ordered by the Board in the absence of the consent of the union involved.[140]

In enforcing the Board's order, the court attempted to set forth the rationale behind this policy. On one hand, recognizing that the Act permits the Board to establish its own election procedures, the court indicated that although the Board may permit a representative of the employer to assist in identifying eligible employees, "such assistance is not essential to a fair election" because "identification of voters may be obtained by other means."[141] On the other hand, the court continued, because the presence of employer representatives is a matter of Board discretion anyway, the Board rationale "that considerations in favor of the presence of an employer representative are outweighed by the possibility that his presence may act as an inhibiting influence on the employees' freedom of choice" is sufficient justification for the Board's policy of denying permission unless the labor organization involved consents.[142]

In contrast to elections conducted pursuant to a Board order, each party in an election held under a consent agreement has the privilege to appoint an observer. The Board's standard forms for consent election agreements expressly provide that each party to the agreement is permitted to station an equal number of authorized observers at the polling places to assist in the conduct of the election.[143] Persons designated as observers for the employer, *must be selected from among his nonsupervisory employees.*[144] Moreover, the right to have observers present at an election conducted pursuant to a consent agreement is not absolute, and may be waived. The Board has frequently held that it will not set aside an election, where prior to the election, the objecting party had not requested the right to designate

---

[140] *Id.* at 588, 7 L.R.R.M. at 355.

[141] *Id.,* 7 L.R.R.M. at 355.

[142] *Id.,* 7 L.R.R.M. at 355.

[143] *Cf.* Breman Steel Co., 115 N.L.R.B. 247, 249, 37 L.R.R.M. 1273, 1274 (1956).

[144] *See* note 152, *infra.*

an observer,[145] nor where the opportunity to do so was not denied.[146] Furthermore, where the grounds for objection are based on the failure of the party asserting the claim to have an *equal* number of observers present, the objection will be overruled when the alleged insufficiency can be traced to that party's own lack of diligence.[147]

In *Westinghouse Appliance Sales & Service Co.*,[148] the Board extended the waiver concept to its farthest limits. In that case, the Board indicated that even though the employer may have reached a prior, oral understanding that only one observer would represent each party, the fact that the union involved in the election had two observers, constituted an immaterial variation in election conduct and in no way compromised the fairness of the election.[149] A fairly plausible argument can be advanced, as done by the employer in *Westinghouse Appliances,* that the imbalance in the number of observers might create an impression that the Board favored the party with the most observers. Nonetheless, this variation in election conduct, viewed in isolation—especially in an election which was not very close—probably would not create the prejudicial effect alleged by the employers.

The Board's conception of when a waiver has occurred is not without limits. Indeed, it has held that the rights created by a consent agreement are based on contract.[150] Therefore, if a party to the election fails to select any observers, in reliance upon a prior understanding to its own detriment, the Board will be estopped from certifying the results of the election.[151]

---

[145] Q-F Wholesalers, Inc., 87 N.L.R.B. 1085, 1087, 25 L.R.R.M. 1254 (1949).

[146] Interboro Chevrolet Co., 113 N.L.R.B. 118, 119, 36 L.R.R.M. 1277 (1955).

[147] *See, e.g.*, Westinghouse Appliance Sales & Service Co., 182 N.L.R.B. 481, 74 L.R.R.M. 1204 (1970); Bordo Products Co., 119 N.L.R.B. 79, 80, 41 L.R.R.M. 1045, 1046 (1957).

[148] 182 N.L.R.B. 481, 74 L.R.R.M. 1204 (1970).

[149] *Id.* at 481 n.1, 74 L.R.R.M. at 1204.

[150] Bremen Steel Co., 115 N.L.R.B. 247, 249, 37 L.R.R.M. 1273, 1274 (1956). *See also* Semi-Steel Casting Co. v. NLRB, 160 F.2d 388, 19 L.R.R.M. 2458 (8th Cir.), *cert. denied*, 332 U.S. 758, 20 L.R.R.M. 2673 (1947); Capitol Greyhound Lines, 49 N.L.R.B. 156, 159, 12 L.R.R.M. 198, 199 (1943), *enforced*, 140 F.2d 754, 13 L.R.R.M. 778 (6th Cir.), *cert. denied*, 322 U.S. 763, 14 L.R.R.M. 952 (1944).

[151] 115 N.L.R.B. at 249, 37 L.R.R.M. at 1274.

Observers for the Employer

As has been previously stated, absent consent by the participating labor organization, it is a matter of Board policy that observers for the employer be selected from among his "nonsupervisory employees," [152] and not be persons "closely identified with the employer." [153] Early in the history of the Board, this principle was approved by the Supreme Court in *Southern Steamship Co. v. NLRB*,[154] wherein the Court indicated that the policy was "wholly reasonable [as an attempt] to remove any possibility of intimidation by conducting the election in the absence of the employer's representatives." [155] Apparently, the underlying rationale of this policy is that the mere presence of representatives of the employer at the polls will intimidate the employees because such observers would be subjectively linked, in the minds of the employees, with the employer's power over their jobs—*i.e.* the power to hire and fire, and set wages.[156] The fact that supervisors or other persons closely identified with the company, may be the only persons actually qualified to act as observers for the employer, because of their peculiar knowledge as to the identity and eligibility of employees by both name and sight, is viewed as insufficient to warrant the use of such persons.[157]

Since the excluded class of supervisors are also employees of the company, the fate of many objections to the conduct of the election, claiming that supervisory employees have been utilized as observers, is tied directly to the actual capacity in which

---

152 NLRB Field Manual, § 11310; Worth Food Market Stores, Inc., 103 N.L.R.B. 259, 31 L.R.R.M. 1527 (1953); The Ann Arbor Press, 88 N.L.R.B. 391, 25 L.R.R.M. 1339 (1950); Parkway Lincoln-Mercury Sales Co., Inc., 84 N.L.R.B. 475, 24 L.R.R.M. 1274 (1949); Burrows & Sanborn, Inc., 84 N.L.R.B. 304, 24 L.R.R.M. 1228 (1949); Paragon Rubber Co., 7 N.L.R.B. 965, 2 L.R.R.M. 106 (1938).

153 *E.g.*, Watkins Brick Co., 107 N.L.R.B. 500, 33 L.R.R.M. 1176 (1953); Herbert Men's Shop Corp., 100 N.L.R.B. 670, 30 L.R.R.M. 1330 (1952); Peabody Engineering Co., 95 N.L.R.B. 952, 28 L.R.R.M. 1391 (1951).

154 316 U.S. 31, 10 L.R.R.M. 544 (1942).

155 *Id.* at 37, 10 L.R.R.M. at 547.

156 *Cf.* Paragon Rubber Co., 7 N.L.R.B. 965, 966, 2 L.R.R.M. 106, 108 (1938).

157 Watkins Brick Co., 107 N.L.R.B. 500, 33 L.R.R.M. 1176 (1953).

the alleged supervisor is employed. In this context, the test applied as to whether an observer can qualify as a nonsupervisory employee is quite similar to the statutory definition of the term in Section 2 of the Act.[158] A convenient rule of thumb utilized by the Board is whether the employee alleged to be a supervisor is authorized by the employer to exercise independent control over any of the aspects of the "economic welfare" of th employees. Thus, the Board in *Herbert Men's Shop Corp.*,[159] held that an employee who had attended all of the negotiations of the employer dealing with labor relations and who took part in the final steps of employee grievances, was not qualified as a nonsupervisory employee to act as the employer's observer.[160] On the other hand, if the alleged supervisory status of the employer's observer is only the result of a temporary expedient, the Board has held that he will qualify as a "nonsupervisory employee." [161] The second class of persons, who are precluded from being observers for the employer, are those people who can be "too closely identified with the employer." The Board

---

[158] 29 U.S.C. § 152 (11) (1970) defines supervisor as:

. . . any individual having authority, in the interest of the employer, to hire, transfer, suspend, lay-off, recall, promote, discharge, assign, reward, or discipline other employees, or responsibility to direct them, or to adjust their grievances, or effectively to recommend such action, if in connection with the foregoing exercise of such authority is not of a merely routine or clerical nature, but requires the use of independent judgment.

[159] 100 N.L.R.B. 670, 671, 30 L.R.R.M. 1330 (1952).

[160] *But see* Westinghouse Electric Corp., 118 N.L.R.B. 1625, 40 L.R.R.M. 1440 (1957), wherein the Board held that an "Industrial Relations Assistant" was a nonsupervisory employee, even though, as in the *Herbert's Men's Shop* case, he also participated in labor negotiations and the grievance process. The distinction drawn by the Board in *Westinghouse* was apparently based on the grounds that he could not act as an agent for his employer.

[161] Cooper Supply Co., 120 N.L.R.B. 1023, 1025, 42 L.R.R.M. 1094, 1095 (1958); *see also* Milwaukee Cheese Co., 112 N.L.R.B. 1383, 36 L.R.R.M 1225 (1955) (accountant in employer's office); Werman & Sons, 106 N.L.R.B. 1215, 32 L.R.R.M. 1053 (1953) (payroll clerk who had acted as an observer for the employer in a prior election without objection); Northrop Aircraft, Inc.,106 N.L.R.B. 23, 32 L.R.R.M. 1390 (1953) (employees of Industrial Relations Department who were not supervisors); Silver Knit Hosiery Mills, 99 N.L.R.B. 422, 30 L.R.R.M. 1077 (1952) (production clerk who exhibited sample ballot during employer's antiunion speech who had no supervisory authority).

has held that this category includes relatives of the employer,[162] officers of the company,[163] and the employer's attorney.[164]

Observers for the Union

The strict limitations on the status of observers who may be used by the employer, do not carry over into the selection of observers for the union. Indeed, as the Board [165] and courts [166] have stated many times, the mere fact that an employee is also a union official, does not disqualify him to act as an observer. This policy of permitting persons closely identified with the union to act as its observers is also extended to include employees who have been active in the organizational campaign preceding the particular election.[167]

The justification for the Board's policy of permitting union officials to act as observers is somewhat ambiguous. In some instances, the Board has reasoned that as long as the union official or organizer is a "nonsupervisory employee," his status as observer is not impaired, since he is a member of the class of personages specifically chosen by the Board to act as observers.[168] Nonetheless, the Board has indicated that "supervisory

---

162 International Stamping Co., Inc., 97 N.L.R.B. 921, 922-23, 29 L.R.R.M. 1158, 1159 (1951) (son and sister-in-law); Wiley Mfg., Inc., 93 N.L.R.B. 1600, 1601, 27 L.R.R.M. 1623 (1951) (wife).

163 Watkins Brick Co., 107 N.L.R.B. 500, 33 L.R.R.M. 1176 (1953) (vice-president, treasurer, and office manager); Parkway Lincoln-Mercury Sales, Inc., 84 N.L.R.B. 475, 24 L.R.R.M. 1274 (1949) (vice-president).

164 Peabody Engineering Co., 95 N.L.R.B. 952, 953, 28 L.R.R.M. 1391, 1392 (1951); The Union Switch & Signal Co., 76 N.L.R.B. 205, 211, 21 L.R.R.M. 1169, 1170 (1948).

165 *E.g.*, Bordo Products Co., 119 N.L.R.B. 79, 42 L.R.R.M. 1045 (1957); Dallas City Packing Co., 110 N.L.R.B. 8, 34 L.R.R.M. 1588 (1954); Goodyear Tire & Rubber Co., 85 N.L.R.B. 135, 24 L.R.R.M. 1373 (1949); United States Gypsum Co., 80 N.L.R.B. 1205, 23 L.R.R.M. 1208 (1948).

166 *E.g.*, NLRB v. E-Z Davies Chevrolet, 395 F.2d 191, 192-93, 68 L.R.R.M. 2228, 2230 (9th Cir. 1968); NLRB v. Zelrich Co., 344 F.2d 1011, 1015, 59 L.R.R.M. 2225, 2227-28 (5th Cir. 1965); Shoreline Enterprises of America, Inc. v. NLRB, 262 F.2d 933, 942, 43 L.R.R.M. 2407, 2413 (5th Cir. 1959); NLRB v. Huntsville Mfg. Co., 203 F.2d 430, 434, 31 L.R.R.M. 2637, 2640 (5th Cir. 1953).

167 *See* Dallas City Packing Co., 116 N.L.R.B. 1609, 39 L.R.R.M. 1054 (1956); Stokely Foods, Inc., 81 N.L.R.B. 449, 23 L.R.R.M. 1364 (1949).

168 *Cf.* Stokely Foods, Inc., 81 N.L.R.B. 449, 23 L.R.R.M. 1364 (1949); United States Gypsum Co., 80 N.L.R.B. 1205, 23 L.R.R.M. 1208 (1948).

personnel" would be permitted to act as observers for the union if the circumstances show that the use of a supervisor as an observer for the union could not be construed by the employees as an endorsement of that union by the employer.[169] Thus, the fact that the observer of the union is also a non-supervisory employee is not the sole criterion for establishing the requisite credentials of a union observer.

It is clear that the Board's policy is not based on a matter of fairness between employer and labor union—but instead rests on the Board's concept of what factors may exert undue influence on the individual employee as he casts his ballot. Indeed, the Board itself has recognized that a "union official should not ordinarily be designated to act as an observer at an election." [170] The difference is found in the Board's belief that, absent evidence to the contrary, the conduct of the union official will be—in the terminology of the Board—"exemplary." [171] In summary, the mere status of observers closely identified with the employer, is considered to be so influential in the minds of the voters that the election must be set aside. In the case of observers closely identified with the union, the fact that they are also employees, and theoretically "in the same boat" as their fellow employees,[172] nullifies any presumption that their presence will influence the employees' freedom of choice. Instead, the burden of preventing their use as observers is shifted to the employer who must raise the objection at the pre-election conference.

Interference in the Conduct of the Election by Observers

The concern of the Board over election observers is not confined to determining the legality of their status as observers, but also extends to regulating their conduct. Unlike the prior consideration of whom may be used as an observer, in resolving

---

[169] Howard Cooper Corp., 121 N.L.R.B. 950, 951, 42 L.R.R.M. 1511 (1958); Plant City Welding and Tank Co., 119 N.L.R.B. 131, 132, 41 L.R.R.M. 1014, 1015 (1957). The "circumstances" under which the Board will permit a supervisor to act as an observer for the union are apparently dependent upon a union victory in the election.

[170] United States Gypsum Co., 80 N.L.R.B. 1205, 1206, 23 L.R.R.M. 1208 (1948).

[171] *Id.* at 1206, 23 L.R.R.M. at 1208; *accord*, Stokely Foods, Inc., 81 N.L.R.B. 449, 451, 23 L.R.R.M. at 1364 (1949).

[172] 81 N.L.R.B. at 451, 23 L.R.R.M. at 1364.

issues of alleged interference, observers for either the union or the employer must abide by the same code of conduct. In performing their primary functions of watching the ballot box and identifying eligible voters, observers are endowed by the Board with a quasi-official status as its representatives. Thus, misconduct on the part of an observer reflects on the Board itself, casting a shadow of doubt on the integrity of the NLRB's electoral processes. To maintain its appearance of neutrality, the Board regulates the conduct of observers, prohibiting implicitly coercive conduct and overt electioneering.

Eligibility Lists. It has long been a rule of NLRB election procedure to prohibit the maintenance of any lists of employees who have or have not voted, other than the official eligibility list secured by the Board agent for his use in the election.[173] However, this prohibition does not apply against the retention, by the observer of either party, of a list of prospective voters whose ballots he intends to challenge.[174] Like all Board rules pertaining to the electoral processes, the prohibition against the maintenance of a "voting list" is explained as a necessary limitation in the interest of promoting free elections.[175] Since accurate record keeping of participation in the election is provided for by giving the agent in charge a list of voters, a supplementary count by the observers is deemed unnecessary. Therefore, the Board has reasoned that if observers do keep track of those voting in the presence of the employees, such a practice may have the effect of a veiled threat, by either party, that it intends to use such a voting list for postelection retribution against the employees.

This prohibition deals with the employee's state of mind at the time of the election—*i.e.* what the employee might perceive

---

[173] *E.g.*, Milwaukee Cheese Co., 112 N.L.R.B. 1383, 36 L.R.R.M. 1225 (1955); International Stamping, Inc., 97 N.L.R.B. 921, 29 L.R.R.M. 1158 (1951). *See also* NLRB Form 722, entitled "Instruction to Election Observers" which directs observers *not* to "keep a list of those who have and have not voted."

[174] *See* Tom Brown Drilling Co., Inc., 172 N.L.R.B. 1267, 68 L.R.R.M. 1473 (1968); The Kendall Co., 115 N.L.R.B. 1401, 1403, 38 L.R.R.M. 1078, 1079 (1956); Bear Creek Orchards, 90 N.L.R.B. 286, 26 L.R.R.M. 1204 (1950).

[175] International Stamping, Inc., 97 N.L.R.B. 921, 29 L.R.R.M. 1158 (1951); *accord*, Belk's Department Store of Savannah, Ga., Inc., 98 N.L.R.B. 280, 29 L.R.R.M. 1325 (1951); *cf.* Piggly-Wiggly #011, 168 N.L.R.B. 792, 66 L.R.R.M. 1360 (1967).

to be true, rather than the actual purpose for keeping such a list. Therefore, the objecting party must show that the employees were in fact aware that their names were being recorded.[176] Absent this showing, such a breach in the conduct of the election will not constitute grounds for setting aside the election.[177]

The focus of the inquiry regarding the keeping of voting records is illustrated in *Craddock-Terry Shoe Corp.*[178] In that case, the employer contended that at one polling place the Board agent in charge permitted the union's observer to call headquarters, reporting names of union members who had not yet voted, and asking that they be brought in.[179] Stating that it was unnecessary to resolve the dispute over whether the agent actually granted the observer permission to call union headquarters, the Board found that the conduct complained of was nonprejudicial. It reasoned that since it is normal in representation elections for both parties to have access to the eligibility list, utilizing that accessibility for the purpose of "getting out the vote" is merely a traditional part of the election procedure.[180] Consequently, the Board overruled the objections because "the conduct complained of was not coercive in its effect nor could it tend to exercise undue influence upon any voter." [181] Therefore, in order to object successfully to an observer's use of an eligibility list, evidence of partisan conduct alone is insufficient. Instead, the impermissible nature of the observer's actions are limited to those within the polling area, in plain view of the employees.

Wearing Campaign Buttons and Similar Insignia. Although the Board's instructions direct observers not to wear or display buttons and other insignia in the polling place, a breach of these

---

[176] 168 N.L.R.B. at 792-93, 66 L.R.R.M. at 1360; *see also* Tom Brown Drilling Co., 172 N.L.R.B. 1267, 68 L.R.R.M. 1473 (1968) ; A.D. Juilliard and Co., 110 N.L.R.B. 2197, 2199, 35 L.R.R.M. 1401 (1954).

[177] 172 N.L.R.B. at 1267, 68 L.R.R.M. at 1473; 110 N.L.R.B. at 2199, 35 L.R.R.M. at 1401.

[178] 80 N.L.R.B. 1239, 23 L.R.R.M. 1215 (1948).

[179] *Id.* at 1240, 23 L.R.R.M. at 1216.

[180] *Id.* at 1241, 23 L.R.R.M. at 1216.

[181] *Id.,* 23 L.R.R.M. at 1216. *Cf.* The Kendall Co., 115 N.L.R.B. 1401, 1403, 38 L.R.R.M. 1078 (1956).

instructions has been considered insufficient to constitute interference with the election to warrant a second election.[182] This
policy is based on the rationale that because "the identity of
election observers, as well as the fact that they represent the
special interests of the parties, is generally known to employees,"
the fact that an observer wears any insignia in support of the
party he represents, is not prejudicial enough to have affected the
results of the election.[183] In addition, the presence of the additional word "vote," followed by a union designation, will not
invalidate the election.[184] In *Larkwood Farms*,[185] the Board extended this principle to include antiunion insignia worn by the
employer's observer. In so doing, the Board stated:

> The identity and special interests of employer observers may not
> reasonably be presumed to be less well known to [the employees]
> than that of union observers. We are of the opinion that the im-
> pact on voters is not materially different whether the observers
> wear prounion or antiunion insignia of this kind.[186]

In reaching this conclusion, the Board in *Larkwood* conceded
that employees are sophisticated enough in the political processes
to recognize that antiunion propaganda by the employer's observer is a natural incidence of the interests which that observer
represents.

Electioneering. Board policy concerning electioneering by observers may be roughly divided into two phases—pre- and post-
1968. Until 1968, the standard of conduct with which an observer was required to conform was extremely marginal. For
example, the Board upheld an election in which the union's
observer, during the polling period, reported to union headquarters with a list of known union supporters who had not
voted, urging that they be sought to vote.[187] In other cases,

---

[182] *See* Larkwood Farms, 178 N.L.R.B. 226, 72 L.R.R.M. 1057 (1969).

[183] Western Electric Co., 87 N.L.R.B. 183, 185, 25 L.R.R.M. 1099, 1100
(1949); *accord*, NLRB v. Laney & Duke Storage Warehouse Co., 369 F.2d
859, 865, 63 L.R.R.M. 2552, 2554 (5th Cir. 1966). *See also* Larkwood Farms,
178 N.L.R.B. 226, 72 L.R.R.M. 1057 (1969).

[184] Electric Wheel Co., 120 N.L.R.B. 1644, 42 L.R.R.M. 1244 (1958).

[185] 178 N.L.R.B. 226, 72 L.R.R.M. 1057 (1969).

[186] *Id.*, 72 L.R.R.M. at 1058.

[187] Craddock-Terry Shoe Corp., 80 N.L.R.B. 1239, 1241, 23 L.R.R.M. 1215,
1216 (1948).

solicitation by the observer of employees who had not yet voted, was permitted subsequent to the expiration of the observer's shift at the polls.[188] Allegations of campaigning based on mere inference, were overruled. Instead, the Board required that a factual showing of "electioneering, interference, or coercion" must be set forth in order to substantiate charges of prejudicial campaigning by observers sufficient to set aside an election.[189]

Abruptly, in 1968, the Board ended its permissive policy vis-à-vis electioneering by observers in *Star Expansion Industries Corp.*[190] A companion case of *Milchem, Inc.*,[191] the *Star Expansion* case, implemented the new, "get tough" policy of the Board, enunciated in *Milchem*, that prohibited electioneering near the polls.[192] In *Star Expansion*, an observer of the union, not conducting his official duties at the polls, engaged in electioneering activities in close proximity to the polls during a substantial part of the voting period, in defiance of the Board agent's instructions, warning him to stay at least 50 feet away from the polling area.[193] Disagreeing with the regional director's conclusions, the Board held that the observer's electioneering activities, consisting of urging the employees to cast ballots for the union, did constitute coercion when coupled with the fact that the remarks were directed to employees waiting to vote.[194]

Subsequently, the Board in *Modern Hard Chrome Service Co.*,[195] held that the rule enunciated in *Milchem* was not meant to be limited "to situations where a party's conversations with voters in the polling place were shown to have constituted electioneering." Instead, the rule was meant to be prophylatic

---

[188] *E.g.*, The Kendall Co., 115 N.L.R.B. 1401, 1403, 38 L.R.R.M. 1078, 1079 (1956); East Texas Pulp & Paper Co., 114 N.L.R.B. 885, 888, 37 L.R.R.M. 1053, 1054 (1955).

[189] *See* Bordo Products Co., 119 N.L.R.B. 79, 80, 41 L.R.R.M. 1045 (1957); *cf.* Miami Paper Board Mills, Inc., 115 N.L.R.B. 1431, 1432-33, 38 L.R.R.M. 1091 (1956).

[190] 170 N.L.R.B. 364, 67 L.R.R.M. 1400 (1968).

[191] 170 N.L.R.B. 362, 67 L.R.R.M. 1395 (1968).

[192] *Id.* at 362-63, 67 L.R.R.M. at 1395.

[193] 170 N.L.R.B. at 365, 67 L.R.R.M. at 1401.

[194] *Id.*, 67 L.R.R.M. at 1402.

[195] 187 N.L.R.B. 82, 75 L.R.R.M. 1498 (1970).

in nature, without requiring an inquiry into the actual content of such conversations, but rather presuming that all conversations were prejudicial in nature.[196] The Board deemed this presumption necessary in order to avoid burdensome investigations into the substance and effect of the conversations, observing "that parties should, to assure complete compliance with the rule, instruct their agents simply to refrain from conversation with prospective voters in the polling area." [197]

In *Modern Hard Chrome Service Co.*, the Board set aside the election because of the electioneering engaged in by the union's observer. In addition to conversing repeatedly with the voters over the admonitions of the agent in charge, he actually offered to loan one of the employees several dollars out of his own pocket.[198] In reaching its conclusions, the Board reviewed the services to be performed by observers, stating, somewhat acidly, that:

> The Board jealously guards its election process as the keystone of the Act. Observers are supposed to watch the ballot box, identify and check off voters on the eligibility list, and perform other services as requested by the Board agent. *Their functions do not include offering small loans to prospective voters as they stand in line.*[199]

---

[196] *Id.*, 75 L.R.R.M. at 1498.

[197] *Id.*, 75 L.R.R.M. at 1498. Of course, as the Board in *Milchem* stated, a chance "hello" will not suffice to set aside an election. 170 N.L.R.B. at 363, 67 L.R.R.M. at 1395.

[198] 187 N.L.R.B. at 83, 75 L.R.R.M. at 1498.

[199] *Id.*, 75 L.R.R.M. at 1498 (emphasis added).

CHAPTER XV

Deficiencies In The Election Processes

Although pre- and postelection safeguards are legion, the Board is "especially zealous in preventing intrusions"[1] during the actual polling period of a representation election. Although most election standards have been promulgated to regulate the conduct of the participants, the behavior of Board agents is also subject to regulation. Improper conduct on the part of a Board agent which may invalidate an election includes: (1) fraternizing with the representatives of one of the parties; (2) improper handling of ballots and the ballot box; (3) abuses of discretion in conducting the election; and (4) personal expressions of preference or similar statements. In addition, Board agents are charged with determining the validity of each ballot in arriving at a final tally.

IMPROPER CONDUCT BY BOARD AGENTS

Two factors must be considered in assessing the conduct expected of Board agents. First is the extremely specialized vocation of the interested parties. Since representation elections are specialized activities within an already limited field—administration of the NLRA, it is not unlikely that the principals involved in the election (*e.g.*, Board agents, employers, union organizers, and attorneys) may be professional acquaintances. As a result, it is often difficult to determine when common courtesy exceeds its bounds and impairs the neutrality of the electoral process.[2] Secondly, certification elections differ in their consequences from civil elections. Usually the latter involves voter decisions concerning the board outlines of social policy and are binding only upon a given electorate. NLRB representation elections, however, may result in the imposition upon the

---

[1] Claussen Baking Co., 134 N.L.R.B. 111, 112, 49 L.R.R.M. 1092, 1093 (1961).

[2] *E.g.*, Queen City Foundry, Inc., Case No. 11-RC-3018, 73 L.R.R.M. 1345 (1970).

participants of a specific, comprehensive set of legal rights and duties, which bind not only the electorate but also the nonvoting employer and union. Because the Board remains responsible for administering all possible future allegations concerning violations of the NLRA, or supervising subsequent elections, misconduct or suggestions of partiality by the Board agents conducting an election could tend to impair future cooperation among the parties and the Board, and possibly between the parties themselves.

Fraternizing

In cases where Board agents have been accused of fraternizing with either party, the possibility that the alleged fraternization is only an exchange of social amenities between acquaintences is ever present. For example, in *Queen City Foundry, Inc.,*[3] the regional director found that infrequent exchanges between the Board agent conducting the election and a union representative did not constitute a substantial departure from Board procedures relating to the conduct of an election. The Board and union agent had engaged in small talk during the entire stay of the union representative. Conversation between the two began upon the arrival of the Board agent, and continued during a walk through the plant to the polling area. In addition, the organizer had assisted the agent in setting up a portable election booth. When the union representative left, he had observed the Board agent's car, and exchanged greetings with the agent's wife.

Although such familiarities might well raise suspicions of favoritism in the employer's mind, the regional director dismissed the conversations as ". . . nothing more than an exchange of amenities between two persons who had had previous contact in connection with their jobs."[5] Alternatively, the *Queen City* decision might be justified on the basis that the Board agent did not initiate, but was rather the "passive recipient" of the union representative's attentions. In such circumstances,

---

[3] *Id.*

[4] *Id.*

[5] *Id.*

the agent's conduct would be less likely to be construed by the employer as evidence of partiality.[6]

If the alleged misconduct of the agent in *Queen City* was insufficient to raise material objections concerning his neutrality, under what circumstances will an agent's conduct tend to destroy confidence in the Board's election process? In 1967, the Board formulated a minimum standard of conduct expected of all Board agents in their dealings with either party to a representation election.

In *Athbro Precision Engineering Corp.*,[7] the NLRB set aside an election because of conduct on the part of the Board agent in charge which could be construed as partial by an independent observer. Upon the completion of the initial polling period of the "split-session" election, an employee, who had already voted, observed the Board agent drinking beer with one of the union's representatives in a nearby cafe.[8] The employer, upon discovery of this incident, filed timely objections with the regional director, alleging that the behavior of the Board agent gave an appearance of irregularity to the conduct of the election. Although the regional director agreed on principle with the employer's claim that Board agents should not fraternize with representatives of one of the parties during the hiatus between balloting, he found that the objection was insufficient to set aside the election.[9]

The Board, however, directed a second election even though the employer had neither alleged that the conduct violated the integrity of the ballot box, nor that the conduct had influenced the four employees who cast ballots in the second session.[10]

---

[6] *Cf.* NLRB v. Dobbs Houses, Inc., 435 F.2d 704, 76 L.R.R.M. 2120 (5th Cir. 1970), wherein the court refused to invalidate an election where a Board agent made statements partial to the union in answer to questions posed by the employer's observer. In enforcing the Board's order, the court stated:

> An employer cannot through *his* agent lead the Board Agent to make improper statements and then rely on such statements to void the election without a showing of prejudice. *Id.* at 706, 76 L.R.R.M. at 2121.

[7] 166 N.L.R.B. 966, 65 L.R.R.M. 1699 (1967).

[8] *Id.*, 65 L.R.R.M. at 1699.

[9] *Id.*, 65 L.R.R.M. at 1699.

[10] *Id.*, 65 L.R.R.M. at 1699.

Instead, the Board reasoned that:

> The commission of an act by a Board agent conducting an election which tends to destroy confidence in the Board's election process, or which could reasonably be interpreted as impugning the election standards we seek to maintain, is a sufficient basis for setting aside that election.[11]

Although the Board's formulation is vague, several factors do stand out as guidelines for determining acceptable behavior by a Board agent. The decision indicates that misconduct by a Board agent, sufficient to invalidate an election, need only exhibit a "tendency to destroy confidence in," or "reasonably impugn election standards." In addition, the objecting party need not prove that such behavior has materially affected the outcome of the election.

Subsequently, the union sought and obtained an injunction against the Board's ruling from the District Court of the District of Columbia.[12] Disregarding the Board's claim of need to internally police itself, the court found that since the behavior of the Board agent neither affected the outcome of the election nor did it provide an extra advantage to either party, the election was valid and the union was entitled to certification.[13] Holding that the Board's refusal to grant certification had been arbitrary and capricious conduct in violation of Section 9(c)(1), the court ordered the employer to bargain with the now certified union.[14]

The Board declined to appeal the court's injunction, and accepted the district court's order as the law of the case.[15] Subsequently, the NLRB found *Athbro* in violation of its duty to bargain, as the company still maintained that the union had been unlawfully certified.[16] Athbro appealed the unfair labor practice finding to the Court of Appeals for the First Circuit

---

[11] *Id.*, 65 L.R.R.M. at 1699.

[12] IUE v. NLRB, 67 L.R.R.M. 2361 (D.D.C. 1968).

[13] *Id.* at 2363.

[14] *Id.*

[15] Athbro Precision Engineering Corp., 171 N.L.R.B. 21, 68 L.R.R.M. 1001 (1968).

[16] Athbro Precision Engineering Corp., 173 N.L.R.B. 995, 69 L.R.R.M. 1512 (1968).

which upheld the Board order.[17] The circuit court's holding, however, did not constitute an approval of the district court's declaratory judgment.[18] Indeed, the court stated that the original Board decision was correct.[19] In other circumstances,[20] the circuit court implied, it would have held that since the "Board's public image provides the basis for its existence," the NLRB's role in supervising representation elections should not be limited to mere ballot counting, but should extend to establishing procedures and safeguards to insure fairness.[21]

Shortly after the Board's first decision in *Athbro,* it again faced the issue of fraternization in *Delta Drilling Co.*[22] There, the employer filed an objection based upon alleged misconduct that occurred when the Board agent conducting the election stopped off at the motel room of a union representative to "freshen up" while driving between polling places located at a number of drilling rigs maintained by the employer.[23] The Board upheld the determination of the regional director not to set aside the election on the grounds of the employer's allegations.

The Court of Appeals for the Fifth Circuit, however, denied enforcement of the Board's subsequent bargaining order on the grounds that the Board, in upholding the election, had departed from the policy it had announced in *Athbro* and thereby violated the understanding of the parties in entering into a consent election agreement.[24] Before the court of appeals,

---

[17] NLRB v. Athbro Precision Engineering Corp., 423 F.2d 573, 73 L.R.R.M. 2355 (1st Cir. 1970).

[18] *Id.* at 575, 73 L.R.R.M. at 2356.

[19] *Id.,* 73 L.R.R.M. at 2356.

[20] The "other circumstances" alluded to by the court referred to the procedure followed by Athbro in litigating its claim. Apparently, the court felt that Athbro's failure to appeal directly to the circuit courts following the issuance of the district court injunction was a dilatory tactic calculated to delay either certification or an order directing a second election. *Id.* at 575, 73 L.R.R.M. at 2357.

[21] *Id.* at 575, 73 L.R.R.M. at 2356. *See generally* NLRB v. A. J. Tower, 329 U.S. 324, 330, 19 L.R.R.M. 2128, 2131 (1946).

[22] 169 N.L.R.B. 617, 67 L.R.R.M. 1251 (1968).

[23] *Id.,* 67 L.R.R.M. at 1251.

[24] The consent agreement provided that the determinations of the regional director would be "final and binding upon any question . . . relating in any

the Board had argued that the *Athbro* decision was distinguishable because the "motel stopover was observed, not by an eligible voter, . . . but by a Company supervisor," thereby insulating the employees, whose rights were primarily at stake in the election.[25] Further, the Board's brief stated that ". . . Board's refusal to apply these principles here [*Delta Drilling*], where no impairment of *voter confidence* in the election process is shown, is not a failure to conform to the *Athbro* policy, but rather, a declination to extend that policy."[26] The court, however, was plainly eager to sanction the Board's abortive attempt in *Athbro* to establish a high standard of impartiality to be maintained by Board agents conducting representation elections. Unlike the Board, the court felt no qualms in extending that policy to protect company supervisors, as well as eligible voters, from any impairment of confidence in the impartiality of the Board's agents.

Accordingly, the court interpreted the Board's policy in *Athbro* as entitling the employer, as well as the voters, to an election

---

manner to the election." It also provided that the election would be conducted in accordance with the Act, the Board's Rules and Regulations, and the "applicable procedures and policies of the Board." Delta Drilling Co. v. NLRB, 406 F.2d 109, 111-112, 70 L.R.R.M. 2272, 2274 (5th Cir. 1969).

Pursuant to the Board's Rules and Regulations, objections to the conduct of consent elections are considered "on the basis of an administrative investigation or, if it appears . . . that substantial and material factual issues exist . . . (a) hearing on said issues." 29 C.F.R. § 102.69(d), *see also* NLRB *Statements of Procedure*, 29 C.F.R. § 101.19(a)(4). Thus, where the parties have entered into a consent election agreement, the regional director's findings are binding unless they are arbitrary or capricious, or contrary to Board policy or statutory requirements. *See* Manning, Maxwell & Moore, Inc. v. NLRB, 324 F.2d 857, 858, 54 L.R.R.M. 2659, 2660 (5th Cir. 1963); NLRB v. J. H. Matthews & Co., 342 F.2d 129, 131-32, 58 L.R.R.M. 2392, 2394 (3d Cir.), *cert. denied*, 382 U.S. 832, 60 L.R.R.M. 2234 (1964). The purposes served by refraining from review of determinations pursuant to a consent agreement are: to provide for final settlements of disputes without delay, NLRB v. Continental Nut Co., 395 F.2d 830, 832, 68 L.R.R.M. 2350, 2352 (9th Cir. 1969); prevent frivolous objections from becoming dilatory tactics, Sonoco Products Co. v. NLRB, 399 F.2d 835, 839, 69 L.R.R.M. 2037, 2040 (9th Cir. 1968); and fulfill the statutory requirement that the objections be resolved prior to the establishment of the bargaining relationship, NLRB v. O.K. Van Storage, Inc., 297 F.2d 74, 76, 49 L.R.R.M. 2218, 2220 (5th Cir. 1961).

[25] Brief for NLRB at 9, Delta Drilling Co. v. NLRB, 406 F.2d 109, 70 L.R.R.M. 2276 (5th Cir. 1969).

[26] *Id.* at 14-15 (emphasis added).

conducted "free of so much as the appearance of evil." [27] And since the employer in *Delta* had entered into a consent agreement,

> . . . relying upon the unflinching preservation of Board policy, [he] is entitled to the benefit of that reliance, especially when the questionable activity of a Board agent occurs without [the employer's] knowledge or participation. [28]

As further support for the imposition of a broad requirement of ethical appearances in the conduct of elections, the court indicated the belief that such a standard was necessary to preserve the practice of consent election agreements:

> If the benefits and advantages of consent elections are to be maintained, preserved, and utilized, the employer is entitled to that same degree of confidence in the election process as counsel concedes the employee is entitled to have. [29]

In cases involving fraternization, it may be difficult to justify the necessity for a second election because of the economic and psychological burdens it places upon the parties. After all, it was the conduct of the Board's representative, not that of employer or union, that formed the basis for the objection. Further, as illustrated by *Athbro* and *Delta Drilling*, the alleged misconduct need not even affect the outcome of the election. Quite logically, the question that arises is: why must the parties pay the penalty for what amounts to a Board deficiency? In terms of labor policy, the answer is implicit in the nature and implementation of the Act itself. As the circuit court in *Athbro* quite accurately observed, "the Board's public image provides the basis for its existence." [30] Consequently, it is the integrity of the Board's election processes, and derivatively, all of the Board's administrative functions, that are at issue. Surely it is absurd for the Board to insist upon the maintenance of

---

[27] 406 F.2d at 114, 70 L.R.R.M. at 2276.

[28] *Id.*, 70 L.R.R.M. at 2275. Chronologically, the court's assumption that *Athbro* was the applicable Board policy at the time the employer signed the consent agreement is refutable. Indeed, it is impossible that even the regional director in *Delta Drilling* could have relied upon *Athbro* because his decision was announced on November 7, 1966, while *Athbro* was not decided until August 1, 1967. Further, the Board determination in *Delta Drilling*, February 2, 1968, followed upon the heels of the district court's injunction, January 17, 1968, of the Board order in *Athbro*.

[29] 406 F.2d at 114, 70 L.R.R.M. at 2275.

[30] 423 F.2d at 575, 73 L.R.R.M. at 2356.

"laboratory conditions" by the parties and ignore activity by its agents that may create the impression that the "experiment" has been rigged. As Member Kennedy has recently stated

> When unions and employers invest substantial time, effort, and money in an organizational campaign, it is incumbent upon the Board to conduct an election in a manner which inspires confidence in the impartiality and competence of the Board and its agents. *There is no function or mission of this agency of greater importance than running fair elections.*[31]

Improper Handling of Ballots and the Ballot Box

The Board has consistently held that its agents may maintain possession of ballots and the ballot box during an election.[32] Nonetheless, because the agent is called upon to maintain order and resolve disputes which arise during the actual polling period, his surveillance of the ballot box may be less than ideal at all times. In addition, the necessity of conducting a "split-session" election or one by mail ballot often extends the period of time for which he is charged by the Board to maintain carefully his custodianship of the ballot box. Consequently, the involved nature of certain types of elections increases the likelihood that irregularities in the Board's election processes may occur. Indeed, the Board has set aside elections wherein the ballots have been mishandled,[33] or doubt has been cast upon the integrity of the ballot box because it was either unsealed,[34] or unattended[35] for a period of time.

Maintaining the Integrity of the Ballot Box. Although there has been extensive litigation involving alleged lapses in the integrity of the ballot box, no uniform standard has emerged which can be readily applied in all cases. For example, the court in *Polymers, Inc. v. NLRB,*[36] attempted to rest its decision

---

[31] Wald Sound, Inc., 203 N.L.R.B. No. 61, 83 L.R.R.M. 1125, 1127 (1973).

[32] *E.g.*, Continental Smelting & Refining Co., 117 N.L.R.B. 1388, 40 L.R.R.M. 1015 (1957); Fairmont Mills, Inc., 87 N.L.R.B. 21, 25 L.R.R.M. 1068 (1949); Robbins Tire & Rubber Co., 72 N.L.R.B. 157, 19 L.R.R.M. 1154 (1947).

[33] New York Telephone Co., 109 N.L.R.B. 788, 34 L.R.R.M. 1441 (1954).

[34] Hook Drugs, Inc., 117 N.L.R.B. 846, 39 L.R.R.M. 1331 (1957); Tidelands Marine Services, Inc., 116 N.L.R.B. 1222, 38 L.R.R.M. 1444 (1956).

[35] Austill Waxed Paper Co., 169 N.L.R.B. 1109, 67 L.R.R.M. 1366 (1968).

[36] 414 F.2d 999, 71 L.R.R.M. 3107 (2d Cir.), *cert. denied,* 396 U.S. 1010, 73 L.R.R.M. 2121 (1969).

on the basis of a review of prior cases of objections arising from the alleged failure of Board agents to adhere to appropriate safeguards in handling the ballot boxes. Failing to find a common denominator, the court hedged, stating:

> This line of conflicting precedents reflects the principle that each possibility must be assessed upon its own unique facts and circumstances, under expert analysis by the Board, to determine whether to certify or set aside.[37]

In reliance upon this Board "expertise," the court adopted the NLRB's holding which set forth the requisite standard of behavior for a Board agent in handling the ballot box. Although the agent in charge had not complied with all of the Board's own recommended procedures for sealing and guarding the ballot box between voting sessions, the Board had certified the election, concluding that "no reasonable possibility of irregularity" was present.[38] Enlarging upon this theme, the Board stated:

> We do not think however, that the word "possibility" could ever be construed in this context to have the connotation of "conceivable." The concept of reasonableness of the possibility must be imported into this test in order for it to have meaning.[39]

Consequently, the Board had declined even to hold a hearing on the employer's objection.

The "reasonable possibility" approach taken in *Polymers,* however, is contrary to the standard set forth by the Board in *Austill Waxed Paper Co.*[40] In *Austill,* the Board set aside an election in which a ballot box had been left unsealed and unattended for approximately two to five minutes.[41] In reaching its conclusion, the Board stated that any objection to the above circumstances was not the "proper subject for litigation on and

---

[37] *Id.* at 1004, 71 L.R.R.M. at 3109.

[38] *Id.* at 1002, 71 L.R.R.M. at 3108.

[39] *Id.,* 71 L.R.R.M. at 3109.

[40] 169 N.L.R.B. 1109, 67 L.R.R.M. 1366 (1968). *Cf.* Tidelands Marine Services, Inc., 116 N.L.R.B. 1222, 38 L.R.R.M. 1444 (1956); New York Telephone Co., 109 N.L.R.B. 788, 34 L.R.R.M. 1441 (1954).

[41] 169 N.L.R.B. at 1109 & n.2, 67 L.R.R.M. at 1366. The ballot box had been left unattended by election officials when an altercation occurred outside the polling place, drawing away the agents' attention.

[sic] *ad hoc* basis." [42] Consequently, the Board ordered a new election rather than engaging in "speculat[ion] on whether something did or did not occur while the ballot box was unattended." [43] The rationale of the Board in *Austill* was twofold. First, it indicated that the very fact of the unattended ballot box cast a "doubt or cloud over the integrity of the ballot box itself." [44] Secondly, alluding to the Board's responsibility "to certify to the validity of its own balloting procedures," the Board indicated that it must be free from doubt that the highest standards of integrity have been maintained before an election could be certified. [45]

No profitable comparison of the standards annunicated in *Polymers* and *Austill* can be made in order to formulate one overriding principle. The case-by-case approach advocated in *Polymers* is rejected in *Austill* in favor of a *per se* rule requiring strict compliance with all proper ballot-handling procedures. Clearly, a uniform Board policy for evaluating election irregularities concerning an unattended or unsealed ballot box is nonexistent. As a result of formulating two sets of standards, the Board is afforded the opportunity first to reach a decision, and then to support it with the reasoning appropriate to that result. To set aside an election, the Board will reiterate its policy in terms of electoral integrity, [46] the rationale advanced in *Austill;* to uphold an election, it will resort to the "reasonable possibility" approach of *Polymers.* [47]

The objecting party has the initial burden of proof in charging that some irregularity in the election process has occurred which impairs the integrity of the ballot box. [48] The difficulty in de-

---

[42] *Id.* at 1109, 67 L.R.R.M. at 1366.

[43] *Id.,* 67 L.R.R.M. at 1366.

[44] *Id.,* 67 L.R.R.M. at 1366.

[45] *Id.* at 1109-1110, 67 L.R.R.M. at 1366.

[46] *E.g.,* Hook Drugs, Inc., 117 N.L.R.B. 846, 39 L.R.R.M. 1331 (1957); Tube Distributors Co., Inc., 113 N.L.R.B. 381, 36 L.R.R.M. 1306 (1955); New York Telephone Co., 109 N.L.R.B. 788, 34 L.R.R.M. 1441 (1954).

[47] *E.g.,* Capitan Drilling Co., 167 N.L.R.B. 144, 66 L.R.R.M. 1015 (1967); General Electric Co., 119 N.L.R.B. 944, 41 L.R.R.M. 1206 (1957); Filtrol Corp., 91 N.L.R.B. 93, 26 L.R.R.M. 1458 (1950); Clark Shoe Co., 83 N.L.R.B. 782, 24 L.R.R.M. 1136 (1949).

[48] "[T]he party seeking a hearing [must] clearly demonstrate that factual issues exist which can only be resolved by an evidentiary hearing. . . ."

termining what *quantum* of evidence is necessary to meet that burden, however, is illustrated by the problems posed by the *Austill* and *Polymers* cases. In both cases, the Board denied an evidentiary hearing on the alleged irregularity. This denial is inexplicable, since in each instance, it could have been dispositive of the merits of the objection.

A more generous policy with respect to the granting of hearings in such cases would provide a desirable alternative to the frustrating dualism exhibited in the *Polymers* and *Austill* cases. Thus, a hearing could be granted whenever the preliminary evidence showed that some breach of proper election procedure made tampering a physical possibility.[49] At the hearing, a factual determination would be made as to whether or not actual tampering had occurred. Since this latter determination, like any other finding of fact, would depend upon the circumstances and inherent possibilities of the case, the standard applied at this stage might actually be more lenient than the *Polymers* "reasonable possibility" test, but by giving the objecting party a "day in court" rather than simply brushing aside its agents' alleged default, the Board would do much to preserve the parties' confidence in the fairness of its procedures.[50]

The use of this physical possibility standard in *Polymers, Inc.* would have resulted in the direction of a hearing, since the

---

NLRB v. Tennessee Packers, Frosty Morn. Div., 379 F.2d 172, 178, 65 L.R.R.M. 2619, 2622 (6th Cir.), *cert. denied,* 389 U.S. 958, 66 L.R.R.M. 2507 (1967). The implication of the requirement is twofold. On one hand, a hearing is unnecessary when "the Board accepts the factual allegations of [the charging party] and no additional facts remain to be developed." 414 F.2d at 1005, 71 L.R.R.M. at 3110 (2d Cir. 1969); NLRB v. Bata Shoe Co., 377 F.2d 821, 65 L.R.R.M. 2318 (4th Cir.), *cert. denied,* 389 U.S. 917, 66 L.R.R.M. 2370 (1967). On the other hand, to be entitled to a hearing, the objection must contain *prima facie* evidence which would warrant setting aside the election. *Cf.* NLRB v. Mattison Machine Works, 365 U.S. 123, 47 L.R.R.M. 2437 (1961). The requisite burden of proof is not met by "conclusory allegations," "nebulous and declaratory assertions," or "equivocal hearsay," but rather by evidence of "specific events about specific people." *See generally* NLRB v. Difco Laboratories, Inc., 389 F.2d 663, 67 L.R.R.M. 2585 (6th Cir.), *cert. denied,* 393 U.S. 828, 69 L.R.R.M. 2434 (1968); Macomb Pottery Co. v. NLRB, 376 F.2d 450, 452, 65 L.R.R.M. 2055, 2056 (7th Cir. 1967); United States Rubber Co. v. NLRB, 373 F.2d 602, 606, 64 L.R.R.M. 2393, 2396 (5th Cir. 1967).

[49] *Cf.* NLRB v. Lowell Corrugated Container Corp., 431 F.2d 1196, 1197, 75 L.R.R.M. 2346, 2347 (1st Cir. 1970); Wald Sound, Inc., 203 N.L.R.B. No. 61, 83 L.R.R.M. 1125, 1127 (1973) (Member Kennedy, dissenting).

[50] *See* Peoples Drug Stores, 202 N.L.R.B. No. 166, 83 L.R.R.M. 1763 (1973).

employer had made a preliminary showing of procedural deficiencies which made tampering with the ballot box physically possible.[51] However, unless a showing of complicity on the part of the Board agent had been made at the hearing, it is unlikely that a finding of actual tampering would have resulted.[52] Therefore, the election would probably have been sustained.

In *Austill*, once the possibility of tampering had been established because the box had been left unattended, evidence could have been produced to show whether or not any other adequate safeguards against tampering were present. For example, in *K. Barthelmes Mfg. Co., Inc.*,[53] although the box was unattended, it was proven that the ballot box was inside a trailer while the observers and agent who had vacated the trailer for a conference over challenges, stood in front of the only door.[54]

Ballot Mishandling. In addition to their more general duty of maintaining the integrity of the ballot box, Board agents are also held accountable for the security of individual ballots prior to the tally. For example, in *New York Telephone Co.*[55] 25 percent of the ballots received in a vote by mail were mislaid during the initial count and were not found until three days later. Since the number of missing ballots was sufficient to affect the outcome of the election and the temporary loss created grave questions as to the security of the ballots, the Board set aside the election.[56]

---

[51] 414 F.2d at 1002, 71 L.R.R.M. at 3108. In *Polymers* the employer alleged that the following irregularities had occurred: (1) the ballot box had been sealed with easily removable tape; (2) the requisite signatures of Board agents were not continued onto the surface of the ballot box; (3) the tape did not extend onto the cardboard surface of the box; (4) the agents failed to obtain approval of the observers as to the sufficiency of the seal; and (5) the agent failed to retain personal custody of the box between polling periods.

[52] The case of NLRB v. Capitan Drilling Co., 408 F.2d 676, 70 L.R.R.M. 3258 (5th Cir. 1969) that was asserted as controlling by the court in *Polymers, Inc.* also involved an alleged irregularity, which although physically possible, was dependent upon a showing that any tampering could only have occurred through complicity by the Board agent.

[53] 71 N.L.R.B. 513, 19 L.R.R.M. 1026 (1946).

[54] *Id.* at 516, 19 L.R.R.M. at 1026.

[55] 109 N.L.R.B. 788, 34 L.R.R.M. 1441 (1954).

[56] *Id.* at 790, 34 L.R.R.M. at 1442. *See also* Kerona Plastics Extrusion Co., 196 N.L.R.B. No. 179, 80 L.R.R.M. 1231 (1971).

As in the case of ballots which have been temporarily mislaid, a permanent loss of ballots sufficient in number to affect the outcome of the election will result in a Board order for a new election. In *Tube Distributors Co., Inc.*,[57] the Board, relying on its prior decision in *New York Telephone Co.*, ordered a new election when it was discovered that certain ballots placed in challenge envelopes could not be found.

In another case involving challenge ballots, *D & N Delivery Corp.*,[58] the Board set aside an election in which the regional director's behavior was deemed to have prejudiced any attempt of conducting a postelection hearing. Following an election in which 9 of 15 ballots cast were challenged by the union, the regional director sustained a challenge to one ballot, ordering that the remaining ballots be opened and counted. The union objected to the regional director's method of handling the challenge ballots, claiming that the opening was premature and, therefore, constituted an irregularity of sufficient consequence to set aside the election.[59]

In vacating the election, the Board reasoned that although its Rules and Regulations state generally that a request for review of the election shall not stay any action taken by the regional director, he is not permitted, in absence of a waiver to "count any challenge ballots until the Board has ruled upon any request for review which may be filed."[60] Concluding that the "breach of the Rules and Regulations may create the appearance that the Board has prejudged the issues," which were the subject matter of the union's objections, it ordered a new election.[61]

As is apparent, the Board utilizes a different standard in evaluating any irregularity concerning the security of its ballots than it does in an alleged breach in the integrity of the ballot box. On one hand, irregularities in the handling of the ballots become significant only when the number of ballots affected are sufficient to influence the results of the election. On the other

---

[57] 113 N.L.R.B. 381, 36 L.R.R.M. 1306 (1955). *See also* American Export Lines, 84 N.L.R.B. 134, 24 L.R.R.M. 1238 (1949).

[58] 201 N.L.R.B. No. 37, 82 L.R.R.M. 1208 (1973).

[59] *Id.*, 82 L.R.R.M. at 1209.

[60] *Id.*, 82 L.R.R.M. at 1209.

[61] *Id.*, 82 L.R.R.M. at 1209.

hand, such a showing is not a prerequisite to vacating an
election when the integrity of the ballot box is questioned. The
difference in standards reflects the difference in the issues raised.
In the case of the former, only the validity of a specific number
of ballots, which are readily identifiable, is at stake. The latter
situation, however, involves a threat to the overall appearance
of neutrality of the Board's election process; hence, the potential impact of such a breach on individual voters is irrelevant.

Abuses of Discretion by Board Agents in Conducting Elections

One of the principal duties of the Board agent in charge of
an election is to ensure the unit employees the opportunity to
vote. When a Board agent denies an eligible employee's right
to vote, through either lackadaisical or inflexible methods amounting to an abuse of discretion, the election may be set aside.

In *NLRB v. Bata Shoe Co.*,[62] the Court of Appeals for the
Fourth Circuit refused to enforce a Board order certifying
an election that had been conducted in a remarkably slipshod
manner. At the stipulated closing hour of the polls, the Board
agent directed the last three employees in line to ensure that
no other employees were permitted to enter the voting line.
Nonetheless, at least thirty employees did subsequently get
on the end of the line, while one employee, who arrived one
hour and fifteen minutes late, was permitted to vote without
question. On the other hand, another employee who was in line
before the closing hour, stepped out to go to the washroom
and when he returned was denied the opportunity to cast even
a challenge ballot.[63] The court refused to validate the results
of the election due to the irregularities in the electoral process
caused by substantial omissions by the Board agent which
precluded all of the employees from a fair and equal opportunity
to vote.[64]

Although the careless conduct condemned in *Bata Shoe Co.*
provides a prominent illustration of abuse of discretion, in
Hanford Sentinel, Inc.[65] the Board set aside an election in which

---

[62] 377 F.2d 821, 65 L.R.R.M. 2318 (4th Cir.), *cert. denied*, 389 U.S. 917,
66 L.R.R.M. 2370 (1967).

[63] 377 F.2d at 831-32, 65 L.R.R.M. at 2326.

[64] *Id.*, 65 L.R.R.M. at 2326.

[65] 163 N.L.R.B. 1004, 64 L.R.R.M. 1482 (1967).

the agent's conduct was literally letter perfect. In that case, two eligible employees of the newspaper company, who were on the way to the darkroom for film processing, overheard the Board agent's announcement that the polls were about to open. The employees asked the agent if it would be possible for them to vote slightly ahead of time. The agent responded negatively, indicating they could either wait until the polls opened or come back during the scheduled voting period. The two employees decided to complete their darkroom work first, but when they appeared to vote they found that the polls had just closed. The Board agent indicated he was sorry they had missed their opportunity to cast their ballots, but stated that nothing could be done because the polls had closed.[66]

The regional director found that since the polls had been open as scheduled,[67] both employees had read the notice of the election, and the employees could have interrupted their work to vote, there was no abuse of discretion to vote.[68] The Board, however, reversed the regional director's determination, stating that the Board agent should have allowed the two employees to cast their ballots as a proper exercise of his discretion.[69] The Board emphasized that only the special circumstances involved caused it to reverse the regional director's decision. The Board cited three factors contributing to the special circumstances: (1) the brief duration of the election period; (2) the fact that the agent was aware of the two employees' prior request to vote; and (3) the fact that the employees' second attempt occurred only minutes after the polls closed and before the ballot box had been opened or the votes tallied.[70] Under these conditions, the Board concluded that the only adequate remedy available was to order a second election.

Although the Board based its decision in *Hanford Sentinel* on the Board agent's exercise of discretion, the real effect of the decision is to undercut any discretion on the part of the

---

[66] *Id.*, 64 L.R.R.M. at 1482.

[67] The duration of the polling period was extremely brief, lasting only 15 minutes.

[68] 163 N.L.R.B. at 1004, 64 L.R.R.M. at 1482.

[69] *Id.* at 1005, 64 L.R.R.M. at 1482.

[70] *Id.*, 64 L.R.R.M. at 1482.

agent. The very nature of a discretionary standard is to allow latitude for the agent in charge to decide whether extraordinary circumstances are present which justify a departure from rigid application of the usual election rules. To hold that the agent was *required* to grant an exception in *Hanford Sentinel* where the loss of opportunity was primarily the fault of the employees themselves, is tantamount to saying he had no real discretion over the matter at all. For the Board to so freely substitute its judgment for that of the agent in charge simply encourages postelection litigation, since the possibility of a successful objection and second election is always present. Although allowing the Board agent to employ challenge ballots in a situation wherein he has a good faith doubt as to the allowable extent of his discretion has a certain surface appeal,[71] its rationale is both impractical[72] and contrary to the Board's election procedures.[73]

Discretionary action by a Board agent is sometimes necessary, even if it is exercised in direct violation of NLRB established election procedures. For example, recently in *NLRB v. Schwartz Bros., Inc.,*[74] the Court of Appeals for the District of Columbia refused to set aside an election, although the agent conducting the election violated a provision of the NLRB Field Manual.

The literal language of section 11338 of the NLRB Field Manual prohibits ". . . challenges in behalf of the parties, whether

---

[71] For example, the agent in *Hanford Sentinel* might have utilized challenge ballots for the two employees. Hence, the Board could have determined that since the number of challenged ballots was sufficient to affect the outcome of the election, and the agent acted within his discretion in permitting them to cast challenged ballots, the ballots could be opened, thereby obviating the need for a second election.

[72] *See, e.g.,* NLRB v. Bata Shoe Co., 377 F.2d 821, 65 L.R.R.M. 2318 (4th Cir. 1967). Considering that the agent in this case did not detect the tardy appearance of some 30 voters even though he caught one voter who had stepped out of line to use the washroom, it is highly unlikely that he could have properly used challenged ballots—assuming he could have found the right voters to challenge.

[73] *E.g.,* T & G Mfg., Inc., 173 N.L.R.B. 1503, 70 L.R.R.M. 1038 (1969). In this case, the Board voided an agreement of the parties to put a particular ballot in a challenge envelope on the basis that the choice of the voter was known, creating ". . . the very opportunity for collusion, coercion, and election abuse the Board is committed to prevent." *Id.* at 1504, 70 L.R.R.M. at 1038.

[74] 475 F.2d 927, 82 L.R.R.M. 2376 (D.C. Cir. 1973).

or not such parties have observers present." [75] In *Schwartz*, the agent, accepting a roster of desired union challenges, did in fact challenge the votes of the seven employees listed therein. The employed filed timely objections to the agent's conduct charging that the challenges made by the Board representatives on behalf of the union tended to destroy the desired neutrality and objectivity of the conduct of the election by implication to the employees that the Board favors the union. [76] The court rejected the employer's objections, fashioning three guidelines to be followed in similar cases. In condensed version, these standards are: (1) the Board agent must be completely impartial in stating the challenges; (2) he may only make challenges when necessitated by an unexpected occurrence; and (3) the charging party assumes the burden of proof in showing partiality. [77] Briefly, the procedural result of this decision is that the presumption of partiality arising from an agent's failure to adhere to section 11338, may be negated upon the showing of an unexpected, necessary use of discretion by the Board agent, thereby shifting the burden of proof to the objecting party.

In summarizing the discretionary action cases, it is clear that concrete rules of election procedure are not practical in all situations. In order to profitably conduct elections that will yield results, rather than becoming mere exercises in futility, the agent must be given some degree of discretion. Therefore, only when an agent's conduct amounts to an unreasonable abuse of discretion, when viewed in the context of the totality of the election process, should the election be set aside.

Partisan Statements By Board Agents

Because Board agents are entrusted with the direct supervision of representation elections, they have the primary responsibility for maintaining the fairness and impartiality of

---

[75] NLRB Field Manual § 11338.

[76] *See* Kerona Plastics Extrusions Co., 196 N.L.R.B. No. 179, 80 L.R.R.M. 1231 (1972). In *Kerona* the Board agreed to set aside an election upon the employer's contention that the inadvertent early closure of the polls by the Board agent gave rise to rumors that the Board representatives favored the employer thereby creating an atmosphere of confusion, bias, and prejudice against the employer.

[77] 475 F.2d at 930, 82 L.R.R.M. at 2378.

the Board's election machinery. The unique position of the Board agent, therefore, should not be used by the agent as a forum for airing his personal views regarding either the desired outcome of the election or the character of the participants. The purpose of the representation election is to ascertain the wishes of the employees regarding self-organization, which will in turn be binding upon the parties. Thus, the Board agent has no personal stake in the outcome of the election, and any conduct on his part that might be construed as favoring one party over the other must be closely scrutinized. Recently, in *NLRB v. Dobbs Houses, Inc.*,[78] the Court of Appeals for the Fifth Circuit, upheld a Board determination,[79] which had refused to set aside an election wherein the agent in charge had made remarks in support of the union. The employer had charged that the electoral process was tainted because during the balloting the agent had told the observers that he felt the union would win and that if they did it would "do the people a lot of good." [80]

The gravamen of the employer's appeal was that in making his determination, the regional director had applied the wrong standard of review. Instead of finding that the election was not tainted by the agent's behavior "because it caused no prejudice in the voting," the company contended that the *Athbro* rationale [81] should have been utilized in condemning the conduct of the agent.

Although neither the Board nor the company had explicitly referred to *Athbro* or any of its progeny,[82] the court indicated that the standards annunciated in those cases were accurate statements of the law whenever the question of alleged interference by the Board's agent with the integrity and imparitality of Board election procedures arose. The court then attempted to apply the *Athbro* standard of misconduct which it stated to be a "public act inconsistent with the Board agent's required

78 435 F.2d 704, 76 L.R.R.M. 2120 (5th Cir. 1970).

79 172 N.L.R.B. 1781, 69 L.R.R.M. 1171 (1968).

80 435 F.2d at 705, 76 L.R.R.M. at 2120. In addition, the agent stated that the union represented about 20 places and was trying to get more.

81 *See* discussion of the *Athbro* rationale at pp. 341-46, *supra*.

82 *E.g.*, Delta Drilling Co. v. NLRB, 406 F.2d 109, 70 L.R.R.M. 2276 (5th Cir. 1969).

impartiality." [83] In doing so, *Athbro* was distinguished upon its facts. First, the court found that the alleged improper acts of the agent in *Dobbs Houses, Inc.* were not as public as those in *Athbro*. Secondly, the court felt it reasonable to distinguish between acts of fraternization and expressions of personal feelings to limited audiences. Finally, the court determined that because the agent's remarks were not part of a proselytizing effort on his part, but merely given in answer to the employer's observer who had solicited the agent's response, the statements had no evidentiary value in establishing that the agent's attitude was biased. [84]

The first two factors mentioned by the court deserve little weight. The public nature of the statements is of limited value in determining their propriety. [85] Instead, the issue under *Athbro* is whether the agent's actions failed to maintain the integrity and neutrality of the Board's election procedures, *not* the potential of such behavior on the outcome of the election. In similar cases, the number of individuals who were witnesses to the alleged misconduct, [86] and the identity of these individuals [87] has been considered immaterial to the objection.

Moreover, why there should be any distinction between fraternization and prejudicial statements is unexplained by the court, except for its comment that "the former smacks much more of irregularity than the latter." [88] As a practical matter, it is difficult to imagine why an employer (or any other party to an election) would perceive a greater possibility of irregularity. He is confronted on one hand, by an agent who indicates he has prounion sentiments, and on the other hand, by an agent who drank beer with a union representative or who briefly stopped

---

[83] 435 F.2d at 705, 76 L.R.R.M. at 2121.

[84] *Id.* at 705-706, 76 L.R.R.M. at 2121.

[85] Although the improper conduct condemned in *Athbro* could be deemed "public" because the fraternization occurred in a cafe, the misconduct in *Delta Drilling Co.* took place in a closed motel room.

[86] In *Athbro*, only one employee, who had already voted, was a witness to the improper behavior. 166 N.L.R.B. at 966, 65 L.R.R.M. at 1699.

[87] In *Delta Drilling Co.*, the court indicated that since the conduct itself was partial, it was irrelevant that the witness had been a company supervisor, rather than an employee. 406 F.2d at 113, 70 L.R.R.M. at 2275.

[88] 435 F.2d at 706, 76 L.R.R.M. at 2121.

in at the representative's motel room. Either of these situations is serious enough to raise an inference of partiality on the part of the agent and probably casts a shadow of doubt over the integrity at the election itself. While the latter two of the foregoing acts of misconduct are suspicious, the former is almost self-indicting.

Only the final rationale—*i.e.* that the agent's statements were in a response to the questions of the employer's own observer—'s a valid ground for upholding the Board's certification. The agent's remarks were not self-initiated or even an "improvoked indiscretion," but rather elicited by another party. As the court states, "[a]n employer cannot through *his* agent lead the Board agent to make improper statements and then rely on such statements to void the election without a showing of prejudice." [89] Only on this ground is *Dobbs Houses, Inc.* distinguishable from the *Athbro* rationale.

Since the court in *Dobbs Houses, Inc.* relied on other rationale in addition to that discussed immediately above, it left open the question of whether the election would have been set aside had the Board agent volunteered the prejudicial statements, absent any inductment by the employer. In support of its conclusion, the court had said that ". . . the Board agent's improper statements were not part of a proselytizing effort on his part or even a simple unprovoked indiscretion." [90] This dictum raises the following questions. In calling the statements improper, did the court mean that such statements, standing alone, could constitute a showing of partiality similar to the proscribed conduct in *Delta Drilling Co.* and *Athbro?* Or, in the alternative, is the requisite impartiality destroyed only if coupled with a showing of attempted influence upon the voters?

A partial answer to this question was available as early as 1948. In that year, in a three to two decision, the Board in *Craddock-Terry Shoe Corp.*[91] overruled an employer's objections to the conduct of the agents conducting a representation election. In *Craddock,* the employer had protested that an employee who had been discharged for drunkenness several times and who was also intoxicated on the day of the election be not

---

[89] *Id.,* 76 L.R.R.M. at 2121.

[90] *Id.,* 76 L.R.R.M. at 2121.

[91] 80 N.L.R.B. 1237, 23 L.R.R.M. 1215 (1948).

allowed to vote. The agent let the employee vote anyway, although he had to be assisted into the voting booth. Later, two Board agents discussing the incident made remarks, which may have been heard by other employees, ridiculing the employer for raising the issue about the drunkenness of the voter.[92] In dismissing the objection, the majority stated that neither seeing the employee helped into the polls by the Board agent, or overhearing the allegedly derogatory statements would tend to restrain or influence the voters.[93]

Referring to these incidents in their dissent, Chairman Herzog and Member Gray said that "[a]s the integrity of the Board's own processes is involved, we would . . . apply a stricter standard to this case than our colleagues seem to think necessary."[94] Thus, as early as this, Board members indicated a willingness to take agents to task when issues of electoral integrity and neutrality were created by the agents of the Board itself.

In 1973, two additional cases arose in which allegedly partisan statements were attributable to Board agents. In both *Wabash Transformer Corp.*[95] and *Wald Sound, Inc.*,[96] Members Fanning and Penello, who comprised the majority in each case, found that although the agents' remarks were "unfortunate," the import of the statements did not destroy the appearance of the Board's neutrality. Dissenting in *Wabash Transformer*, Chairman Miller was unwilling to excuse "this particular deviation"[97]

---

[92] *Id.* at 1240-41, 23 L.R.R.M. at 1215. Since the NLRB has gone to great lengths to ensure what it has termed, "laboratory conditions," by means of myriad rules and regulations governing the conduct of the parties in a representation election, it is unfortunate, in some circumstances, that the attitude of certain employees vis-á-vis the election is less than ideal. Only recently, in Crown Machinery Co., 205 N.L.R.B. No. 49, 83 L.R.R.M. 1587 (1973), the Board in a two to one decision, upheld an election in which a number of employees, sufficient to affect the results, arrived at the polls in an intoxicated condition. In his dissent, Chairman Miller lamented the fact that ". . . the balloting was conducted in an atmosphere of crude joking, threats, and in general, fell considerably short of the orderly and serious-minded atmosphere which [the Board] earnestly [tries] to maintain as a standard for NLRB election." *Id.*, 83 L.R.R.M. at 1588.

[93] 80 N.L.R.B. at 1241, 23 L.R.R.M. at 1215.

[94] *Id.* at 1245, 23 L.R.R.M. at 1217.

[95] 205 N.L.R.B. No. 38, 83 L.R.R.M. 1545 (1973).

[96] 203 N.L.R.B. No. 61, 83 L.R.R.M. 1125 (1973).

[97] 205 N.L.R.B. No. 38, 83 L.R.R.M. at 1545.

on the majority grounds that the "Board's preelection notices and the employer's campaign literature . . . adequately neutralized any prejudicial effect the Board agents' statements may have [had] on the prospective voters." [98] Instead, Miller stated that he was:

> . . . of the view that where a representative of this Board, even unwittingly, fails to preserve not only the fact of neutrality, but also the appearance of neutrality, we must rerun the election.[99]

In *Wald Sound*, Member Kennedy, also in dissent, argued that allegedly prejudicial remarks by Board agents must be carefully scrutinized to determine whether they have destroyed the "confidence in the impartiality and competence of the Board and its agents." [100] He felt that at the very least, a hearing should be held to determine what the Board agent intended by the remark.[101] Urging his colleagues to consider the importance of maintaining the appearance of fairness in the Board's election processes, Member Kennedy indicated that he believed "[t]he re-running of an occasional election is a small price to pay for the preservation of public respect." [102]

In each of the foregoing cases, an agent of the Board made a partisan statement. It is not enough for the Board to dispose of these cases as involving only "unfortunate" remarks, for they are more, they impugn the integrity of the Board's election processes. In evaluating the coercive nature of statements by the parties to the election, a defense based upon the unfortunate nature of the remark would be quite unacceptable to the Board. For the same reasons, this explanation asserted on behalf of the Board's agents is unacceptable to the parties.

Concluding Remarks

Through the years, the Board has employed two different standards in determining whether to set aside an election because of a Board agent's alleged misconduct in the election

---

[98] *Id.*, 83 L.R.R.M. at 1545.

[99] *Id.*, 83 L.R.R.M. at 1545-46.

[100] 203 N.L.R.B. No. 61, 83 L.R.R.M. at 1127.

[101] *Id.*, 83 L.R.R.M. at 1127.

[102] *Id.*, 83 L.R.R.M. at 1127.

procedures. On one hand, the Board has looked to the effect of such improper behavior on the outcome of the election. On the other hand, the Board has utilized the criterion of the possible detrimental effect of the agent's misconduct upon the integrity of the Board's election processes, regardless of the outcome.

When the Board employs the "effect on the outcome of the election" standard, it behaves as a pragmatist. This cause-effect analysis is justified on the following grounds: (1) that a "bad-faith" employer might use such objections as dilatory tactics in order to delay eventual bargaining or gain time to render the union ineffective by the date of a second election; (2) that the cost in money and possibly employee morale is unduly burdensome to the government, as well as the parties, and a subsequent election should be avoided; and (3) similar to the use of challenge ballots, alleged improper conduct should only be considered when it can be shown that it had a possible demonstrative affect on the outcome of the election that could have *changed the results*.

The Board, however, assumes the role of idealist when it uses the "impugnment of the integrity of the Board's election processes" standard in deciding a case. This rationale of requiring that the Board agent, like the parties, must not upset the oft-referred to "laboratory conditions" is supported by: (1) the importance of instilling in the parties the appearance of Board neutrality; and (2) the dramatic effect of the election results upon the subsequent legal rights and duties.

The consequences of these dual philosophies are not without effect upon the litigants as well as the courts themselves. Indeed, after considering a number of prior cases dealing with the legal aspects of agent misconduct, the court in *Polymers, Inc.* was unable to untangle the inconsistent policy of the Board and was forced to defer to the Board's "expertise."

As suggested earlier, the objectives of both the "pragmatic" and "idealistic" approaches might be advanced by the greater use of hearings in cases of alleged misconduct. By granting the party which has alleged that the election has been unfairly conducted an opportunity to subpoena witnesses, cross-examine the agent involved, and generally air the facts surrounding the claim of impropriety, the Board would do much to overcome the notion that it actually is partial in election matters. Such hearings would also dispel any suspicions that the Board is more concerned with concealing the mistakes of its own staff members than with fairly effectuating the election procedures of the Act. At the same time, it may be assumed that most allegations of partiality and election tampering would prove unfounded if tested through the hearing process. Hence, the election results could be certified in most cases without the greater delay and uncertainty of rerun elections.

IMPROPERLY MARKED BALLOTS

Agents of the Board are charged with the responsibility of passing upon the validity of ballots which have not been cast or marked in the usual manner. Prior to the election, the Board supervises the preparation of the ballots which must be furnished by the Board. To preserve the legitimacy of the election, the color of the ballot for any particular election will not be disclosed to the parties prior to the voting; and write-in votes are not counted.[103]

Upon the commencement of the polling period, a voter must identify himself and have his eligibility ascertained by Board agents before he receives a ballot. The voter then marks his choice on the ballot and deposits it directly into the ballot box. As an aid to the agents in arriving at the initial tally, the Board has developed a set of guidelines to be used in determining the validity of each ballot. Only those ballots, which have been validly cast, are counted for the purpose of determining the necessary majority of votes required for certification.[104] Generally, a ballot is valid when both the intent of the voter is clearly indicated, and the secrecy of the ballot has not been impaired.

Determining the Clear Intent of the Voter

All ballots that are supplied by the Board instruct the voters to place an "X" in the appropriate box to indicate their choice. As early as 1947, however, the Board recognized that even if

---

[103] Woodmark Industries, Inc., 80 N.L.R.B. 1105, 23 L.R.R.M. 1209 (1948).

[104] *See* Great Lakes Pipe Line Co., 57 N.L.R.B. 369 (1944); American Tobacco Co., Inc., 10 N.L.R.B. 1171 (1938); Sorg Paper Co., 9 N.L.R.B. 136, 3 L.R.R.M. 249 (1938).

the "X" is placed outside the box, the ballot may still be valid if it clearly indicates the intent of the voter.[105]

A common problem that arises occurs when the usual "X" appears in one box, while the other box contains some other marking. For example, in *Bon Tool & Die Co.*,[106] a ballot containing an "X" in one box and an unfinished diagonal line in the other box was held invalid by the Board. Relying upon an earlier case,[107] the Board held that it could not certify the validity of the ballot, since the additional markings concealed the clear intent of the voter in casting his ballot.[108] Moreover, the Board reasoned that since the voter had quite obviously "spoiled" his ballot, it was incumbent upon him to request a new one, thus avoiding any ambiguities.[109] A short time later in *Belmont Smelting & Refining Works*,[110] the Board reconsidered the principle announced in *Bon Tool* and overruled it, stating that it now believed that a diagonal line in one box *does not* cancel a clear "X" in the remaining box and it *does* reveal the clear intent of the voter.

The use of markings other than an "X" may raise issues of both intent and secrecy. On one hand, the Board has held that when a voter writes the name of a participating union— *e.g.*, C.I.O. in the C.I.O. affiliates box of the ballot—the ballot is valid because the markings clearly reveal the intent of the voter,[111] while they do not impair the secrecy of the ballot.[112] On the other hand, the nature of the markings may raise doubts as to the actual intent of the voter. For example, in *Burlington Mills Corp.*[113] a ballot contained the word "union" in the "No"

---

[105] National Kaolin Products Co., 73 N.L.R.B. 1161, 20 L.R.R.M. 1073 (1947) ("X" placed one-half inch above the word "Yes").

[106] 115 N.L.R.B. 103, 37 L.R.R.M. 1254 (1956).

[107] Iroquois China Co., 55 N.L.R.B. 290 (1944) (Board held that diagonal line in one box, and an "X" in the other box, voided the ballot, since the clear intent of the voter was not revealed).

[108] 115 N.L.R.B. at 104, 37 L.R.R.M. at 1254.

[109] *Id.* at 105, 37 L.R.R.M. at 1254.

[110] 115 N.L.R.B. 1481, 38 L.R.R.M. 1104 (1956).

[111] Garod Radio Corp., 32 N.L.R.B. 1010, 8 L.R.R.M. 240 (1941).

[112] Western Electric Co., Inc., 97 N.L.R.B. 933, 29 L.R.R.M. 1187 (1951).

[113] 56 N.L.R.B. 365, 14 L.R.R.M. 148 (1944).

box. Although the company contended that the marking evinced a clear intent to vote against the union, the Board found that the ballot was void, since the marking "union" indicated a choice at variance with the "No" square in which it appeared, and thus appearing ambiguous.[114]

Unlike the *Burlington Mills* case, the voter in *Crucible Steel Co.*[115] had written the word "union" immediately following the word "NO" on his ballot. The regional director had made the somewhat narrow finding that the ballot was void even though there was a "distinct possibility," bordering on a "probability," that the employee intended to vote against the union.[116] Taking notice of the preelection campaign, wherein the employees were urged to vote "for the union" or for "no union," the Board reversed the decision of the regional director. Instead, the Board stated that the intent of the voter should be ascertained by examining the markings upon the ballot through the eyes of the employees who interpreted the voting instructions and marked the ballot, rather than by becoming overly technical in searching for ulterior motives.[117]

Recent decisions have evidenced a tendency towards a more liberal construction of the voter's intent than the more narrow approach taken by the Board in its earlier *Burlington Mills* case. For example, the Board in *Greg Moore Co., Inc.*[118] upheld the validity of a ballot which had been marked "No" in the "Neither" box. In so deciding, the Board reasoned that because the voter appeared at the polls and cast a marked ballot, it is apparent that he wished to register a preference.[119] Accordingly, his ballot was construed as a vote against union representation.[120]

Despite the more lenient attitude of the Board, it has not totally abandoned the *Burlington Mills* test regarding the in-

---

[114] *Id.* at 368, 14 L.R.R.M. at 148.

[115] 117 N.L.R.B. 1616, 40 L.R.R.M. 1054 (1957).

[116] *Id.* at 1617, 40 L.R.R.M. at 1054.

[117] *Id.* at 1618, 40 L.R.R.M. at 1054.

[118] 178 N.L.R.B. 483, 72 L.R.R.M. 1137 (1969).

[119] *Id.* at 484, 72 L.R.R.M. at 1137.

[120] *Id.*, 72 L.R.R.M. at 1138. *But see* Semi-Steel Casting Co., 66 N.L.R.B. 713, 17 L.R.R.M. 343 (1946), *enforced*, 160 F.2d 388, 19 L.R.R.M. 2458 (8th Cir.), *cert. denied*, 332 U.S. 758, 20 L.R.R.M. 2673 (1947) (ballot marked both for and against union held invalid).

validity of ballots which are ambiguous on their face. How long the Board may be able to maintain this position, however, is uncertain. In 1973, the Court of Appeals for the Second Circuit in *Spaulding Fibre Co. v. NLRB*,[121] found that the Board had erred in invalidating a ballot which contained no markings except the word "No" written on the "Yes" side of the ballot under the "Yes." Stating that since "[o]nly one question was presented on the ballot—whether the voter wished to be represented by the union," the written "No" "expresses a clear preference on the part of the voter."[122] As the Board in *Crucible Steel* had done, the court pointed out that the primary message of the management campaign had urged the worker to vote "No," while union literature urged him to vote "Yes." Consequently, the court concluded that "the vote of 'No' meant a vote against union representation, *wherever* the worker placed the word."[123]

Generally, the courts have taken a more liberal stance in construing the intent of the voter in collateral areas as well. Interestingly, the use of pencils in certification elections has raised a number of issues involving attempted erasures by the voters. In its decision in *NLRB v. Whitinsville Spinning Ring Co.*,[124] the Court of Appeals for the First Circuit reversed the Board policy which held that ballots containing a partial erasure were void *per se*.[125] The court reasoned that as long as the intent of the voter is clear, there is no justification for the Board to single out ballots containing erasures as being automatically void in view of the Board's more generous policy of construction regarding other types of unorthodox markings on ballots. More significantly, the court indicated that excepting the Board's policy on ballots which bear signatures, any *per se* rule regarding the invalidation of a ballot would be closely scrutinized.[126]

---

[121] 481 F.2d 1044, 83 L.R.R.M. 2650 (2d Cir. 1973) (per curiam).

[122] *Id.* at 1045, 83 L.R.R.M. at 2652.

[123] *Id.* at 1045, 83 L.R.R.M. at 2652 (emphasis added).

[124] 199 F.2d 585, 31 L.R.R.M. 2051 (1st Cir. 1952).

[125] *Id.* at 588, 31 L.R.R.M. at 2053. *See* Palmetto Cotton Mills, Inc., 63 N.L.R.B. 421 (1945), for another example of previous Board policy.

[126] 199 F.2d at 588, 31 L.R.R.M. at 2053.

In 1951, the Board in *Western Electric Co., Inc.*[127] held that a ballot, which contained no markings on the front, while the letters "AFL" appeared on the back of the ballot, was void because it impaired the secrecy in the election. Nineteen years later, the Court of Appeals for the Fifth Circuit in *NLRB* v. *Titche-Goettinger Co.*,[128] refused to enforce a Board order subsequent to an election in which three ballots were invalidated because they had been marked "No" by the voter on the blank reverse side and not in the designated square.[129] The court rejected the Board's claim under the *Bridgeton Transit* rule,[130] a marking on the reverse side of the ballot is too radical a departure from the norm to permit conjecture as to the intent of the voter. Instead, the court invoked the principle recommended by the First Circuit in *Whitinsville Spinning Ring Co.*, that any *per se* invalidation of ballots should be carefully scrutinized. In view of this caveat and the admitted policy of the Board to give effect to the intent of the voter whenever possible, the court held that there was no excuse for not counting the ballots, since the clear intent of the voter could be readily determined.[131]

In *Columbus Nursing Home, Inc.*,[132] the Board attempted to refute the Fifth Circuit's criticism in *Titche-Goettinger* concerning the inadvisability of the Board's policy of not counting ballots marked on the reverse side. The Board argued that even though its policy is to implement the clear intent of the voter, any conclusion based upon markings on the back of the ballot must be entirely speculative.[133] In addition, the Board cited several administrative reasons why counting ballots that contained markings on the reverse side would be impractical

---

127 97 N.L.R.B. 933, 29 L.R.R.M. 1187 (1951).

128 433 F.2d 1045, 75 L.R.R.M. 2561 (5th Cir. 1970).

129 *Id.* at 1047, 75 L.R.R.M. at 2561.

130 For a full statement of the *Bridgeton Transit* rule see p. 369, *infra.*

131 433 F.2d at 1048, 75 L.R.R.M. at 2562-63.

132 188 N.L.R.B. 825, 76 L.R.R.M. 1417 (1971).

133 *Id.*, 76 L.R.R.M. at 1418. More recently, the Court of Appeals for the Second Circuit in Spaulding Fibre Co. v. NLRB, 481 F.2d 1044, 83 L.R.R.M. 2650 (2d Cir. 1973) has specifically approved the rationale advanced in both the *Titche-Goettinger* and *Whitinsville Spinning Ring Co.* cases.

in the administration of the NLRA. As an example of these "difficulties," the Board posited that some of the blank ballots may be counted and others would not. Moreover, the Board indicated that it doubted the wisdom of a rule requiring Board agents to look at the back of ballots because it would not only double the time spent in counting ballots, but it might increase the number of challenges to ballots containing unusual markings.[134]

The Board's rebuttal in *Columbus Nursing Home* is less persuasive than the Fifth Circuit's analysis in *Titche-Goettinger*. Policy based on administrative case which may deny an effective voice to employees who have attempted to register their intent regarding union representation is of dubious value.[135] It is of far greater consequences to preserve the employees' right of self-determination, when the extra burden of supervision placed upon the Board is inconsequential.

Maintaining Ballot Secrecy

Markings on a ballot which reveal the identity of a particular voter raise the possibility of improper influence by the employer or union in contravention of Section 7 guarantees of the right to choose or reject self-organization free from restraint and coercion. Clearly then, any ballot which bears the signature of a voter is void *per se*.[136]

Over a period of years, a doctrine has been developed for the purpose of determining whether a marking on a ballot breaches the secrecy of the ballot. The evolution of this doctrine began in 1949, with the Board's decision in *J. I. Case Co.*[137] In that

---

[134] 188 N.L.R.B. at 826, 76 L.R.R.M. at 1418.

[135] In establishing the simple majority rule, the Board in R.C.A. Mfg. Co., Inc., 2 N.L.R.B. 168 (1936), stated that the rule was based upon the principle that those not voting in an election are deemed to have assented to the wishes of the majority. Therefore, in a situation such as *Titche-Goettinger*, where in an employee has attempted to vote, the Board should make all efforts to ascertain his desires in order to effectuate the corollary principle that those who do participate in an election are entitled to every effort to enable them to make their vote count. *Cf.* Greg Moore Co., Inc., 178 N.L.R.B. 483, 484, 72 L.R.R.M. at 1137 (1969).

[136] *See, e.g.,* George K. Garrett Co., Inc., 120 N.L.R.B. 484, 41 L.R.R.M. 1519 (1958); Northwest Packing Co., 65 N.L.R.B. 890, 17 L.R.R.M. 249 (1946).

[137] Case No. 18-RC-139, 23 L.R.R.M. 1667 (1949).

case, a group of employees improperly voted at nonchallenge tables, affixing stickers of the union, which they were voting for, upon their ballots. After the ballots had been voided by the regional director, the union offered affidavits from the employees who had cast them in order to prove their validity. The Board, however, upheld the employer's objections to the admission of the affidavits, ᴏ. the grounds that permitting such testimony to be offered by voters at a postelection hearing would violate the principal of secrecy in Board elections.[138]

The *J. I. Case Co.* decision effectuates the principal that post-election affidavits would neither be required nor permitted as a means of proving the validity of objections.[139] The principle itself is of course fundamental in preserving the secrecy to which every employee is entitled in casting his or her ballot.[140]

The following year, in *Ebco Mfg. Co.*,[141] the Board held invalid a ballot that had been marked "No," but which contained an additional marking identifiable as the letter "R" which had been encircled. The union alleged that the ballot was attributable to an employee who had marked ballots in a similar manner in other elections. In agreeing that the ballot was void, the Board took the opportunity to overrule its prior *Estee Bedding*[142] standard, in which it had held that the identity of the voter must be established before a ballot would be voided. Instead, the Board indicated that as long as the marking in question was made deliberately and *may* serve to reveal the identity of the voter, it is sufficient to render the ballot invalid.[143] Shortly thereafter, in *Laconia Malleable Iron Co., Inc.*,[144] the Board

---

[138] *Id.* at 1668.

[139] *See* Johnson City Foundry & Machine Works, Inc., 71 N.L.R.B. 825, 19 L.R.R.M. 1074 (1946); Russell-Miller Milling Co., 15 N.L.R.B. 1093, 5 L.R.R.M. 199 (1939).

[140] *But see* F. J. Stokes Corp., 117 N.L.R.B. 951, 39 L.R.R.M. 1338 (1957), where the Board pointed out that although the affidavits may be impermissible, challenges concerning the validity of a ballot, are a right of the parties which is not waived unless the objections are not timely raised.

[141] 88 N.L.R.B. 983, 25 L.R.R.M. 1326 (1950).

[142] 73 N.L.R.B. 825, 20 L.R.R.M. 1034 (1947).

[143] 88 N.L.R.B. at 985, 25 L.R.R.M. at 1427.

[144] 95 N.L.R.B. 161, 28 L.R.R.M. 1290 (1951).

broadened the *Ebco* rule, stating the requirement that the marking would no longer be applied, but rather the ballot would be voided if the marking may have been deliberate and may serve to identify the voter.[145]

Concluding Remarks

As we have seen, two major avenues of inquiry, voter intent and ballot secrecy, are weighed by the Board in determining the validity of the ballots in a representation election. This two-pronged analysis was integrated by the Board in the *Bridgeton Transit*[146] case wherein the current rule concerning irregular markings that may serve to invalidate ballots was established. In that case, the Board stated that a ballot is valid if: (1) it indicates the voter's choice; and (2) does not inherently reveal the identity of the voter; or (3) constitute such a departure from the usual ways of marking ballots as to warrant the conclusion that it is an identifying mark; *unless (4) it can be shown that the mark was used for identification purposes, or at the urging of a participating union or the employer.*[147]

The major question which remains, however, is not the narrow one concerning what rules have been established to determine the validity of a ballot, but rather why, at this late date, the issue is still being litigated? In nearly 40 years of experience in conducting representation elections, one can but wonder why concrete rules regarding this most fundamental of issues have not emerged long ago. For example, no really clear standard for determining the consequence of printing errors on the ballots which may confuse voters as to the identity of the parties has been established.[148]

---

[145] *Id.* at 162, 28 L.R.R.M. at 1290. *But see* Standard-Coosa-Thatcher Co., 115 N.L.R.B. 1790, 38 L.R.R.M. 1165 (1956), wherein the Board held that the extremely large number of participants served to preserve the anonymity of a ballot which would have been ruled invalid under a strict application of the *Laconia Malleable Iron Co.* rule.

[146] 124 N.L.R.B. 1047, 44 L.R.R.M. 1580 (1959).

[147] *Id.* at 1048, 44 L.R.R.M. at 1581.

[148] Printing errors on the ballots rendered the election in Dedman Foundry & Machine Co., 52 N.L.R.B. 609, 13 L.R.R.M. 35 (1943), so confusing that the Board ordered a second election. In V. LaRosa & Sons, Inc., 121 N.L.R.B. 671, 42 L.R.R.M. 1418 (1958), however, a similar printing error did not

Unlike the situation in the preceding section in which agent misconduct was discussed, wherein the Board, augmented by the courts, is presently engaged in rewriting the standards regulating the conduct of its own agents; issues concerning the validity of the ballot are not new, or are they unique. Indeed, the recent reversal of Board doctrine by two different circuit courts in both the *Titche-Goettinger* and *Spaulding Fibre* cases further illustrates the uncertain principles which still abound in this area. This state of flux, unlike other areas of conflict cannot be attributed to changing philosophies, politics, or differing views, as to the problems of regulating the conduct of the parties. Since the issues involving the validity of ballots are subject to an objective analysis based on the principles ennunciated in *Bridgeton Transit*, concrete rules of procedure should be readily forthcoming.

---

invalidate the results of an election even though the ballots confused the names of two unions which had very similar names and the same local number as the result of a prior schism. *See also* Bayliss Trucking Corp., 177 N.L.R.B. 276, 71 L.R.R.M. 1636 (1969); *enforced*, 432 F.2d 1025, 75 L.R.R.M. 2501 (2d Cir. 1970).

CHAPTER XVI

Mail Balloting

It is within the descretion of the regional director to conduct a ballot by mail, in whole or in part, whenever he determines that the efficient utilization of the so-called "manual election" is in jeopardy. The rationale for such a determination is that in certain situations it is physically impractical for eligible voters to cast their ballots at one or more centralized polling stations.[1] The decision to conduct a mail ballot implements Board policy which recognizes that the "circumstances surrounding working conditions in various industries require an adaptation of established standards to those conditions."[2] For example, if the eligible voters of a potential bargaining unit work in widely scattered locations,[3] or travel a great deal,[4] the regional director will provide for a mail ballot for these employees. In addition, war,[5] or even potentially adverse weather conditions,[6] may be sufficient grounds for conducting a mail ballot. In the great majority of instances, however, the necessity of holding a representation election by mail is dictated by industry structure alone. For this reason, mail balloting is generally restricted

---

[1] See NLRB Field Manual § 11336; McGUINESS, HOW TO TAKE A CASE BEFORE THE NATIONAL LABOR RELATIONS BOARD § 9-20 (Washington: BNA Books, 1967).

[2] Shipowner's Ass'n of the Pacific Coast, 110 N.L.R.B. 479, 480, 35 L.R.R.M. 1077 (1954).

[3] Consumers Power Co., 9 N.L.R.B. 742, 3 L.R.R.M. 327 (1938) (employees stationed at various power stations).

[4] Pacific Lumber Inspection Bureau, Inc., 7 N.L.R.B. 529, 534, 2 L.R.R.M. 303, 305 (1938) (lumber inspectors who traveled between different mills in the states of Washington and Oregon).

[5] Isbrandsten Steamship Co., Inc., 51 N.L.R.B. 883, 885, 12 L.R.R.M. 287 (1943).

[6] Continental Bus System, Inc., 104 N.L.R.B. 599, 601, 32 L.R.R.M. 1135, 1136 (1953) (mid-winter election among operators of a Rocky Mountain bus line).

to the transportation industry—*e.g.*, bus,[7] trucking,[8] and maritime [9]—the utilities, such as the telephone company [10] and the electric company,[11] and certain types of oil companies.[12]

DISCRETIONARY AUTHORITY OF THE REGIONAL DIRECTOR TO CONDUCT A MAIL BALLOT

When the decision of the regional director to conduct a mail ballot is not arbitrary or capricious, he has broad discretion in determining the method of conducting the election.[13] Because of this delegation of authority to the regional director by the Board, an objection to the use of mail ballots is limited to an affirmative showing of *clear abuse* on the part of the regional director.[14]

The consolidation of the regional director's authority to conduct elections by mail was the end product of a series of Board decisions which granted him the right to act both independently of the participants' requests and the NLRB's orders of election. In *E. I. DuPont de Nemours* [15] the Board held that it was within the authority of the regional director to utilize mail ballots in the absence of any proviso in the NLRB's direction of election which empowered him to do so.[16] In effect, the decision con-

---

[7] *Id.*, 32 L.R.R.M. at 1136.

[8] Central Freight Lines, Inc., 58 N.L.R.B. 263, 267, 15 L.R.R.M. 46, 47 (1944).

[9] Pacific Maritime Ass'n, 112 N.L.R.B. 1280, 1281, 36 L.R.R.M. 1193, 1194 (1955).

[10] Southern Bell Telephone & Telegraph Co., 55 N.L.R.B. 1058, 1077, 14 L.R.R.M. 59, 61 (1944).

[11] Consumers Power Co., 9 N.L.R.B. 742, 3 L.R.R.M. 327 (1938).

[12] Magnolia Pipe Line Co., 61 N.L.R.B. 723, 731, 16 L.R.R.M. 117, 118 (1945).

[13] The regional director employs any one or combination of the factors enumerated above as the basis for making his determination to conduct a mail ballot in whole or part.

[14] *Cf.* National Van Lines, 120 N.L.R.B. 1343, 42 L.R.R.M. 1176 (1958).

[15] 79 N.L.R.B. 345, 22 L.R.R.M. 1396 (1948).

[16] *Id.* at 346, 22 L.R.R.M. at 1396.

stituted a partial delegation of the Board's Section 9 mandate, that had granted the NLRB sole authority to conduct representation elections.[17] The Board reasoned that this was entirely proper, since the regional director acts ". . . as an agent of the Board . . . in arranging the details of an election, including, where appropriate, the determination of whether to conduct the election in whole or part by mail." [18] The Board's decision has a sound practical basis in that the proximity of the regional director, who is directly involved in organizing the election, gives him a greater command of all the facts pertaining to a successfully run election than a more remote Board.

Two years later, the Board expanded the *DuPont* rationale in *Pacific Gas & Electric Co.*,[19] wherein it held that the regional director's use of a mail ballot did not constitute prejudice to any party, although that party had not previously agreed to such a method. Through negative inference, the Board's opinion indicated that the decision to conduct an election by mail was solely within the discretion of the regional director, regardless of a party's failure to ratify the mail ballot procedure.[20]

In *Johnson Transport Co.*[21] the Board took the final step in entrusting complete control of the use of the mail ballot to the discretion of the regional director. In this case, the Board refused to set aside an election, conducted in part by mail, despite the employer's objection to the use of mail ballots prior to the election.[22]

This rapid growth of the regional director's authority to conduct elections by mail reflects the success of the Board's policy, first annunciated in *DuPont,* to leave the administrative task of arranging an election within the discretion of the regional director. Thus, in five years, the Board had reduced the restraints upon the regional director by (1) providing for a

---

[17] *See* 29 U.S.C. § 159(c)(1) (1970), which directs the Board to conduct an election upon the conclusion of a hearing in which the Board finds a question of representation exists.

[18] 79 N.L.R.B. at 346, 22 L.R.R.M. at 1396.

[19] 89 N.L.R.B. 938, 940, 26 L.R.R.M. 1056 (1950).

[20] *Id.*, 26 L.R.R.M. at 1056.

[21] 106 N.L.R.B. 1105, 32 L.R.R.M. 1621 (1953).

[22] *Id.* at 1106, 32 L.R.R.M. at 1621.

mail ballot independent of the Board's direction of election;[23] (2) allowing a ballot by mail without the approval of the parties;[24] and (3) permitting him to act even over the objections of one of the participants.[25] Finally, the regional director's discretionary authority in conducting a mail ballot is not precluded by a manual ballot previously conducted among the same parties.[26]

The Board has set forth a rather broad outline of the factors to be considered by the regional director before he conducts a subsequent ballot by mail in whole or part. First, the agent must consider all the ". . . circumstances surrounding the working conditions in various industries [before] requir[ing] an adaptation of established standards to those conditions." [27] Secondly, it must appear that one or more of the employees eligible to vote in an election may be disenfranchised if he is not permitted to vote by mail.[28] Finally, if the Board finds that the explanations set forth by the regional director in conducting a mail ballot are sufficient and not clearly arbitrary, the Board will sanction the mail ballot as a proper exercise of discretion.[29]

In determining when to conduct a mail ballot, the regional director must offer some explanation for his decision to avoid charges of acting in an arbitrary manner. For example, in *Shipowner's Ass'n of the Pacific Coast*[30] the regional director explained that he had utilized mail ballots in response to a Board decision that had set aside the results of a prior manual ballot, instructing him to determine how best a free election could be conducted. Further, the regional director in *Continental*

---

[23] 79 N.L.R.B. 345, 22 L.R.R.M. 1396 (1948).

[24] 89 N.L.R.B. 938, 26 L.R.R.M. 1056 (1950).

[25] 106 N.L.R.B. 1105, 32 L.R.R.M. 1621 (1953).

[26] *E.g.*, Shipowner's Ass'n of the Pacific Coast, 110 N.L.R.B. 479, 480, 35 L.R.R.M. 1077 (1954); Continental Bus System, Inc., 104 N.L.R.B. 599, 601, 32 L.R.R.M. 1135, 1136 (1953).

[27] 110 N.L.R.B. at 480, 35 L.R.R.M. at 1077.

[28] *Id.* at 480, 35 L.R.R.M. at 1077; 104 N.L.R.B. at 601, 32 L.R.R.M. at 1136.

[29] *See* cases cited at note 26, *supra*.

[30] 110 N.L.R.B. 479, 35 L.R.R.M. 1077 (1954).

Bus System, Inc.,[31] claimed that his determination to conduct an election by mail took into account the fact that the electorate consisted of over-the-road bus drivers, working for a Rocky Mountain bus company in the middle of winter. Therefore, only when the objecting party can show that the regional director's determination was wholly that of his own will, enforced by virtue of his office, and without a rational basis, will the Board set aside the election. In view of the integrity of the regional directors, such a standard effectively precludes objections claiming that the determination was arbitrary and capricious.

MAIL BALLOTING BY ABSENTEE VOTERS

The extensive use of mail ballots by absentee[32] voters in a manual election has grown in a direct relationship to the Board's general acknowledgement of mail ballots as being an acceptable form of conducting an election.[33] In *E. I. DuPont de Nemours,*[34] the Board rejected the challenges of an employer to the validity of two mail ballots cast in a representation election. The ballots had been cast by two eligible voters—the first, on a three month leave of absence, the second on vacation at the time of the election. The Board reasoned that the regional director's determination to use the mail ballots was justifiable in view of the small number of eligible voters in the prospective bargaining unit. Because this factor rendered the two ballots more important than usual, the interests of conducting the most representative election as possible were served by permitting the absentee voters to cast mail ballots.[35]

---

[31] 104 N.L.R.B. 599, 601, 32 L.R.R.M. 1135, 1136 (1953).

[32] In this section, the term "absentee voter" is used to refer to an employee, absent from work on the day of the election, but who will or may be reinstated with a reasonable expectation of employment. Permanently replaced strikers and employees who have been discriminatorily discharged are excluded from this discussion even though the striker, under Board regulations is eligible to vote in an election held within 12 months of the commencement of the strike, 29 U.S.C. § 159(c)(3) (1970); as is the discriminatorily discharged employee, Tampa Sand & Material Co., 137 N.L.R.B. 1549, 50 L.R.R.M. 1438 (1962).

[33] *See* text accompanying notes 23-25, *supra.*

[34] 79 N.L.R.B. 345, 22 L.R.R.M. 1396 (1948).

[35] *Id.* at 345, 22 L.R.R.M. at 1396.

Shortly thereafter, however, in the *Ann Arbor Press* [36] case, the Board refused to set aside an election where it was shown that one of the employees was ill and unable to go to the polls. Because of this illness, the employer argued that the Board should have provided the employee with a mail ballot. The NLRB found no merit in this objection, stating that in manual elections it is the Board's practice to require the eligible employees to present themselves in person at the polls.[37] The Board's decision did not amount to a total ban against the possible use of mail ballots for sick employees. The holding in *Ann Arbor Press* was limited to objections made subsequent to the election. Had the employer requested a mail ballot for the sick employee prior to the election, the result may have been different.[38]

In the meantime, the Court of Appeals for the Seventh Circuit, in *NLRB v. Fresh'nd Aire Co.*,[39] approved the use of mail ballots by laid-off employees even though they were able to vote manually. In so deciding, the court indicated that since the Board customarily directs that temporary laid-off employees are eligible to vote, there is no rationale for precluding the use of the mail in casting their votes.[40]

In the same year that *Fresh'nd Aire* was decided, the Board in *Kresge-Newark, Inc.*[41] had another opportunity to rule on whether it is permissible for sick employees to cast mail rather than manual ballots. In *Kresge-Newark* the employer had requested a partial mail ballot for sick employees, subsequent to signing a stipulation regarding election procedure. The regional director indicated that because the stipulation provided only for a time and place, but *not* for mail balloting, the employer's request could be granted only with union consent. The

---

[36] 88 N.L.R.B. 301, 395, 25 L.R.R.M. 1339, 1340 (1950).

[37] *Id.* at 395, 25 L.R.R.M. at 1340. Indeed, even if the sick employees had voted by mail, the addition of a single vote to the tally would have been insufficient to affect the outcome of the election.

[38] *Cf.* Kresge-Newark, Inc., 112 N.L.R.B. 869, 39 L.R.R.M. 1116 (1955). *See also* discussion following to p. 378, *infra.*

[39] 226 F.2d 737, 36 L.R.R.M. 2732 (7th Cir. 1955), *denying enforcement on other grounds to* 111 N.L.R.B. 158, 35 L.R.R.M. 1418 (1955).

[40] 226 F.2d at 740, 36 L.R.R.M. at 2734.

[41] 112 N.L.R.B. 869, 36 L.R.R.M. 1116 (1955).

union refused to agree, whereupon the regional director gave the employer an opportunity to withdraw from the stipulation. The employer, however, chose to proceed with the election. After the election, the employer alleged that the regional director erred in refusing to send mail ballots to employees who were ill and in the hospital at the time of the election. Under the circumstances, however, the Board had no difficulty in inferring that the employer had waived any objection to the possible use of mail ballots when he failed to withdraw from the stipulation.[42]

Because of the factual situations involved, the Board in both the *Ann Arbor Press* case and *Kresge-Newark* evaded any definitive answer as to whether employees on sick leave should be permitted to vote by mail upon the request of one of the parties as a matter of right.[43] Sick employees may vote by mail if the parties, as well as the regional director, agree to a mail ballot procedure prior to the election. Moreover, it is consistent with NLRB policy to allow sick employees to cast mail ballots if any one of the parties *or* the regional director makes this request prior to the election.[44] For example, if both employer and union requested a mail ballot for employees on sick leave, a determination by the regional director not to allow a mail ballot would be an arbitrary decision, since the director's refusal to furnish mail ballots protects the interests of no one. Furthermore, it follows that even if only the regional director ordered the use of mail ballots for employees on sick leave, absent a contrary

---

[42] *Id.* at 870, 36 L.R.R.M. at 1116.

[43] To avoid potentially onerous administrative burdens on the part of Board agents conducting the election, the responsibility of furnishing mail ballots to sick employees is of necessity that of the parties. Indeed, in a case involving failure of notice to certain laid-off employees, the Board asserted that it would be "an almost impossible burden on the agent to investigate and uncover on his own initiative all conceivably eligible voters. . . ." Rohr Aircraft Corp., 136 N.L.R.B. 958, 959-60, 49 L.R.R.M. 1886 (1962). Moreover, since each of the parties possesses an *"Excelsior* list" of all eligible voters within seven days of the direction of election (*see* discussion in Chapter XIV, *supra*), they are in a much better position to ascertain whether an employee may be absent on the day of the election because of illness.

[44] In establishing other rules of election procedure, the Board has consistently analogized representation elections to political elections. *E.g.*, Excelsior Underwear, Inc., 156 N.L.R.B. 1236, 1242, 61 L.R.R.M. 1217, 1219 (1966) (rule requiring an employer to furnish a list of the names and addresses of all eligible employees); R.C.A. Mfg. Co., 2 N.L.R.B. 168, 177-78 (1936) (simple majority rule). Therefore, it is in line with Board policy to furnish mail ballots to employees who are ill, as absentee ballots are furnished in a political election.

stipulation by the parties,[45] this partial mail ballot should be upheld on the principles of the *DuPont* case.[46]

If only one of the parties requests a mail ballot for sick employees, and is opposed by the other party and the regional director, the following policy considerations dictate the use of the requested mail ballot. First, the disagreement would lead only to a postelection hearing regarding the conduct of the election, thus delaying the finanlity of the result. Secondly, the parties would run afoul of the Board policy announced in *T & G Mfg., Inc.*,[47] if the mail ballot were cast as a challenge ballot for subsequent determination. Lastly, since the Board is willing to permit a mail ballot by vacationers, employees on leaves of absence, or laid-off employees—all of whom could presumably vote in person—it would be unreasonable to preclude employees incapacitated by illness from voting by mail because to do so would make these employees' opportunity to vote contingent upon a circumstance beyond their control.

IMPROPRIETIES IN THE USE OF MAIL BALLOTS

An election by mail ballot, in whole or part, is proper only when adverse circumstances militate against utilizing the more preferable manual ballot procedure.[48] Because a mail ballot is but a substitute procedure,[49] the rules governing conduct in manual elections are paramount; and thus, the Board has attempted to implement these standards in a mail ballot situation.

---

[45] *See* Kresge-Newark, Inc., 112 N.L.R.B. 869, 36 L.R.R.M. 1116 (1955), wherein the stipulation bound the parties to a manual election.

[46] *See* discussion at p. 375, *supra.*

[47] 173 N.L.R.B. 1503, 70 L.R.R.M. 1038 (1969). In *T & G Mfg.*, the Board voided an agreement of the parties to put a particular ballot in a challenge envelope on the basis that the choice of the voter was known, thereby creating an opportunity for collusion or coercion.

[48] *See, e.g.*, North American Aviation, Inc., 81 N.L.R.B. 1046, 23 L.R.R.M. 1460 (1949), wherein the Board indicated that alleged irregularities in the election process were attributable to merely the "*normal hazards associated with mail balloting.*" (emphasis added).

[49] *See* Shipowner's Ass'n of the Pacific Coast, 110 N.L.R.B. 479, 35 L.R.R.M. 1077 (1954), wherein the Board indicated that the totality of circumstances surrounding the working conditions of a particular industry may require an adaptation of the standard manual election.

Failure to Provide a Ballot

One of the problems faced by the Board in setting the standards for elections by mail is what constitutes adequate and proper procedure for guaranteeing the employees' opportunity to vote. This issue is raised when the Board fails to provide a mail ballot to eligible employees.

In *Star Baking Co.*,[50] the Board upheld the regional director's determination to set aside an election wherein one employee had not been sent a ballot. The election had produced a total of twenty-eight ballots, equally divided between "union" and "no union." The regional director had concluded that since the employees had not received a mail ballot, ". . . [his] rights as a voter were prejudiced and that the inconclusiveness of the results might be due to his failure to receive a ballot."[51] To say that the election was "inconclusive," of course, is inaccurate. To be certified, a union must receive a majority of the votes cast. Hence, a tie vote in this situation amounted to a conclusive rejection of representation. More precisely, the regional director's ruling seems to hinge on the fact that the additional ballot could have changed the result.

The director's comment that the individual's rights were prejudiced is clearly a makeweight. Before the Board, the employer claimed that since twenty-eight of thirty-four eligible voters in the unit had participated in the election, it was representative in fairly reflecting the desires of the unit. The Board responded, picking up the theme of the director's comment, that its responsibility is to ensure the opportunity to vote to all members of the electorate, not just a representative number. However, the Board gave the game away by adding that it was "particularly important" to remedy this failure in its procedure here because the missing ballot could have affected the outcome of the election.[52]

In fact, in cases lacking a potential impact upon the result of the election, the Board has not viewed the denial of an individual's right as sufficient to set aside an election. In *Seattle Bakers' Bureau, Inc.*,[53] the Board refused to set aside

---

[50] 119 N.L.R.B. 835, 41 L.R.R.M. 1178 (1957).

[51] *Id.* at 836, 41 L.R.R.M. at 1179.

[52] *Id.*, 41 L.R.R.M. at 1179.

[53] 104 N.L.R.B. 270, 32 L.R.R.M. 1070 (1953).

an election even though thirteen eligible employees had been denied their opportunity to vote through inadvertance. In this case, however, their votes could not have changed the outcome. Any objection based upon the failure of an opportunity to vote in a mail ballot is thus limited by the requirement that the missed opportunity have a possible affect on the outcome of an election. Considering the hazardous and often confused nature of a ballot by mail, the Board is justified in limiting successful objections to an election on the rationale of administrative necessity and practicality.

Failure to Sign Ballot Envelope

Upon the determination of the regional director to conduct a mail ballot, in whole or part, each employee deemed eligible to vote by mail is sent a balloting kit. In addition to the instructions to be followed in casting a mail ballot, the kit includes a preaddressed envelope to the election site, a secret ballot envelope, and a ballot. The envelope addressed to the election site has a perforated stub that must be signed by the voter as a means of determining the validity of the ballot upon receipt.

In *Central Freight Lines, Inc.*,[54] eleven ballots which did not bear the signatures of the voter were challenged as void. The Board reasoned that since, in the absence of signatures, it was impossible to determine whether the ballots were returned by eligible employees, the ballots were invalid.[55] This issue also arose as a collateral matter in the subsequent case of *Northwest Packing Co.*,[56] in which the Board, without comment, upheld the prior action of the regional director in voiding the ballot contained in the unsigned envelope. Since it is axiomatic that valid ballots may be cast only by eligible employees, the Board's stance is well justified and the rule is susceptible to a purely mechanistic application.[57]

---

[54] 58 N.L.R.B. 1523 (1944).

[55] *Id.* at 1524.

[56] 65 N.L.R.B. 890, 17 L.R.R.M. 249 (1946).

[57] *But cf.* NLRB v. Groendyke Transport, Inc., 372 F.2d 137, 64 L.R.R.M. 2270 (10th Cir.), *cert. denied*, 387 U.S. 932, 65 L.R.R.M. 2364 (1967). It does not follow that the automatic invalidation of unsigned ballots is so broad, however, that it encompasses issues raising the authenticity of

Breach of Ballot Secrecy

As in manual elections, a ballot by mail is subject to the express statutory requirement that it be cast in secret. In this respect too, however, the Board may actually give greater weight to practical considerations, such as the effect on the outcome, than to the specific impairment of any individual's statutory voting rights.

In *Northwest Packing Co.*[58] two ballots were not placed within the secret ballot envelope and two other ballots bore signatures on the secret ballot envelopes.[59] The regional director had refused to void these four ballots because he felt that the secrecy of the voter's identification could be preserved, but the Board rejected the director's findings and voided the ballots. The reason given by the Board for its decision was that the ballots:

> . . . were too closely identified with the names of the voters concerned, and that the ballots cannot be opened and adequate protection afforded to the secrecy of the ballots cast, which every voting employee is entitled to expect.[60]

It should be noted, however, that the Board's ruling in this respect was essentially academic, since the Board had decided for other reasons not to certify the election results.

The requirement of secrecy in an election is not absolute, as indicated by the Board in *Jacksonville Journal Co.*[61] In that case, the only employee who voted by mail was provided with a blue ballot, whereas employees who voted manually were furnished with pink ballots. Citing the case of *Machinery Overhaul Co., Inc.*,[62] the regional director found that although the allegations were true and the ballot might be considered in-

---

ballots that do bear signatures. In the latter case, the issue is not procedural, but rather questions the validity of the individual ballots to which they objected. *Id.* at 143, 64 L.R.R.M. at 2274.

[58] 65 N.L.R.B. 890, 17 L.R.R.M. 249 (1946).

[59] *Id.* at 891, 17 L.R.R.M. at 249.

[60] *Id.*, 17 L.R.R.M. at 249.

[61] 117 N.L.R.B. 1828, 40 L.R.R.M. 1098 (1957).

[62] 115 N.L.R.B. 1787, 38 L.R.R.M. 1168 (1957).

valid, the result of the election was unaffected and therefore it should not be set aside.[63]

Before the Board, the employer contended that the right to a secret ballot is absolute, however, the Board disagreed. Although it acknowledged that the rationale for requiring secrecy is to assure the voter's exercise of franchise without fear of reprisal, the Board held, in effect, that since there was no evidence of voter apprehension either of the employer or union, as a result of their selection of a collective bargaining agent, the deleterious effects of reprisal were not present; hence, the need for secrecy was obviated.[64]

It is highly probable that the Board's rationale is colored by the peculiar nature of the outcome of this election. Of twenty-six eligible voters in the unit, twenty-five voted for the union and only one employee cast his ballot against the union.[65] Thus, the Board must have felt that since the original election was so one-sided, a second election would be reduced to a mere formality.

Although the use of mail ballots had long been part and parcel of Board election procedures, an employer, in *NLRB v. Groendyke Transport, Inc.,*[66] challenged the use of the mail ballot procedure as being *per se* illegal because it violates the secrecy of the ballot. The court affirmed the Board's position [67] that since mail balloting is not forbidden either by statute or regulation, it is an acceptable means of conducting representation elections.[68]

In *Groendyke,* the employer had contended that a mail ballot by its very nature could not be conducted secretly. In support of this claim, he alleged that in one instance a voter had marked his ballot in the presence of two other employees. In addition, the employer claimed that in many situations, wives and family members had not only signed for the ballot which came by

---

[63] 117 N.L.R.B. at 1829, 40 L.R.R.M. at 1098.

[64] *Id.* at 1830, 40 L.R.R.M. at 1098.

[65] *Id.* at 1829, 40 L.R.R.M. at 1098.

[66] 372 F.2d 137, 64 L.R.R.M. 2270 (10th Cir.), *cert. denied,* 387 U.S. 932, 65 L.R.R.M. 2364 (1967).

[67] Groendyke Transport, Inc., 154 N.L.R.B. 1040, 60 L.R.R.M. 1174 (1965).

[68] 372 F.2d at 142, 64 L.R.R.M. at 2272.

registered mail, but had also signed the ballot stub itself.[69] In response to the employer's arguments, the court held that with adequate proof, the validity of *individual* ballots might be challenged successfully.[70] The court added that the use of the mails, however, was not a *per se* illegal procedure for conducting elections, stating that the "[i]rregularities in the conduct of the election . . . went to the validity of individual ballots and not to the procedure by which they were cast." [71]

In summary, it appears that, although secrecy is a specific statutory requirement of mail ballot elections, it is not an absolute standard which will negate an entire election if a breach of secrecy is proven. Instead, the principle of ballot secrecy will only be applied to void identifiable individual ballots, not the election as a whole.

Receipt of Ballots After Deadline

As a general rule, mail ballots that are received after the deadline set forth in the notices of the election are void.[72] The only significant limitation of this principle occurs when the receipt of mail ballots subsequent to the closing date is of evidentiary value in showing one factor of a totality of circumstances that cause the election itself to be deemed unrepresentative.[73]

An interesting application of the general rule arises when employees in a certification election have an option to vote either manually or by mail. For example, in *Cooper's Inc.*,[74] the Board found itself faced with a situation in which an employee first voted by mail and a few days later voted manually. The mail ballot was received one day before the manual ballot was cast. The Board held that since the employee had already cast a valid ballot by mail, as evidenced by its receipt of the mail ballot, the employee was thereby precluded from casting a valid ballot

---

[69] *Id.* at 142-43, 64 L.R.R.M. at 2273.

[70] *Id.* at 143, 64 L.R.R.M. at 2273.

[71] *Id.*, 64 L.R.R.M. at 2274.

[72] *See, e.g.*, National Van Lines, 120 N.L.R.B. 1343, 42 L.R.R.M. 1176 (1958).

[73] Mechling Barge Lines, 69 N.L.R.B. 838, 18 L.R.R.M. 1270 (1946). *See* discussion in Chapter XVII, *infra.*

[74] 94 N.L.R.B. 1554, 1556, 28 L.R.R.M. 1212, 1213 (1951).

manually.[75] Although the result in the case has a solid basis in law and policy, one might wonder whether the result would have been different if the mail ballot had been received after the manual ballot was cast, but before the deadline for the receipt of mail ballots had expired.

A variant of the foregoing question did arise in the case of *Seattle Baker's Bureau, Inc.*[76] Here, the Board's regional office received 15 ballots after the deadline for mail ballots had expired, but before the termination date for manual voting. Since seven of the 15 had subsequently voted before the time for manual balloting expired, the Board agent proposed to open the remaining eight ballots. The remaining ballots were never opened, however, since the parties could not agree upon this.[77]

In its decision, the Board dismissed the intervening union's request to have the remaining eight ballots counted, since they were insufficient in number to affect the eventual outcome of the election. Because the general rule states that any mail ballots received after the deadline are void, a principle clearly within the ken of the Board, one can infer that the Board implied that these eight ballots could have been counted had they been sufficient to affect the outcome of the election.

If the inference is correct, it may show a Board tendency toward leniency in its application of the general rule when competing equitable considerations arise. Thus, in *Seattle Baker's,* knowing that its own agent had suggested the ballots be counted, the Board itself may have felt that refusing to count the ballots was inequitable because the employees could have cast a subsequent valid manual ballot.[78]

In retrospect, a major defect in a rule that voids ballots received after a published date of receipt becomes apparent. The principle itself may operate to disenfranchize voters through no fault of their own. Because the current Board rule is to determine the validity of a mail ballot on the basis of receipt, once an employee has dispatched his ballot, its ultimate validity rests upon the efficiency of an independent instrumentality—the postal service. Perhaps a better rule to apply would be to de-

---

75 *Id.* at 1557, 28 L.R.R.M. at 1213.

76 104 N.L.R.B. 270, 32 L.R.R.M. 1070 (1953).

77 *Id.* at 271, 32 L.R.R.M. at 1071.

78 *Cf.* Cooper's Inc., 94 N.L.R.B. 1554, 28 L.R.R.M. 1212 (1951).

termine the validity of individual ballots upon the date of their dispatch rather than their receipt. Under such a system, the postmark would constitute evidence of whether the employee had in fact voted before the deadline. In effect, the proposed rule change would preserve the Board's policy of providing for a final tally as soon as possible, while at the same time, affording the individual employee adequate opportunity to cast his ballot.

In addition, a rule which sets forth the final dispatch date as the deadline for mailing would afford actual notice to every voter as to the exact end of the polling period. The Board could then arbitrarily set a date such as five days after the final mailing deadline to open the ballots. Any ballots received by the Board after the tally, but postmarked before the dispatch date would be added to the count. The five-day filing period for objections could still be retained and objections based on ballots received after the initial five-day waiting period could be used to either amend a prior objection or constitute an exception to the filing limitation for the purpose of subsequent objections.

MAIL BALLOTS AND THE PEERLESS PLYWOOD RULE

In 1953, the Board promulgated its *Peerless Plywood* rule prohibiting both employer and union representatives from making election speeches on company time to massed assemblies of employees within 24 hours before the scheduled time of the election.[79] Six years later in *Oregon Washington Telephone Co.*[80] the Board first applied the so-called *Peerless Plywood* rule to elections by mail. Pointing out that the same policy considerations[81] delineated in *Peerless Plywood* were just as relevant to

---

[79] Peerless Plywood Co., 107 N.L.R.B. 427, 33 L.R.R.M. 1151 (1953). *See* discussion in Chapter X, *supra*.

[80] 123 N.L.R.B. 339, 43 L.R.R.M. 1430 (1959).

[81] *Id.* at 340-41, 43 L.R.R.M. at 1431. The policy considerations underlying the *Peerless Plywood* rule are as follows:

> [1] last-minute speeches . . . have an unwholesome and unsettling effect and tend to interfere with that sober and thoughtful choice which a free election is designed to reflect . . . ; [2] the real vice is in the last-minute character of the speech coupled with the fact that it is made on company time; and [3] because of its timing, [the speech] tends to create a mass psychology which overrides arguments made through other compaign media and gives an unfair advantage to the party . . . who in this manner obtains the last most telling word. . . .

the mail ballot situation, the Board stated the rule as follows:

> [T]he Regional Director will give the parties written notice setting forth the time and date on which "mail in" ballots will be dispatched to the voters, and also setting forth a terminal time and date by which the ballots must be returned. . . . Such notice will be given the parties 24 hours before the . . . ballots will be dispatched. . . . Employers and unions alike will be prohibited from making election speeches on company time to massed assemblies of employees within the period set forth in the notice. . . . Violations of this rule by employers or unions will cause an election to be set aside whenever valid objections are filed.[82]

Any violation of the rule does not result in an unfair labor practice, but is limited to merely providing the grounds for setting aside and directing a new election.[83] In addition, the Board has strictly construed this rule, and requires that the notice of the election may neither be given orally nor be implied, but rather must be given in written form.[84]

In *Samson Tug and Barge Co.*[85] an employer sought to have an election set aside because the union concluded a campaign meeting after the mail ballots were received by the voters. The employer, in support of his objections, pointed to the standard instructions accompanying the mail ballot, which stated in part:

> From the time you open the envelope containing the ballot you should consider yourself in the same position as though in a voting booth in a manually conducted election. You should therefore follow the instructions below and drop your ballot in the United States mail before discussing it with anyone.[86]

Based on this language, the employer argued that the *Peerless Plywood* rule should be supplemented by the principles governing manual elections previously announced by the Board in *Milchem, Inc.*[87] In *Milchem* the Board had proscribed "prolonged conversations of any party to the election and voters waiting [in the polling area] to cast ballots" on the grounds that "[t]he final minutes before an employee casts his vote

---

[82] 123 N.L.R.B. at 341, 43 L.R.R.M. at 1431.

[83] *Id.*, 43 L.R.R.M. at 1431.

[84] Interstate Hosts, Inc., 130 N.L.R.B. 1614, 1621-22, 47 L.R.R.M. 1573, 1575 (1961).

[85] 194 N.L.R.B. No. 46, 78 L.R.R.M. 1606 (1971).

[86] *Id.*, 78 L.R.R.M. at 1607.

[87] 170 N.L.R.B. 362, 67 L.R.R.M. 1395 (1968).

should be his own . . ." and that a "preventive device" was necessary "to enforce the ban against electioneering in polling places. . . ." [88] The company contended that the campaign meeting, attended by employees who had not yet mailed in their ballots, and therefore were "in the same position as though in a voting booth," was a logical equivalent of the electioneering prohibited in *Milchem.*

Had the Board accepted the employer's contentions, the outcome would have been a ban on all campaigning in mail ballot elections during the period in which the ballots were in the hands of the employees. Such a decision would not only have been contrary to the existing law, but even more important, would have severely restricted electioneering, by limiting it to the period prior to the receipt of mail ballots by the employees.

First, the existing law as set forth in *Peerless Plywood* and adapted to mail ballot elections by the Board in *Oregon Washington Telephone Co.*, only proscribes campaigning before massed assemblies on company time for a period beginning 24 hours before the election. The electioneering in *Samson Tug* was not conducted on company time, but rather during the employees off hours. Moreover, the Board's rules in a manual election are not violated even if during the time the polls are open, the parties hold meetings that the employees attend voluntarily and on their own time.[89]

Since the law clearly permits electioneering on the employees own time, the company had to fall back on a broad interpretation of *Milchem.* The safeguards promulgated in *Milchem,* however, proscribe electioneering only during "[t]he final minutes before an employee casts his ballot." [90] In subsequent decisions, the Board has narrowly construed *Milchem* to apply to only those final minutes when the employees are either actually within the polling place or in line waiting to vote or within a "no-electioneering area" demarcated by the Board agent conducting the election.[91] Thus, despite the broad language of the instruc-

---

[88] *Id.* at 362-63, 67 L.R.R.M. at 1395. For an extensive discussion of the *Milchem* rule see Chapter XI, pp. 265-267, *supra.*

[89] *E.g.*, Lach-Simkins Dental Laboratories, Inc., 186 N.L.R.B. 671, 75 L.R.R.M. 1385 (1970).

[90] 170 N.L.R.B. at 363, 67 L.R.R.M. at 1395.

[91] *See, e.g.*, Volt Technical Corp., 176 N.L.R.B. 832, 836, 71 L.R.R.M. 1608 (1969).

tions directing the employees to behave as though in a voting booth, the "final minutes" referred to in *Milchem* could hardly have been expanded to the entire period in which the employees held their ballots as advocated by the employer in *Samson Tug*.

Recently, in *Chotin Transportation, Inc.,*[92] the Board declined to set aside an election in which a maritime company refused to permit union organizers aboard its ships for the purpose of campaigning among its employees on the ground that the employees were already in possession of their mail ballots. Perhaps because of the brevity of the Board's opinion, the decision raised questions as to the continued validity of the *Samson Tug* case. The apparent conflict arose because of the following Board language

> The logistics involved in granting the request [permitting union organizes to board the employer's vessels] would have put the [union] representatives aboard the vessels at or about the same time that the employees were receiving their mail ballots. It follows, therefore, that to have granted [the organizers] access to the employees on board for the purpose of campaigning among them *would inevitably have created conflicts with the Board's instructions that voters refrain from discussions about the election while the mail ballots were still in their possession.*[93]

On its face, the italicized language could be interpreted as a bar to all campaigning during the period in which the employees had mail ballots in their possession, in which case, *Samson Tug* would be in contravention of this newly announced principle. Upon the release of the Board's opinion in *Chotin*, the General Counsel, in a written memorandum, asked the Board if he should go to the Ninth Circuit and ask for a remand of the *Samson Tug* case which was before that circuit on appeal. The Board decided not to ask for a remand, stating that it would distinguish the two cases in later decisions. Subsequently, the Ninth Circuit has enforced the Board's order in *Samson Tug*,[94] and denied the employer's request to reconsider the case in light of *Chotin*.[95]

More recently, the Board in *Ingram Barge Co.,*[96] was presented

92 203 N.L.R.B. No. 73, 83 L.R.R.M. 1131 (1973).

93 *Id.*, 83 L.R.R.M. at 1132 (emphasis added).

94 NLRB v. Samson Tug and Barge Co., Docket No. 72-1365 (9th Cir., June 11, 1973) (unreported).

95 *Id.*

96 204 N.L.R.B. No. 17, 83 L.R.R.M. 1311 (1973).

with a factual situation similar to the *Chotin* case, wherein union organizers were refused permission to board the employer's vessels. The union's request for access had been received by the employer only two days prior to the time at which the ballots would be mailed.[97] In dismissing the union's objection, the Board emphasized the importance of considering the timing of such requests as they relate to the overall pattern of events. In conclusion, the Board citing *Chotin* and *Oregon Washington Telephone Co.* stated that although a union representative was legally entitled access to the employer's vessels, its failure to request access until the last moment "would have inevitably invited a considerable risk of violations of the Board's instructions to voters not to discuss the election with anyone prior to mailing the ballots back to the Board." [98]

Thus, it is apparent that the Board's distinction between *Samson Tug* and *Chotin* rests upon the timeliness of the union's request for access. Future cases in this area will be decided upon the following three principles. First, when the request is made well in advance of the polling period, a refusal by the employer to permit union access to his vessels will constitute interference.[99] Secondly, if the request is so tardy as to constitute a bad faith attempt by the union to violate the *Peerless Plywood* rule, the employer may justifiably prohibit any union representatives from boarding his vessels.[100] Finally, where a union's campaign activities are not tied to access to the employer's vessels, but are undertaken ashore and outside the contemplation of the *Peerless Plywood* rule, such electioneering is permissible.[101]

---

[97] *Id.*, 83 L.R.R.M. at 1312.

[98] *Id.*, 83 L.R.R.M. at 1312.

[99] The Interlake Steamship Co., 174 N.L.R.B. 308, 309, 70 L.R.R.M. 1177, 1178 (1969).

[100] Ingram Barge Co., 204 N.L.R.B. No. 17, 83 L.R.R.M. 1311 (1973).

[101] Samson Tug and Barge Co., 203 N.L.R.B. No. 73, 83 L.R.R.M. 1131 (1973).

CONCLUDING REMARKS

As we have seen, the NLRB's utilization of mail ballots as a substitute procedure for a manual election is primarily dependent upon certain industry structures within the electorate is scattered over a wide geographical area. The Board has delegated to the regional director, broad discretionary authority to make the initial decision to conduct a mail ballot in whole or part; a review of such a determination is severely limited.

As a general rule, breakdowns in the mail balloting procedure are significant only if the ballots in question are sufficient in number to affect the outcome of the election. Thus, claims premised upon the failure of an employee to receive a ballot, the receipt of unsigned ballots, and even ballots whose secrecy has been breached, are sustained only when the alleged irregularity has a potential impact upon the election results. Without proof of such an impact, the ballots affected are treated as invalid and consequently have no bearing on the representation question.

The disposition of the cases concerning a violation of the *Peerless Plywood* rule in a mail ballot election warrant special notice, for it suggests the importance of the posture in which the issue of potential interference with the voter's freedom of choice is raised. In *Samson Tug* the question was whether the meeting, having actually occurred while the mail ballots were outstanding, had such an inherent potential for interference that, even without any showing of a specific impact, it necessitated the invalidation of the election. By contrast, in *Chotin* the issue was whether the possibility that such meetings, if allowed, might have resulted in interference was sufficient to justify the employer's precautionary refusal to grant the union's last-minute request to board the ships. Certainly a finding that such a meeting occurred in one case without coercive results does not necessitate a holding that it is an affirmative act of interference to prohibit such meetings in other circumstances.

CHAPTER XVII

Representative Character Of The Vote

Section 9(a) of the NLRA provides *inter alia*, that representatives for the purposes of collective bargaining shall be selected by "the majority of the employees in a unit appropriate for such purposes."[1] This deceivingly simple language has given rise to a host of litigation concerning what constitutes a "majority" in a labor election. At the outset, controversy arose over how the term majority was to be defined for these purposes. For example, assuming a hypothetical appropriate bargaining unit composed of 100 employees, there are three possible means of determining what number of employees would represent a majority for purposes of union certification. These three formulations are represented in Table 1. Because the Wagner Act contained no numerical definition of the term "majority," shortly after its inception, the Board was called upon to construe the statute and formulate a rule to be applied in subsequent cases.

WHAT CONSTITUES A MAJORITY—THE R.C.A. DOCTRINE

In one of the early landmark cases in the federal labor law, the Board in *R.C.A. Mfg. Co., Inc.*,[2] resolved the ambiguity of the term "majority" within the context of Section 9(a). The Board carefully considered each of the three aforementioned definitions of the term "majority" before reaching its decision. To understand properly the Board's rationale in reaching the conclusion it did, it is advisable to relate briefly the surrounding circumstances in which the case was decided.

The case arose in 1936, one year after the Wagner Act had been passed. With the passage of the Act, many informal as well as previously clandestine, union organizations attempted to establish themselves as the legal statutory representatives of millions of employees around the country. Formal Board certification for these nascent unions, however, was beset with the com-

---

[1] 29 U.S.C. § 159(a) (1970).

[2] 2 N.L.R.B. 168 (1936).

TABLE 1. *Formulas for Determining the Majority Under Absolute, Quorum, and Simple Majority Rule*

Type of Rule	Voting Formula	Range of Employees Required to Elect Union Representation
Majority of all eligible employees (absolute majority rule)	$N/2 + 1$	51 to 100
Majority of ballots cast if a majority of employees have voted (Quorum Rule)	$V/2 + 1 > N/4$	26 to 100
Majority of ballots cast by participating voters (simple majority rule)	$V/2 + 1$	2 to 100

Note: N=total number of eligible employees.
       V=number of employees actually voting.

plexities and difficulties of the then existing labor situation. Not only were the majority of employers opposed to any form of unionism, but the labor movement itself was fragmentized into warring camps, the major combantants being the American Federation of Labor and the Committee for Industrial Organization.[3] Finally, the Great Depression still gripped the nation and many of the legislators who had supported the Act fervently hoped that institutionalized collective bargaining would be a partial solution to that all-encompassing dilemma.

Confronted with these difficulties, the Board found itself faced with a contested election at RCA's Camden, New Jersey plant. The controversy had arisen over numerous charges of misconduct involving a representation election in which only 3,163 ballots had been cast out of a possible 9,752 employees who were eligible to vote.[4] In the election, the United Electrical, Radio and Machine Workers, C.I.O. (UE), recipient of 3,016 of the 3,163 ballots cast, claimed to be the legal representative of all the RCA employees. During the election, however, a local, independent labor organization, known as the Employees' Committee Union, which was comprised solely of Camden, New Jersey

---

[3] For a more extensive discussion of the impact of the split in the labor movement upon the Board's election procedures see NORTHRUP AND BLOOM, GOVERNMENT AND LABOR 57-61 (1963).

[4] 2 N.L.R.B. at 168.

plant workers, had urged its members to boycott the election, asserting that the UE would not win unless it received a number of votes equal to the majority of all eligible voters.[5] In furtherance of this objective, the Employees' Committee Union instituted a massive propaganda campaign directed at employees to discourage their participation in the election.

The issue, thus presented for Board consideration, was whether the UE could be certified as exclusive bargaining representative despite the organized boycott of the Board's election process. First, the Board rejected the employer's argument that "majority of employees" refers to an absolute majority of the employees eligible to vote.[6] In reaching its decision, the Board chose to borrow from decisions involving the Railway Labor Act. Citing the famous *Virginia Railway Co. v. System Federation No. 40* [7] case, the Board pointed out that the Fourth Circuit had rejected this construction of the term "majority" in a Railway Labor Act case in which the union had received a majority of the votes cast, but not a majority of those qualified to vote.[8]

The second possible reading of the term majority is the so-called quorum rule. Under this interpretation, the phrase a "majority of employees," refers to the number of employees actually participating in the election, so that a labor organization can only claim victory in an election in which at least a majority of the eligible voters participate. Again the *Virginia Railway* case afforded precedent on this issue, but the Board refused to accept the district court's interpretation [9] that the phrase

---

[5] Presumably, the independent's campaign to boycott the election was based upon the rules of election procedure of the Railway Labor Act that was the early source of so many NLRB policies and procedures.

[6] 2 N.L.R.B. at 173.

[7] 84 F.2d 641 (4th Cir. 1936).

[8] 2 N.L.R.B. at 173. Commenting upon the applicability of the *Virginia Railway* case, the Board pointed to the similarity in language of the two Acts, adding that:

> [T]here is nothing in the legislative history to offset the normal presumption that the Congress intended to apply the same principles to the fields covered by the respective Acts, and the Board has followed these decisions [citing cases] and has not required that an organization must receive a number of votes equal to a majority of the eligible employees in order to be certified as exclusive representative. *Id.* at 174.

[9] System Federation No. 40 v. Virginia Railway Co., 11 F. Supp. 621 (D.C. Va. 1935).

"majority of any craft or class" referred to the number of employees participating in the election by anology to the quorum rule in corporate law.[10] In rebuttal to the district court's ruling, the Board cited the appellate court's decision in the same case in which the Fourth Circuit implied that it did not approve of the district court's quorum rule interpretation of the term "majority."[11] It is interesting to note that although the Board was willing to adopt principles of the Railway Labor Act, such borrowings would be selective in that the Board did not consider itself bound by all of the prior determinations pursuant to the railroad law.

Since the Board had rejected both the "absolute majority" rule and the "quorum rule" definitions of the term "majority," the only standard left, and the one formally adopted by the Board, was the principle that a union would be certified as long as it received a majority of the votes cast.[12] In support of this standard, the Board in *R.C.A. Mfg.* set forth two major policy considerations. First, the Board stated that it had rejected the quorum doctrine because it "place[d] a premium upon tactics of intimidation and sabotage," which could be utilized to thwart a definitive election by deterring enough employees from voting in order to prevent the requisite 50 percent participation.[13] Secondly, the Board asserted that its adoption of a simple majority rule was based upon the generally accepted principles of democratic elections—*i.e.* all qualified voters who absent themselves from the polls are deemed to assent to the will of the majority of those voting.[14] Of these two justifications, the former has

---

[10] 2 N.L.R.B. at 175.

[11] *Id.* Although the precise issue of the "quorum rule" had not been presented on appeal, thereby precluding the circuit court from passing upon its substantive validity, the court did comment that:

> The rule applied by the judge below would, on the principles applicable to a quorum in legislative assemblies, limit the choice by the majority of those voting to cases where a majority of the qualified voters participate in the election. 84 F.2d at 653.

[12] 2 N.L.R.B. at 177-79.

[13] *Id.* at 176.

[14] *Id.* at 177; *cf.* Carroll County v. Smith, 111 U.S. 556, 565 (1884); County of Cass v. Johnston, 95 U.S. 360, 369 (1878).

eroded over the years,[15] while the latter has become the keystone of the Board's majority rule.

The analogy to political elections rationale has enjoyed widespread support ever since its inception because it is based on far sounder policy, as well as practical considerations. Although both the Board and the courts have regularly recited the principle that those not voting in an election are considered to have assented to the wishes of the majority, a collateral justification of major importance is generally ignored. The Board's sister agency, the National Mediation Board (NMB), adopted the quorum rule as the statutory definition of the term "majority" as used in the Railway Labor Act.[16] Under the election procedures of the NMB, ballots include spaces for voting for named unions or individuals, or for "others," but a ballot marked "no representation" is considered invalid. Thus, in order for an employee to vote "against" a union, he either casts a blank ballot or simply does not vote. The implications of the NMB's electoral policy of refusing to permit employees to register affirmatively their opposition to union representation are so patently prounion, one commentator has been prompted to remark that:

> The NLRB procedure encourages voting; the NMB procedure does not. . . . The NMB quite frankly states that its "ballot was drafted to permit employees to secure some form of representation" . . . . The assumption used by the NMB to rationalize its restrictions on employee rights is that employees always will prefer some union representation to none. In a society in which 45 percent of the elections requested by unions under the jurisdiction of the NLRB find "no union" in a majority, the rationale of the NMB is as dishonest as it is nonsensical.[17]

On the other hand, in an early case, the NLRB adopted a change in ballot procedure which permitted employees to vote

---

[15] The Board last emphasized the prevention of unlawful conduct as an underlying basis for the "simple majority" rule in the early 1940's. *See* NLRB v. National Mineral Co., 134 F.2d 424, 12 L.R.R.M. 567 (7th Cir.), *cert. denied*, 320 U.S. 753, 13 L.R.R.M. 850 (1943); N. Y. Handkerchief Mfg. Co. v. NLRB, 114 F.2d 144, 6 L.R.R.M. 918 (7th Cir.), *cert. denied*, 311 U.S. 704, 7 L.R.R.M. 325 (1940).

[16] *See generally* Virginia Railway v. System Federation No. 40, 300 U.S. 515, 1 L.R.R.M. 743 (1937).

[17] Northrup, *The Railway Labor Act: A Critical Reappraisal*, 25 INDUST'L AND LAB. RELS. REV. 3, 23-24 (1971). *See also* Risher, *Selection of the Bargaining Representative Under the Railway Labor Act*, 17 VILL. L. REV. 246 (1971).

"no union." [18] The import of this seemingly minor procedural modification, when coupled with the Board's majority rule, serves to encourage participation in an election by all employees.[19] At the same time, the NLRB's ballot alerts employees to the fact that although a representation election is being conducted, the Board as an agency of the federal government, does not endorse or oppose the selection of a representative,[20] as is implicit in the NMB ballot which prevents an employee from voting against representation. Even under a system designed to encourage participation in elections, breakdowns do occur that seem to test the wisdom of the Board's "majority" standard. Thus, in one case in which only 32 percent of the eligible employees cast ballots, the Board rued the fact that more employees had not sought to exercise their franchise, but went on to state in defense of the "simple majority" rule that:

> [I]t is a well-established principle that in the conduct of a democratic election, where adequate opportunity to participate in the balloting is provided all those eligible to vote, the decision of the majority actually voting is binding on all. *The indifference or neglect of those failing to exercise the right given them by law should not be permitted to invalidate an otherwise properly conducted election.*[21]

BOARD STANDARDS FOR DETERMINING THE REPRESENTATIVE CHARACTER OF THE VOTE

Had the Board in *R.C.A. Mfg. Co.* adopted the more rigid rule requiring a majority of all eligible voters to vote for union

---

[18] Interlake Iron Corp., 4 N.L.R.B. 55 (1937). In this case, the Board refused to adopt the cumbersome NMB procedure, criticizing it by implication in its statement that it:

> . . . see[s] no advantage in forcing employees who disapprove of the nominees to adopt the rather ambiguous method of expression involved in casting a blank ballot, when their choice can be clearly indicated by providing a space therefore. *Id.* at 61-62.

[19] NLRB elections have averaged 80 to 90 percent participation by those eligible, while national elections draw only 50 to 65 percent of the electorate.

[20] Indeed, the Board jealously guards its neutrality, prohibiting the distribution of sample ballots which have been altered to indicate a proposed choice. *See* Allied Electric Products, Inc., 109 N.L.R.B. 1270, 34 L.R.R.M. 1538 (1954); *see also* discussion in Chapters XIV & XV, *supra.*

[21] S. W. Evans & Sons, 75 N.L.R.B. 811, 813, 21 L.R.R.M. 1081 (1948) (emphasis added).

representation in order for certification, the issue of whether an election was clearly representative, so as to justify certification for the purpose of collective bargaining, may never have arisen. Under the actual standard, however, the potentiality always exists that the Board may become embroiled in an election dispute that is essentially a "numbers game."

Preserving Flexibility: The Board's Refusal to Establish Objective Standards

The Board standard for testing the "representativeness" of an election can be stated succinctly. An election is deemed representative if there is sufficient notice and adequate opportunity to vote and there is no evidence of intereference with the electoral process. While the standard is essentially a three-step analysis, its application in a purely mechanistic manner may result in apparent inequities. For example, in *Valencia Service Co.,*[22] only five votes were cast in a bargaining unit comprised of sixteen eligible employees. Of the five, a bare majority of three cast votes for union representation.[23] Thus, a subsequent certification was based on an election in which only 31 percent of the employees participated and moreover, a mere 19 percent of the potential electorate was sufficient to impose union representation on the entire unit.

In most cases, however, the Board's pattern of decision-making reflects the reality of the election process in that as the percentage of voter participation rises, the likelihood of the election being set aside as unrepresentative declines. For this reason, when the percentage of voter participation is low, the Board's equitable conscience may induce the NLRB to color its judgment to the extent that very minor breaches of notice or opportunity will be considered objectionable; hence, the election will be set aside.[24]

As the government agency entrusted with the regulation of representation elections, the Board enjoys a wide degree of discretion in determining whether or not a particular vote has been representative. For example, in *Standard Lime and Stone*

---

[22] 99 N.L.R.B. 343, 30 L.R.R.M. 1074 (1952).

[23] *Id.* at 344, 30 L.R.R.M. at 1074.

[24] *See, e.g.,* Mechling Barge Lines, 69 N.L.R.B. 838, 18 L.R.R.M. 1270 (1946) (21 percent participating); Weldmaster Co., 56 N.L.R.B. 168 (1944) (18 percent participating).

Co.,[25] after upholding an election in which less than one-half of the employees had participated, the Board elaborated on the grounds upon which the issue of whether an election is representative could be raised. Briefly, the Board stated that where a majority of the electorate does not participate, a question is raised concerning the representative character of the vote but such minority participation does not operate *ipso facto* to render the results of a minority election invalid.[26] As in all representative vote cases, the Board, in *Standard Lime and Stone*, declined to set forth any numerical standard, stating that an election would be deemed representative if a "substantial" number of employees participated.

Although the lack of any definitive standard for establishing whether an election is representative produces uncertainty, the exercise of such discretion by the Board is supported by the courts and Congress. In *NLRB v. A.J. Tower Co.*[27] the Supreme Court affirmed the Board's ability to employ discretionary standards in conducting certification elections, stating that its discretion was limited only by the general principles of democratic elections.

Furthermore, even though the discretionary character of the Board's role sometimes results in conflicting decisions, the need for flexibility in this area of election objections far outweighs the desirability of mechanical rules to ensure certainty and uniformity. Since the issue of whether an election has been representative is ultimately a question of fact [28] as opposed to one of law, each case is unique. An inflexible approach would serve only to obscure the issues, since the Board would be forced to categorize rather than analyze the factual situation.

---

25 56 N.L.R.B. 522, 14 L.R.R.M. 220 (1944).

26 *Id.* at 523, 14 L.R.R.M. at 220.

27 329 U.S. 324, 19 L.R.R.M. 2128 (1946). Setting forth the bounds of the Board's discretionary authority pursuant to the NLRA, the Court stated that:

. . . Congress has entrusted the Board with a wide degree of discretion in establishing the procedure and safeguards necessary to insure the fair and free choice of bargaining representatives by employees. . . . In carrying out this task, of course, the Board must act so as to give effect to the principle of majority rule set forth in § 9(a). . . . *Id.* at 330-31, 19 L.R.R.M. at 2131.

28 *See* NLRB v. Central Dispensary & Emergency Hospital, 145 F.2d 852, 854, 15 L.R.R.M. 643, 645 (D.C. Cir. 1944).

Because the Board's authority in determining whether a particular vote has been truly representative is of a discretionary nature, its findings are subject to judicial review in the event that the judgment of the Board is arbitrary.[29] Thus, in *NLRB v. N.Y. Handkerchief Mfg. Co.*,[30] the Court of Appeals for the Seventh Circuit conceded that the Board had the authority to make a certification upon the results of a minority election, where an employer had interfered with the right of his employees to participate and thus was directly responsible for the small voter turnout. The court, however, added that "[i]t does not follow . . . that the Board could justify itself in the exercise of such authority in every case regardless of the number who participated in the election."[31] Had the Board adopted the Seventh Circuit's limitation, a minority election could be representative only if there was an insufficient opportunity to vote, inadequate notice, or, as in *N.Y. Handkerchief,* evidence of employer interference.

Four years later, in *NLRB v. Central Dispensary & Emergency Hosp.*,[32] the D. C. Circuit enforced a Board order[33] enjoining an employer from further refusals to bargain with a union which had been certified as bargaining representative on the basis of a minority election. The employer's objections were based in part on the *N.Y. Handkerchief* case, claiming that the Seventh Circuit's proposed limitation on Board discretion in minority election cases precluded enforcement of the Board's bargaining order, since there were none of the interferences in the election process which the court had enumerated as grounds for enforcement. The D. C. Circuit, however, rejected this argument, stating that the limitation set forth in *N.Y. Handkerchief* was restricted to that case, therefore, no rigid rule requiring a majority of all employees in the absence of employer interference should be adopted.[34] Instead, the court indicated that the real test is

29 *Id.*, 15 L.R.R.M. at 645.

30 114 F.2d 144, 6 L.R.R.M. 918 (7th Cir. 1940).

31 *Id.* at 149, 6 L.R.R.M. at 923.

32 145 F.2d 852, 15 L.R.R.M. 643 (D.C. Cir. 1944), *cert. denied,* 342 U.S. 847, 16 L.R.R.M. 917 (1945).

33 Central Dispensary & Emergency Hospital, 50 N.L.R.B. 393, 12 L.R.R.M. 222 (1943).

34 145 F.2d at 854, 15 L.R.R.M. at 645.

whether the vote is representative, and this is always a question of fact.[35]

The Board crystallized its policy regarding the representative character of minority elections in *Stiefel Construction Corp.*[36] In this case, the Board initiated its reasoning with the proposition that its concern over elections was twofold: (1) each employee must be afforded a reasonable opportunity to cast a secret ballot if he desires; and (2) no compulsion should be put on any employee to exercise his vote.[37] If these two conditions are fulfilled, the Board went on to say that:

> [Because t]he only purpose of an election is to resolve the majority issue, [where] an election is fairly conducted and employees eligible to vote are freely permitted to do so, the results of the election must be deemed conclusive, if the vote cast be a "representative vote." [38]

Finally, the Board focused on the issue of the representative character of the vote itself, concluding that absent a showing that any employee has been denied his right to vote or prevented from fully exercising his choice, the election is by definition representative, and any other "reasons for neglect to vote are not material to the issue." [39]

THE PARAMETERS OF A "REPRESENTATIVE ELECTION"

Since an election is *prima facie* representative absent evidence to the contrary, the "representative character of the vote" can be best explained by analyzing the various objections which the Board has recognized as constituting the metes and bounds of a "representative" election. The overwhelming majority of these objections arise in four types of cases involving the effects of (1) employer interference; (2) a fluctuating bargaining unit; (3) participation by one employee; and (4) inclement weather. The Board concerns itself with the affirmative duties of the parties in assessing objections to the representativeness of the

---

35 *Id.*, 15 L.R.R.M. at 645.

36 65 N.L.R.B. 925, 17 L.R.R.M. 251 (1946).

37 *Id.* at 926, 17 L.R.R.M. at 251.

38 *Id.* at 926-27, 17 L.R.R.M. at 251.

39 *Id.* at 927, 17 L.R.R.M. at 252.

vote. Since the only duty imposed upon a union is of a negative character—*i.e.* to refrain from interference with the election, the issue of union misconduct which results in an unrepresentative vote never arises.

Employer Interference

When an alleged failure of an election to produce a representative vote can be traced directly to acts of the employer, the Board has formulated a principle of estoppel that serves to bar the employer from asserting lack of representativeness as a basis for an objection. For example, in *Butler Specialty Co.*[40] the Board rejected an employer's contention that an election, which drew only 71 participants out of a possible electorate of 203, was not representative because the company, which now considered the vote insufficient, had not only refused to participate in the arrangements for the election but had also failed to post notices. In effect, the company's own obstructive conduct estopped it from asserting that the election was not representative.

In determining whether the employer's conduct has contributed to a minority election, the Board will look to circumstances that it feels are a critical part of the employer's obligation to assist the Board in conducting a representative election. For example, the refusal of an employer to post notices of an election is probably the single, most crucial factor which will negate an employer's contention that the vote was not representative. An intentional failure to perform this obligation apparently precludes *per se* any objection by an employer based on non-representativeness.[41] Under the same rationale, when an employer urges his employees to boycott an election through notices of his own, he cannot then contend that the subsequent election has not been representative.[42] Of secondary import, the refusal on the part of an employer to furnish an eligibility list, or alternatively, to seek an injunction against the election, may also estop an employer, on the basis of his

---

[40] 29 N.L.R.B. 430, 7 L.R.R.M. 245 (1941).

[41] *See generally* NLRB v. National Mineral Co., 134 F.2d 424, 12 L.R.R.M. 567 (7th Cir. 1943); Atlantic Basin Iron Works, 72 N.L.R.B. 508 (1947); Butler Specialty Co., 29 N.L.R.B. 430, 7 L.R.R.M. 245 (1941).

[42] NLRB v. Singleton Packing Co., 418 F.2d 275, 72 L.R.R.M. 2519 (5th Cir. 1969).

interfering conduct, from claiming the election has not been representative in character.[43]

Fluctuations in the Bargaining Unit

Pursuant to Board policy, which requires that elections be representative, the Board has adopted the principle that elections conducted among employees of seasonal industries, notably the food-packing industry, must be conducted at the "peak of the season."[44] The Board adopted this rule regulating the timing of an election in *San Fernando Heights Lemon Ass'n*.[45] In that case, only 56 of an average 113 workers employed at the peak of the season were actually employed during the payroll period used to establish the eligibility date, and of these employees, only 44 were engaged at the plant at the time of the election.[46] Because only one-half of the potential voters were eligible, the Board found that the election could not be considered representative of the desires of the entire bargaining unit and, therefore, set aside the election, directing a second election for the peak of the next packing season.[47]

While the Board requires that an election be held at the "peak of the season" because of the special problems of voter eligibility and participation posed by seasonal industries, the right of the employees of these industries to organize for the purpose of collective bargaining remains intact. For example, the employer in *California Almond Growers' Exchange*,[48] whose business was seasonal, contended that the nature of his operation rendered collective bargaining difficult, if not impossible, because of the shortness of the season and the high turnover of employees both within a particular season and between operating seasons. The Board overruled both of these objections, finding

---

43 NLRB v. National Mineral Co., 134 F.2d 424, 427-28, 12 L.R.R.M. 567, 570-71 (7th Cir. 1943).

44 *E.g.*, Camp & Felder Compress Co., 121 N.L.R.B. 871, 42 L.R.R.M. 1481 (1958); Richard A. Glass Co., 120 N.L.R.B. 914, 42 L.R.R.M. 1087 (1958); Grower-Shipper Vegetable Ass'n, 112 N.L.R.B. 807, 36 L.R.R.M. 1112 (1955).

45 72 N.L.R.B. 372, 19 L.R.R.M. 1174 (1947).

46 *Id.* at 376, 19 L.R.R.M. at 1176.

47 *Id.* at 377, 19 L.R.R.M. at 1176.

48 73 N.L.R.B. 1367, 1370, 20 L.R.R.M. 1102, 1103 (1947).

that the evidence showed that the length of the employer's season was no different from any other seasonal operations wherein elections for the purpose of determining a collective bargaining representative had been held. Furthermore, the fact that the company made it a practice to notify former employees of the resumption of the season indicated its interest in maintaining the same complement of employees which should serve to maintain some stability within the designated unit.[49]

In view of the Board rule requiring elections in seasonal industries to be held at the "peak of the season" in order to encompass the widest possible electorate within the appropriate unit, by analogy, one might anticipate that an election in an expanding unit would be postponed until a relatively stable complement of employees had been attained. Other than in an exceptional instance, this has not been the case.

In *Rowe-Jordan Furniture Corp.*[50] an unique situation did arise in which the Board set aside an election because of the unit expansion which had occurred at the time of the election and continued for several months thereafter. Resolving challenges to the ballots of all 88 participants in the election, the Board found that only 18 ballots had been cast by eligible voters.[51] The large number of invalid ballots were attributable to a change in the national labor laws coupled with a permanent replacement of strikers by the employer.[52] Since the normal work force within the unit had reached approximately 106 at the time of the post-election hearing, the Board ordered a new election to be taken among the full complement of employees.[53]

The *Rowe-Jordan* case is atypical and must be limited to the special circumstances which had decimated the ranks of eligible voters at the time of the election. Shortly before *Rowe-Jordan* was decided, the Board had rejected several claims by employers that elections be set aside because of the alleged nonrepresentative character of the employee complement who participatd in

---

[49] *Id.* at 1370-71, 20 L.R.R.M. at 1103.

[50] 81 N.L.R.B. 190, 196, 23 L.R.R.M. 1310, 1312 (1949).

[51] *Id.* at 194-196, 23 L.R.R.M. at 1312.

[52] *Id.* at 192, 23 L.R.R.M. at 1310.

[53] *Id.* at 196, 23 L.R.R.M. at 1312.

the election.[54] For example, in *New Era Shirt Co.*[55] the Board refused to set aside an election even when the number of full-time employees had increased from 42 at the time of the election, to 62 at the time of the hearing. Subsequently, the Board has reiterated its position that a postelection expansion in the unit is irrelevant in determining whether an election has been representative or not.[56]

Recently, the Board in *Business Aviation, Inc.*[57] was presented with an opportunity to review its position regarding the effect of employee turnover on the representative character of an election. The employer's objection was based on the fact that subsequent to the Board's Direction of Election, the number of eligible employees was reduced from five to two by voluntary termination in a unit normally comprised of five employees.[58] The Board listed four factors as determinative in its decision to certify the election over the employer's objection. These factors are as follows: (1) there was no expansion or contraction in the size of the unit; (2) the business was not seasonal with recognizable peaks of employment; (3) there was no destruction of the unit through transfer or relocation of the business; and (4) there were no improprieties in the election nor were any voters prevented from voting.[59]

Even a complete turnover in employees between the election and time at which a petition for certification is filed, will not bar a union from being designated the statutory representative of the unit. Thus, in *Orleans Storage Co.*,[60] the Board refused to set aside an election after all five eligible employees who had cast ballots were no longer members of the bargaining unit.[61] In

---

54 *E.g.*, New Era Shirt Co., 79 N.L.R.B. 213, 22 L.R.R.M. 1388 (1948); Cities Service Oil Co. of Pennsylvania, 77 N.L.R.B. 853, 22 L.R.R.M. 1100 (1948).

55 79 N.L.R.B. at 216, 22 L.R.R.M. at 1389.

56 Guidry's Auto Service, 108 N.L.R.B. 103, 104, 33 L.R.R.M. 1494 (1954).

57 202 N.L.R.B. No. 151, 82 L.R.R.M. 1710 (1973).

58 *Id.*, 82 L.R.R.M. at 1711.

59 *Id.*, 82 L.R.R.M. at 1711.

60 123 N.L.R.B. 1757, 44 L.R.R.M. 1226 (1959).

61 Of the five, three had resigned, one had been discharged for cause, and one had been promoted to a supervisory position. *Id.* at 1758, 44 L.R.R.M. at 1226.

support of its decision, the Board stated that the employer, by stipulating to a consent election, had contractually agreed that a representative vote could be taken among the employees eligible to vote on the election date. Furthermore, the Board added that there had been no change in the essential character of the bargaining unit since the election.[62] The Board rationalized that when fortuitous circumstances precipitate a complete turnover of employees, it should not be a valid basis for voiding an election. The Board felt that if it held otherwise, the finality sought to be given representative elections would be destroyed, especially in cases where employee turnover could affect the election results.[63] Implicit in the Board's decision is its realization of the possibility that an employer, through hiring and firing, may be able to forestall the consequences of a union victory at the polls.

Participation by One Employee

An interesting problem within the general category of the representative character of an election occurs when only one employee participates in an election and casts his ballot for the union. In the first place, pursuant to the principle of collective bargaining, which presupposes that there is more than one eligible person who desires to bargain, the Board will not certify a labor organization seeking to represent a one-man unit.[64]

A similar situation arises when only one eligible voter in the entire unit actually participates and casts his ballot for the union. Initially, the Board in *Williams Dimond & Co.*,[65] took the position that pursuant to the principle established in *R.C.A. Mfg.*, the majority of employees referred to in the NLRA is a majority of those participating; thus, the one vote which was cast represented this majority. Subsequently, the Board changed its position in 1942,[66] and has held ever since that when only one em-

---

[62] *Id.*, 44 L.R.R.M. at 1226.

[63] *Id.*, 44 L.R.R.M. at 1226.

[64] Luckenbach Steamship Co., 2 N.L.R.B. 181, 1 L.R.R.M. 91 (1936). *See also* Al & Dick's Steak House, Inc., 129 N.L.R.B. 1207, 47 L.R.R.M. 1147 (1960); Foreign Car Center, 129 N.L.R.B. 319, 46 L.R.R.M. 1538 (1960).

[65] 2 N.L.R.B. 859, 870, 1 L.R.R.M. 116 (1937). *See also* Aluminum Line, 9 N.L.R.B. 72, 3 L.R.R.M. 231 (1938).

[66] S.A. Kendall, Jr., 41 N.L.R.B. 395, 9 L.R.R.M. 314 (1942) (three-man unit).

ployee in the unit participates in the election, no certification will be issued because the one vote is not considered representative of the desires of the employees.[67]

Recently, the Board in *Gemco Automotive Center # 507*,[68] certified a union subsequent to an election in which of the two eligible employees within the proposed unit, one cast his ballot for the union and the other ballot was void. The Board reasoned that since both employees eligible to vote had done so, the fact that one of them cast a void ballot does not alter the fact of his participation. Moreover, the Board felt that although a second election might yield a different result, it could not be more representative.[69] Pursuant to Board doctrine, however, certification of a representative is based on a *majority of valid votes cast, not on the majority of all votes cast.*[70] Thus, in an election in which ten employees participate, if four votes are cast for union representation, three are cast for "no union" and three are void, the union will be certified, although it has not received a majority of all ballots.

Inclement Weather

In 1950, the Board in *Red Wing Potteries, Inc.*,[71] refused to set aside an election that was alleged to be nonrepresentative on the grounds that inclement weather and hazardous road conditions at the site of the balloting prevented an adequate opportunity to vote for 40 eligible employees who resided in rural areas. Although the vote separating the competing unions was less than 2 percent,[72] the Board held that since nearly 91 percent of the

---

[67] *E.g.*, Kit Mfg. Co., 198 N.L.R.B. No. 131, 81 L.R.R.M. 1136 (1971) (two-man unit); Firestone Tire & Rubber Co., 57 N.L.R.B. 868 (1944) (four-man unit); Gold & Baker, 54 N.L.R.B. 869, 13 L.R.R.M. 235 (1944) (two-man unit).

[68] 198 N.L.R.B. No. 128, 81 L.R.R.M. 1020 (1972).

[69] *Id.*, 81 L.R.R.M. at 1021.

[70] *See, e.g.*, Semi-Steel Casting Co. v. NLRB, 160 F.2d 388, 19 L.R.R.M. 2458 (8th Cir. 1947); Albion Malleable Iron Co., 104 N.L.R.B. 225, 32 L.R.R.M. 1084 (1953).

[71] 87 N.L.R.B. 1234, 1235, 25 L.R.R.M. 1458 (1950).

[72] The C.I.O. affiliate had carried the election with a total of 208 votes versus the 201 ballots received by the AFL affiliate. *Id.* at 1234, 25 L.R.R.M. at 1458.

eligible voters had participated, the election could be deemed as a representative reflection of the desires of the employees.

The same issue was raised in a 1971 election, wherein the Sixth Circuit, in *NLRB v. Wolverine World Wide, Inc.,*[73] held that despite inclement weather conditions during the election, the 71 percent who did participate constituted a representative majority. Although *Red Wing Potteries* was put forth by the Board as authoritative, the court held that it was not dispositive of the *Wolverine* case because it is conceivable that a party could show that weather conditions had caused an otherwise valid election to be nonrepresentative.[74] The weather, legally an "Act of God," constitutes an uncontrollable instrumentality which can only be forestalled by use of a mail ballot.[75] The Sixth Circuit suggested that an investigation, conducted upon the introduction of proper evidence, would be a workable means of ensuring that an election be representative.[76]

NOTICE OF ELECTION

Prior to the date on which the election is scheduled, a Board agent attempts to arrange adequate publicity of the election "by the posting of official notices in the [employer's] establishment whenever possible or in other places, or by the use of other means considered appropriate and effective. These notices reproduce a sample ballot and outline such election details as location of polls, time of voting, and eligibility rules."[77] In general, the Board agent attempts to have the notices placed in conspicuous places, such as on a bulletin board or on a timecard rack. As previously indicated,[78] one of the primary determinants of whether an election is in fact representative, is that the parties receive sufficient notice prior to the election. Generally, the Board

---

[73] 477 F.2d 969, 83 L.R.R.M. 2309 (6th Cir. 1973).

[74] *Id.* at 972, 83 L.R.R.M. at 2311.

[75] *See* Continental Bus System, Inc., 104 N.L.R.B. 599, 601, 32 L.R.R.M. 1135, 1136 (1953), wherein the Board upheld a regional director's decision to conduct a ballot by mail because of potentially adverse weather conditions.

[76] *Cf.* P.D. Gwaltney, Jr., and Co., Inc., 74 N.L.R.B. 371, 20 L.R.R.M. 1172, 1173-74 (1947).

[77] NLRB *Statements of Procedure,* Series 8, *as amended,* § 101.19(a)(1).

[78] *See* p. 397, *supra.*

emphasizes the extent of employee participation actually achieved whenever lack of notice is raised as an objection to an election. Consequently, the success of this type of objection is dependent upon the objecting party's ability to show that a group of employees, sufficient in number to have affected the final outcome of the election had they voted, were in fact prevented from voting because of a failure of notice.[79]

Notice to Employees

The issue of adequate and sufficient notice is not restricted to the narrow question of whether it reached the employee participants, but also whether the exactitude, quality of information, and neutrality of the notification conform to Board standards of election procedure. Furthermore, the notice requirement is not limited to employees only, but extends to labor organizations when they are able to show a sufficient interest among a substantial number of employees.

Proper Time Period of Pre-election Notification. Until quite recently, there has never been any standard establishing a definite period of time for which a notice must be posted in order to be considered sufficient.[80] Since the scheduling of elections has always been deemed to be within the discretionary authority of the regional director,[81] the Board has refrained from attempting to fix any objective standards for notification. Instead, the Board has fallen back on the principle that if a vote could be deemed representative in character, the actual time period required for posting is irrelevant.[82]

When set against this background, the Board's recent decision in *Kilgore Corp.*[83] is a marked contrast. Reviewed by the entire five-member Board, the *Kilgore* case produced a remarkedly sharp

---

[79] *E.g.*, Atlas Imperial Diesel Engine Co., 93 N.L.R.B. 268, 269-71, 27 L.R.R.M. 1368, 1369-70 (1951).

[80] *See* G. R. Garrett Co., 72 N.L.R.B. 1260, 19 L.R.R.M. 1264 (1947).

[81] Postex Cotton Mills, Inc., 73 N.L.R.B. 673, 677 & n.6, 20 L.R.R.M. 1028, 1029 (1947) (citing cases).

[82] Lloyd A. Fry Roofing Co., 121 N.L.R.B. 1433, 1435, 43 L.R.R.M. 1013, 1014 (1958); G. R. Garrett Co., Inc., 72 N.L.R.B. 1260, 1263, 19 L.R.R.M. 1264, 1265 (1947); American France Line, 6 N.L.R.B. 311, 312, 2 L.R.R.M. 237, 239 (1938).

[83] 203 N.L.R.B. No. 28, 83 L.R.R.M. 1010 (1973).

and incongruous split of opinion.[84] Although it is premature to engage in speculation as to whether the majority opinion in *Kilgore* actually set forth the objective standards which the dissent claimed it did,[85] it certainly provided a fresh perspective in analyzing objections grounded on insufficient time of notice posting.

The procedural background in the *Kilgore* case may be summarized as follows: The tally of ballots issued by the regional director following the election revealed that of approximately 272 eligible voters, 132 cast ballots for union representation, 132 votes were cast for "no union," one ballot was void, and four were challenged. Pursuant to the rulings of the regional director on the challenged ballots, it was shown that although the petitioning union had not received a majority of the ballots cast, the union's objection, that the employer's failure to post notices until one day prior to the election constituted insufficient notice to the employees, was sustained. Subsequently, the employer took exception to the regional director's findings on two grounds: (1) that the notice was sufficient, since all but three out of a possible 272 voters had participated in the election; and (2) that the union waived its right to object over the tardy posting because it had declined to delay the election to cure the defect in posting.[86]

In *Kilgore* the regional director had mailed ten official notices to the employer, two weeks prior to the election, with instructions that they be posted immediately "at conspicuous [and] usual posting places easily accessible to the eligible employees." The employer delayed, finally posting one in the personnel office two to three days before the election and a second one in the employee cafeteria the day before the election.[87]

In its criticism of the majority action which sustained the

---

[84] In a departure from the usual majority composition of the Board, Chairman Miller joined Members Fanning and Jenkins in the majority opinion.

[85] 203 N.L.R.B. No. 28, 83 L.R.R.M. at 1012.

[86] *Id.*, 83 L.R.R.M. at 1010.

[87] *Id.*, 83 L.R.R.M. at 1010. The notice posted in the personnel office was considered inconspicuous because few employees ever visited the office. Consequently, the cafeteria notice was the only one which was actually accessible to the employees, and even it could be seen only during the three work breaks and two lunch periods immediately preceeding the election.

union's objection on the basis of insufficient notice, the minority claimed that the majority would:

> require at the very least, [1] that the posting be in areas housing the employee's work stations, [2] for a period which allows more than five opportunities to observe the notice before the election, and [3] time to ask questions and discuss the election issues.[88]

The first two of these purportedly new standards are elements of the definitional dispute over the meaning of the term "conspicuous." Whether the posting in the employee cafeteria could be deemed conspicuous in other circumstances is a question of fact and thus establishes no real new standards of election conduct. Indeed, the failure, or in this case the extreme delay of the employer, to post notices of an election has always been construed as electoral interference.[89]

Ironically, it is the third factor—*i.e.* providing time to the employees "to ask questions and discuss the election issues"— that is new. Time and again, objections have been raised to no avail that the failure to post notices for an adequate period of time prior to the election precluded employees from fully discussing and acquainting themselves with the issues in an upcoming election.[90] In considering this point, the Board squarely confronted the issue implicit in many cases in the notice area—*i.e.* if the Board is going to enforce strictly the requirement that *official* notification must be given, it must, therefore, serve some purpose. Elaborating upon this theme, the Board stated:

> Apart from information . . . as to the date, time and place of polling, eligibility requirements, and the type of ballot used, the official election notices . . . contain important information with respect to the rights of employees. . . . All these matters should have been brought to the employees' attention sufficiently in advance of the election that by the day of the election, they could have asked any

---

[88] *Id.*, 83 L.R.R.M. at 1012.

[89] *E.g.*, NLRB v. National Mineral Co., 134 F.2d 424, 12 L.R.R.M. 567 (7th Cir. 1943); Atlantic Basin Iron Works, 72 N.L.R.B. 508 (1947); Butler Specialty Co., 29 N.L.R.B. 430, 7 L.R.R.M. 245 (1941). *See also* pp. 401-402, *supra*, for a brief discussion of the estoppel principle that the Board utilizes in cases involving the failure of an employer to post official notices of an upcoming election.

[90] *See, e.g.*, General Plywood Corp., 83 N.L.R.B. 197 (1949); Griffin-Goodner Grocery Co., 73 N.L.R.B. 1332, 20 L.R.R.M. 1099 (1947); G. R. Garrett Co., 72 N.L.R.B. 1260, 19 L.R.R.M 1264 (1947); United States Gypsum Co, 70 N.L.R.B. 1322, 18 L.R.R.M. 1450 (1946); Proximity Print Works, 11 N.L.R.B. 379, 3 L.R.R.M. 587 (1939).

questions that bothered them . . . and could discuss the election issues with their fellow employees and friends so they might come to a reasoned decision by the date of the election.[91]

Since the Board has often held that the employees have an obligation to inquire as to the nature of the notice as it applies to them,[92] it is not unreasonable to provide a period of time for this purpose. Implicit in Section 7 of the Act, which grants employees the right either to engage in efforts at self-organization or to refrain from the activities of labor organizations, is the presumption that they will be given reasonable time in which to evaluate their options in order to reach an intelligent decision.[93] This important policy consideration militates against those cases in which the Board has held that notification is sufficient as long as it conveys the very limited information of time and place of the election.[94]

Failure of Employer to Post Notices Within His Establishment

Clearly, when an employer has received and subsequently refuses to post the official election notices, he is in effect, estopped from claiming that the official election is nonrepresentative because the employees did not receive adequate notice. Nonetheless, such an objection must be considered by the Board because the employer

---

[91] 203 N.L.R.B. No. 28, 83 L.R.R.M. at 1010-1011.

[92] *E.g.*, NLRB v. Singleton Packing Corp., 418 F.2d 275, 72 L.R.R.M. 2519 (5th Cir. 1969) (it was incumbent upon employees to disregard their employer's notice urging them to refrain from voting); Rohr Aircraft Corp., 136 N.L.R.B. 958, 49 L.R.R.M. 1886 (1962) (laid-off employees who were not included on any eligibility list, absent any notification that they were in fact eligible, should have attempted to cast challenge ballots or protests in some other manner to the Board); Boeing Airplane Co., 88 N.L.R.B. 227, 25 L.R.R.M. 1314 (1950) (where notice of election did not include any eligibility date, all employees should have attempted to vote anyway).

[93] *See* Overland Hauling, Inc., 168 N.L.R.B. 870, 67 L.R.R.M. 1003 (1967), wherein the Board held that the purpose of including the section on "Rights of Employees" in the official notice was to alert employees of their rights under the Act and in order to warn unions and management alike against conduct impeding fair and free elections.
Since the Board in *Overland Hauling* considered the information contained in this part of the notice necessary to maintain the "laboratory conditions" essential for the election process, it follows that employees should have the opportunity not only to read the notice, but also to weigh it in reaching their decision.

[94] *E.g.*, Griffin-Goodner Grocery Co., 73 N.L.R.B. 1332, 20 L.R.R.M. 1099 (1947).

does not have an absolute duty to post notices of the election on his premises.[95] Since the employer's objection is probably triggered by a union victory at the polls, the Board's findings appear *pro forma*, considering what alternate means of notification were used to inform the employees of the election, and finding that these alternatives have been an effective substitute, thereby ensuring a representative election.

Two other situations involving an employer's failure or refusal to post notices of the election may also arise. The first instance occurs when an employer is seeking either to postpone the election or to dispute the eligibility of certain employees. Secondly, an employer may simply not have received the official notices of the election from the Board and in turn posts notices of his own to inform his employees of the election.

Alternate Notification. Alternate means of notification to employees may be undertaken by the union as well as by the Board agent(s) in charge of the election. Thus, the union may supplement the efforts of the Board to publicize an election in the face of an employer refusal to cooperate by posting notices.[96] The forms of supplementary notification by the union which the Board has approved range from a series of radio messages, telegrams, and public address system announcements in a maritime case,[97] through union-sponsored meetings and handbills,[98] to distributing copies of the official election notice to employees.[99] Presumably, alternate notification based solely upon supplementary notices by the union, will be insufficient unless participated in by Board agents to some extent.[100] Indeed, the Board has stated that "[b]y no stretch of the imagination will campaign literature of

---

[95] *E.g.*, Kingsport Press, Inc., 146 N.L.R.B. 1111, 56 L.R.R.M. 1007 (1964).

[96] *See generally* The Root Store, 88 N.L.R.B. 289, 25 L.R.R.M. 1316 (1950); Cities Service Oil Co. of Pennsylvania, 87 N.L.R.B. 324, 25 L.R.R.M. 1112 (1949); Stonewall Cotton Mills, 78 N.L.R.B. 28, 22 L.R.R.M. 1167 (1948).

[97] Cities Service Oil Co. of Pennsylvania, 87 N.L.R.B. 324, 329, 25 L.R.R.M. 1112 (1949).

[98] Stonewall Cotton Mills, 78 N.L.R.B. 28, 29, 22 L.R.R.M. 1167 (1948).

[99] The Root Store, 88 N.L.R.B. 289, 290, 25 L.R.R.M. 1316 (1950).

[100] *See* The Falmouth Co., 115 N.L.R.B. 1533, 38 L.R.R.M. 1124 (1956). In *Falmouth*, the Board held that distribution of election notices among the employees, and the posting of notices on utility poles in front of the employer's plant by agents of the Board and the union constituted adequate notice. *Id.* at 1536, 38 L.R.R.M. at 1125.

the parties take the place of an official Board notice." [101] Consequently, if the Board agents fail to attempt any means of alternate notification to the employees, the Board should conclude that sufficient notice has not occurred, where the sole source of information is comprised of union handbills and the like. The rationale for this policy is apparent when one considers that it is highly probable that such partisan literature would most likely be directed toward union members and supporters rather than the entire unit.

Substitute Notification by an Employer. Since the Board alone is charged with maintaining the proper conduct of an election,[102] a question arises as to whether an employer is able to maintain adequate safeguards of the electoral process through the substitution of his own notice if he fails to receive an official Board notice before the election takes place. This situation first arose in *McKesson & Robbins, Inc.*,[103] wherein the company substituted notices it had in its possession from a previous election. The sample ballot contained therein, however, was the standard sample ballot used for union-authorization elections rather than representation elections. Under these circumstances, the Board found that the employees were not properly apprised of the issue in the election and, therefore, there was "substantial doubt" as to whether proper election standards had been maintained.[104]

Three years later, in *Pegwill Packing Co.*[105] the Board again considered whether an election should be set aside when an employer posted a substitute notice because he had not received the official notices. In this case, however, prior to the election the employer had called a meeting of his employees to explain the situation and inform them as to the time and place of the election, the composition of the appropriate unit, that the election would be conducted by secret ballot, and that it would be supervised by Board agents.[106] The notice which the employer substi-

---

[101] Kilgore Corp., 203 N.L.R.B. No. 28, 83 L.R.R.M. 1010 (1973).

[102] *E.g.*, NLRB v. A. J. Tower Co., 329 U.S. 324, 330, 19 L.R.R.M. 2128, 2131 (1946); NLRB v. Southern S.S. Co., 316 U.S. 31, 37, 10 L.R.R.M. 544, 547 (1942); NLRB v. Falk Corp., 308 U.S. 453, 458, 5 L.R.R.M. 677, 680 (1940).

[103] 106 N.L.R.B. 1220, 32 L.R.R.M. 1654 (1953).

[104] *Id.*, 32 L.R.R.M. at 1655.

[105] 115 N.L.R.B. 1151, 38 L.R.R.M. 1009 (1956).

[106] *Id.* at 1152, 38 L.R.R.M. at 1009.

tuted had failed to include certain information as to the employee's Section 7 rights. The regional director, relying upon *McKesson & Robbins*, recommended that a new election be directed because the failure to include the statement concerning employee rights created a "substantial doubt" that proper election standards had been met.[107]

Rather surprisingly, the Board upheld the employer's exceptions to the recommendations of the regional director, finding that despite the absence of the section pertaining to employee rights, the official notices, did in fact, adequately apprise the employees of the issue in the election—namely, whether the employees wished to be represented by the petitioning labor organization.[108] The Board distinguished *McKesson & Robbins* on the grounds that unlike the situation in *Pegwill*, the notice utilized in the former case was calculated to mislead the employees as to the purpose of the election. The Board concluded that even if the employees were not informed of their basic Section 7 rights—to organize, bargain collectively, and engage in concerted activities —it could presume, in the absence of evidence to the contrary, that the employees were aware of these "long-established rights of labor." [109]

In light of more recent developments, if an employer finds it necessary to post a substitute notice, it should be designed to correspond to official notices as nearly as possible. This practice of strict adherence to the Board's official notice should be followed because of the uncertain affect which the Board's decision in *Overland Hauling, Inc.*[110] has exerted on the continuing validity of *Pegwill*. In *Overland Hauling*, the employer had turned the section entitled "Rights of Employees" underneath the remaining portions of the Board's official notice. The Board held that in view of the intended purpose of the section, which was designed to alert employees of their rights under the Act *and* warn unions and management alike against engaging in conduct that would impede fair and free elections, the employer's method of posting was a patent attempt to minimize the effect of the

---

107 *Id.* at 1153, 38 L.R.R.M. at 1009-1010.

108 *Id.*, 38 L.R.R.M. at 1010.

109 *Id.* at 1154, 38 L.R.R.M. at 1010.

110 168 N.L.R.B. 870, 67 L.R.R.M. 1003 (1967).

Board's notice.[111] Furthermore, in a few cases the Board has overruled employer objections to the inclusion of the employee rights section on the grounds that the language contained therein is unfair to management.[112] Therefore, the precedential value of the *Pegwill* case is probably minimal today since the Board would most likely construe any omission of the section on employee rights as an attempt to withhold this information from the employees.

Employer Interference with Notification. A third type of situation, which arises when an employer fails to post an official notice, can only be loosely categorized as a form of interference by the employer with the notification process. This interference is attributable to some underlying motivation other than simply attempting to prevent the notice of election from reaching the employees. In *F. H. Vahlsing, Inc.*[113] an employer attempted to notify only those employees that *he* deemed to be eligible. In defense of his conduct, the employer contended that he had not posted notices of the election because there were no employees in the unit whose eligibility could be positively established from the payroll period utilized for that purpose. In lieu of physical posting at all company plants, the employer called the election to the attention of three employees he believed might be eligible, handing them copies of the notice to read and telling them to go to the polls and vote.[114] The Board found that the employer's violation of the instructions to post the notice in the plant resulted in inadequate publication of the election to interested employees, which thereby prevented them from voting.[115]

Assuming arguendo that in *Vahlsing* the only motive of the employer was his good faith belief that the eligible voters in the bargaining unit included only the three employees that he notified personally, he would still fall afoul of the Board's requisite election procedures. Any doubts as to the eligibility of any voter can be resolved at a postelection hearing after a proper challenge has been made during the election. Therefore, the employer is

---

[111] *Id.*, 67 L.R.R.M. at 1003.

[112] *E.g.*, The Smith Co., 192 N.L.R.B. No. 162, 78 L.R.R.M. 1266 (1971).

[113] 114 N.L.R.B. 1451, 37 L.R.R.M. 1194 (1955).

[114] *Id.*, 37 L.R.R.M. at 1194.

[115] *Id.* at 1452, 37 L.R.R.M. at 1194. At the employer's three plants, only six employees attempted to vote.

not precluded from asserting his uncertainties as to the eligibility of any particular employee. Since an established procedure exists, an employer cannot and should not be allowed to engage in the type of self-help practiced in *Vahlsing*.

In addition to posting the usual official notices, the employer in *NLRB v. Singleton Packing Corp.*,[116] posted "counter-notices" of his own urging his employees to boycott the election. The purpose of these notices was part of a plan to enable the employer to obtain judicial review of the *Excelsior* rule.[117] In the meantime, however, the Supreme Court in *NLRB v. Wyman-Gordon Co.*[118] had directed the enforcement of an *Excelsior* type subpoena, thus rendering the employer's attempt moot.

The certification in the *Singleton* case was based on the outcome of a second election, in which of approximately 506 eligible voters, 136 voted for representation, and only one employee voted against representation.[119] In the first election, however, only 180 votes had been cast for representation, while there were 237 "no union" votes, and 30 ballots were challenged, all out of a total eligibility of 503 employees.[120] Thus, it is manifest that the employer's "counter-notice" prior to the second election radically changed the character of eventual employee participation. Nevertheless, citing the familiar principle that those employees not voting in a representation election are assumed to "assent to the will of the majority who do participate," [121] the Board and court found that the second election should be certified, since it was well publicized and all employees had had an opportunity to participate if they had wanted to do so.[122]

A third case in the area of employer interference, *Postex Cotton Mills, Inc.*,[123] revolved around an employer's failure to

---

[116] 418 F.2d 275, 72 L.R.R.M. 2519 (5th Cir. 1969).

[117] For an extensive discussion of the origin, development, and ramifications of the *Excelsior* rule, see Chapter XIV, *supra*.

[118] 394 U.S. 759, 70 L.R.R.M. 3345 (1969).

[119] 418 F.2d at 277, 72 L.R.R.M. at 2520. In addition, one vote was void and fourteen ballots were challenged.

[120] 418 F.2d at 277, 72 L.R.R.M. at 2519.

[121] *See* R.C.A. Mfg. Co., Inc., 2 N.L.R.B. 168, 177-79 (1936).

[122] 418 F.2d at 279, 72 L.R.R.M. at 2521.

[123] 73 N.L.R.B. 673, 20 L.R.R.M. 1028 (1947).

post notices, as an integral part of an attempt to postpone an election for a few days. The Board held that since the regional director has broad discretion in setting the date of an election, the employer's design to postpone the election constituted interference with the Board's own authority to conduct elections.[124]

Notice to Absentee Employees

The Board will set aside an election wherein it is asserted that absentee employees did not receive adequate notice, only in very special circumstances. First, the number of absentee employees, who allegedly did not receive notification, must be sufficient in number to have affected the outcome of the election had they participated.[125] The reason for this rule is obvious, since the alleged lack of notice would be irrelevant if the affected employees votes could not have influenced the ultimate result of the election.[126]

Secondly, the Board agents conducting a representation election are under no obligation to send individual notices to the absentee employes.[127] Instead, individual notification is a matter of discretion with the Board's regional offices and agents, depending upon the circumstances of the case.[128] If notices of election have been prominently displayed in the plant, absentee employees may be considered by the Board to have constructive notice of such posting,[129] where it is shown that a large percentage of all

---

[124] *Id.* at 676-77, 20 L.R.R.M. at 1029.

[125] *Compare* Jacksonville Journal Co., 117 N.L.R.B. 1828, 1832, 40 L.R.R.M. 1098, 1099 (1957) (Board refused to set aside election where number of part-time employees, who allegedly had not received notice of the election, were insufficient in number to affect the outcome), *with* J.R. Simplot Produce Co., 57 N.L.R.B. 1258, 1260 (1944) (election invalidated where eligible employees, temporarily employed elsewhere, were sufficient in number to affect the results).

[126] *See* Cities Service Oil Co. of Pennsylvania, 87 N.L.R.B. 324, 25 L.R.R.M. 1112 (1949).

[127] Rohr Aircraft Corp., 136 N.L.R.B. 958, 959-60, 49 L.R.R.M. 1886 (1962); Cities Service Oil Co. of Pennsylvania, 87 N.L.R.B. 324, 25 L.R.R.M. 1112 (1949); National Silver Co., 71 N.L.R.B. 594, 600, 19 L.R.R.M. 1028, 1030 (1946).

[128] 136 N.L.R.B. at 959, 49 L.R.R.M. at 1886.

[129] *Cf.* National Silver Co., 71 N.L.R.B. 594, 600, 19 L.R.R.M. 1028, 1030 (1946).

eligible employees have voted, thereby indicating that the notice must have been widespread among the employees to produce such a highly representative vote.[130]

The rationale for the Board's practice of discretionary use of individual notification is that, whereas in some situations it will be feasible to send each absentee employee notice of the election, particularly when their status is made known to the agent in charge at a reasonable period prior to the election, in other instances the Board may not know of the existence [131] or whereabouts [132] of such employees. Consequently, the Board has refused to make it mandatory that its agents notify all absentee employees individually because of the impossible burden on the agent to uncover all eligible voters under the penalty of having the election set aside.[133]

Contents of the Official Notice

Objections to the contents of official election notices fall into three major categories: (1) those based on errors or omissions; (2) the failure to furnish bilingual ballots; and (3) those charging that the impact of the language used is in itself prejudicial. The Board's analysis of allegedly prejudicial errors in notification proceeds on two levels. First, the magnitude of the error and attempts to correct it are evaluated, and secondly, the probability that the error influenced the conduct of the employees to anyone's detriment is considered.

Errors and Omissions. The most serious mistake that might occur in an official election notice is an error in the designation of the appropriate unit. All other significant information, such as time, date, and place are matters of common knowledge that require a minimum amount of interpretation. The definition of the appropriate unit, however, is one of the most problematic as

---

[130] *Id.*, 19 L.R.R.M. at 1030.

[131] In *Rohr Aircraft*, none of the parties to the election informed the Board agent as to the existence of certain eligible employees who had been temporarily laid off. 136 N.L.R.B. at 959-60, 49 L.R.R.M. at 1887.

[132] In *National Silver Co.*, the Board found no merit in an objection grounded on the failure of notice where some of the notices sent to striking employees were returned because of the incorrect addresses furnished by the employer. 71 N.L.R.B. at 600, 19 L.R.R.M. at 1030.

[133] 136 N.L.R.B. at 960, 49 L.R.R.M. at 1886.

well as important areas of labor law.[134] Once the notice of the election has been posted, the employees usually have a very limited period of time in which to ascertain their eligibility to participate in the election. Thus, it is imperative that any errors in the description of the appropriate bargaining unit in the official notice be corrected as quickly as possible.

The deleterious effects, which an error in notifying employees as to the proper scope of the electorate can cause, were illustrated in *Angelus Chevrolet Co.*[135] In that case, the Board agent charged with conducting the election misconstrued the scope of the unit and advised the employer not to post a notice which could be seen by five eligible employees at another plant location.[136] As a result of the agent's error, these five employees did not receive notice of the election and did not participate therein. Under the circumstances, the Board felt it advisable to direct a new election because of the "substantial doubt as to whether the proper election standards had been met." [137]

Because it was easy to identify the omission and its consequences, the Board in *Angelus Chevrolet* had no difficulty in setting aside the election. In subsequent cases, however, the Board has shown great reluctance in permitting errors in notification to be the grounds upon which an election is set aside. Apparently, this unwillingness is often directly related to the fact that the error, despite being asserted as misleading, could not logically be reconciled with the coincident high percentage of participation in the election.[138]

---

[134] Discussing the profound impact which unit determination may have on the outcome of a subsequent representation election, Dean Derek Bok remarked that:

[I]t is disturbing to note how few writers have paid attention to the problem of defining an appropriate unit despite the fact that a unit determination may profoundly affect labor management relations and constitute a heavy proportion of the work of the NLRB.

Discussion, *Proceedings of the 19th Annual Winter Meeting, Industrial Relations Research Association* 99-104 (1966).

[135] 90 N.L.R.B. 1142, 26 L.R.R.M. 1320 (1950).

[136] *Id.* at 1142-43, 26 L.R.R.M. at 1320.

[137] *Id.* at 1143, 26 L.R.R.M. at 1320.

[138] *See, e.g.,* Continental Baking Co., 122 N.L.R.B. 1074, 43 L.R.R.M. 1249 (1959). In *Continental Baking,* fully 97.6 percent of all eligible employees participated in an election in which only one of the two plants comprising

Furthermore, the Board has always permitted the regional director to correct minor, inadvertant errors in official notices.[139] Consequently, any errors in the description of the bargaining unit will not be deemed prejudicial unless it is affirmatively shown that: (1) the objecting party detrimentally relied on such notice;[140] or (2) protested to no avail prior to the election;[141] and (3) a substantial number of employees, sufficient in number to affect the eventual outcome of the election, did not participate because of the error or omission in notification.[142]

Another type of problem arises when the Board has inadvertantly omitted the statement concerning the applicable payroll period which has been utilized to establish eligibility. In *Boeing Airplane Co.*,[143] the Board held that the omission of the eligibility date from the official notice of election does not give rise to a meritorious objection. In reaching that decision, the Board reasoned that since the eligibility date is only a limitation, " . . . its lack might have led employees who were not eligible to vote to try to do so, [but] it could not have caused eligible voters to stay away from the polls." [144] Assuming *arguendo*, that employee interest in the election is so strong that every employee would attempt to vote if possible, this rationale is valid. Where employee interest is only moderate, however, this policy places a rather onerous affirmative obligation on every employee to present himself at the polls to protect his interest in the election, even when he thinks that he may not, in fact, be eligible. The

---

the appropriate unit was listed on the official notice. Furthermore, of all the workers employed at the second plant who were eligible, only one failed to vote, and he was on vacation! Although the Board lamented the breakdown in adherence to the established election standards, it concluded that it could safely presume that the omission was not misleading. *Id.* at 1076, 43 L.R.R.M. at 1249.

139 *Cf.* Landis Tool Co., 203 N.L.R.B. No. 143, 83 L.R.R.M. 1270 (1973); West Texas Utilities Co., 100 N.L.R.B. 1012, 30 L.R.R.M. 1389 (1952).

140 Angelus Chevrolet Co., 90 N.L.R.B. 1142, 26 L.R.R.M. 1320 (1950).

141 Landis Tool Co., 203 N.L.R.B. No. 143, 83 L.R.R.M. 1270 (1973); Continental Baking Co., 122 N.L.R.B. 1074, 43 L.R.R.M. 1249 (1959)

142 West Texas Utilities Co., 100 N.L.R.B. 1012, 30 L.R.R.M. 1389 (1952); *see* cases cited at note 141, *supra*.

143 88 N.L.R.B. 227, 25 L.R.R.M. 1314 (1950).

144 *Id.* at 229, 25 L.R.R.M. at 1314.

absence of an eligibility date on the election notice makes every employee a judge of his own eligibility even though he is ignorant of the terms of the Board's "Direction of Election." Consequently, the Board's recent formulation in *Kilgore Corp.*,[145] which would give the employee a short respite before the election to ascertain his eligibility, has a strong foundation in policy.

Where a union is able to show that a mistake in the election notice involving its name is prejudicial, the Board will direct a second election. In *Walker Vehicle Co.*,[146] the "Walker-Automatic Independent Labor Association," successfully objected to an election in which it had been inadvertently designated as *"Walker's Automatic Independent Labor Association."* The Board agreed with the objecting labor organization, an "inside union," competing on the ballot with a C.I.O. affiliate, that the error may have placed an unintended stigma upon the association in the minds of some voters.[147]

In a subsequent case, in which the word "International," the first term in the union's name, was deleted from the notice of election, the Board found that the union was not prejudiced by any alleged confusion among the employees caused by the omission.[148] The Board reasoned that the omission could hardly have created any confusion among the employees, since the union was the only labor organization on the ballot.[149]

Failure to Furnish Bilingual Notices and Ballots. Recently, the Board has formulated a new standard regarding the content of election notices that requires bilingual notices or ballots be provided upon the request of either party to the election.[150] For example, in *Fibre Leather Mfg. Co.*,[151] the Board set aside an election on the basis that it had not been conducted "with due regard

---

[145] 203 N.L.R.B. No. 28, 83 L.R.R.M. 1010 (1973).

[146] 7 N.L.R.B. 827, 2 L.R.R.M. 345 (1938).

[147] *Id.* at 833, 2 L.R.R.M. at 348.

[148] Bridgeport Moulded Plastics, Inc., 115 N.L.R.B. 1751, 1752, 38 L.R.R.M. 1164, 1165 (1956).

[149] *Id.*, 38 L.R.R.M. at 1165.

[150] *E.g.*, Alamo Lumber Co., 187 N.L.R.B. 384, 76 L.R.R.M. 1126 (1970), *affirmed without opinion*, 455 F.2d 607, 78 L.R.R.M. 2966 (5th Cir. 1971); Facs, Snack Foods Division, Case No. 23-RC-3394 (May 1, 1970).

[151] 167 N.L.R.B. 393, 66 L.R.R.M. 1056 (1967).

to the needs of Portuguese-speaking employees who could not read English." At a pre-election conference, the employer had called this handicap of some of his employees to the attention of the Board's agent.[152] After learning that the notices and ballots were issued in English only, the employer continued to press for a solution to the language problem. The stop-gap measures utilized to meet this difficulty failed to impress the Board that adequate safeguards had been maintained.[153] In setting aside the election, the Board stated that it had not been "satisfied that the conditions under which the election was conducted were such as to assure the effective and informed expression by all employees of their true desire." [154]

Shortly after *Fibre Leather,* a number of cases arose in Region 13 (Chicago) which had maintained a policy of consistently refusing all requests for either bilingual notices or ballots. Region 13 policy came under sharp attack by the Court of Appeals for the Fifth Circuit in *Marriott In-Flight Service Div. of Marriott Corp.* v. *NLRB.*[155] In a strongly worded opinion, the court took the Board to task for permitting the contradictory standards of Region 13 to stand. First, the court pointed out that of eighteen other regions which had considered the issue, all were unanimous in stating that they had or would, when the occasion arose, employ foreign language ballots.[156] Then, the court recited a statement by the Associate Executive Secretary of the Labor Board, who had declared that "the Agency does have a uniform policy" regarding such ballots.[157]

Before the court, the NLRB argued that its decision in *Marriott* was based upon the precedent afforded in *Fibre Leather*

---

152 *Id.,* 66 L.R.R.M. at 1057. Some 15 to 20 employees of the 86 man unit could not speak English.

153 *Id.,* 66 L.R.R.M. at 1057. Although an arrangement had been made whereby each party provided an additional bilingual observer, not all the Portuguese-speaking employees had been advised of the purposes of the special observers.

154 *Id.,* 66 L.R.R.M. at 1057.

155 417 F.2d 563, 72 L.R.R.M. 2455 (5th Cir. 1969), *cert. denied,* 397 U.S. 920, 73 L.R.R.M. 2538 (1970).

156 417 F.2d at 565 & n.2, 72 L.R.R.M. at 2457.

157 *Id.* at 565, 72 L.R.R.M. at 2357.

Mfg. Corp.,[158] and *Trio Metal Cap Co.*[159] The Board contended that: (1) *Fibre Leather* was distinguishable, since it had applied to *both* notices and ballots, whereas in *Marriott*, only the ballots had not been bilingual; and (2) consequently, the Board's decision in *Trio Metal Cap Co.* was determinative, since in that case, like *Marriott*, only the ballots were entirely English.

Rejecting both of the Board's contentions, the court pointed to the conflict with the position statement issued by the Associate Director "which was written after [*Trio Metal Cap Co.*] and which speaks explicitly of the need for foreign-language notices and ballots."[160] Further, the court indicated that the *Trio Metal Cap Co.* case had little precedential value, since it had also arisen in Region 13.[161]

In subsequent cases, the Board and courts have erected a consistent policy structure concerning the use of bilingual ballots.[162] Under the standard that has emerged, an election will be set aside due to the failure of the regional director to furnish bilingual notices and ballots *only* where the objecting party has requested their use *prior* to the election. The rationale for requiring the objecting party to assert the defect prior to the election is founded upon the Board's general policy which favors the election as the final determinant of the representation question,[163] while disallowing either frivolous or self-serving objections after the election has been held.[164] For example, in *NLRB v. Lowell Corrugated Container Corp.,*[165] the Court of Appeals for the First Cir-

---

[158] 167 N.L.R.B. 393, 66 L.R.R.M. 1056 (1967).

[159] 168 N.L.R.B. 802, 66 L.R.R.M. 1382 (1967).

[160] 417 F.2d at 566, 72 L.R.R.M. at 2458.

[161] *Id.,* 72 L.R.R.M. at 2458.

[162] *E.g.,* NLRB v. Lowell Corrugated Container Corp., 431 F.2d 1196, 75 L.R.R.M. 2346 (1st Cir. 1970); General Dynamics Corp., 187 N.L.R.B. No. 96, 76 L.R.R.M. 1540 (1971).

[163] *Compare* NLRB v. Continental Nut Co., 395 F.2d 830, 832-33, 68 L.R.R.M. 2350, 2352 (9th Cir. 1968), *with* NLRB v. O.K. Van Storage, Inc., 297 F.2d 74, 76, 49 L.R.R.M. 2218, 2221 (5th Cir. 1961).

[164] *See generally* NLRB v. Difco Laboratories, Inc., 389 F.2d 663, 67 L.R.R.M. 2585 (6th Cir.), *cert. denied,* 393 U.S. 828, 69 L.R.R.M. 2434 (1968); Sonoco Products Co. v. NLRB, 399 F.2d 835, 839, 69 L.R.R.M. 2037, 2039 (9th Cir. 1968).

[165] 431 F.2d 1196, 75 L.R.R.M. 2346 (1st Cir. 1970).

cuit enforced a Board order over postelection objections to the failure of the regional director to furnish bilingual ballots, stating:

> . . . [T]he inescapable fact is that there was full knowledge of the coming election, and the notices, with sample ballots, were posted for the customary week. During this period the [employer] and the second union, which lost the election, were silent as to employee problems in understanding the choices offered. *Their failure to object may be termed laches, or perhaps, preferably, compelling evidence that the proposed procedure was sufficient.*[166]

The Fifth Circuit's opinion in *Marriott* dealt in some depth with the problem of inconsistency among the regions in applying different standards to identical problems. The court stated that "[t]he agency [had failed] to explain why the difficulties Chicago [Region 13] employees have with English condemn them to more restricted voting rights than those enjoyed by similarly handicapped workers in Milwaukee [Region 30]."[167] Despite all attempted Board explanations, the court claimed that it could not "escape the fact that while Region 13 followed one rule, Washington and the other regions were following another."[168] Instead, the court argued that "the requirement that minimum standards of fairness must be met for the election to be valid" outweighed any claims that the consistency sought in uniformity was merely a "hobgoblin of little minds."[169]

In view of the fact that the NLRA is the major source of "federal" labor policy, there is little justification for maintaining a separate set of local standards other than those which are of a purely administrative character. When such standards have any potential material effect on the election, the necessity for maintaining a uniform national labor policy comes to the fore.

Region 13 was not the only region to utilize a different standard regarding bilingual notices and ballots. Region 8 also has its own unique rule, in that it "provides foreign language ballots only when all members of the unit speak the same foreign language."[170] In view of the criticism of and subsequent change in

---

166 *Id.* at 1197, 75 L.R.R.M. at 2347 (emphasis added).

167 417 F.2d at 565, 72 L.R.R.M. at 2457.

168 *Id.* at 566, 72 L.R.R.M. at 2458.

169 *Id.* at 566-67, 72 L.R.R.M. at 2458.

170 *Id.* at 565 n.2, 72 L.R.R.M. at 2457.

policy initiated by Region 13,[171] the standard employed in Region 8 is subject to similar defects. Should the voters be composed of more than one foreign-language group, some portion of the electorate will be discriminated against on the sole basis of its inability to understand the English language. As the court in *Marriott* stated, "[a]n election in which [a substantial segment] of the electorate has no access to ballots [and/or notices] in language that it can understand necessarily falls below the minimum laboratory standards of fairness." [172]

Alleged Prejudice Contained in the Official Notice. Another type of objection to the contents of the official notice of election, which has been raised without success, has been the claim that certain aspects of the language therein is highly prejudicial to the employer, in that it portrays the company as a party not to be trusted.[173] The most serious type of this alleged bias arises when the notice of a second election includes a statement advising the employees that the new election is being conducted because the employer interfered with the employees' freedom of choice in the first election.[174]

In the *Lufkin Rule Co.*[175] case, pursuant to a motion by the petitioning union, the Board ordered that the following paragraph be included in the notices of the "Decision and Direction of a Second Election":

NOTICE TO ALL VOTERS

The elections conducted on June 25, 1963 were set aside because the National Labor Relations Board found that certain conduct of

---

[171] *Id.* at 565, 72 L.R.R.M. at 2457.

[172] *Id.* at 567, 72 L.R.R.M. at 2458.

[173] *See* The Smith Co., 192 N.L.R.B. No. 162, 78 L.R.R.M. 1266 (1971), wherein the employer asserted that the Board's official notice, especially the section entitled "Rights of Employees," unfairly creates an atmosphere of bias and prejudice against an employer. Moreover, the company in Overland Hauling, Inc., 168 N.L.R.B. 870, 67 L.R.R.M. 1003 (1967), apparently felt that the language of that section was so prejudicial that the company actually turned under the "Rights of Employees" section of the notice when it was posted.
Cf. The Item Co., 110 N.L.R.B. 1061, 35 L.R.R.M. 1216 (1954) (employer alleged that certain explanatory information in the official notices had the effect of enhancing the position of one union on the ballot over another).

[174] *E.g.*, Morgan Dyeing & Bleaching, Inc., Case No. 13-RC-9658, 56 L.R.R.M. 1223 (1964).

[175] 147 N.L.R.B. 341, 56 L.R.R.M. 1212 (1964).

the employer interfered with the employee's exercise of a free and reasoned choice. Therefore, new elections will be held in accordance with the terms of this notice of election. All eligible voters should understand that the National Labor Relations Act, as amended, gives them the right to cast their ballots as they see fit, and protects them in the exercise of this right, free from interference by any of the parties.[176]

In the employer's objections to the conduct of the second election, the Board rejected the company's claim that the notice had caused it undue prejudice. The gist of the employer's objection was that such a statement, having the imprimatur of the Board, would suggest to the employees that in view of the employer's misconduct, the Board favored a vote for the union in the second election.[177] In response to this charge, the Board stated that the notice does not favor the union, but rather, is designed to provide official notification to all eligible voters, without detailing the unlawful conduct involved, as to the reason why the election was set aside.[178]

Although it is true that the notice does not overtly suggest to the employees that the Board favors the union over the employer, there is little doubt that it does warn the employees to beware of their employer. Since the Board ruled that the employer had interfered with the electoral process, it is reasonable that some official notification should be forthcoming to explain why a second election is necessary. The possibility of prejudice occurs not in what the notice says, but rather in what it omits. The only information that the notice gives the employees is that the employer had interfered with their right to a free election. Perhaps a more evenhanded approach would be to permit the employer (or union) to accompany such a notice with the official text of the Board decision. In this way, the prejudicial affects of rumors, plant gossip, and misrepresentations would be forestalled, since the official notice would contain an explanation for the necessity of conducting a second election.

Notice to the Union

Unlike the nearly automatic notification to a company, which can be deemed to have received constructive notice of an up-

---

[176] *Id.* at 342, 56 L.R.R.M. at 1212.

[177] *Id.*, 56 L.R.R.M. at 1212.

[178] *Id.*, 56 L.R.R.M. at 1212.

coming election,[179] a labor organization need only be notified when
it has claimed an interest in the election that is substantiated by
evidence of employee support within the proposed election unit.
Thus, in *Southeastern Illinois Gas Co.*,[180] the Board set aside an
election where it found that a second interested union, was denied adequate time to inform the employees of its last-minute inclusion on the ballot. Furthermore, where a labor organization
claims to be the representative of the employees, and communi-
cates this claim to the employer, any omission by the company
to relay this claim to the Board will constitute grounds for setting aside the election.[181] This is based on the concept that it is
for the "regional director of the Board and not the parties, to
determine whether a claim has sufficient validity or vitality to
require that notice of the proceeding be given to the claimant." [182]

On the other hand, when the union states that it has no interest in being placed on the ballot prior to the election, it is estopped from subsequently objecting that it had no notice of the
election.[183] Similarly, in the *Dairymens' League Cooperative
Ass'n, Inc.*,[184] the Board refused to set aside an election in which
a union claimed that it had been prejudiced, since it had no
representatives present at the time the ballots were tallied because of an alleged failure of notice. The Board held that the
union was prevented from asserting such an objection where
prior to the election, it had made no protests or inquiries to the
Board's agents revealing that the union had not received such a
notice.[185]

Finally, the issue of whether "alternate notification" to a union
will be sufficient, as in the case of alternate notice to the em-

---

[179] *E.g.*, Simplot Fertilizer Co., 107 N.L.R.B. 1211, 33 L.R.R.M. 1357 (1954).

[180] 119 N.L.R.B. 1665, 41 L.R.R.M. 1366 (1958).

[181] U.S. Chaircraft, Inc., 132 N.L.R.B. 922, 48 L.R.R.M. 1448 (1961);
accord, General Motors Corp., 133 N.L.R.B. 1063, 48 L.R.R.M. 1767 (1961).

[182] 132 N.L.R.B. at 923, 48 L.R.R.M. at 1448. *See also* Somerville Iron
Works, Inc., 117 N.L.R.B. 1702, 40 L.R.R.M. 1073 (1957).

[183] *E.g.*, Altoona Brewing Co., 72 N.L.R.B. 1320, 1321 (1947); Armour and
Co., 71 N.L.R.B. 1501, 1504, 19 L.R.R.M. 1157 (1947).

[184] 121 N.L.R.B. 124, 42 L.R.R.M. 1313 (1958).

[185] *Id.* at 125, 42 L.R.R.M. at 1313.

ployees,[186] is a question of fact. In *Tennessee Copper Co.*,[187] a union asserted that the failure of the regional director to notify it formally until two days prior to the election constituted prejudicial error. In this case, the Board found that the union had ample notice of the election where (1) it was clear that the union had general notice that the election would be held in the near future, (2) the regional director had contacted its organizers over two weeks prior to the election by telegraph, and (3) four newspapers in the area, including one sponsored by the parent union, had published articles announcing the date of the election 5 to 15 days prior thereto.[188]

In a subsequent case, however, even though a competing union was able to show that the objecting union had actual notice through radio and newspaper publicity, as well as through the business agent of a sister local, the Board held that its failure to receive official notice introduced error into the electoral process and was sufficient cause to set aside the election.[189]

ADEQUATE OPPORTUNITY TO VOTE

Just as the requirement that employees be given sufficient notice of an election is one of the elements of a representative vote, affording the employees an adequate opportunity to vote is also a determinant of the election's representative character.[190] Objections to representation elections grounded on inadequate opportunity to vote are of two varieties: (1) those concerned with the time and place an election is held; and (2) those dealing with a postponement of a previously scheduled election.

In accordance with accepted Board procedures, an election is held when it is likely that the greatest number of eligible employees will be present and able to vote; *e.g.*, a pay day or a day in the middle of the work week. Although an election may be held on company time with the consent of the employer, the actual time set for voting is designed to afford all employees adequate opportunity to vote, and at the same time, cause the

---

186 *See* pp. 412-413, *supra*.

187 10 N.L.R.B. 1433, 3 L.R.R.M. 547 (1939).

188 *Id.* at 1433, 3 L.R.R.M. at 548.

189 Ravenna Arsenal, Inc., 98 N.L.R.B. 1, 2-3, 29 L.R.R.M. 1283, 1284 (1952).

190 *See* discussion at p. 397, *supra*.

minimum amount of interference with the work day. The polls themselves should be situated so as to afford easy accessibility and convenience to the employees.[191] If it appears that there has been an impairment in the opportunity to vote of a significant number of employees, the Board will set aside the election.[192]

Time and Place of Election

When any party can show that the failure of a significant number of eligible employees to participate in the election is traceable to an outside—*i.e.* out of town—work assignment of the employer, the Board will set aside the election.[193] Thus, in a series of cases in which employees engaged in trucking operations were working elsewhere at the time of the election, the Board has invalidated elections where otherwise eligible voters did not have an adequate opportunity to cast their ballots.[194] The rationale employed in setting aside these elections arises primarily from the Board's authority to regulate the processes of representation elections.[195] Thus, the Board has stated that as part of its responsibility in establishing the "proper procedure for the conduct of its elections, that such procedure requires that all eligible employees be given an opportunity to vote." [196] The purpose is to guarantee employees that the opportunity afforded all eligible voters "was sufficiently 'adequate' or 'equal' as to reflect accurately the 'majority' required by the

---

[191] Manchester Knitted Fashions, Inc., 108 N.L.R.B. 1366, 34 L.R.R.M. 1214 (1954).

[192] *See* NLRB v. W.S. Hatch Co., 474 F.2d 558, 82 L.R.R.M. 2662 (9th Cir. 1973); Yerges Van Liners, Inc., 162 N.L.R.B. 1259, 1260, 64 L.R.R.M. 1173 (1967); Star Baking Co., 119 N.L.R.B. 835, 836, 41 L.R.R.M. 1178, 1179 (1957); Alterman-Big Apple, Inc., 116 N.L.R.B. 1078, 38 L.R.R.M. 1406 (1956).

[193] *Cf.* Wagner Electric Corp., 125 N.L.R.B. 834, 45 L.R.R.M. 1240 (1959); Dornback Furnace & Foundry Co., 115 N.L.R.B. 350, 37 L.R.R.M. 1304 (1956).

[194] NLRB v. W.S. Hatch Co., 474 F.2d 588, 82 L.R.R.M. 2662 (9th Cir. 1973); Yerges Van Liners, Inc., 162 N.L.R.B. 1259, 1260, 64 L.R.R.M. 1173 Alterman-Big Apple, Inc., 116 N.L.R.B. 1078, 38 L.R.R.M. 1406 (1956).

[195] *See* NLRB v. A. J. Tower Co., 329 U.S. 324, 330-31, 19 L.R.R.M. 2128, 2131 (1946).

[196] 162 N.L.R.B. at 1260, 64 L.R.R.M. at 1173; 116 N.L.R.B. at 1080, 38 L.R.R.M. at 1406. *See also* Repcal Brass Mfg. Co., 109 N.L.R.B. 4, 34 L.R.R.M. 1277 (1954).

statute." [197] Since this is a matter of Board responsibility, it cannot be waived by any of the parties.[198]

Of all the situations in which lack of adequate opportunity to vote is alleged, those involving employees engaged in a work assignment in another locale constitute the clearest violation of the employees' opportunity to vote; hence, they are the easiest to decide. Less obvious, are those cases in which an eligible voter, although working elsewhere at the time of the eelction, is not engaged in a work assignment by the employer, but instead, holds another job. In the *Alaskan Glacier Sea Food Co.*[199] case, an election was held at the height of the canning season. Many of the eligible employees were working temporarily at other canning companies on an 18-hour-a-day schedule. A large number of the employees affected had only their lunch hour in which to travel approximately one-half mile to the ballot box and back. Furthermore, ten of the eligible voters were working for canneries in other parts of Alaska and had not been notified.[200] In view of the foregoing circumstances, the Board held that the balloting failed to result in a representative vote because a significant number of employees were not given the same voting opportunity as the other employees in the employer's plant.[201]

In another case involving eligible voters employed elsewhere at the time of the election, the Board held that these employees had been given an adequate opportunity to vote. Although the Court of Appeals for the Ninth Circuit sustained the Board's determination in *International Tel. & Tel. Corp. v. NLRB*,[202] the court opined that the Board might have been better advised to order a new election.[203] The employees, who had allegedly been denied an opportunity to vote were engaged as night janitors at the company and worked elsewhere during the daytime when the

---

[197] International Tel. & Tel. Corp. v. NLRB, 294 F.2d 393, 395, 48 L.R.R.M. 2952, 2954 (9th Cir. 1961).

[198] 116 N.L.R.B. at 1080, 38 L.R.R.M. at 1406; *accord*, Active Sportswear Co., Inc., 104 N.L.R.B. 1057, 32 L.R.R.M. 1189 (1943).

[199] Case No. 19-RC-272, 25 L.R.R.M. 1346, 1347 (1950).

[200] *Id.* at 1347.

[201] *Id.*

[202] 294 F.2d 393, 48 L.R.R.M. 2952 (9th Cir. 1961).

[203] *Id.* at 395, 48 L.R.R.M. at 2954.

election was held. In two previous elections, these janitors had taken time off from their daytime jobs in order to vote, thereby losing time and pay. By the time the third election was scheduled, they were in danger of losing their jobs if they took more time off in order to participate.[204]

The rationale which the Ninth Circuit in *International Tel. & Tel. Corp.* used to enforce the Board order was rooted in the discretion authorized to the Board in carrying out its duty to supervise representation elections.[205] The court found that the Board had not abused its discretion in determining that the opportunity afforded all eligible voters to exercise their right to vote was adequate. Instead, the court held that in view of the Board's expertise, it was better equipped than the courts in determining whether the opportunity given the employees to vote was adequate *"unless clear error was shown."* [206]

In view of the extreme hardship that the two janitors had been subjected to in order to vote in the prior elections, one can but wonder why neither the company, the two unions seeking recognition, nor the Board itself, offered to provide mail ballots for these two employees. The decision to conduct a partial mail ballot is *within the discretion of the regional director* [207] and could have been authorized here.

The Effect of Postponement of a Previously Scheduled Election on the Employees' Opportunity to Vote

Commenting on the basic thrust of the official notice of election, the court in *NLRB v. Conlon Bros. Mfg. Co.,*[208] stated that "[t]he only purpose of the notice of an election is to advise the employees of the fact that an election is to be held so that all

---

[204] *Id.* at 394, 48 L.R.R.M. at 2953.

[205] *Id.* at 395, 48 L.R.R.M. at 2954.

[206] *Id.,* 48 L.R.R.M. at 2954 (emphasis added).

[207] *See* Shipowner's Ass'n of the Pacific Coast, 110 N.L.R.B. 479, 35 L.R.R.M. 1077 (1954), wherein the Board, speaking of the utilization of mail ballots, stated that the ". . . circumstances surrounding working conditions in various industries require an adaptation of established standards to those conditions." *Id.* at 480, 35 L.R.R.M. at 1077. For an extensive discussion of the Board's use of mail ballots see Chapter XVI, *supra.*

[208] 187 F.2d 329, 27 L.R.R.M. 2407 (7th Cir. 1951).

may have an opportunity to vote." [209] Therefore, it is conceivable that this purpose may be thwarted by a last minute cancellation of the election. Such a postponement may serve to vitiate the original notification and deprive eligible voters of their opportunity to participate in the rescheduled election. For example, in the *Conlon Bros.* case, an election was postponed for one day because a number of the part-time employees had already left the plant before the Board agent in charge arrived.[210] A "split-session" election had originally been scheduled in order to provide these part-time employees with ample opportunity to vote, but because of the agent's tardy arrival, the first polling session had already passed. The agent then decided to hold the election on the following day during the same hours and at the same place "and so informed the parties." [211] At the election held on the next day, 42 of approximately 44 eligible employees participated. One ballot, being void, was not counted, and another ballot was challenged. Of the remaining valid ballots, 21 were cast for representation by the labor organization and 19 were cast against the union.[212]

After the tally, the employer objected to the conduct of the election, claiming that since some of the part-time employees had already left the plant after the election was postponed, if any one of them did not appear for work on the following day, he of course, would not even know that an election had been held.[213] On appeal, the court reasoned that where 42 of a total of 44 eligible voters had participated, the Board could assume, under the circumstances that the other two nonvoting employees also knew of the election.[214] Moreover, the employer failed to offer any proof that the nonvoters were also part-time employees.[215]

The *Conlon Bros.* court's third rationale, that the execution by the employer's representative of a stipulation stating that the

---

[209] *Id.* at 332, 27 L.R.R.M. at 2409.

[210] *Id.* at 331, 27 L.R.R.M. at 2409.

[211] *Id.*, 27 L.R.R.M. at 2409.

[212] *Id.*, 27 L.R.R.M. at 2409.

[213] *Id.* at 332, 27 L.R.R.M. at 2409.

[214] *Id.*, 27 L.R.R.M. at 2409.

[215] *Id.*, 27 L.R.R.M. at 2409.

election was fairly conducted and afforded all eligible employees an opportunity to vote and thereby effectively barred any objection on the grounds of inadequate opportunity to vote,[216] is in direct contravention of Board election policy. Indeed, in *Alterman-Big Apple, Inc.,*[217] the Board held that since it is the Board's responsibility alone, to protect the opportunity of all eligible employees to vote, any breach of this safeguard "is not subject to waiver by the parties." [218] Therefore, the written certification by the employer's representative would not be binding in the event that evidence could be brought forward to show that the oportunity to vote of a significant number of employees was impaired.

The teachings of *Conlon Bros.,* and similar cases in the area do, however, provide a workable standard. Briefly, an election will be set aside, after a postponement has occurred of the previously scheduled election where the objecting party can show that a number of employees, sufficient to affect the result of the election, were, *in fact,* denied adequate opportunity to vote in the rescheduled election. Because of collateral considerations which favor certification of the election results, the emphasis is on the ability of the objecting party to bring forth actual proof of the lack of opportunity, without the aid of presumption or inference on the part of the Board.

---

[216] *Id.,* 27 L.R.R.M. at 2409.

[217] 116 N.L.R.B. 1078, 38 L.R.R.M. 1406 (1956).

[218] *Id.* at 1080, 38 L.R.R.M. at 1406. *See also* Active Sportswear Co., Inc., 104 N.L.R.B. 1057, 32 L.R.R.M. 1189 (1954).

PART SIX
Conclusion

CHAPTER XVIII

Conclusion

Viewed in their entirety, the NLRB's rules and standards for regulating representation election conduct form an enormously complex maze. As we have seen, the varieties of conduct which may serve as bases for postelection objections are practically infinite. At the same time, the policies and principles applied by the Board in ruling on such objections are, for the most part, quite narrow and limited. Thus, in the nearly four decades since the passage of the Wagner Act, few broadly applicable basic rules have emerged to guide election participants in determining what they may say and do during the campaign period, or to govern Board agents in deciding whether proper standards have been maintained in the conduct of elections. Indeed, as illustrated in the foregoing chapters, even in the relatively few instances in which the Board has attempted to devise broad rules applicable to all elections, those rules have often proven to be so short-lived, ambiguous, and riddled with exceptions that it is difficult to judge whether they have eliminated as much uncertainty as they have introduced into the election process.

The sheer complexity of the Board's election rules has been cited as a factor seriously undermining their effectiveness.[1]

> The utility of elections lies in final, definitive and unchallenged results; elections become useless when the results are challenged, uncertain, or rejected. Elections are intended to establish and stabilize representation, not leave it unsettled and in dispute.[2]

Regrettably, widespread acceptance of the results of NLRB elections has not been achieved.[3] Nor is it realistic to expect a high level of acceptance of election results as long as the standards for determining the validity of elections remain so complicated.

---

[1] Samoff, *NLRB Elections: Uncertainty and Certainty*, 117 U. PA. L. REV. 228 (1968).

[2] *Id.*

[3] Objections were filed in 1,095 of the 9,226 elections conducted in representation cases closed by the Board in fiscal 1972. 37 NLRB ANN. REP. 244 (1972).

It is difficult even for well-intentioned election participants to be certain of all the rules by which they must abide. For those seeking to delay the resolution of representation issues or avoid the results of an election, there may be a real tactical advantage in the complexity of the Board's rules. For, as this study indicates, there is scarcely any phase of election conduct regarding which a determined party cannot raise at least some colorable issues concerning the applicability of the Board's rules or the interpretation of Board precedents.

The Board's readiness to intervene and set aside elections upon so wide a variety of grounds has been self-defeating in another sense. It has led to the expenditure of large and increasing amounts of the agency's time and resources in dealing with postelection questions in a period in which the Board's members as well as its critics have been protesting its inability to cope adequately with an ever-expanding caseload.[4] If caseload pressures and the delays attendant thereto tend to impair the effectiveness of the Board's processing of unfair labor practice cases, clearly they must have at least as destructive an impact on the handling of representation questions, whose prompt resolution demands particularly high priority. Thus, for the Board to intervene and to invalidate elections unnecessarily not only has an adverse effect on the interest of the parties immediately involved; it also diminishes the overall ability of the Board to provide effective regulation of the election proces where it is needed.

Unlike other aspects of its caseload dilemma, this is one which the Board itself has considerable latitude to control. The Act, as we have noted, does not specify either the standards which should be applied in regulating election conduct or the manner in which the Board should enforce them. It simply states that elections shall be conducted "by secret ballot,"[5] and leaves it to the Board to determine the procedures to be followed and conditions required. All of the rules, policies, and principles discussed in the foregoing chapters have thus been developed by the Board itself through the case-by-case method. We have witnessed, in this study, frequent exercises of Board discretion to change these rules and

---

[4] *See, e.g.*, Miller, *Toward an Improved Labor Judiciary*, 80 LAB. REL. REP. 143 (1972) ; Fanning, *The Viability of NLRB Regulation in the Future*, in COLLECTIVE BARGAINING: SURVIVAL IN THE '70's? 36-38 (1972).

[5] 29 U.S.C. § 159(c)(1) (1970).

policies, and except where those changes appeared to be arbitrarily selective, they have generally been approved by the courts.

There does not appear, then, to be any external obstacle to prevent the Board from revising its overall approach to the regulation of election conduct. It could, if it chose, sharply reduce its involvement with issues of campaign conduct and accord greater finality to the results of elections conducted under its auspices. Indeed, in our discussion of cases we have noted periodic instances in which Board members have expressed sentiments in favor of such a course. But the Board as a whole has not been persuaded to abandon the view that active agency regulation of all phases of the election process is truly necessary to preserve the freedom, rationality, and fairness of that process. Consequently, although Board opinions have occasionally given lip-service to the need for restraint in setting aside the results of completed elections, the Board's overall approach to the regulation of campaign conduct has been far from restrained.[6]

On the contrary, we have found that the Board has greatly expanded its role as overseer of election conduct over the years. Prior to the Taft-Hartley amendments, the Board appeared to view representation elections as comparable in many respects to ordinary political elections. It would, even then, generally sustain objections where unfair labor practices or overt acts of coercion had occurred. It also applied the Wagner Act notion that employers were obliged to maintain complete neutrality regarding unionization. But in other respects, the Board's involvement with questions of campaign conduct was quite limited. Most importantly, the Board did not undertake, during that early period, to regulate the substance of campaign statements and propaganda of the parties. It flatly prohibited employers from making such statements, but it credited employees with the ability to evaluate union campaign statements, speeches and literature for themselves, just as they would propaganda in any ordinary civil election.

We have traced how the Congressional effort in the Taft-Hartley amendments to secure greater freedom for employers to express their views concerning unionization led ironically to a decrease of freedom of expression for unions and little increase for employers, as both parties' campaign statements came to be evaluated under the unrealistic "laboratory conditions" standard. Further, we

---

[6] In recent years, the Board has annually invalidated between 22.1 and 34.8 percent of all elections in which objections have been filed. *See* Tables 11B and D, NLRB Annual Reports for fiscal years 1964 through 1972.

have seen that the movement toward greater control over the substance of pre-election speech has tended to take on a momentum
of its own, as reviewing courts have applied a stricter standard
to union statements as the only available means of counter-
balancing the Board's strict treatment of employers' statements.
Throughout this process, the early commonplace presumption that
employees have the ability to evaluate campaign propaganda and
to act reasonably in their own interests has been largely forgotten.

The most recent irony in this progression is that the current
Board, in seeking to justify a slight relaxation of its present
tight control over campaign speech, has cited, as reasons for doing
so, "improvements in our educational processes" and a higher
"degree of employee sophistication" in regard to NLRB elections
than prevailed "during the [early] years of the Act's existence." [7]
In truth, if the Board were only to credit employees today with the
same degree of perceptivity it attributed to voters in its elections
during the Wagner Act period vis-á-vis union campaign statements,
it would go a long way toward reducing its role as a campaign
censor and freeing itself from the burden of excessive involvement
with propaganda issues.

Actually, the Board has never had any reliable basis for assuming that active government regulation of campaign speech and
conduct can make the voting process any more rational or intelligent. The benefit to employees, employers, unions, and the public
from prompt, final settlement of representation questions is clear
and identifiable. But whether any countervailing benefit is gained
from setting aside one election and ordering another in the hope
that the second will be a freer or more rational process is, in most
instances, a matter of pure conjecture. As we have repeatedly
pointed out in discussing the Board's application of speculative
theories about the influence of particular campaign tactics upon the
voters' mental processes, the Board's credentials as experts in
election psychology are exceedingly slim. Indeed, the only empirical
data presently available in this area, while not conclusive, suggest
that the Board's assumptions about the impact of election conduct on voting behavior are off target substantially more than
they are on. [8]

---

[7] Modine Mfg. Co., 203 N.L.R.B. No. 17, 83 L.R.R.M 1133 (1973).

[8] Getman & Goldberg, *The Myth of NLRB Expertise*, 39 U. CHI. L. REV.
681 (1972). *See also*, Brotslaw, *Attitude of Retail Workers Toward Union
Organization*, 18 LAB. L. J. 149, 170 (1967).

All of these considerations weigh in favor of a fundamental revision of the Board's approach to the regulation of election conduct. It is our conclusion, after studying the NLRB's rulings on all categories of election conduct throughout the span of its existence, that the Board's energies are best spent when they are concentrated on promoting order, efficiency, and fairness in the election process itself, rather than attempting to regulate the pre-election speech and conduct of the participants. In the foregoing chapters, we have suggested a number of specific areas in which Board rules and policies could be modified in accordance with these priorities.

Rules aimed at preserving public confidence in the impartiality of the Board's agents and the fairness of its election procedures provide a necessary foundation for public acceptance of election results and the rights and obligations which flow therefrom. We have suggested the continued application of strict standards in cases of alleged improper conduct by Board agents, since rerun elections would seem particularly justifiable in this area. We have also suggested that the Board could eliminate suspicions of impropriety without invalidating election results in many cases by adopting a more liberal policy of granting hearings in such cases.

Rules designed to effectuate the mechanical details of the election process—*e.g.*, providing sufficient notices and ballots, handling the ballots and the ballot box properly, ensuring ballot secrecy, affording an adequate opportunity for all eligible employees to vote, etc.—are necessary to efficient, routine resolution of representation issues. To the greatest extent possible, such rules should be clear, simple, consistent, and constant. Perhaps, it is an inevitable outgrowth of the Board's insistence upon regulating elections through a case-by-case, quasi-judicial method that its rules regarding the mechanics of the election process have not come close to these objectives.

Since the Board's rules are generally fabricated piecemeal in response to particular fact situations, overall consistency is undoubtedly difficult to achieve. But, particularly where the mechanical aspects of the election process are involved, the establishment of firm, reasonable rules for all cases would seem to be of greater overall importance than the precise weighing of the circumstances of each case. This is an area of election regulation in which administrative rule-making offers especially promising possibilities.[9]

---

[9] *See generally* Bernstein, *The NLRB's Adjudication-Rulemaking Dilemma Under the Administrative Procedure Act*, 79 YALE L. J. 571 (1970); Shapiro,

To the extent possible, the Board should strive to decrease its involvement with the campaign statements and tactics of election parties. Voters in Board elections are indeed better educated and more sophisticated today than they were in the 1930's, and even then the Board was probably well-justified in avoiding entanglement in the substance of campaign statements. In lieu of its quixotic attempt to enforce rationality in the election process, the Board should concentrate on eliminating unnecessary impediments to campaign communication by either party. One of the fundamental assumptions of a system calling for democratic elections is, after all, that voters exposed to a free flow of information, opinions, and ideas, from the competing sides can be trusted to make a rational choice for themselves, without the necessity for censorship.

Some continued agency involvement with campaign speech and conduct is undoubtedly necessary in order to redress cases involving actual coercion of such magnitude as to have clearly rendered the election results unreliable. Outright bribes and threats by either party, for example, certainly should not be condoned, and where they are sufficiently widespread to have had a clear impact on the election results, such conduct should be considered grounds for ordering a rerun election. But the Board should temper its reflex to read "implied" or "veiled" threats into routine expressions of partisan opinion and to infer an adverse impact upon the voters' choice from such remarks. Here again, it is time for the Board to recognize that the voters in its elections are generally mature, responsible individuals, capable of taking the campaign boasts and bluffs of both parties with an appropriate grain of salt.

In addition, the Board should reevaluate its presumptions about the relative economic strengths of employers and unions in light of the realities of present-day labor-management relations. Where it exists, the economic power of a union to compel or to prevent particular management actions should be recognized as just as real an ingredient in determining the impact of pre-election conduct as the employer's technical authority to "decide" upon the action. Above all, and regardless of what specific standards are applied, the Board's treatment of election conduct should be equal and even-handed as between labor and management.

Any movement to revise the rules and standards governing representation election conduct will almost certainly have to origi-

---

Choice of Rule Making or Adjudication in the Development of Administrative Policy, 78 HARV. L. REV. 921 (1965).

nate with the Board itself. Meaningful Congressional action in this highly specialized area is unlikely. Indeed, if the effectiveness of Congress' attempt to eliminate restrictions on free speech through the addition of Section 8(c) in 1947 is any guide, Congressional intervention would only further complicate the regulation of election conduct. Nor can any basic reform be expected to originate with the courts. Appellate review of Board rulings on election objections is too infrequent to do more than check isolated abuses of discretion. Moreover, as we have pointed out, because of the peculiar procedural structure of the Act, under which only those elections which the Board has upheld normally ever progress to the stage of judicial review, court reversals tend to have distorted and probably unintended effects on the agency's overall approach to the issues involved.[10]

Because of the potentiality of court review, however, the Board should observe certain precautions if it does undertake to revise its election standards in future cases. As noted, the courts have generally granted the Board wide leeway to state in the first instance what the applicable policies should be, as long as it does not appear that the Board has acted arbitrarily to favor one side in the labor-management arena over the other. Consequently, if the Board wishes to adopt a new basic approach, it should make it unequivocally clear in its decisions that it is doing so, rather than just bending the old standards to favor particular parties. Where it is necessary to overrule existing precedents, this should be done forthrightly.

It will undoubtedly be necessary for the Board to surrender much of the flexibility it has jealously defended in the past in order to achieve clear-cut election rules for the future. But the benefits to the Board, as well as to the public, from a thorough revision of the policies and standards governing representation elections would more than compensate for the loss. As we have observed, the Board's current concern over its caseload dilemma would provide an excellent occasion to set this process of revision into motion.

---

[10] *See* discussion at pp. 7-9, *supra*.

Index

445

Racial Policies of American Industry Series

Order from: Kraus Reprint Co., Route 100, Millwood, New York 10546